ENVIRONMENTAL ETHICS

An Introduction to
Environmental Philosophy

Third Edition

JOSEPH R. DES JARDINS
College of Saint Benedict

WADSWORTH
———✦———™
THOMSON LEARNING

Australia • Canada • Mexico • Singapore • Spain
United Kingdom • United States

WADSWORTH

THOMSON LEARNING

Philosophy Editor: Peter Adams
Assistant Editor: Kara Kindstrom
Editorial Assistant: Mark Andrews
Marketing Manager: Dave Garrison
Print Buyer: Tandra Jorgensen
Permissions Editor: Joohee Lee

Production Service: Gustafson Graphics
Copy Editor: Jeanie Orlandi; Linda Ireland
Cover Designer: Bill Stanton
Cover Photo: The Image Bank/Jo Van Os
Compositor: Gustafson Graphics
Text and Cover Printer: Webcom, Limited

Library of Congress Cataloging-in-Publication Data

Des Jardins, Joseph R.
 Environmental ethics : an introduction to environmental philosophy / Joseph R. Des Jardins.—3rd ed.
  p. cm.
 Includes bibliographical references and index.
 ISBN 0-534-51966-0
  1. Environmental ethics. I. Title

 GE42 .D48 2000
 179'.1—dc21
                                                    00-043848

Wadsworth/Thomson Learning
10 Davis Drive
Belmont, CA 94002-3098
USA

For information about our products, contact us:
Thomson Learning Academic Resource Center
1-800-423-0563
http://www.wadsworth.com

International Headquarters
Thomson Learning
International Division
290 Harbor Drive, 2nd Floor
Stamford, CT 06902-7477
USA

UK/Europe/Middle East/South Africa
Thomson Learning
Berkshire House
168-173 High Holborn
London WC1V 7AA
United Kingdom

Asia
Thomson Learning
60 Albert Street, #15-01
Albert Complex
Singapore 189969

Canada
Nelson Thomson Learning
1120 Birchmount Road
Toronto, Ontario M1K 5G4
Canada

DEDICATION

One summer morning, while driving through the countryside, my four-year-old son asked, "Daddy, what are trees good for?" Sensing a precious moment of parenthood, I began gently to explain that as living things they don't need to be good for anything, but that trees do provide homes to many other living things, that they make and clean the air that we breathe, that they can be majestic and beautiful. "But daddy, I'm a scientist and I know more than you because you forgot the most important thing. Trees are good for climbing."

I hope that I have not missed too many other such obvious truths in writing this book, which I dedicate to Michael and Matthew.

CONTENTS

PREFACE

One winter evening several years ago I reread Aldo Leopold's *A Sand County Almanac*. This occurred a few months after I had moved to rural Minnesota from suburban Philadelphia. I came upon Leopold's entry for February:

> There are two spiritual dangers in not owning a farm. One is the danger of supposing that breakfast comes from the grocery, and the other that heat comes from the furnace. To avoid the first danger, one should plant a garden, preferably where there is no grocer to confuse the issue. To avoid the second, he should lay a split of good oak on the andirons, preferably where there is no furnace.

This passage struck me in a way that it never could have had I still been living in a metropolitan area. The fact that it was twenty-seven degrees below zero outside and I was sitting in front of a roaring oak fire might have had something to do with this. I recognized that there are more than just two spiritual dangers in not owning a farm; one other concerns divorcing your life from your work. That evening, I realized that teaching courses on environmental and ecological issues would mean more to me now, personally and professionally, than it could have in the city. This book grows out of a commitment to integrate more fully my life with my work.

The primary aim of this book is simple: to provide a clear, systematic, and comprehensive introduction to the philosophical issues underlying environmental and ecological controversies. At the start of the twenty-first century, it is fair to say that we face environmental challenges unprecedented in human history. Largely through human activity, life on Earth faces the greatest mass extinctions since the end of the dinosaur age 65 million years ago. Some estimates suggest more than one hundred species a day are becoming extinct and that this rate could double or triple within the next few decades. The natural resources that sustain life on this planet—air, water, and soil—are being polluted or depleted at alarming rates. Human population growth is increasing exponentially. The 2000 world population of 6 billion people will likely increase by one billion people by the year 2010. The prospects for continued degradation and depletion of natural resources multiply with this population growth. Toxic wastes that will plague future generations continue to accumulate worldwide. The world's wilderness areas, its forests, wetlands, mountains, and grasslands, are being developed, paved, drained, burned, and overgrazed out of existence. With destruction of the ozone layer and the potential for a greenhouse effect, human activity threatens the atmosphere and climate of the planet itself.

The tendency in our culture is to treat such issues as simply scientific, technological, or political problems. But they are much more than this. These environmental and ecological controversies raise fundamental questions about what we as human beings value, about the kind of beings we are, the kinds of lives we should live, our place in nature, and the kind of world in which we might flourish. In short, environmental problems raise fundamental questions of ethics and philosophy. This book seeks to provide a systematic introduction to these philosophical issues.

OVERVIEW

A significant amount of philosophically interesting and important research on environmental and ecological issues has been conducted during the past few decades. The structure of this book tells the story of how the fields of environmental ethics and environmental philosophy have been developing during that period.

Two initial chapters introduce the relevance of philosophy for environmental concerns and some traditional ethical theories and principles. Chapters 3 and 4 survey topics that essentially fit an "applied ethics" model. Traditional philosophical theories and methodologies are applied to environmental issues with the aim of clarification, analysis, and evaluation. The applied ethics model, it seems to me, accounts for much of the early work in environmental ethics.

Many philosophers came to believe that traditional theories and principles were inadequate to deal with new environmental challenges. In response, philosophers began to extend traditional concepts and principles so that they might become environmentally relevant. The next three chapters examine attempts to extend moral standing to such things as individual animals, future generations, trees, and other natural objects. Within much of this thinking, traditional theories and principles remain essentially intact, but their scope and range have extended to cover topics not previously explored by philosophers.

In recent years, many philosophers working in this field have come to believe that ethical extensionism itself is an inadequate philosophical response to environmental issues and controversies. To many of these thinkers, traditional ethical theories and principles are part of a worldview that has been responsible for much environmental and ecological destruction. What is needed, in their eyes, is a more radical philosophical approach that includes rethinking metaphysical, epistemological, and political, as well as ethical, concepts. At this point, the field once identified as environmental ethics is better conceived of as environmental philosophy. The final five chapters examine several of these more comprehensive environmental and ecological philosophies. These views include biocentrism (the view that all living things deserve moral standing), ecocentrism (the view that shifts away from traditional environmental concerns to a more holistic and ecological focus), Deep Ecology, social ecology, and ecofeminism.

THE THIRD EDITION

My primary goal for this book remains to provide a reasonably clear and straightforward introduction to the philosophical issues underlying environmental controversies. I have been very pleased to learn that this book has been adopted for use in classes ranging from high school to graduate-level seminars. I take this fact as evidence that, to some modest degree at least, I have met this goal. Yet despite this success there is a great temptation to try to do more, especially to expand the book into applied areas of environmental policy. But that would be to write a different book. Thanks in no small part to the advice of reviewers, I have refrained from making any such wholesale changes in this edition.

This edition tries to correct mistakes, of both commission and omission, without sacrificing the primary goal. I have tried to keep major changes to a minimum. Chapter 4 has been revised so that the debate over consumption and population, rather than the more narrow debate concerning energy policy, provides a context for the philosophical examination of ethical responsibilities to future generations. I have also added new sections on recent debates over the idea of wilderness and on environmental pragmatism. I also include several new discussion cases and have tried to integrate the discussion cases into each chapter more explicitly. Most other changes are relatively minor updates, additions, corrections, and clarifications.

TO STUDENTS AND TEACHERS

Writing a book like this carries two intellectual dangers. One is the danger of supposing that students are as motivated by and interested in abstract philosophical issues as their teachers. The other is that in pointing to the immense practical relevance of environmental ethics, I ignore or understate the importance of careful and rigorous conceptual analysis. I have tried to address these dangers in a number of ways.

Each chapter begins with a description of one or two issues that can be used as an entry into the philosophical discussion that follows. These discussions describe issues that are at the forefront of the contemporary environmental scene, and they implicitly raise fundamental ethical and philosophical questions. My hope is that after some directed reflection and discussion, students will see the need to address philosophical questions in developing their own environmental and ecological positions. Each chapter also ends with a series of discussion questions that can be used either as the basis for a chapter review or as the basis for further study.

To avoid the second danger, I have tried to follow the philosophical debates far enough to provide an accurate example of how philosophers reason and how reasoning can make progress. There can be no substitute for a careful study and reading of the many primary sources that I have used in this book. But the nature of this book requires that these debates not be so developed that readers get lost in, or bored by, the detail.

I have not always been successful in my own teaching at balancing a relevant introduction to the issues with an in-depth analysis. Without a clear context to motivate the need to know, students often get lost in philosophical analysis. On the other hand, without depth students can become convinced too easily that they now know all the answers. Class time spent providing context, of course, takes away from time spent developing analysis; time spent following through on the debates prevents the forest from being seen for all the trees.

I wrote this book to address that tension. I suspect that for many teachers, the book provides a context and introduction, allowing them to use class time for fuller development of selected issues. They might do this in a number of ways: by reading classic or contemporary primary sources, by studying more empirical resources like the Worldwatch publications, by using some of the many excellent videos on environmental topics that are now available, by addressing the claims of more activist groups, ranging from the Sierra Club to Earth First! However individual instructors choose to develop their courses, I hope that this book can provide a context to ensure that students remain as connected to the important philosophical issues as they so often are to the practical environmental ones.

ACKNOWLEDGMENTS

I owe my greatest debts to those thinkers who are doing the original research in this field. I have tried to acknowledge their work at every turn, but if I have missed someone, I hope this general acknowledgment will suffice.

The reviewers who read this book for Wadsworth provided thorough, insightful, and tremendously helpful advice. I must especially acknowledge Claudia Card of the University of Wisconsin, Arthur Millman of the University of Massachusetts in Boston, and Ellen Klein of the University of North Florida for very helpful and detailed advice for the first edition. Although their advice improved this book immeasurably, the usual disclaimers of responsibility apply. My thanks also to Ned Hettinger, College of Charleston; Dale Jamieson, University of Colorado; Donald C. Lee, University of New Mexico; Jon McGregor, Arizona State University; Charles Taliaferro, Saint Olaf College; Douglas Browning, University of Texas, Austin; Wade Robinson, Rochester Institute of Technology; and William O. Stephens, Creighton University for thoughtful advice for the second edition. I have also benefited from advice offered by Holmes Rolston and Ernie Diedrich. Most recently I wish to thank the following reviewers for the advice that they offered for this third edition: Donald Hubin, Ohio State University; Kathie Jenni, University of Redlands; Eugene Troxell, San Diego State University; and Charles Verharen, Howard University.

My students at the College of St. Benedict and St. John's University worked through early versions of this text. We were all students in those classes, and their comments helped substantively and pedagogically. The College of St. Benedict has provided financial support for research during the writing of this book.

Everyone associated with Wadsworth Publishing proved once again why they are simply the best textbook publishers around. My oldest debts at Wadsworth are to Ken King for his initial enthusiasm for this project and to Tammy Goldfeld and Kelly Zavislak for their help, good humor, and patience. Peter Adams continues this great tradition of editors who blend humanity with professionalism. For help with the second edition, I wish to thank Clay Glad, Angela Mann, and Polly Kummel for their professionalism and support. For this third edition, I have been fortunate to work with Jerry Holloway, Sara Dovre Wudali, and Linda Ireland. Thank you all for your help.

I

BASIC CONCEPTS

Science, Ethics, and the Environment

Technological Solutions to Environmental Problems

In the early 1970s, scientists discovered an area in the Gulf of Mexico, off-shore from the Mississippi delta, that was suffering from a condition called "hypoxia." Hypoxia occurs in a body of water when dissolved oxygen levels are too low to sustain marine life. This condition occurs when too many nutrients, particularly nitrogen and phosphorus, trigger excessive algae growth resulting in decreased sunlight, loss of aquatic vegetation, and ultimately, a significant decrease in dissolved oxygen. Few aquatic species can survive under these conditions.

After the Mississippi River floods in 1993, this hypoxic area doubled in size from previous years, reaching an estimated 18,000 square kilometers, and remained in this range through 1997. In 1998, the area had shrunk to an estimated 13,000 square kilometers or approximately the size of the state of Connecticut. It remains the largest zone of coastal hypoxia in the Western Hemisphere.

This Gulf of Mexico hypoxia has had significant economic and ecological impact. Many marine species have suffered drastic declines in population and fisheries, tourism, and recreational industries have suffered as a result. Forty percent of all U.S. shrimp catch, the most commercially valuable U.S.

marine species, is harvested from the Gulf region. Commercial and recreational fishing in this region is a $2.8 billion annual business.

Some nutrients are, of course, essential for a healthy marine ecosystem. The natural nutrient load flowing down the Mississippi River is perhaps the major reason this area has been such a productive fisheries region. Too much nutrient, on the other hand, can lead to hypoxia. The cause of this increase and the resulting hypoxia is human activity all along the Mississippi watershed.

Scientists have identified three major causes for the excessive nutrient load carried into the Gulf of Mexico by the Mississippi: nutrient runoff from agricultural uses along the entire Mississippi watershed, channelization of the river increasing the flow rate of the river, and loss of natural vegetation and wetland along the riverbanks.

Each of these activities is the direct result of technological innovations and actions aimed at controlling the natural world in order to improve human well-being. Increased fertilizer use has significantly contributed to the productivity of American farms, more than 50 percent of which are located along the Mississippi River basin. Dredging channels and constructing levees, most of which has been done under the supervision of the U.S. Army Corps of Engineers, has contributed greatly to flood control and improved commercial transportation along the river. Agricultural productivity has also benefited from programs that drained hundreds of thousands of acres of wetlands and other activities that turned natural areas into farmland. The recognition that major harmful environmental consequences can result from technological innovations aimed at controlling nature occurred perhaps most famously just a generation ago.

With the publication of *Silent Spring* in 1962, Rachel Carson focused international attention on the deadly effects of DDT and other chemical pesticides. The continued indiscriminate use of these "elixirs of death" would, according to Carson, lead us to a time when death and poisoning would silence the "voices of spring." This book had a profound influence on the public's attitude concerning chemical pollution and environmental protection.

Although chemical agents have been used to control pests since the beginning of agriculture, the decades immediately after World War II witnessed tremendous development in the discovery, production, and use of chemical pesticides. (For simplicity's sake, *pesticide* can be defined as any agent that kills a "pest" or undesirable form of life. Insecticides target insects, herbicides target plants, fungicides target fungi, and so forth.) Increasing population growth and a corresponding increase in demand on agriculture, along with a decrease in the number of farmers, led to intense pressures to increase agricultural productivity. One large part of this involved the use of chemicals to limit crop loss from pests, estimated to be as high as 37 percent of all planted crops. Before the publication of *Silent*

Spring, the only question generally asked about chemical pesticides, by both scientists and the public, concerned their effectiveness: Do they eliminate undesirable pests without harming humans or their crops? After Carson's work, the long-term consequences as well as the political and ethical implications of pesticide use came to the forefront.

At first glance, the benefits of these pesticides seemed clear. Insecticides like DDT and other chlorinated hydrocarbons were quite effective in killing mosquitoes and other insects that transmitted such diseases as malaria, typhus, and bubonic plague. Pesticides also cut crop loss, enabling farmers to meet demand without raising prices. In short, pesticides were an effective, economical, and technologically feasible answer to a variety of health and agricultural questions.

But other questions—ecological, political, and ethical—were not even being asked: What effects were pesticides having on other living things throughout the food chain? Who should decide levels of safety and risk? Are the benefits worth the risks?

Silent Spring challenged scientists, industry, farmers, and the public to examine the long-term ecological effects of pesticide use. For example, many of these chemicals were designed to resist breaking down in the environment, keeping them effective for longer periods. DDT, for one, is insoluble in water but soluble in fat. Thus, it not only remains in an ecosystem for a long time but can build up and become concentrated in the fatty tissues of living organisms. As a result, minute amounts of DDT in a body of water will, through a process called "biological amplification," become concentrated in microorganisms such as plankton, more concentrated in the small fish that feed on plankton, and increasingly concentrated all the way up the food chain. In the decades after World War II, when pesticide use increased dramatically, many birds at the top of the food chain—bald eagles, peregrine falcons, ospreys, and pelicans—were severely threatened. Accumulated residues of DDT in the birds caused a decrease in the calcium content of their egg shells, which meant that the shells were too thin to protect the unhatched chicks. Today, a similar process of biological amplification of such toxins as PCBs, mercury, and lead has made many fish dangerous for human consumption.

But harm to other species was not the only unforeseen danger. Evidence shows that, over the long term, pesticides have not been effective in reducing crop loss from pests. In fact, despite a tenfold increase in pesticide use since the 1940s, the rate of overall crop loss has actually increased. Several factors help explain how this happened.

First, few pesticides are so precise that they destroy targeted pests without also killing their natural predators. An insecticide aimed at aphids, for example, may also kill ladybugs and preying mantis, which ordinarily feed on aphids. Without natural enemies, the pests that do survive can quickly reproduce. Second, the surviving organisms that are reproducing will be more resistant to the pesticide. By random genetic chance, some organisms will be naturally resistant to the specific pesticide. Through natural selection, these organisms will rapidly increase as less resistant members of the species, as well as natural predators, are killed. Over a short period of time (a generation for many insect species is simply a matter of days), pests can develop a genetic resistance that makes the original pesticide ineffective. As a result, there is a strong incentive to increase the frequency and concentration of pesticide use or turn to new chemicals and begin the process over again.

Defenders of pesticide use within the chemical and agricultural industries can point out that this remains merely a scientific and technological challenge. Can new chemical pesticides be developed that are safe for human use and that will prove to be effective in the fight against pests?[1]

1.1 INTRODUCTION: WHY PHILOSOPHY?

Upon entering the twenty-first century, it is fair to say that human beings face environmental challenges unprecedented in the history of this planet. Largely through human activity, life on Earth faces the greatest mass extinctions since the end of the dinosaur age 65 million years ago. Some estimates suggest more than 100 species are becoming extinct every day and that this rate could double or triple within the next few decades.[2] The natural resources that sustain life on this planet—air, water, and soil—are being polluted or depleted at alarming rates. Human population growth is increasing exponentially. In 1999, world population reached 6 billion people. While it was not until 1804 that world population first reached 1 billion people, the most recent 1 billion increase took just twelve years. The rate of population increase is slowing somewhat. Estimates are that it may take 15 years to add another 1 billion people. The prospects for continued degradation and depletion of natural resources multiply with this population growth. Toxic wastes that will plague future generations continue to accumulate worldwide. The world's wilderness areas, its forests, wetlands, mountains, and grasslands, are being developed, paved, drained, burned, and overgrazed out of existence. With destruction of the ozone layer and the potential that the "greenhouse effect" will lead to global warming, human activity threatens the very atmosphere and climate of the planet Earth.

Faced with such a potentially catastrophic future, we are challenged with momentous decisions. But, how do we start making the right decisions? As the cases outlined previously show, many of our present problems are the result of decisions made in good faith by previous generations. In fact, many of those decisions did have very beneficial consequences to both prior and present generations. But they also had devastating consequences as well. How can we be sure that the decisions we make, likewise made in good faith, will not have equally ambiguous consequences? Before making these decisions, it seems only reasonable that we should step back to reflect on the decision-making process itself.

In many ways, philosophical ethics is just that. Ethics involves a self-conscious stepping back from our lives to reflect on what we should do, how we should act, and what kind of people we should be. This textbook, like all philosophical ethics, will introduce environmental ethics by working at two levels: the practical level of deciding what we should do and how we should live and the more abstract and academic level of *thinking about* how we decide what to do and what to value.

While this textbook relies on philosophical ethics for guidance, many others look to science and technology for answers. If only we can develop safe, inexpensive, and effective chemical pesticides. If only we could engineer more efficient solar panels or harness the energy potential of geothermal, wind, or tidal power. If only we could develop hydrogen fuel cell technology as an alternative to the internal combustion engine. If only we could master cold fusion. If only we could arrange economic incentives to discourage pollution.

For many people in our culture and especially for many in policy-making positions, science and technology offer the only hope for solving environmental problems. Because environmental problems often involve highly technical matters, it is only reasonable to turn to experts in these technical areas for answers. Who better than chemists to tell us about the safety and effectiveness of pesticides? For example, a task force working to address the Gulf of Mexico hypoxia problem includes experts from agricultural economics, engineering, agronomy, animal ecology, biogeochemistry, biology, environmental research, limnology, marine science, oceanography, and soil science.[3] For many people, because science offers objective and factual answers in an area in which emotions run high and controversies abound, science is the obvious place to look to for help with environmental concerns. The only alternative seems to be a pessimistic surrender to controversy and disagreement.

Unfortunately, turning to science with the optimistic hope for a quick fix is not much different from taking a pessimistic attitude. Each involves individual citizens relinquishing the authority to make decisions about their world. Although turning to science and technology in the hope of a quick fix is tempting, environmental challenges are neither exclusively, nor even primarily, problems of science and technology. Environmental issues raise fundamental questions about what we as human beings value, the kind of beings we are, the kind of lives we should live, our place in nature, and the kind of world in which we might flourish. Turning to science and technology to address the hypoxia in the Gulf of Mexico or pesticide use should occur only after we have thought through why we should do these things. Environmental problems raise fundamental questions of ethics and philosophy, about the ends we should pursue. Science and technology, at best, can provide us with some means for attaining these ends.

Western philosophy was born 2,500 years ago with Socrates's questioning of Athenian society and an individual's role within it. "We are dealing with no small thing," Socrates said, "but with how we ought to live." Environmental issues, even seemingly innocuous issues such as fertilizer and pesticide use, raise philosophical questions about how we ought to live. For example, do we have any ethical responsibility to preserve the various life-forms around us? Is there anything wrong with defining some living organisms as pests and working to eradicate them? Philosophical assumptions are involved wherever we stand in this debate. Again, should pesticides be proved safe before they are used, or should the burden rest with those who predict danger? Answering this question also involves issues in ethics and political philosophy.

Relying on science or technology (or economics or the law) without also considering the ethical and philosophical issues can raise as many problems as it solves. Leaving environmental decisions to the "experts" in science and technology does not mean that these decisions will be objective and value neutral. It means only that the values and philosophical assumptions that do decide the issue will be those that these experts hold.

This textbook introduces the many ways in which philosophy can contribute to the creation of a sane and judicious environmental policy. Environmental issues raise fundamental questions about how we should live. These are philosophical and ethical questions and need to be addressed in a philosophically sophisticated way. Environmental policy ought to be decided in the political arena and not in scientific laboratories, corporate boardrooms, or government bureaucracies. Thus, a further goal of this textbook is to empower citizens to become full participants in these critical public policy debates. Familiarity with the philosophical issues involved in these debates is a necessary first step in this direction.

1.2 SCIENCE AND ETHICS

As Rachel Carson's writing suggests, we take risks when we treat environmental problems merely as technical problems awaiting solution from some specialized discipline. This is partly because the dimensions of environmental issues are seldom limited to the specific boundaries of any one particular discipline. Pesticide pollution, for example, involves agriculture, various branches of biology and chemistry, medicine, economics, politics, and law. Oceanic hypoxia involves an equally diverse group of disciplines. But it is equally impossible to find an environmental issue that does not raise basic questions of value. Approaching any serious environmental issue with the hope of finding a technical quick fix guarantees only a narrow and parochial understanding of what is at stake. Carson's *Silent Spring* testifies to the dangers inherent in this approach. As seen in the examples at the beginning of this chapter, technological or scientific "solutions" have often resulted in as many new problems as they have solved.

But the danger in overreliance on science and technology goes beyond this simple point of technological complexity. Science is not as value neutral as many assume. Our culture has a deep belief in science as the ultimate authority on questions of knowledge and truth. This belief is so deep and unexamined that it takes on the dimensions of a cultural myth. According to this myth of scientific objectivity, our beliefs are mere opinion—personal, subjective, arbitrary, and biased—unless they are validated by science. Although it is important not to overstate this point—science does have tremendous potential for helping us to understand and solve environmental problems—science is not the purely objective and value-neutral resource that so many assume it to be.

This is not the place for a full discussion of the issue of scientific objectivity. However, several points should give us pause when we are tempted to turn solely to science and technology for solutions to environmental problems.

In some ways, science is nothing more than a detailed, precise, and documented approach to knowledge. Science demands that its practitioners minimize assumptions, seek to eliminate bias, verify results, and limit conclusions to what the evidence supports. In this sense, the scientific method has a real "ethic" that aims to ensure an impartial, accurate, and rational result. To the degree that scientific practice measures up to this ethic, we can have confidence in the rationality of its result.

Nevertheless, this method may have hidden assumptions that can influence scientific practice. For example, Chapter 10 will consider the claim that modern science is dominated by models imported from physics. In that view, we best understand something (a physical object, for example) when we reduce that object to its simplest elements (such as atoms, electrons, and so forth) and investigate the forces that work on those elements (for example, gravity and electromagnetism). But, according to critics, that approach is inappropriate for other fields. Social sciences such as economics, sociology, and political science may well distort reality if they reduce "society" to a mere collection of individuals mechanically driven by the forces of self-interest.[4] What is more relevant to our concerns is that some biologists believe that the physics model is particularly misleading in the study of ecosystems. The reductionist tendency can ignore or distort the complex relations that exist within an ecosystem. Reductionism literally fails to see the forests for the trees.

Likewise, a commitment to mechanistic explanations can also distort our understanding of ecological relationships. For example, debates that concern our understanding of animal behavior are sometimes framed in mechanistic terms. *Either* animal behavior is caused by environmental conditioning, *or* it is controlled by genetic programming. Either way, the explanation can be stated as invariable, deterministic, mechanistic "laws of nature." Again, for many biologists this represents a distorted and oversimplified account of animal behavior. Even the simplest organism is capable of changing its environment as much as it (and its progeny) is changed by the environment. Biological and environmental changes seem to occur as much through random chance as according to deterministic laws.[5] Accordingly, a policy of wildlife management based on a mechanistic model of animal behavior would have different consequences and recommendations from a policy that assumes that change rather than constancy is the norm. Thus, despite the commitment of science to the values of impartiality and objectivity, the practice of science is not always the unbiased procedure it is taken to be.

Science is also sometimes understood not as a method or procedure but as a body of information or facts. Surely facts are objective, and if science discovers the facts, scientific knowledge must be objective, or so the myth of scientific objectivity would have us believe.

How comfortable should we be when we rely solely on scientific information to meet environmental challenges? Assuming that the facts are established through a careful, methodical, and verified procedure, we need to recognize that the facts seldom tell the whole story. Reliance on well-established scientific information can be risky if that information fails to give us a complete explanation. Perhaps the biggest obstacle to getting the whole story is not science's inability to get answers but science's limits in asking questions. Before relying on scientific answers to resolve environmental problems, we need to know what questions the scientists are asking, and the questions they ask are often determined by factors that lie outside the realm of science.

Amory Lovins, an internationally recognized energy scientist, makes a similar point by reminding us that the "answers you get depend on the questions you ask."[6] Lovins uses an example from energy policy to develop this point. If we define our energy problem as a supply problem, we can easily conclude that we are running out of energy and need new energy sources. Science can document the facts of resource depletion; calculate the known reserves of coal, oil, and uranium; compare the technological advantages of various energy sources; and predict the costs and efficiencies of coal, oil, nuclear-powered generating plants, and so forth. We might thus imagine collecting a significant amount of relevant scientific data on the various alternatives of energy production. We can also imagine that, given these facts, one alternative (for example, breeder nuclear fission reactors) might emerge as the most reasonable option. This decision, we can well imagine, is based on the objective neutral facts of science.

But if we define our energy problem as a question of demand, we will come up with different answers. Defined this way, we begin to ask questions about energy use, about matching energy sources with energy use, energy efficiencies, appropriate technologies, and the like. A scientist who asks these questions is more likely to focus on such issues as home heating, insulation, efficiency of electric motors, lighting, appliances, fuel-efficient cars, or mass transportation, hydrogen fuel cells, solar power, and so forth. Clearly, the information emerging from these questions, as factual and objective as the information coming from supply questions, will suggest different energy policies. These facts might well prove that heating homes with electricity is quite unreasonable, even if the source of that electricity is safe and efficient when compared to alternative sources.

Thus, we have a situation in which two sets of facts, each equally valid and objective from a scientific point of view, lead to quite different policy recommendations. One set supports building new power plants, and the other set supports a greater emphasis on appropriate technologies. In such a scenario, the scientific facts alone tell us nothing about which alternative we ought to choose. Later chapters examine the more general difficulties involved with reasoning from facts to values. Philosophers have long recognized that descriptions of the world do not, in themselves, commit us to particular conclusions about how the world should be. Simply acknowledging the gap between statements of fact and statements of value is enough to caution us about an overreliance on science and technology.

We need to be especially careful in determining which questions the environmental scientists are asking. If the questions are limited, so too will the answers be and so too will be the policy recommendations that society adopts based on those answers.

So where do scientists get their questions? The answer is that scientific questions are formed to a large degree by the people who pay for scientific research. Contemporary, state-of-the-art scientific research is an expensive enterprise. Typically, it is funded by government and private industry. The projects that get funded are the projects that answer the questions being asked by government and industry. We should not be surprised, for example, when scientists working for the chemical industry respond to the problem of resistant strains of insects by recommending use of new (and typically more expensive) chemical pesticides. Science conducted under these conditions may not always supply the answers that government and industry want, but the likelihood of it supplying radically different answers is seriously restricted.

Continuing with the Lovins energy example, most of what is known about nuclear energy is the result of research supported by the U.S. government. Specifically, the Department of Defense has spent billions of dollars developing nuclear weapons. In fact, the standard design for a nuclear power plant is a modified version of the nuclear reactor that powers submarines. Thus, the knowledge that we possess about nuclear energy is directly traceable to political decisions made in a quite different context. (So too is our knowledge about chemical pesticides. Much of that research began during the world wars with research on chemical weapons.)

This is not to suggest that such knowledge is somehow less reasonable or valid than it might be. However, we need to acknowledge that the environmental decisions that we make are dependent on the information and technology that we have available and that these are dependent on the types of questions the scientists are asking. Imagine the knowledge and technology that we would have about solar power, for example, if the money spent on nuclear weapons and nuclear research in the last fifty years had been spent instead on solar energy research.

Intellectual honesty demands that we not overgeneralize the expertise of scientists. We should not deceive ourselves into thinking that because science demands objectivity and neutrality that all its uses are objective and value neutral. Even if the scientific enterprise is committed to impartial and objective methods and even if its findings are reasonable and true, the practical *uses* that we make of scientific information may not be. We should also not deceive ourselves into thinking that because many environmental problems involve technical issues, they do not raise ethical questions as well. The myth of objectivity that sometimes surrounds science can obscure these points. One role of environmental philosophy is to make explicit the hidden value assumptions of alternative environmental policies. Sometimes this will require examining the value assumptions implicit in science and technology.

Nevertheless, it also would be a mistake to think that some abstract ethical theory can resolve environmental controversies. Ethical and philosophical analysis done in the abstract, ignorant of science, technology, and other relevant disciplines, will not have much to contribute to the resolution of environmental problems. The alternative to looking to science for some quick fix is not to look to philosophical ethics instead.

How we understand our world and, therefore, how and what we value is significantly shaped by what science tells us about that world. The only serious alternative is to recognize that both science and ethics are essential if we hope to make meaningful progress in meeting the environmental challenges that confront us. We can capture this perspective by adapting an old philosophical adage: "Science without ethics is blind; ethics without science is empty." This textbook is a survey of the variety of ways in which philosophers attempt to provide such a vision for environmental science and environmental policy.

1.3 WHAT IS ENVIRONMENTAL ETHICS?

In general, environmental ethics is a systematic account of the moral relations between human beings and their natural environment. Environmental ethics assumes that moral norms can and do govern human behavior toward the natural world. A theory of environmental ethics, then, must go on to explain what these norms are and to whom or to what humans have responsibilities and show how these responsibilities are justified.

Different theories of environmental ethics offer differing answers to these questions. A brief survey of some of the answers provides an overview of this textbook.

Some philosophers argue that our responsibilities to the natural environment are only indirect, that the responsibility to preserve resources, for example, is best understood in terms of the responsibilities that we owe to other humans. *Anthropocentric* ("human-centered") *ethics* holds that only human beings have moral value. Thus, although we may be said to have responsibilities *regarding* the natural world, we do not have direct responsibilities *to* the natural world.

Many controversies in the early decades of the environmental movement, such as air and water pollution, toxic wastes, and the abuse of pesticides, arose because of a perspective of anthropocentric ethics. Pesticide-contaminated food and polluted drinking water pose direct threats to human well-being. Thus, anthropocentric environmental ethics involves simply applying standard ethical principles to new social problems. Chapter 3 provides some examples of this approach.

An extension of anthropocentric ethics occurs by considering future generations of human beings as objects of our moral responsibilities. This approach remains anthropocentric in that only human beings count morally, but it extends our responsibilities to include some to humans who do not (yet) exist. Again, various problems highlighted by the early environmental movement, such as resource conservation and nuclear waste disposal, were regarded from this ethical perspective.

Other philosophers have argued that we do have direct responsibilities to natural objects other than human beings. *Nonanthropocentric ethics* grants moral standing to such natural objects as animals and plants. Typically, this approach requires further extensions and revisions of standard ethical principles. Controversies surrounding the ethical treatment of animals and the threatened extinction of many plant and animal species are among the best-known issues of nonanthropocentric ethics. Chapters 5 through 7 examine a variety of nonanthropocentric systems of ethics.

A further development of environmental ethics occurs by shifting from a focus on individual living things—for example, spotted owls or redwood trees—to a focus on collections or "wholes" such as species, populations, or ecosystems. *Holistic ethics* holds that we have moral responsibilities to collections of (or relationships between) individuals rather than (or in addition to) those individuals who constitute the whole. For example, holistic environmental ethics might allow selective hunting of individual animals so long as the population of that species is not endangered. Holism, greatly influenced by the science of ecology, raises more serious philosophical challenges than do more individualistic ethics. For example, standard criteria for moral standing—that something is alive, can feel pain, is conscious, and so forth—apply plausibly to individuals but less plausibly to collections. The presentation of holistic, nonanthropocentric ethics in Chapters 8 through 11 considers how recent environmental philosophers have met these challenges. Typically, the development and justification of these environmental ethics require defenders to move into the areas of epistemology, metaphysics, and political philosophy. The later chapters provide an introduction to these broader environmental philosophies.

One final caution is in order before we leave this discussion. It is fair to say that many philosophers think of ethics as providing the same general type of practical guidance as does science and technology. Many believe that the role of ethics is to provide a general principle or theory that can be applied in specific cases and from which we can deduce specific practical conclusions. Thus, for example, an ethical principle might direct us to act so as to maximize the overall happiness. Ethical behavior, therefore, involves determining which of two acts, A or B, will in fact maximize overall happiness. With this done, we can then deduce the ethically responsible act. From this perspective, ethics is capable of offering the same kind of objective and unambiguous conclusions as science. But be forewarned. Ethical issues of any type, including environmental issues, are seldom open to such unambiguous resolution. The world is not as simple as we would like it to be.

1.4 SUMMARY AND CONCLUSIONS

This textbook tells a story within a story. Its primary emphasis is surveying the wide variety of contributions that philosophers have been making to environmental debates. These represent the philosophical "visions" being offered to environmental scientists and policy makers. But within this story is a description of how philosophical ethics itself is challenged and extended by its encounter with the contemporary environmental and ecological crisis. For many philosophers, traditional philosophical theories have proved inadequate for resolving environmental problems. Thus, this textbook introduces philosophical ethics as an ongoing intellectual activity in which readers are encouraged to become active participants rather than passive observers.

Notes

1. Resources used for the outline of the Gulf of Mexico hypoxia include the National Ocean Service, National Oceanic and Atmospheric Administration (*http://www.nos.noaa.gov/products/pubs_hyox.html*), The Council for Agricultural Science and Technology (*http://www.cast-science.org/hypo/hypo_nr.html*), and the lower Mississippi River Conservation Committee (*http://www.lmrcc.org/Library/1297hypoia.html*). See also David Pimental, "Is Silent Spring Behind Us?," in *Silent Spring Revisited*, ed. Gino Marco, Robert Hollingworth, and William Durham (Washington, D.C.: American Chemical Society, 1987), p. 183.
2. E. O. Wilson offers estimates like these in a number of places. See, for example, "Threats to Biodiversity," *Scientific American* 261 (September 1989): 108–16.
3. See The Council for Agricultural Science and Technology (CAST), *http://www.cast.org*.
4. Jane Mansbridge, *Beyond Self-Interest* (Chicago: University of Chicago, 1990), is a helpful collection of essays on this topic.
5. See, for example, Daniel Botkin, *Discordant Harmonies* (New York: Oxford University Press, 1990), for a critique of a mechanistic view of science from an ecological perspective.
6. Amory Lovins, "Technology is the Answer (But What was the Question?)," published as a guest essay, pp.56–57, in G. Tyler Miller, *Environmental Science*, 3d ed. (Belmont, CA.: Wadworth, 1991).

Discussion Questions

1. When evaluating the safety of chemical pesticides, who should determine levels of acceptable risk? Is "risk" a matter of scientific fact, or is it a matter of value? What makes an issue a value issue?
2. When deciding how to address an issue such as the hypoxia region in the Gulf of Mexico, should some groups or individuals such as local residents or local fisheries workers have greater authority than others?
3. Identify as many different uses of the words *natural* and *nature* as you can. Which, if any, have value connotations? Are all things that are "natural" also good? What about "human nature"? What is not natural about human beings? What would be the difference between "natural" fertilizers and "nonnatural" ones? Could there be such a thing as a "natural" pesticide?

4. Is there a difference between good science and bad science? We often hear that science should be value neutral. Is this true? Can you think of any values involved in the practice of good science?

5. How is reasoning about ethical matters different from reasoning about scientific matters? How do scientists evaluate controversial claims in science? How would we evaluate controversial ethical claims?

6. What makes a belief or statement objective? Contrast this with subjective beliefs or statements. What statements about, for example, a tree are objective? Which are subjective?

Further Reading

The field of environmental ethics continues to flourish with books, textbooks, and essays appearing in many disciplines. The journal *Environmental Ethics* remains the single best source for following the philosophical debates surveyed in this textbook.

G. Tyler Miller, *Environmental Science,* 5th ed. (Belmont, Calif.: Wadsworth, 1994), is an accessible introduction to all relevant scientific issues.

A number of major anthologies in environmental ethics have been published since the first edition of this book. Among them are Susan Armstrong and Richard Botzler, *Environmental Ethics: Divergence and Convergence* (New York: McGraw-Hill, 1993); Louis Pojman, *Environmental Ethics* (Boston: Jones and Bartlett, 1994); James Sterba, *Earth Ethics* (Englewood Cliffs, N.J.: Prentice-Hall, 1995); Donald VanDeVeer and Christine Pierce, *The Environmental Ethics and Policy Book* (Belmont, Calif.: Wadsworth, 1994); Michael Zimmerman, *Environmental Philosophy* (Englewood Cliffs, N.J.: Prentice-Hall, 1993); and Joseph R. DesJardins, *Environmental Ethics: Concepts, Policy, Theory* (Mountain View, CA: Mayfield, 1999).

The International Society for Environmental Ethics (ISEE) publishes a newsletter updating publications, meetings, and activities of interest to people concerned with environmental ethics. The Master Bibliography in Environmental Ethics has been composed by Holmes Rolston at Colorado State University and can be accessed from the ISEE's World Wide Web Site at *http://www.cep.unt.edu/ISEE.html.* This site has many links to other environmental resources. It is maintained by the Center for Environmental Philosophy at the University of North Texas.

2

Ethical Theory
and the Environment

Individual Rights
and Social Goods

Much of the most significant environmental legislation in the United States was enacted during the 1970s. The Clean Air Act of 1970 (amended and renewed in 1977), Federal Water Pollution Act of 1972 (amended and renewed as the Clean Water Act of 1977), and Endangered Species Act of 1973 were part of a national consensus for addressing environmental problems. Each law was originally enacted by a Democratic Congress and signed into law by a Republican president.

These laws shared a common approach to environmental issues. For the most part, before this legislation was enacted, only individuals who could prove that they had been harmed by the pollution could legally address air and water pollution. This public policy placed the burden on the person who was harmed and at best offered compensation for the harm only after the fact. Except for the incentive provided by the threat of compensation, U.S. policy did little to prevent the pollution in the first place. Because endangered species themselves had no legal standing, the policy did even less to prevent harm to plant and animal life.

Each law enacted during the 1970s established standards that effectively shifted the burden from those threatened with harm to those who would cause the harm. The executive branch established regulatory standards to try to prevent the occurrence of pollution or species extinction rather than compensation after the fact. Think of these laws as establishing a moral minimum. The country set minimum standards to ensure air and water quality and species preservation. Private, governmental, and commercial activity is allowed only after these minimum standards are met.

In recent years, critics have charged that the environmental regulations go too far. Criticism of these laws has been a part of the "wise use" movement, the Republican *Contract with America*, and various "takings" legislation (from the so-called takings clause of the Fifth Amendment: "nor shall private property be taken for public use without just compensation") at the federal and state levels. These critics have focused on two charges: environmental legislation fails to consider the full consequences of regulation, including the economic costs, and this legislation violates the rights of private property owners.

Critics point out that environmental legislation has been expensive for individuals and business. Regulations require expensive pollution control technology, prohibit economic development, control land use, and so forth. However, these regulations never consider whether the overall social benefits are worth the costs. For example, the wise use movement argues that government regulation should recognize that various constituencies compete for the use of national resources. Wilderness and species preservation is one public goal for the use of western lands but so are agriculture, cattle grazing, mining, oil exploration, recreation, and development. These lands should be used "wisely," in ways that provide maximum satisfaction of the public's goals. The goal of environmental policy should be to maximize public benefits and minimize public costs.

Further, according to these critics, much environmental regulation violates the rights of individuals. In this view, government has an obligation to protect the rights of its citizens and, when this cannot be done, provide compensation to those whose rights have been violated. In recent years, various states and Congress have considered takings legislation that would require compensation for the loss of property value arising from government regulation. Thus, for example, if a farmer is prohibited from filling in a wetland to gain more agricultural land, the government would have to pay the farmer for the loss of the use of that land. As another example, if developers are prohibited from building a housing project in an area that provides habitat to an endangered species, the government might owe those developers for the profits they would have made had they developed the land. Defenders of such legislation argue that if government action denies people that to which they are entitled, fairness and justice demand that the government compensate them for the loss.

Construction of new nuclear power plants has come to a virtual standstill in the United States. No new plants have been ordered since the Three Mile Island accident in 1979. Significantly rising costs, largely the result of strong public opposition, and concerns about waste disposal continue to pose major obstacles to new construction. But earlier decisions to build, license, and locate nuclear power plants provide helpful examples of ordinary ethical decision making.

To receive a license to construct a nuclear plant, a power company must first demonstrate to government regulators that its customers need more power. Typically, the companies did this by demonstrating the existence of consumer demand for more electricity. The implicit assumption was that *social need* is the same as *consumer demand*.

The next step required the company to show why nuclear fuel, rather than coal or oil, should be used to meet the demand. Again, cost-benefit analysis was the typical way to accomplish this. The company would compare the costs and benefits of the alternatives, and if its analysis showed that a nuclear plant was more cost effective than oil or coal, the company had met the second condition.

The third step, taken in consultation with various government bodies, involved choosing a location for the plant. Again, the company would propose various alternative sites and conduct a cost-benefit analysis to decide among the alternatives. Such an analysis might proceed as follows.

One proposed site would be in a rural area, some distance from the major population center that was home to the increasing consumer demand for electricity. The costs for this site would include building and maintaining power lines, as well as the small loss of electricity that occurs through transmission. On the other hand, land costs typically would be lower in a rural area, as would costs for labor and materials. Additionally, of course, *if* an accident was to occur, a rural location would put a smaller number of people at risk.

On the other hand, building the plant within a metropolitan area would save transmission costs and provide efficiencies. However, labor, land, and material costs would likely be higher in a metropolitan area. Finally, in the remote case of an accident, hundreds of thousands of people would be put at risk. The actual location of nuclear power plants across this country is the best evidence we have for determining how and why government and industry made these decisions.

2.1 INTRODUCTION

Implicit within the descriptions of these controversies are the fundamental categories and language of ethics: rights, fairness, justice, and utility. These controversies call out for the type of careful analysis that is most at home in philosophical ethics. Throughout history, philosophers have sought to develop systematic and comprehensive accounts of the ethical life. These ethical theories provide a basis from which to understand, analyze, evaluate, and guide ethical behavior. This chapter considers the relevance of such theories and briefly describes several that are important for much of what is discussed in this textbook.

The word *ethics* is derived from the Greek word *ethos*, meaning "custom." In this sense, ethics refers to *the general beliefs, attitudes, or standards that guide customary behavior*. Thus, any society will have its own ethics in the sense that it will have certain typical beliefs, attitudes, and standards that determine what is customary. But from the earliest days of Greek philosophy, *philosophical ethics* has not been satisfied simply to accept as right that which is customary. Ethics as a branch of philosophy seeks a reasoned examination of what custom tells us about how we ought to live. Indeed, it is fair to say that Western philosophy was born in Socrates' lifelong critical examination of the customary norms of Greek society.

This critical examination involves two levels of stepping back or abstracting ourselves from ordinary experience. (Perhaps this explains the common perception of philosophy as "too abstract.") We all hold certain beliefs, attitudes, and values about our ordinary, customary experience. Philosophy asks us to step back from this experience to reflect critically on it: Why do we believe the things we believe? Should we change our attitudes? Are our values justified? At this first level of abstraction, customary behavior is examined by appeal to some norm or standard of what *ought* or *should* be done. The difference between ordinary experience and the first level of philosophical abstraction is the difference between what *is* done (or valued or believed) and what *ought* to be done (or valued or believed).

One of the first and most serious challenges in any study of ethics involves identifying an issue as an ethical issue. We all need to practice this stepping back in order to recognize ethical issues in our everyday experience. For example, in the classic environmental essay *The Land Ethic*, Aldo Leopold retells the story of Odysseus's return from the Trojan War.[1] Odysseus hanged a dozen women slaves whom he suspected of misbehavior. Because Greeks saw slaves as property, they apparently saw nothing ethically wrong with this action. Leopold uses this example to call for an "extension of ethics" to include human relations to the land. Just as Odysseus was ethically insensitive to the evil of killing slaves, we fail to notice the wanton destruction of the land. Leopold's point is that sometimes we need to work intellectually in order to be capable of noticing an ethical issue. A major contribution of such notable environmental writers as Aldo Leopold and Rachel Carson was precisely this ability to get us to notice ethical and philosophical issues where previously we were limited by our customary beliefs, attitudes, and values.

Uncovering the limitations of our ethical and environmental consciousness is a regular theme in the chapters that follow. This may also turn out to be the cause of some of the frustration that characterizes ethical discussions and, therefore, prevents us from following through on the careful thinking required in ethics. Many environmental controversies rest on different attitudes and values concerning our world. Few things are as frustrating as having our fundamental perspectives challenged. But we need to be open to the possibility that, like Odysseus, we might suffer from an ethical ignorance. A primary goal of philosophical ethics is to constantly stretch our understandings, shift our perspective and consciousness, and help us escape the limitations implicit in customary ways of thinking.

To make ethical judgments, give advice, and offer evaluations of what ought or should be is to engage in *normative ethics*. This first level of abstraction is the type of ethical reasoning that most people associate with ethics.

Normative judgments prescribe behavior. "Pesticide use should be reduced." "Factories ought not pollute the air and water." "Endangered species ought to be protected." "Nuclear power plants should not be located in residential neighborhoods." Normative judgments implicitly or explicitly appeal to some norm or standard of ethical behavior.

Many environmental controversies involve disputes of normative ethics. One side believes that nuclear power plants are hazardous and the other side believes that nuclear power is necessary to maintain our lifestyle. Each side cites evidence and appeals to certain norms to support its judgments. Normative disputes can be frustrating when ethical discussions are left at this level, with disagreements and controversies abounding.

However, we must not remain at the level of normative ethics. Resolving controversy requires us once again to step out of or to abstract ourselves from specific disagreements in order to examine the values in conflict and the competing factors that underlie the conflict. Moving to this more abstract level of thinking is to move from normative to philosophical ethics.

Philosophical ethics is the third level of ethical reasoning. Philosophical ethics is a higher level of generality and abstraction in which we analyze and evaluate normative judgments and their supporting reasons. This is the level of the general concepts, principles, and theories to which we appeal in defending and explaining normative claims. This is the level at which philosophers are most comfortable and have the most to offer. Generally, evaluating reasons that support or criticize a normative judgment, or seek to clarify the concepts involved is the essence of philosophical ethics. In this sense, environmental ethics is a branch of philosophy involving the systematic study and evaluation of the normative judgments that are so much a part of environmentalism.

As used here, *ethical theory* refers to any attempt to provide systematic answers to the philosophical questions raised by descriptive and normative approaches to ethics. These questions are raised from both an individual moral point of view and the point of view of society or public policy. Individual moral questions would include: What should I do? What kind of person should I be? What do I value? How should I live? Questions of social philosophy or public policy include: What type of society is best? What policies should we follow as a group? What social arrangements and practices will best protect and promote individual well-being? What should be done when individuals disagree? From the earliest days of Western philosophy, ethics has included questions of both individual and social morality. Thus, in this broad sense, ethical theory would include philosophical analyses of moral, political, economic, legal, and social questions.[2]

2.2 WHY ETHICAL THEORY?

Chapter 1 discussed in general terms why the study of ethics is necessary for any complete evaluation of environmental controversies. This section considers why the study of *ethical theory* is also relevant.

Four general considerations make theory relevant to the study of environmental ethics. First, ethical theories provide a common language for

discussing and understanding ethical issues. Environmental ethics is characterized by deep and numerous controversies. Clearly, a necessary first step in
examining and resolving controversy is to understand these disputes fully
and accurately. The basic concepts and categories of ethics—rights, responsibilities, utility, the common good, and the relationships among these concepts—can provide a basis for mutual understanding and dialogue. Ethical
theories make explicit and systematize the common beliefs and shared values
that are often implicit in specific controversies. By learning the language of
philosophical ethics, we become better able to understand, evaluate, and
communicate. This, in turn, can empower us to become full participants in
environmental debates. Philosophical ethics can contribute to the common
language that is essential to reasoned dialogue.

Second, because various ethical theories have played a major role in our traditions, they tend to be reflected in the ways in which most of us think. By
learning about ethical theories, we become more aware of the patterns and
assumptions in our ways of thinking. We, thus, become better able to articulate our views and better able to defend them. Of equal importance, we gain
a philosophical perspective for a critical examination of our ways of thinking.
By making these patterns explicit, we also are in a position to better see and
understand issues as ethical issues.

Third, one traditional function of an ethical theory is to offer guidance and
evaluation. We can apply theories to specific situations and use them to generate specific recommendations. The long history of ethics gives us a reasonable basis from which to analyze and offer advice. As we work our way
through environmental controversies, it will be helpful if we do not have to
reinvent the wheel at every step. People reason about ethics in standard ways,
many of which match standard ethical theories. Because philosophers have
spent considerable time thinking through these theories and uncovering their
strengths and weaknesses, knowledge of theory is an important resource for
the debates that follow.

Finally, familiarity with ethical theories is important because some com-
mentators claim that these theories, embedded as they are in common ways
of thinking, have been responsible for some of the environmental problems
we face. That is, the practice of environmental ethics sometimes involves challenging the very theories of ethics that philosophers have been busy defending. Some argue that these theories are part of the problem, and that we have
been misled by these theories. Thus, an important part of environmental
ethics is an examination of philosophical theories about ethics. In this way,
environmental ethics not only benefits from traditional ethical theory but contributes to the development of this branch of philosophy.

2.3 ETHICAL RELATIVISM
Before turning to a survey of traditional ethical theories, we need to confront
a common challenge to philosophical ethics. In the view of some people,
studying ethics is futile because ethical values and judgments are, ultimately,

a matter of opinion or personal feelings. As such, ethical controversies cannot have objective and rational answers. This skepticism about ethics, what we shall call "ethical relativism," is often expressed in this rhetorical question: Who is to say what is right or wrong?

Ethical relativism is defined as the view that denies the possibility of making objective ethical judgments. The relativist holds that ethical standards depend on or are *relative to* an individual's feelings, culture, religion, and so forth. A relativist would claim that ethics is merely and exclusively a matter of what is customary. Therefore, relativists deny that there can be objective norms by which we can evaluate ethical behavior and judgments. A person who holds that all ethical beliefs are only a matter of custom is one example of a relativist. "It is all a matter of opinion," and therefore, we are wasting our time trying to find the "correct" or "true" answers to environmental controversies.

Relativism may be the most serious challenge to teachers of ethics. This is not because we lack philosophical refutations of this view. Rather, relativism threatens our most important goal as teachers: to develop in our students the skills of careful and informed thinking. Too often, the relativist challenge is raised at exactly the critical point of an ethical controversy, when calling for careful reasoning. Unfortunately, many people turn to the relativist perspective more as a result of frustration and intellectual laziness than as the result of careful philosophical reasoning. Just when a controversy demands careful and reasoned analysis, relativists shrug their shoulders and dismiss the debate, asking, "Who is to say what is right or wrong?"

The short answer to that rhetorical question is this: anyone who can offer good reasons to support a judgment of right or wrong. Both normative and philosophical ethics provide resources for disputing the relativist claim. The chapters that follow are evidence that reasoning is possible and that relativism is, therefore, wrong. To practice philosophical ethics is to do the hard work of reasoning through ethical controversies. This textbook invites you to participate fully in this hard work.

Of course, some reasons for rejecting ethical relativism go beyond its implications for teachers of ethics. First, we should not confuse the *fact* that people disagree about ethical issues with the philosophical *claim* that objective agreement is impossible. People in different cultures and from differing backgrounds hold different beliefs about many things, including—but not limited to—questions of ethics. But it would be a mistake to conclude that there is no right answer simply because two cultures hold different beliefs. For example, some people may believe that the earth is flat and at the center of the universe. But we have no reason to conclude that because people disagree that there are no objective standards for evaluating these beliefs. So, too, is it a mistake to reason that because cultures disagree about values that no correct answer exists. Believing that the earth is flat does not make it flat or believing that murder is right does not make it right.

We should also be careful not to ask too much of ethical reasoning. Few controversies that are examined in this book can be resolved with moral certainty.

It is tempting to think that if ethics cannot "prove" a conclusion beyond doubt that no objective conclusion exists. But this standard of proof, perhaps applicable in mathematics and a few other areas, is surely inappropriate in ethics. Just as such sciences as medicine, ecology, and meteorology offer rational and objective judgments without proving these judgments beyond any doubt, so too does ethics involve standards of reasoning that are different from those found in mathematics.

Finally, we should point out the implications of relativism. A consistent relativist must believe that there is no objective basis for praising friendship, love, freedom, and democracy while condemning hatred, murder, slavery, and totalitarianism. The relativist must accept the conclusion that no objective grounds exist for denouncing a tyrant or for praising a hero. A consistent ethical relativist must deny that rational persuasion and dialogue in ethics are possible. Although some people may talk like ethical relativists, few of us could live our lives as consistent relativists. Perhaps this practical contradiction is the most telling refutation of the relativist position.

2.4 NATURAL LAW—THE TRADITION OF TELEOLOGY

One of the oldest ethical traditions relevant to environmental ethics is the *natural law* or *teleological tradition*. We can trace the ethical views associated with this tradition to Aristotle (fourth century B.C.) and Thomas Aquinas (thirteenth century A.D.).

Aristotle did not distinguish ethics and science as clearly as we sometimes distinguish them today. Aristotle thought that the study of biology and psychology was an essential part of ethics because this required, at a minimum, knowledge of basic human needs, common capabilities and potentials, and motivation. Further, Aristotle placed the biological sciences at the forefront of knowledge, whereas in the twentieth century physics and math seem to hold sway. This interesting blend of biology and ethics is one reason that this ethical tradition can be relevant to environmental issues.

For Aristotle, to fully understand something was to understand the *causes* for its being the way it is. Science involves more than simply describing what exists. Scientific knowledge requires that we be able to explain *why* something is what it is. To do this requires that we describe four aspects, what Aristotle called the "four causes" of an object's existence—the *material, formal, efficient,* and *final causes.*

An object's material cause is what an object is made from, its matter. The formal cause explains how that matter is organized or structured so that this material is what it is rather than something else that is made from the same material. Thus, a tree and a table have the same material cause, wood, which exists in two different forms. An efficient cause explains how something comes to be what it is. A carpenter would be the efficient cause for some wood becoming a table. Last, a final cause explains the purpose or characteristic activity of the object. The final cause of the table is to provide a place at which to sit and eat. The final cause or characteristic activity of a tree would be that activity which trees do that other living things do not. No doubt, Aristotle would be happy with the type of explanation that modern biology offers: trees take nutrition from their environment and convert it into wood, bark, and leaves in a process of growth and reproduction.

Aristotle's science differed in part from a more modern version in holding that we do not fully understand an object until we understand its final cause or its characteristic or natural activity. Based on his observations of nature, Aristotle believed that all things do have a natural and distinctive activity. The goal of this activity, what it is aiming for (sometimes called its purpose or function), was identified in the Greek as the object's *telos*. Hence, Aristotle's science and his ethics are often called *teleological*. We understand some object fully, according to Aristotle, only when we understand its natural function or activity.

For example, suppose that we seek a scientific explanation of a heart. In Aristotle's view, we do not fully understand the heart until we understand its characteristic activity. A teleological explanation of the heart answers these questions: What is the distinctive activity of hearts? What functions do hearts perform that distinguish them from other bodily organs? We understand the heart when we understand its function in the circulatory system. A teleological explanation would describe the heart as an organ that pumps blood throughout the body.

A more modern explanation might instead explain the heart in terms of its composition (or matter): muscle tissue, cells, and the like. A modern tendency is to reduce the object to be studied to its more simple elements and investigate the physical, mechanical, and chemical forces (efficient causes) that make this object what it is (formal cause).[3]

Aristotle distinguishes two basic types of natural objects: those that are alive and those that are not. The characteristic activity of living things, what we might call the "principle of life itself," is called the "psyche" or, as it was later translated, the "soul." Thus, to say that some body is alive is to say that it has a soul. Aristotle describes three "powers" or fundamental activities of life: nutrition, sensation, and thinking. Some living things possess only one (the "nutritive soul"), whereas others possess two (the nutritive and "appetitive" or "sensitive"), and some possess all three types (the nutritive, appetitive, and thinking). Plants are living things that possess only the nutritive soul. This means that their characteristic activities include only the powers of nutrition, growth, and reproduction. Animals possess appetitive powers in addition to nutrition. This means that their natural activities include the powers of sensation, desire, and motion. Finally, only humans possess the three life activities of nutrition, appetite, and thought.

With this admittedly brief characterization, we can now see how the distinction between scientific fact and ethical value was not as clear for Aristotle as it sometimes seems today. When we understand the characteristic activity of a heart, for example, we also come to understand what a *good* heart is. A good heart is one that pumps blood through the body in a regular, stable, and continuous manner and does so over a long period of time. A good heart is one that performs its characteristic activity well.

Aristotle believed that this teleological framework could be applied to all natural objects, including humans. All things have a natural activity or function. Things are good when they fulfill this function or, in terms more common to this tradition, when they actualize their potential.

In general terms, every living thing can be said to have a good of its own. The good for any living thing is to attain fully its natural activity (or fully actualize its soul). Thus, the good of a plant is to accomplish the nutritive functions of taking in nutrition, growth, and reproduction. The good of animals includes these functions, as well as attaining its desires and fulfilling its appetites. The human good includes all these ends, as well as living a thoughtful and deliberative life.

This teleological system was further developed in the writings of Thomas Aquinas in the thirteenth century. It is perhaps through Aquinas's writings that these views have had the greatest influence on Western thought.

Aquinas attempted to synthesize Christian theology and Aristotle's science and ethics. He interprets the scientific and ethical teleology of Aristotle as evidence that a divine plan operates in nature. The characteristic activity of all natural objects results from God's plan and God's purposes. Because God is assumed to be supremely good and because the purposes discovered in nature are God's purposes, the natural order can be equated with the moral order. Nature itself has a purpose, and the harmonious functioning of nature reveals the goodness of God's plan. In this theory, the laws of nature or natural law include both descriptive regularities that we discover in nature and, because these regularities are part of the divine plan, the normative and prescriptive rules that we ethically ought to follow. In this ethical tradition, fulfilling our natural potential—a potential implicitly in harmony with the rest of nature—is the highest form of ethical activity for an individual.

Several themes in modern environmentalism are reminiscent of this ethical tradition. Basing their views on the findings of some ecologists, many environmentalists assume that natural ecosystems are well-ordered and harmonious. All parts of an ecosystem and especially all its biotic members have a distinctive place in the overall scheme. Each contributes to the natural order in its own way. Nature undisturbed is good. Ecological problems arise when humans interfere with the natural order and treat other natural objects as having value only insofar as they serve human purposes. In this view, the way the world is (or would be if humans did not interfere), is the way the world should be. This ethics would prescribe a general policy of preservationism and nonintervention.

Other environmentalists emphasize the ethical status of all living things and base this status on the fact that every living thing has a good of its own. A version of this view is presented in examining biocentric ethics in Chapter 7. Although the Aristotlean system allows for a moral hierarchy with humans "higher" than animals and animals "higher" than plants, it nevertheless also allows for the possibility of seeing that all living things have a good of their own. Thus, they possess a good that is independent of human interests and uses.

Unfortunately, several major objections to the Aristotlean tradition undermine its relevance to contemporary debates. The first objection denies that all natural objects do have some one definite and distinctive telos. It seems true that some objects have a definite purpose or function. Human artifacts, such as a chair or a computer, are obvious examples. Some *parts* of a natural whole, such as a heart or a chromosome, also seem to have natural functions. But these parts have a purpose only in the sense that they contribute to the function of the whole. It does not seem obvious that these wholes themselves have a purpose. What, for example, is the characteristic activity of a human being? What is the characteristic activity of a spotted owl? Philosophers and scientists in the modern era have thought that they could fully understand and explain natural objects without having to assume some natural purpose or plan. (Interestingly enough, some ecologists are less reluctant to attribute characteristic functions to members of ecosystems.)

A second objection denies that we can conclude that something is good simply because it is natural. Because some natural occurrences seem evil—for example, pain and suffering caused by death, disease, and natural disasters—some reason other than the appeal to nature must show why something is good. It would be a giant leap, for example, to reason from the characteristic natural activity of the HIV virus to the conclusion that this virus is good. In the natural law tradition, the explanation most often given for the connection between natural and good lies in a divine plan. However, this appeal effectively ends the philosophical discussion because it provides a reason only to those people who already assume a divine creator. To people of other religious traditions or to people who do not believe in a supremely good creator, this reason carries little rational weight.

Finally, modern evolutionary science provides a significant and perhaps insurmountable challenge to the natural law tradition. The process of natural selection offers an account of the apparent design found in nature without appealing to any purpose or telos. The order that is found in nature comes not from a divine plan but from the process of species adapting to their environment, typically through a process of random mutation and natural selection. For example, a defender of natural law might explain the long neck of the giraffe by claiming that the long neck exists (or was designed) in order to allow the giraffe to reach food high off the ground. The defender of natural selection, on the other hand, would claim that the giraffe did not develop a long neck in order to reach the leaves high in a tree but that it survived because, having a long neck, it could reach these leaves and was, thus, better adapted to its environment than competing organisms. The long neck is itself the result of random evolutionary change. Thus, the purposive language of teleology can be reduced to the more mechanistic language of the physical sciences. In this view, nature as we find it today is the result of hundreds of millions of years of random evolutionary change. Nature is neither good nor bad; it just is.

Thus, although the natural law tradition provides a framework for thinking and reasoning about relations between nature and ethics, it is not without significant philosophical challenges. This brief review helps us evaluate later occasions when we see various insights from this tradition applied to contemporary environmental issues.

2.5 THE UTILITARIAN TRADITION

A second ethical tradition that is helpful in the study of environmental ethics is *utilitarianism*. The classical statements of this tradition are found in the writings of Jeremy Bentham and John Stuart Mill in the nineteenth century, but utilitarianism continues to be an influential theory today.[4] Utilitarian reasoning is especially influential in the areas of economics, public policy, and government regulation, as the discussions that open this chapter suggest. This means that utilitarianism has also played a significant role in environmental policy.

In general terms, utilitarianism tells us to maximize the overall good or to produce the greatest good for the greatest number. Utilitarian theory, thus, rests on two elements: an account of the good and a rule for judging all acts and decisions in terms of that good. The rule tells us to look to the *consequences* of any particular act and judge the ethical status of that act in terms of those consequences. If the act tends to maximize good consequences, it is an ethically right act, and if it does not, the act is ethically wrong.

Consequently, utilitarians distinguish between two basic types of value: the good, which is valued for its own sake, and all other things, which are valued because of their relation to the good. Thus, all acts or decisions are judged in terms of their utility or their usefulness in producing good consequences. This distinction is sometimes made in terms of *intrinsic* and *instrumental value*. Utilitarians defend some view of intrinsic value (for example, pleasure or happiness) and then judge the value of all other things and activities in terms of how well they serve to achieve the optimal amount of that value.

The challenge to utilitarians, of course, is to successfully defend an account of the good that can serve as the basis of all other values. If this good is to function in this way, it should be *objective* (good independent of particular human interests) and *universal* (good for all people at all times). Different versions of utilitarianism can then be distinguished by how they describe the good.

Two versions of utilitarianism are important for what follows. One type of utilitarianism takes pleasure, or at least the absence of pain, to be the only good valued for its own sake. Pleasure and the absence of pain are universally desired. People who desire pain or avoid pleasure typically are suspected of acting unreasonably. Pleasure would seem to be a plausible candidate for something that is objectively good and universally valued. This version is called *hedonistic utilitarianism*.

A second version of utilitarianism understands the good as the happiness that results from the satisfaction of our desires. In this view, people are happy when they have what they want, when their desires are satisfied. A world in which as many people have as much of what they desire as possible would be the ethically best world. Contemporary defenders of this version often fine-tune this by adding the requirement that individuals are best left to choose and rank their desires. Sometimes called *preference utilitarianism*, this version would direct us to satisfy as many individual preferences as possible. Something close to this was surely operating in the public policy decisions for locating nuclear power plants. As presented in Chapter 3, this ethical theory is closely associated with free-market economic theory, and in that way it has significant implications for environmental policy.

A number of standard challenges are raised against utilitarian thinking, and reviewing several of them will prove helpful. We can group together a set of challenges as *measurement* problems. Utilitarianism essentially involves a process of measurement and comparison. Phrases like "maximize the overall good" and "the greatest good for the greatest number" necessarily require measuring, comparing, and quantifying. However, a tension exists when we attempt to quantify that which is primarily qualitative. The good is taken by utilitarians to be that which has intrinsic value. Yet intrinsic value may not be the sort of thing that can easily be counted, measured, or compared.

These considerations lead to several serious philosophical problems. The first challenges the very possibility of quantifying such things as pleasure, happiness, desires, and so forth. Are we to assume that all pleasures or desires are qualitatively the same? Are all pleasures created equal? Is the pleasure that I receive from breathing clean air equal to the pleasure that you receive from smoking? If not, how can we measure them? According to what scale? In part, preference utilitarianism attempts to overcome this problem because preferences, as opposed to desires, are ranked. I want both more time to finish my work and a vacation, but I *prefer* the vacation to work. However, although this may overcome some problems of comparing an individual's desires, it does not help in making comparisons of two people with conflicting desires.

A second problem follows from this. Because the good is difficult to quantify, utilitarians have a tendency to substitute for the good something that can be quantified. For example, suppose we take good health to be the social goal we seek to maximize. How can we measure and compare the health consequences of various pollution control decisions? In practice, it could become easy to substitute for health some quantifiable considerations such as life expectancy, infant mortality, injury rate, per capita expenditures on health care, and the like. Although such factors may well give us an indication of health, they surely do not give us the whole story. Moreover, in practice it becomes easy to forget the primary goal of health and simply identify these quantifiable factors as the final goal. This problem raises significant questions when we realize that the most easily quantifiable substitute for the good is money.

Critics claim that this is exactly what occurs when environmental regulation is subjected to cost-benefit analysis. Because regulators seem unable to measure the value of health itself, they instead measure various economic factors associated with health and then decide cases by comparing the costs of health to the costs of closing down the source of pollution.

A final measurement problem arises when we consider the *scope* of the people to be considered and the *range* of what counts as a person. In theory, the utilitarian should be concerned with all the pleasure or happiness that is affected by the particular act. In practice, this is all but impossible. We can never know all the consequences of any act. The tendency among utilitarians is to restrict consideration to the expected consequences to people in the immediate vicinity. Further, an act's effects on future generations, for example, on people in other countries, or on animals (who do experience pleasure and pain) are often ignored. Each of these limitations has significant environmental implications.

The criticisms raised so far could be countered by adjusting the application of utilitarian principles. Other criticisms raise more direct challenges to the theory itself and call for abandoning rather than reforming utilitarianism. One such challenge begins with the provisional nature of utilitarian judgments. According to the utilitarian, no particular act, in and of itself, is ever right or wrong. The ethical status of any act always depends on something else: its consequences. Right and wrong always depend upon the context and, therefore, always depend on factors outside the individual's control. But this reasoning seems to miss an important area of ethical concern, namely, those occasions when the ethically correct decision is to act on principle, regardless of consequences. There can be times when we judge an act to be wrong in principle, even if the overall consequences turn out to be good. There are times when we judge an act to be ethically right in principle, even if the overall consequences turn out to be bad. Because utilitarianism seems unable to account for such notable cases, critics charge that this theory is at best incomplete.

Two examples may help illuminate this point. Imagine a situation in which significant and good consequences would result if only I would betray a friend. Imagine also that this friend would never know that I was responsible for the betrayal. In such a scenario, the utilitarian decision would be to betray the friend. However, critics would claim that this betrayal violates an important ethical principle ("do not betray friends") and ought not be done, even if the consequences were bad.

A second example can be developed from a well-known environmental controversy. In recent years, many environmentalists have fought to prevent logging in the old-growth forests of the Pacific Northwest. Logging activities were threatening to destroy the habitat of the spotted owl, an endangered species. The spotted owl was threatened with extinction if the logging continued. On the other hand, significant social benefits would follow from a growth in the logging industry. Because the owl has no known *use* and because it does not contribute to society in any obvious way, a utilitarian calculation might suggest that the logging be allowed. However, environmentalists charged that causing the extinction of a species is wrong in principle, even if doing so would result in a net increase in beneficial social consequences.

At the beginning of this chapter, we suggested that ethical theory should be studied because, among other reasons, some standard theories are embedded in common ways of thinking and reasoning. This is perhaps most true of utilitarianism. In many ways, it is the unofficial ethical theory of public policy in much of North America and Western Europe. Time and time again, environmental debates are cast in utilitarian terms. Recent political debates about the Clean Air Act, Clean Water Act, and Endangered Species Act are clear examples of this, as is the public policy decision making surrounding nuclear power plants and protection of the spotted owl. We hope that this brief introduction helps you recognize utilitarian reasoning and sensitizes you to the implicit strengths and inherent dangers of this common public philosophy.

2.6 DEONTOLOGY: AN ETHICS OF DUTY AND RIGHTS

The final ethical tradition considered emphasizes the notion of acting on principle rather than consequences. In this view, the central concepts of ethics involve duties and rights. (This approach to ethics is sometimes called "deontology" from the Greek word for *duty*.) The classic philosophical defense of this view is found in the writings of the eighteenth century German philosopher Immanuel Kant.[5]

Remember one of the critical concerns raised against utilitarianism: the view that seemed to make the ethical status of our acts depend on factors over which we have no control. My acts are judged by their consequences, yet surely I can neither anticipate nor control all the consequences of my actions. Thus, that ethical theory seems to hold people responsible for things that they cannot control. This would seem to violate a fundamental maxim of ethics. People can be held responsible only for those things within their power or, in the words of an often-used phrase, *ought* implies *can*.

Kantian ethics begins with the claim that we can be held responsible only for those things that we can control. This, argued Kant, means that the focus of ethics should be on those principles (what he called "maxims") on which we choose to act.

We can think of these principles as expressing the intention of our action. Assuming that we are rational beings and do not act merely as a result of instinct or conditioning, we can be held responsible because we have freely chosen or have intended our actions. Thus, Kant held that we are ethical beings because we are rational beings who can freely form intentions and deliberately choose to act on them. Our standing as moral beings is derived from our nature as free and rational beings.

But how do we determine which intentions are ethically correct and which are unethical? Kant argued that we are acting ethically whenever the principle or maxim on which we act is a rational one. A rational principle in ethics, like rationality in other areas, would be found acceptable and binding by all other actors. That is, a rational principle is one that is *categorical* and *universalized*. The fundamental ethical duty, called by Kant the "categorical imperative," is to act only in those ways that all rational beings would find acceptable.

Kant believed that this fundamental ethical duty could be expressed in a number of different ways. The categorical imperative also requires that we treat people as *ends* and never simply as *means* or as *subjects,* and never simply as *objects.* Thus, we are ethically obligated to treat people as rational and autonomous beings. We should never treat a person as a mere thing to be used for our own purposes. People are subjects who have their own purposes and intentions, and we have a moral obligation to respect them as capable of making their own decisions.

Thus, the categorical imperative establishes our fundamental ethical duties: treat people as ends and never as mere means or as objects. However, because other people are equally obligated to treat me in this manner, the categorical imperative can also be seen as establishing our fundamental ethical *rights.* Like all people, I have the right to be treated as an end, not as a means. I have the right to be treated as a free and rational being who has his own purposes and goals. I have the right to pursue those goals so long as I do not in turn treat others as a means to my ends. Following from these considerations, this ethical tradition places primary value on the duty to treat other people with respect and on the rights of equality and freedom. These basic rights and duties all follow from our nature as beings capable of free and rational action.

This discussion of duties and rights gives us another way to understand the major deficiency in utilitarian thinking. Given its focus on consequences, utilitarianism neglects the important role that moral principles can play in ethical decision making. According to Kant, acting on principle is to act in accordance with the categorical imperative. The principle of justice, for example, requires us to fulfill our duties to other people. Justice requires that we respect the rights of other people at all times and under all conditions. (That is what it means to call this imperative "categorical.") Utilitarianism, on the other hand, requires us to fulfill our duties and respect others' rights *only* when doing so maximizes the overall good consequences. But this, argues the Kantian, is the perfect example of injustice: fulfilling duties and respecting rights only when doing so has beneficial consequences.

Thus, rights can trump social utility.[6] If I have a right to some good (or a right to be protected against some harm), denying me this good (or not protecting me from that harm) would be wrong, even if doing so would contribute to the overall social good. This is one way to understand the recent debates concerning takings legislation. If I have a right to private property, taking this property from me simply to satisfy the desires of the wider community would be wrong. Proponents of takings legislation claim that many environmental laws violate the rights of individuals simply to serve the utilitarian goal of maximizing overall happiness. In this view, such acts violate principles of social justice.

Such ideas have had a profound influence on Western ethical and political thought. They are reflected in the central notions of democracy and civil liberties. An ethical theory that does not take seriously the dignity of each person as a free and rational agent would need significant philosophical defense. Nonetheless, we must mention several critical issues at this point.

Some critics claim that the Kantian ethical tradition offers no basis for making substantive value judgments. So long as I am treating other people correctly (which I might accomplish simply by leaving other people alone), no ethical basis exists for evaluating those choices that I do make. In that view, value questions become merely a matter of personal choice or preference. According to some critics, this deontological tradition offers no account of what is good, valuable, or worthy. A life of conspicuous consumption, if autonomously chosen and if done without violating the dignity of other autonomous agents, is ethically no better or worse than a more ecologically sound lifestyle. A life spent competing with others or in solitude and loneliness is ethically no worse than a life of friendships, caring, and community.

A version of this criticism holds that talk of rights amounts to little more than a disguised way of talking about "wants." If people want something strongly enough, they attempt to legitimize their wants by identifying them as rights. One result is an explosion of rights with society becoming a collection of numerous interest groups, each claiming rights against the greater public interest and overall social good.

Other critics see a strong human-centered or anthropocentric bias implicit in this tradition. It seems a short step from treating humans as ends because they are rational to treating nonrational things as mere means. There appears little basis in this tradition for ethical obligations to anything that is not free and rational. Thus, it would seem legitimate to treat other living beings and the environment simply as means to our ends. These things are, after all, the perfect example of objects, not subjects. Some of these criticisms are developed at greater length in later chapters.

2.7 SOCIAL JUSTICE AND PROPERTY RIGHTS

Earlier in this chapter, it was suggested that ethics has traditionally included both individual moral questions (What should I do? What kind of person should I be?) and questions of social justice or public policy (How should we arrange our society? Which political and economic institutions are just?). We should recognize that the ethical traditions of natural law, utilitarianism, and Kantian deontology have had a significant influence on the development of modern political thinking. Indeed, it is fair to see these philosophical theories as providing the intellectual and ethical framework of most modern social and political arrangements. Both classical utilitarianism and Kantian deontology are especially influential in the development of democratic forms of government that provide strong protections of individual freedoms and individual rights.

The political arrangements of a constitutional democracy are a useful example for seeing the connections between these ethical traditions and contemporary politics. A commitment to majority rule can be seen as serving the utilitarian goal of maximizing happiness. If we seek to attain the greatest happiness for the greatest number, we would not go wrong by taking a vote and following the will of the majority. On the other hand, constitutional protections of civil rights and civil liberties can be seen as serving the Kantian goal of respecting individual autonomy. Thus, constitutional rights serve as a check on and limit to the majoritarian decisions of legislature.

Sometimes these social and political dimensions get overlooked in discussions of ethics. It is easy for us to think about ethics only from the inside, as private individuals looking out at the world and asking about our rights and responsibilities. In doing this, we can easily overlook how much our choices, attitudes, and values are influenced and limited by what is outside. Human beings do not only create and shape their social institutions, but these institutions in turn also create and shape human attitudes, beliefs, and values. Ethics must also challenge us to look at our social institutions and ask what are they doing *to* us and *for* us? Are our social institutions just? Are burdens and benefits distributed fairly? Do our social and political arrangements encourage cooperation and community or competition and domination? How is power distributed, and how is it limited? How should we—as a group, not as individuals—live?

The controversies presented in the discussions that begin this chapter are not simply conflicts of self-interest or politics. They are controversies involving conflicting theories of social justice, individual rights, and different visions of the good and just society.

Few individual rights have played a more important role in Western political and philosophical traditions than the right of private property. Unquestionably, no right is more central to a wider variety of environmental issues than private property. Property and the related concepts of ownership and land are fundamental to many debates that we examine in this textbook.

Contemporary Western understanding of property rights is often traced to the seventeenth century English philosopher John Locke.[7] Locke's political philosophy begins by speculating about a "state of nature," the situation in which humans would exist were there no government. In this original natural state, all land is unowned (or, more in line with seventeenth century thinking, owned by God). This unowned land becomes owned, becomes *private* property, when an individual "mixes his labor" with the unowned land. In essence, Locke's argument is as follows:

1. People have exclusive rights over, "own," their bodies and their labor.

2. Land, in its natural state, is unowned—no one individual can rightfully claim exclusive control of it.

3. Therefore, when someone's labor, which is owned, comes to be "mixed" with land that is unowned, the exclusive rights over that person's labor are transferred to the land. The person comes to own the land.

For example, if people travel into the wilderness, clear some land, build homes, till the soil, and grow crops on this land, they come to have a legitimate claim to this land. This legitimate claim is the establishment of private property rights.

A number of powerful objections have been raised against this Lockean view of private property. Some objections stem from the vagueness of the mixing metaphor. If I do mix something owned with something unowned, why assume that I come to own what was previously unowned? Why not assume that I lose ownership of what was previously owned, that I lose my labor in the mixing? Why not assume that I gain ownership over only the improvements that I make, so that I can own the crops that I grow but not the land itself? Suppose that my labor worsens rather than improves the land? What if the goal of the first people on the land is to preserve it, and they, therefore, make a conscious decision not to mix their labor with it? Must all land be developed to be valued and owned?

Other problems arise when we realize that Locke's seventeenth century European image of some vast unowned wilderness does an injustice to historical fact. The image of early American settlers, mixing their labor with the western frontier and laying claim to it, ignores the native peoples who had been using that land for millennia. In effect, the Lockean view of property presupposes an agricultural or industrial conception of property. Nomadic cultures, for example, might travel over broad expanses of land as they follow changing seasons or migrating herds. The idea of laying a private and exclusive claim on the land would be quite outlandish in such a culture.

Finally, according to Locke's ethical principles, private ownership can be justified only when "enough and as good" land remains for others. Lockean property rights are derived from a more fundamental right of personal liberty ("the exclusive rights over one's own body"). Thus, I can justify *my* ownership only when it does not violate the liberty of other people. This will not happen, according to Locke, so long as sufficient land is left in common for others. In the modern world, with a population of almost 6 billion people, it is difficult to see how this condition can be met.

Difficulties like these have led more contemporary accounts to view private property as involving a bundle of associated rights. These include the right to possess, control, use, benefit from, dispose of, and exclude others from the property. The "bundle view" is thought necessary because of the complexity that follows from the attempt to specify the implications of property rights. For example, surely it will not do to say that my right to property means that I can do anything I want with it. The rights of other people restrict my property rights in a number of ways. I cannot turn my backyard into a toxic waste dump, for example. Zoning laws restrict the type of building that I can construct on my property and the uses of that building. Owning stock in a corporation, for example, entitles me to receive certain benefits from that stock in the form of dividends and appreciation. However, stock owners may not have the right to manage or exclude others from using the corporate property, nor in some cases can they even sell the stock to anyone they choose.

By viewing property rights as a bundle of rights, a property right no longer can be seen as an all-or-nothing thing. Just as zoning laws restrict but do not violate my property rights, much legislation aimed at protecting the environment will restrict only some rights in the bundle. Keep this in mind as we review contemporary environmental debates such as those surrounding the wise use movement and takings legislation. The debate seldom, if ever, is that either the environment is harmed or I lose my property rights. Most debates involve the degree and type of control that property owners are allowed to exercise over the various aspects of their interests.

2.8 SUMMARY AND CONCLUSIONS

We might think of this textbook as presenting an ongoing conversation among philosophers, scientists, environmentalists, and citizens. The conversation has been going on for some time, but it clearly has a long way to go before reaching any conclusions. We can think of these initial chapters as providing an introduction to some of the main characters in the conversation and some of the motivation that initiated the conversation. We have also introduced some of the language that they are using and some of what has been said in the past.

By no means have the philosophers had the final word. Do not think that the path is now open for simply applying these philosophical theories and concepts to environmental problems. Rather, now that the introductions have been made, you should see yourself as a participant in this conversation. Join in the conversation, learn as you go, contribute what and when you can, and do not end the discussion too soon.

Notes

1. Aldo Leopold, "The Land Ethic," in *A Sand County Almanac with Essays on Conservation from Round River*, pp. 237–64 (New York: Oxford University Press, 1949).
2. For a insightful critique of a standard understanding of the role of ethical theory and principles in environmental ethics, see Ken Sayre, "An Alternative View of Environmental Ethics," *Environmental Ethics* (fall 1991): 195–213. Sayre argues against what he calls the "inferential" view of ethical theory, a view similar to what we shall be calling "applied ethics." Like Sayre, this textbook suggests that the inferential/applied view of ethical theory is at best incomplete when addressing environmental issues.
3. For Aristotle's account of the four causes, see his *Physics*, book 2, ch. 3. For a critique of the abuse of the more mechanistic model in environmental science, see Daniel Botkin's *Discordant Harmonies* (New York: Oxford University Press, 1990).
4. For the classic statements of utilitarianism, see Jeremy Bentham, *Introduction to the Principles of Morals and Legislation* (Oxford: Clarendon Press) and John Stuart Mill, *Utilitarianism*, edited by George Sher (Indianapolis, Ind.: Hackett, 1979). For a contemporary defense of utilitarianism, see J. J. C. Smart and Bernard Williams, *Utilitarianism: For and Against* (Cambridge, England: Cambridge University Press, 1973).

5. For Kant's views on ethics, see especially his *Groundwork for the Metaphysics of Morals*, edited by James Ellington (Indianapolis, Ind: Hackett, 1993).
6. For a thorough presentation of this view, see Ronald Dworkin, *Taking Rights Seriously* (Cambridge, Mass.: Harvard University Press, 1977).
7. For Locke's defense of private property, see his *Second Treatise on Government*, edited by C. B. Macpherson (Indianapolis, Ind.: Hackett, 1980), especially ch. 5. For a helpful collection of essays on property rights and economic justice see Virginia Held, *Property, Profits, and Economic Justice* (Belmont, Calif.: Wadsworth, 1980). For an excellent collection on land use policy and ethics see Lynton Caldwell and Kristin Shrader-Frechette, *Policy for Land* (Lanham, Md.: Rowman and Littlefield, 1993).

Discussion Questions

1. The United States Constitution prohibits the government from taking private property for public use without just compensation. Do you think that this clause should protect developers when they seek to build housing or a commercial development in an environmentally sensitive area? Do environmental laws that restrict land use violate this constitutional protection? If so, should developers be compensated for the price they paid for the land or for what they could have received if they had been allowed to develop the land?
2. If the price of land in a rural area is less than comparable land in an urban area, is this land less valuable? If not, how do you determine the value of land?
3. Given that society receives benefits from nuclear power, how should we determine the distribution of the burdens that go along with these benefits? Should nuclear waste storage facilities be located where the energy is generated, where the energy is used, even if that means within a large urban center, or should it be located in an area where the risks are lowest, even if the people living in that area do not benefit from nuclear energy?
4. Aristotle suggested that all natural objects could be distinguished in terms of a natural and characteristic activity. Can we apply this approach to an ecosystem? Do different elements of an ecosystem perform different functions within that system? Could you reason from such ecological facts to normative conclusions about what should be? Why or why not?
5. Many environmental controversies are seen as a debate between jobs and environmental protection. For example, the spotted owl controversy in the Pacific Northwest is often framed in terms of owls versus jobs. Are such utilitarian tradeoffs reasonable? Are tradeoffs possible?
6. Nomadic cultures on many continents travel across great distances following migrating herds of animals. Such people never settle permanently on one section of land. How might their understanding of ownership and property differ from yours? Can a concept of "private property" even exist in such a culture?

Further Reading

The original sources mentioned in the footnotes within this chapter are the best places to begin a study of ethical theory, although perhaps only Mill and Bentham are accessible to nonphilosophers on first reading. Aristotle, Aquinas, and Kant require substantial background to be easily followed on first read. However, many helpful secondary sources and textbooks are available.

James Rachels, *The Elements of Moral Philosophy*, 2d ed. (New York: McGraw-Hill, 1993), is a helpful survey text. Tim Robinson, *Aristotle* (Indianapolis: Hackett, 1995), provides a clear introduction to the philosophy of Aristotle. Peter Wenz, *Environmental Justice* (Albany: State University of New York Press, 1988), offers an introduction to environmental issues from the perspective of social justice rather than ethical theory.

ENVIRONMENTAL ETHICS AS APPLIED ETHICS

3

Ethics and Economics: The Cases of Forests and Pollution

Development Versus Preservation

The U.S. Forest Service is charged with managing the national forest lands for "outdoor recreation, range, timber, watershed, and wildlife and fish purposes." This multiple-use responsibility is the primary legal mission of the service. However, as a branch of the Department of Agriculture, the U.S. Forest Service views the trees that it manages primarily as crops to be harvested. In practice, the most serious challenge facing the U.S. Forest Service lies in deciding exactly how to balance the interests of the timber industry with the competing interests of recreational users of various types, preservationists, developers, and farmers.

During the 1960s, the U.S. Forest Service began accepting bids to develop the Mineral King Valley, a wilderness area adjacent to California's Sequoia National Park, for recreational uses. In January 1969, the U.S. Forest Service approved a plan submitted by Walt Disney Enterprises to develop Mineral King as a ski resort. The plan called for creating a complex of motels, restaurants, parking lots, and other structures to accommodate an estimated 14,000 daily visitors to the valley. Ski slopes, ski lifts, a cog-assisted railway, and utility lines would be built onto the mountainside. Walt Disney Enterprises also would build a twenty mile highway and a high-voltage power line crossing the Sequoia National Park.

The Sierra Club objected to these plans and filed suit in federal court seeking to prevent the commercial development of Mineral King Valley. The Sierra Club endorsed only those recreational uses that would be consistent with the preservation of this wilderness area in an undeveloped state. Critics of the U.S. Forest Service's decision offered numerous arguments to support their view. They claimed that the U.S. Forest Service failed to give aesthetic and ecological factors equal weight with economic considerations. They also claimed that the well-being of the animals, plants, rivers, and the mountain itself were being ignored.

In defense of its decision, the U.S. Forest Service argued that more citizens would get more of what they want under the Walt Disney Enterprises plan than under the Sierra Club's alternative. The 14,000 visitors expected daily at the resort would outnumber the people who use the area for hiking, camping, hunting, and fishing. Further, the willingness of skiers to pay more for their activities than wilderness users are willing to pay for theirs, as evidenced by Walt Disney Enterprises's ability to make a greater profit from this use than the Sierra Club could ever hope to make from its proposed uses, shows that the desire for skiing is more intense and widespread than is the desire for wilderness. For an agency of a democratic government, the economic market is a convenient measure of the desires of its citizens.

Water pollution is one of the most visible environmental problems. In 1969, the Cuyahoga River in Cleveland, Ohio was so saturated with petrochemical pollutants that it caught fire and burned. During the summer of 1988, numerous beaches along New Jersey's Atlantic shore were closed when human feces, hospital wastes, and other toxic substances washed ashore. In March 1989, the *Exxon Valdez* ran aground in Prince William Sound, Alaska, spilling approximately 11 million gallons of oil. The final toll on wildlife, the fishing industry, and recreation is still being counted. Every year, according to the World Health Organization, 5 million people, mostly children, die as a result of water-related diseases that are easily eliminated with proper sanitation and clean drinking water.

Like water pollution, air pollution is one of the first environmental issues that average citizens confront in their daily life. Airborne acidic chemicals, commonly called "acid rain," have caused tremendous environmental destruction through North America and Europe. Forests, lakes, rivers, and soil have become so acidified that they can no longer support life. During the record hot summer of 1988, seventy-six cities in the United States registered ozone pollution levels at least 25 percent higher than the maximum safe limit set by the Environmental Protection Agency (EPA). Airborne pollutants continue to destroy the earth's upper atmosphere ozone layer. This results in an increase in the harmful ultraviolet radiation that reaches the earth's surface. Other airborne pollutants, generally called "greenhouse gases," can result in a global warming effect that threatens significant climatic upheaval.

3.1 INTRODUCTION

The philosophical framework introduced in the first two chapters has been applied to a wide variety of public policy issues since the 1970s. "Applied ethics" has contributed to public debates in such fields as medical and business ethics and to such issues as affirmative action, economic justice, abortion, and the nuclear arms race. It is not surprising, then, that much of the philosophical work on environmental issues has followed the applied ethics format of identifying and clarifying ethical issues and analyzing them in terms of ethical theories and principles. At least initially, applying ethics to specific environmental issues was not seen as affecting ethics itself. Application did relatively little to change the theory and principles of the ethics that was applied.[1]

Applied ethics has frequently focused on the use of economic and market analyses in public policy debates. Economics is without question the most common tool of policy analysts, government decision makers, and private sector experts. This chapter examines the contributions that philosophers can make to environmental debates by applying philosophical ethics to economic analysis. Specifically, how economic analysis plays a central role in debates concerning the conservation of national forests and pollution of air and water is examined. Our philosophical evaluation suggests that the uncritical use of economic analysis to resolve environmental debates is seriously problematic.

It is not surprising that economics would play a major role in environmental debates. For example, many environmental problems appear to be fundamentally economic problems. Many environmental problems are easily cast in economic terms: the distribution of scarce resources, allocation of risks and benefits, competing interests, production of desired goods, and so forth. Furthermore, we can trace much environmental destruction to economic factors. To recognize this, we need only review the terrible environmental destruction that took place under the centralized state command economies of central and eastern Europe since World War II.[2]

The relevance of economics to the environment is nicely summarized in the following foreword to a book of economic analyses of U.S. environmental policy:

> A significant social development of the past decade [1968–1978] has been the general realization that important damage may be done to the environment if the economy is permitted to operate in an unfettered way. . . . This certainty of "market failure" has long been known by economists. . . . It is appropriate that economists concern themselves with this general group of problems. Just as the awareness of environmental problems becomes more general, it is now also becoming known more generally that environmental improvement requires more resources and greater sacrifices. Thus an economic problem exists whether lawmakers decide to protect the environment through direct regulation or whether they choose to modify economic incentives that affect the behavior of millions of decision makers in the economic system.[3]

Thus, environmental problems are often understood as economic problems requiring the skills and expertise of economists.

3.2 FORESTS: CONSERVATION OR PRESERVATION?

A pivotal moment in the history of American environmentalism occurred during the first decade of the twentieth century. The specific debates concerned a proposal to build a dam and reservoir in the Hetch Hetchy Valley adjacent to California's Yosemite National Park. Demand for water in San Francisco led to the plan to flood the Hetch Hetchy. Two of the most prominent early American environmentalists, Gifford Pinchot and John Muir, were at the center of these debates, which have come to symbolize two major competing environmental world views.

Gifford Pinchot was head of the U.S. Forest Service, one of the first professionally trained foresters in the United States, and a close friend and adviser to President Theodore Roosevelt. Pinchot was a founder and leader of the conservation movement, which held that forestlands are to be conserved so that they might be wisely used and controlled by all citizens. He was an early defender of the scientific management of national forest lands. His guiding principle was that public lands exist to serve the needs and uses of the public.

> The object of our forest policy is not to preserve the forests because they are beautiful . . . or because they are refuges for the wild creatures of the wilderness . . . but . . . the making of prosperous homes.[4]

He also said,

> Forestry is the knowledge of the forest. In particular, it is the art of handling the forest so that it will render whatever service is required of it without being impoverished or destroyed. . . . Forestry is the art of producing from the forest whatever it can yield for the service of man.[5]

Pinchot supported San Francisco's plan to build the reservoir. Damming the Hetch Hetchy would provide much needed water to millions of people. It would represent the most efficient use of this natural resource.

John Muir was the founder of the Sierra Club and best-known representative of the preservation movement. Muir argued to preserve the Hetch Hetchy. He thought that the conservationist view, treating all natural resources as mere commodities to be used for human consumption, was a serious mistake. Muir defended the spiritual and aesthetic value of wilderness as well as the inherent worth of other living things.[6] In his view, the Hetch Hetchy should be preserved, protected from human activity that would degrade and spoil it.

Thus, this early debate symbolizes the worldviews of two dominant strains of American environmentalism. The conservationists sought to protect the natural environment from exploitation so that humans would receive greater long-term benefits from it. The preservationists sought to protect the environment from any human activity that would disrupt or degrade it. Their goal was to preserve the wilderness in its natural, unspoiled state. This same debate was repeated one-half century later when Pinchot's U.S. Forest Service tangled with Muir's Sierra Club over development of Mineral King Valley.

The ethical justification for the conservationist program was fairly straightforward. The natural environment is valuable as a means for serving human interests. Thus, natural resources have instrumental value. Pinchot argued that these resources were being wasted when they were left undeveloped.

Preservationists, on the other hand, appealed to two different types of reasons to support their goals. One was the instrumental value of wilderness as a source of religious inspiration, refuge from modern life, location for aesthetic experience, and so forth. Thus, leaving the wilderness undeveloped also served human interests. But some preservationists also argued that the wilderness should be recognized as having intrinsic value. We ought to preserve the wilderness not only for its human uses, but also for its own sake.

Contemporary observers could easily cast Muir as the environmentalist and Pinchot as the environmental villain in this dispute. But this would be a mistake. Pinchot's position was quite progressive at the time and considering this claim briefly is helpful.

For much of American history, the forests and wilderness areas of this country represented a threat to be overcome, an enemy to be conquered. The images are common throughout the first 400 years of European settlement of North America. Man against nature. The frontier was to be pushed back, and the wilderness was to be conquered. Life in the wilderness was difficult, and if humans were to survive, they needed to fight and defeat the forces of nature. Nature was seen as the enemy to be subdued and exploited.

By the mid to late nineteenth century, the United States had largely succeeded in these tasks, and most of the American landscape lay open for use. During this period of tremendous industrial growth and urbanization, nature was generally thought to be less an enemy to be conquered and more an inexhaustible resource to fuel the U.S. economy. This often meant that natural resources contributed to the extraordinary wealth of the privileged few who monopolized much of American industry.

Pinchot's conservation movement was part of a more general progressive movement fighting the laissez-faire, monopolistic social Darwinism characteristic of much nineteenth century American economic life.[7] The progressives held that natural resources should benefit all citizens, not just the wealthy few who privately owned vast amounts of property. Government policy should serve this goal by preventing waste, limiting monopolistic control, providing economic opportunity for the many, and keeping prices low.

Pinchot's progressive conservation was in line with the progressivism of nineteenth century utilitarians like Bentham and Mill. Government policy, including economic policy, should aim to provide maximum benefit to all citizens, not to just a privileged few. In Pinchot's words,

The central idea of the Forester, in handling the forest, is to promote and perpet-uate its greatest use to men. His purpose is to make it serve the greatest good of the greatest number for the longest time. . . . The idea of applying foresight and common sense to the other natural resources as well as to the forest was natural and inevitable. . . . It was foreseen from the beginning by those who were respon-sible for inaugurating the Conservation movement that its natural development would in time work out into a planned and orderly scheme for national effi-ciency, based on the elimination of waste, and directed toward the best use of all we have for the greatest good of the greatest number for the longest time.[8]

Thus, Pinchot's conservation movement fits squarely within the utilitarian tradition. Public policy should be directed to "serve the greatest good of the greatest number for the longest time." Consistent with much in the utilitarian tradition, Pinchot encouraged the use of experts who could manage policy so that it might attain this goal. Utilitarian thinking promotes reliance on experts, especially social scientists, who can calculate, measure, compare, pre-dict, and influence the consequences of various policy options. Utilitarians accept the goal of maximally satisfying public welfare. Decision makers then rely on professional managers to determine which of the policy options will result in consequences most closely approaching this goal. This is precisely the role that Pinchot saw for the professional forester. This is fundamentally the same role played by economists and other social scientists in many of today's environmental policy debates. To expand on this, let us turn to a more contemporary version of this practice.

3.3 MANAGING THE NATIONAL FORESTS

By the mid-1980s, Pinchot's U.S. Forest Service was managing 156 different national forests containing more than 191 million acres of land. It was the largest agency in the U.S. Department of Agriculture, employing more than 30,000 people.[9] In the one hundred years of its existence, the U.S. Forest Service has gone through a number of changes. The 1897 Organic Administration Act established the purpose of national forest reserves "to fur-nish a continuous supply of timber." For fifty years, the U.S. Forest Service accomplished this mission primarily through fire suppression, research, and other custodial duties. In the years after World War II, an increase in demand for housing and a decrease in the supply of privately owned timberlands led to a greater focus on managing forests for timber sales. Later, in 1960, Congress enacted the Multiple-Use Sustained Yield Act to require that the U.S. Forest Service manage the forests for "outdoor recreation, range, timber, watershed, and wildlife and fish purposes." Although multiple use remains the primary legal mission of the service, in practice most of its activity today is concerned with timber production, harvesting, and sales.

One controversial activity that follows from this mission is the construction of roads into wilderness areas to provide access to that timber. Although the U.S. Forest Service often defends these construction projects on multiple-use grounds (they provide access for recreational uses as well as for timber companies), critics charge that the roads and the timber harvesting that they promote are responsible for significant environmental damage.[10] These critics fault the U.S. Forest Service for widespread destruction of wilderness areas, loss of old-growth forests, degradation of wildlife habitat, and threatening endangered species with extinction.

Of course, a government bureaucracy responsible for administering a multiple-use policy is likely to be the focus of criticism from its competing constituencies. The timber industry believes that not enough high-quality forests are open for its use. Environmentalists argue that too much wilderness is being sacrificed to timber interests. Ranchers would like to see more forest-land open for grazing. Hunters and anglers decry the loss of habitat. Although the U.S. Forest Service manages assets estimated by some to be worth in excess of $42 billion, the agency costs taxpayers more than $1 billion per year. In the words of one critic,

> In terms of assets, the agency would rank in the top five in *Fortune* magazine's list of the nation's 500 largest corporations. In terms of operating revenues, however, the agency would be only number 290. In terms of net income, the Forest Service would be classified as bankrupt.[11]

Our purpose is not to develop a detailed criticism of the U.S. Forest Service. It is enough for our purposes to recognize that serious environmental controversies surround the management of our national forests. Our immediate interest—seeing the relevance of applied ethics—lies instead with the evaluation of current policies and the alternatives that some environmental critics recommend.

As mentioned, the primary responsibility of the U.S. Forest Service is to serve the oftentimes competing interests of various constituencies. Consistent with the goals of utilitarianism, it seeks to balance these interests in a manner that makes as many people as happy as possible. In this sense, the end or goal is a given, and the challenge is to find the best means for attaining the goal.

Two alternative means compete to answer this challenge. On one hand, consistent with Pinchot's practice, the U.S. Forest Service could rely on the informed judgments of public policy and forestry experts. These people would use their expertise and training to resolve conflict, balance competing interests, and maximize the overall good. On the other hand, the U.S. Forest Service could rely on the workings of a free market with open competition to work out the most efficient uses of the forests. A brief consideration of how markets work follows.

Consider how a free market analysis would decide the Mineral King Valley case. Use of this valley should be assigned to those who are willing to pay most for it, in this case Walt Disney Enterprises. Walt Disney Enterprises would be able to raise the capital to purchase and develop this land because investors believe that Walt Disney Enterprises would be able to make a profit from its proposal and repay their investment with interest. Those same investors would be reluctant to support the Sierra Club's bid because they have little reason to believe that the Sierra Club would be able to raise enough income from its proposal to repay the investment. But, of course, either could profit only if they were supplying consumers (citizens) with goods for which they were willing to pay. Thus, the fact that Walt Disney Enterprises would and the Sierra Club would not make a profit shows quite clearly that more people are willing to pay more for ski slopes than for wilderness experiences. Thus, more people prefer ski slopes to wilderness. Consequently, developing Mineral King Valley as a ski resort will provide more people with what they most want. This demonstrates, according to defenders of the free market, that the most efficient means for allocating scarce resources (that is, the way to give as many people as much of what they want as possible) is to leave this to the workings of a competitive, open, and free market.

According to classical free market economics, markets alone, with minimal government regulation to prevent fraud and coercion, are sufficient to ensure attainment of this goal. But many contemporary economists, particularly those identified with "environmental economics," disagree. They believe that, in practice, markets can fail to reach the goals envisioned in theory. Thus, a new type of expert, one trained in economics, who can determine what should be done to mimic the workings of an idealized market, should shape environmental policy. Although ideal markets do not exist in the real world, environmental economists can develop policies that help actual markets approximate the results of ideal markets. One such environmental economist is Randal O'Toole.

O'Toole has written a sustained critique of U.S. Forest Service management. In his book, *Reforming the Forest Service,* O'Toole summarizes his five years of analyzing the activities of the U.S. Forest Service.

> I've visited national forests in every part of the country and have seen costly environmental destruction on a grand scale. Money-losing timber sales are costing taxpayers at least $250 to $500 million dollars per year. Many of these sales are reducing scarce recreation opportunities, driving wildlife species toward extinction, and polluting waters and fish habitat.[12]

Nevertheless, despite these troubles O'Toole remains optimistic in offering his recommendations.

> My economic research has convinced me that Americans can have all the wilderness, timber, wildlife, fish, and other forest resources they want. Apparent shortages of any of these resources are due solely to the Forest Service's failure to sell them at market prices.[13]

O'Toole's diagnosis of the U.S. Forest Service's problems is consistent with much economic analysis and is a clear example of how economic analysis is used in environmental debates.

The U.S. Forest Service is a large government bureaucracy with little or no incentive to balance revenues and expenses. Economic and environmental problems created by the policies of the U.S. Forest Service owe "not to ignorance or maliciousness but rather to a lack of incentive to be concerned." O'Toole attempts to show that "inefficient management and environmental controversies are not problems in themselves but are merely symptoms of major institutional defects within the Forest Service."[14] In general, the major institutional defects all stem from the fact that the U.S. Forest Service does not operate according to the economic laws that would guide a private, for-profit business operating within a truly free market.

O'Toole's analysis is based on "the fundamental economic assumption that people's decisions are strongly influenced by the incentives affecting the decision makers."[15] The current structure of the U.S. Forest Service provides incentives only to "maximize its budget" and provides little or no incentive to supply Americans with "all the wilderness, timber, wildlife, fish, and other forest resources they want." The laws of economics tell us that if we "change the incentives, the decisions change."

What are the sources of U.S. Forest Service mismanagement? Essentially, there are two. The U.S. Forest Service is primarily responsible to Congress. Like Congress, its decisions reflect an attempt to balance the demands of competing and sometimes contradictory interest groups. Recent debates concerning protection of the spotted owl in the Pacific Northwest demonstrate the type of controversial decisions the U.S. Forest Service faces. Thus, the primary incentive for the U.S. Forest Service is to satisfy these interest groups as much as possible, even if doing so comes at the expense of consistently enforcing a long-range, rational, and efficient policy. Like Congress, which measures its success not in terms of the quality of legislation but in terms of reelection rates, the U.S. Forest Service is left with no measure of its success other than its budgetary retention rates. If its budget is maintained or increased, the U.S. Forest Service must be properly balancing the demands of its constituencies.[16]

The second source of U.S. Forest Service mismanagement lies in its budget, much of which comes from revenues retained from timber sales. An example is the Knutson-Vandenberg Act of 1930, which allows the U.S. Forest Service to retain money collected from timber sales to fund reforestation. Congressional thinking seems to have been that this would accomplish desired goals without costing taxpayers money. However, because this made the U.S. Forest Service's budget dependent on the timber revenues collected, including those collected from below-cost sales of timber, the practice provides an incentive to sell timber at any price. The service has no incentive to balance either revenues and costs or timber sales against other uses of the forests.

Thus, in O'Toole's view, classical economic analysis has uncovered the underlying cause of the U.S. Forest Service's inability to manage national forests in an ecologically sound manner. The bureaucracy is organized in such a way that managers have incentives only to maximize their budget. In short, the U.S. Forest Service does not exist within a free market framework. This is the diagnosis of U.S. Forest Service ills. Now, what is the cure?

The recommendation of environmental economics calls for the "marketization of the Forest Service." That is, the decisions of the U.S. Forest Service should mimic those decisions that would be made by private sector business managers seeking profits in a competitive market. The economic laws of the marketplace would lead to decisions that would best satisfy the diverse demands of the public. The market would "ensure efficient production of most forest resources and an efficient allocation of forestlands." The market will give Americans "all the wilderness, timber, wildlife, fish, and other forest resources they want."

It is interesting to contrast this recommendation with Pinchot's views of the U.S. Forest Service. Both approaches agree on the desirable outcome: using forestlands to provide the greatest good for the greatest number of people. In this way, both apparently accept the utilitarian goal of maximally satisfying individual preferences. The forests should be used to give people as much of what they want as possible. These approaches differ, however, on the correct means for attaining this goal. Whereas Pinchot left it to scientific foresters and other experts to determine the correct policy, O'Toole trusts the workings of a competitive, free, and open market to achieve this goal. Unlike Pinchot's forester, the role of the economist is not to make substantive policy decisions but to help eliminate barriers to the operation of the market. The economic marketplace is the most appropriate means for attaining the utilitarian goal of maximum satisfaction of want.

O'Toole cites the work of the new resource economists, especially John Baden and Richard Stroup, to support his recommendations.[17] According to these economists, it is a mistake to treat natural resources as "public goods" to be managed for the public welfare by experts. Instead, we should recognize that not "every citizen benefits from his share of the public lands and the resources found thereon." In leaving resource decisions to government bureaucrats and asking them to make decisions for the public good, we assume "that culture can rewire people so that the public interest becomes self-interest."[18]

These economists argue that a market would be the most equitable and reasonable means for making these decisions. The market requires only those people affected by a decision to participate in it, which makes it more equitable. Assuming that every person is motivated by self-interest, it is more reasonable. Ignoring the laws of the market has "caused most of the environmental destruction the United States has seen in this century."[19]

Specifically, how should U.S. Forest Service decisions mimic the market? The U.S. Forest Service should manage resources the way a private owner would seek to manage private property. Private owners use their property to maximize their self-interest. Baden and Stroup explain:

> If the buffalo is not mine until I kill it and I cannot sell my interest in the living animal to another, I have no incentive—beyond altruism—to investigate others' interest in it. I will do with it as I wish. But if the buffalo is mine and I may sell it, I am motivated to consider others' value estimate of the animal. I will misuse the buffalo only at my own economic peril.[20]

The U.S. Forest Service should seek to make a profit from its use of the national forests. According to the laws of economics, a profit is evidence that a decision is satisfying demand in an efficient manner. Maximum profit reflects the fact that those people who most value a resource, those who are most willing to pay for it, have control of that resource. Thus, O'Toole recommends that all U.S. Forest Service activities should be funded out of the profits, not the gross receipts, generated by those activities.

This would imply, first, that timber no longer would be offered for sale below cost. Selling timber rights to national forests on the open market would increase the costs of those rights. Following the economic law of supply and demand, this would decrease demand for timber, thereby increasing the amount of forestland available for wilderness, wildlife preservation, and recreation uses. Individuals who wish to use the national forests as wilderness areas or for recreational use will, of course, be required to pay for that use. These "user fees," in effect, will mean that competing users of the forests—timber, wilderness, and recreation—will be bidding against each other for access rights. By seeking to maximize the profits generated by the forests, the U.S. Forest Service will attain equilibrium between these competing interests. The group that most values the resource will be willing to pay most for it, thereby achieving the most efficient use of it. The market optimally satisfies competing consumer demand. It provides Americans with "all the wilderness, timber, wildlife, fish, and other forest resources they want."

Before examining the ethical implications of this view, consider the following similar economic analysis of air and water pollution.

3.4 POLLUTION AND ECONOMICS

As the discussions that open this chapter suggest, water and air pollution are among the most pressing environmental problems that we face. Few people anywhere in the world have not, at least at one point in their lives, been adversely affected by polluted water or air. But, as recent debates in Congress suggest, although people may be in wide agreement about the problem, they are in wide disagreement about the solution.

Part of the challenge in pollution issues lies with specifying the goal. Everyone wants clean water and clean air. But what exactly counts as *clean*, and what would we need to give up in order to attain it? Pure water with absolutely no contaminants exists in laboratories but nowhere in nature. What is clean air? The atmosphere contains nitrogen (78 percent) and oxygen (21 percent) and trace amounts of many other gases, water, and solids. How clean is clean?

Perhaps the only answer is that water and air are clean if they are safe for human consumption. But safety is not an all-or-nothing proposition. To determine safety, we need to identify, describe, and assess risks. To determine safety, we need to balance risks with benefits, something we do in many contexts every day. Is crossing a busy street safe? Is driving a car safe? Is it safe to eat food containing chemical preservatives?

It would seem that something is judged to be safe if its risks are judged acceptable, if its benefits outweigh its potential costs. Phrased in this way, we can see why treating pollution problems as economic problems is so tempting. How should resources be allocated so that maximum benefits are received from minimum costs? What are the costs and benefits of various levels of pollution?

William Baxter's *People or Penguins: The Case for Optimal Pollution* develops an economic analysis of pollution that parallels O'Toole's analysis of forest conservation.[21] In Baxter's words,

> To assert that there is a pollution problem or an environmental problem is to assert, at least implicitly, that one or more resources is not being used so as to maximize human satisfactions. In this respect at least environmental problems are economics problems, and better insight can be gained by application of economic analysis.[22]

Baxter begins his analysis by reviewing some of its basic assumptions. He values individual freedom so long as one person's actions "do not interfere with the interests of other human beings." He assumes that "waste is a bad thing" and, therefore, any resources that are "employed so as to yield less than they might yield in human satisfactions" are wasted.[23] He also assumes that human beings are the source of all value and that environmental policies ought to be "people oriented."

He explains this point while discussing the threat posed to penguins by use of the pesticide DDT.

> My criteria are oriented to people, not penguins. Damage to penguins, or sugar pines, or geological marvels is, without more, simply irrelevant. One must go further, by my criteria, and say: Penguins are important because people enjoy seeing them walk about rocks. . . . I have no interest in preserving penguins for their own sake.[24]

With these assumptions, Baxter turns to an economic analysis of pollution. Denying that there is any "naturally good" state of air or water, he explains that "there is no normative definition of clean air or pure water, hence no definition of polluted air or of pollution, except by reference to the needs of man."[25] In a vein similar to the earlier discussion of risks, Baxter argues that "clean" air and water are whatever is judged acceptable by human beings. Too much pollution would be judged unacceptable by society but so too would too little pollution. Air and water that were totally free of any contaminants *could* be desirable, but their costs would be too high. In essence, society aims at a proper balance of risks, an "optimal level of pollution." This optimal level is

> just those amounts that attend a sensibly organized society thoughtfully and knowledgeably pursuing the greatest possible satisfaction for its human members.[26]

Consistent with much economic thinking, Baxter believes that the functioning of a free and competitive market would yield this "greatest possible amount of human satisfaction." How would this work?

Baxter reminds us that most decisions that we make involve tradeoffs. If I choose to do one thing, I give up something else. Every opportunity pursued involves other opportunities forgone. This captures the classic economic meaning of *costs*. The cost of something is equivalent to what must be given up to attain it. In Baxter's example, if we choose to build a dam, the resources that are used in building the dam cannot be used to build hospitals, fishing poles, schools, or electric can openers. Thus, the cost of the dam is equivalent to alternative uses of those resources—labor, building materials, technological skills, capital, and energy—that have been forgone.

Accordingly, the costs of reducing water and air pollution should be understood in terms of those other goods that we would need to give up to accomplish this goal. In short, we need to make tradeoffs. Every resource devoted to reducing pollution is a resource not devoted to washing machines, hospitals, schools, B-1 bombers, and so forth. Left alone, markets would continue to make these tradeoffs so long as the result is a net increase in human satisfaction and the benefits gained outweigh the additional costs. The optimal level of pollution is that point of equilibrium at which the next tradeoff made to reduce pollution results in a *decrease* of overall satisfaction. This is the point at which the resources used to fight pollution would have a higher value to society if used elsewhere.

Consider the following example of how this process might work. Suppose a community's drinking water showed contamination levels slightly above those recommended by health officials. Lowering the contamination below recommended levels would involve certain costs. In other words, tax monies diverted to this project could not be used to build a new school, fund road construction, and undertake other public works projects. Assume that this community decides that the benefits outweigh the costs. The residents would rather have cleaner drinking water than newly paved roads, and they decide to make this tradeoff. This decision results in a greater satisfaction of the community's desires than either the status quo or other alternatives.

Now, this community might also desire to have drinking water that is absolutely pure, totally free of contaminants. The costs for this goal would be much higher. Other community projects would have to be sacrificed and tax rates raised higher. Eventually, the community must decide when to stop making these tradeoffs. This is the point at which slightly improved water quality is not worth the costs, not worth those other goods that would have to be given up to achieve this goal. At that point, any decision to obtain cleaner water would result in a net *decrease* in community satisfaction.

According to classical economics, this point of equilibrium between diverse and competing community desires should be the goal of public policy decisions. This would be the point at which optimal satisfaction is achieved. People have more of what they want than would occur under any other allocation of resources. This is the "optimal level of pollution."

Baxter acknowledges that this may sound "so general and abstract as to be unhelpful."[27] However, this abstraction has accurately described just what results, at least in theory, from the workings of a free, open, and competitive marketplace. Economic analysis tells us that when people have the opportunity to freely exchange goods and services, when competition ensures that alternative choices exist, and when these individuals seek to maximize their own welfare, the result is an optimal satisfaction of desires. More people get more of what they most want through this process than they would under any other economic arrangement. According to Baxter,

> If individuals in a society are free to engage in whatever exchanges of resources are mutually satisfactory for themselves, then, at least in theory, every resource in society will be deployed in the way that yields the greatest possible human satisfaction.[28]

Thus, Baxter's solution to the pollution problem, like O'Toole's solution to forest conservation problems, rests in the working of the free market. In both cases, economic analysis and methodology offer a diagnosis of environmental ills. Each case offers a particular economic prescription to cure those ills. A society that structures its economy to follow the principles of the free market will successfully meet all its environmental challenges.

3.5 ETHICAL ISSUES IN ECONOMIC ANALYSIS

Before turning to an analysis of these claims, we need to be clear about the issues involved. A first step of applied ethics is to identify and clarify the ethical issues at stake.

As discussed in Chapter 1, turning to technical and objective disciplines like economics can be an attractive option when faced with controversial environmental problems. Part of the reason for this lies in the myth of objectivity that often surrounds scientific and technical disciplines. According to this myth, the scientific method offers precise and objective answers to our problems. Sciences like economics are, in this view, value neutral. A helpful starting point for our ethical analysis, therefore, is to show how these economic analyses are heavily influenced by value assumptions. Our first step is to show that economic analysis is a value-laden analysis.

The ethical framework of classical economic analysis can be understood in terms of *ends* and *means*. The end of economic policy is the maximum satisfaction of individual desires or maximum happiness. The functioning of a free and competitive market is believed to be the ethically best means for attaining that end.

Economic analysis of environmental problems, as represented by the work of people like O'Toole and Baxter, thus assumes an essentially *utilitarian* ethics. The ultimate policy goal implicitly or explicitly assumed throughout these analyses is the utilitarian goal of maximizing the overall good. The specific understanding of that good and the specific means defended to attain that goal locates these views as a version of *preference utilitarianism.* Let us examine these claims more closely.

Perhaps Gifford Pinchot was most explicit in stating the utilitarian goals of his policies. Forest management sought the "greatest good for the greatest number for the longest time." O'Toole is less explicit but no less utilitarian. His recommendations aim to provide the American people with a maximum satisfaction of their wants. Baxter's recommendations seek to ensure that resources are "used so as to maximize human satisfactions." Thus, they all judge environmental policies in terms of their ability to produce certain beneficial consequences.

Pinchot believed that scientific management techniques could best lead us to this goal. O'Toole and Baxter argue that the workings of the marketplace are the most efficient means available. Their reasons for relying on the market suggest further value assumptions. Markets give priority to the wants that people actually express, as opposed to those interests that other people (for example, professional foresters) determine or assume that they have. That is, the market version of utilitarianism assumes the best way to determine what is good for someone is to figure out what that person wants, and the best way to learn this is to see what that person is willing to pay for in the marketplace.

To say that the market is the best way to determine what people want is not only to claim that it is the most efficient (although for economists it certainly is that), but also that it is the best way ethically. Why *should* public policy give priority to those preferences expressed in the market? We can find at least three philosophical answers to this question in O'Toole and Baxter.

First, market utilitarianism is thought to promote individual freedom. Baxter takes it as a "basic tenet of our civilization" that "every person should be free to do whatever he wishes in contexts where his actions do not interfere with the interests of other human beings."[29] He acknowledges that his market solution to environmental problems "stems from" this criterion. O'Toole explains that the market "preserves individual freedom since those who support and wish to participate in each activity may do so on the basis of willing consent."[30] The market is preferable to government regulation, for example, because the government "is based on coercive activity." Thus, O'Toole and Baxter would reject Pinchot's reliance on experts as a threat to individual freedom of choice.

A second reason for supporting market solutions rests with a commitment to the value of private property rights. O'Toole tells us that "the marketplace is centered around the notion of private property. . . . For the market to work, private property rights to resources must be easily transferable. . . . The market works when rights are both privately held and easily transferable." Indeed, "most environmental problems, such as lack of protection for wildlife, air pollution, and poor water quality, are due to the lack of transferable property rights."[31] Therefore, market solutions to public policy questions will be reasonable only within a society that recognizes and values private property rights.

Finally, market solutions are consistent with certain philosophical assumptions about human nature. O'Toole identifies a major problem with the U.S. Forest Service as the "lack of incentive to be concerned." "The fundamental economic assumption," he tells us, is that "people's decisions are strongly influenced by the incentives affecting the decision makers" and that if we "change the incentives, the decisions change." As it stands, this seems trivially true. But what are these incentives? The answer can be found when O'Toole quotes the reasons offered by the new resource economists, Baden and Stroup, for rejecting Pinchot's nonmarket version.

> The national forests, for example, were created with the idea that "scientific foresters" employed by the public could objectively determine the method of management that best meets the public interest. But to assume that managers will be altruistic, say Stroup and Baden, it must be assumed "that culture can rewire people so that the public interest becomes self-interest." Instead, "Property rights theorists assume that the decision maker will maximize his own utility . . . in whatever situation he finds himself."[32]

The fundamental assumption about human nature is that human beings act, primarily if not solely, on the basis of self-interest. Self-interest then is understood in the classic utilitarian sense of maximizing our own satisfactions or "utilities." Altruism or acting for the best interests of others would require that human nature be "rewired." In Baxter's words,

> It may be said by way of objection to this position, that it is very selfish of people to act as if each person represented one unit of importance and nothing else was of importance. It is undeniably selfish. Nevertheless I think it is the only tenable starting place for analysis for several reasons. First, no other position corresponds to the way most people really think and actually corresponds to reality.[33]

Thus, underlying the economic analyses described in this chapter are commitments to the values of individual freedom and private property rights and philosophical assumptions about human nature. Along with the clear utilitarian goal of providing the greatest good for the greatest number, these commitments clearly show the ethical and philosophical nature of economic analysis. Despite common opinion, economic analysis and methodology do not claim to offer us ethically neutral answers to environmental controversies. These recommendations clearly make philosophical assumptions concerning several value issues. Thus, this type of analysis lies within the domain of philosophical ethics. Following the applied ethics model, we now need to ask whether these analyses offer justifiable answers and recommendations.

3.6 COST-BENEFIT ANALYSIS

Cost-benefit analysis, a technique for deciding among alternative courses of action, is one essential aspect of much economic analysis. It is implicit in the evaluations of both O'Toole and Baxter. It is also at the center of recent public policy debates in the U.S. Congress concerning the Clean Air Act, Clean Water Act, and Endangered Species Act, as well as being crucially involved in takings legislation and the wise-use movement. Critics argue that the environmental laws all need to be revised in ways that require government regulators to incorporate cost-benefit analysis in their decisions. For example, critics of the Endangered Species Act argued that before banning logging to protect the spotted owl, government regulators should have been required to prove that the benefits of protecting the owl outweighed the costs to loggers, timber companies, local communities, and others.

To its defenders, cost-benefit analysis requires an obvious and simple step: before deciding on some course of action, we should determine that the benefits of that act outweigh the costs. But cost-benefit analysis is neither as simple nor as value neutral as it may seem.

Cost-benefit analysis is different from what is sometimes called "cost effectiveness," and the distinction is important. Cost effectiveness directs us to pursue the most effective means to a given end. Thus, to use a simple example, if we are seeking to reduce the amount of contaminants in drinking water, a cost-effective analysis might compare the relative costs of a centralized water treatment plant to the installation of filters on home faucets. We should pursue whichever is more effective, that is, the alternative that attains our ends at lower cost.

Cost-benefit analysis directs us to determine whether a given end is worth pursuing in light of its costs. In this strategy, both the means and the ends of our decisions are subjected to economic analysis. When we distinguish cost effectiveness from cost benefit, we can see that much of the commonsense appeal of cost benefit may actually be the result of a confusion with cost effectiveness. Consider the following example.

Imagine that a child is diagnosed with an illness for which a variety of equally effective treatments are available. Cost effectiveness would direct us to follow the lowest cost treatment (for example, choosing a generic version of a name brand prescription). On the other hand, a cost-benefit approach would require that we compare the benefits (the child's health) with the costs and pursue whichever strategy maximizes net benefits. We would need to ask whether the child's health is worth the cost. Now, although sometimes, sadly this question must be asked, it is by no means the obvious and commonsensical way to proceed.

This raises a second major challenge to cost-benefit analysis. It is far from clear that all our values or goals can be or should be expressed in economic terms. Cost-benefit analysis requires that we compare the "benefits" with the costs. To avoid the old "apples and oranges" problem, the benefits and costs must be in the same category. That is, they must be expressible in economic terms. Ultimately, this means that we must express both in terms of dollars and cents. Despite some clever work by economists, it is not at all clear that this is possible.

For example, several years ago I was on a canoe trip in Canada's Quetico Park. To preserve this wilderness area, entrance is by permit alone and motorized boats are prohibited. As we checked in with a park ranger, we were asked to fill out a short questionnaire that would be used to help determine future park policies, including price and availability of permits. Among other things, this questionnaire asked what we would be willing to pay for permits if we could be assured of such benefits as not seeing other campers or seeing bald eagles and moose. Because no free and open market exists for such goods as permits, eagles, or moose and because a cost-benefit analysis requires that these goods have a price, someone must devise an elaborate scheme to figure out (some might say create) a cost for these benefits.

This only hints at the difficulty in trying to establish the costs for those benefits that are not traded on economic markets. But it also hints at another danger. Because markets do not exist for many environmental goods like clean air and water or an endangered species, use of cost-benefit analysis seems to require that we rely on economists and other social scientists to tell us what the cost would be if there were markets for such goods. But in determining forest policy, for example, this means that we still rely on the decisions of "experts" rather than markets. However, this time the experts are economists (usually working in universities and industry) rather than foresters trained in science and ecology. Thus, one alleged benefit of economic analysis—that it takes decisions out of the hands of "experts" and government bureaucrats and gives them back to individual citizens—is soon violated when economists are required to determine a price for nonmarket goods.

Finally, besides questioning whether we can establish the cost of many environmental benefits, there is a serious question about whether we should be doing this at all. As the example of the child's health suggests, we should resist the move to reduce certain values to their economic costs. Imagine conducting a cost-benefit analysis of democracy, or of friendship, or the Grand Canyon. Further, cost-benefit analysis is usually totally anthropocentric. You will seldom hear economists speak of either the costs or benefits to animals or other natural objects. Perhaps we should not. But to adopt cost-benefit analysis without addressing these questions is to ignore important value-laden questions.

3.7 ETHICAL ANALYSIS AND ENVIRONMENTAL ECONOMICS

To the degree that contemporary economic analyses of environmental problems reflect a utilitarian ethics, philosophers have much to offer in the evaluation of this ethical theory.[34] Several standard criticisms, mentioned briefly in Chapter 2, are a useful starting point for this evaluation.

Utilitarians face several problems when they attempt to quantify and measure consequences. These problems arise again in the use of cost-benefit analysis. One aspect involves the attempt to quantify qualitative goods. We have seen, for example, the challenge posed by trying to determine clean or safe water and air quality standards. These qualitative goods find no place in the economic approach because they cannot be easily quantified. A second problem is the resulting tendency to translate qualitative goods into categories that can be measured. Thus, we find Baxter translating discussions of clean and safe into a discussion of risks, the probabilities of which can be quantified and calculated. We find O'Toole, consistent with typical applications of the cost-benefit method, translating qualitative goods into economic terms. The value of wilderness or recreation areas is understood as measurable by the willingness of users to pay for them. A final measurement problem involves the tendency to artificially restrict the range of relevant subjects. As presented in the chapters that follow, some critics claim that this tendency systematically ignores the well-being of animals, future generations, trees, the biosphere, and the like. We examine the charge that the economic approach is overly anthropocentric or human centered in greater detail elsewhere. The general point of these measurement problems is to raise the possibility that economic analysis seriously distorts or ignores important environmental issues.

In a series of articles culminating in the book *The Economy of the Earth,* Mark Sagoff develops an insightful and convincing case against the use of economic analysis as the dominant tool of environmental policymakers.[35] In the remainder of this chapter, we will use Sagoff's evaluation as an example of the best that applied ethics has offered. Although his book offers a variety of subtle and powerful arguments, we concentrate on three major challenges to the use of economic analysis.

Sagoff argues that much economic analysis rests on a serious confusion between wants or preferences, on one hand, and beliefs and values on the other. Economics deals only with wants and preferences because these are what get expressed in an economic market. The market can measure the intensity of our wants by our willingness to pay (by price), measure and compare individual wants (through cost-benefit analysis), and determine efficient means for optimally fulfilling wants. But markets cannot measure or quantify our beliefs or values. Because many environmental issues involve our beliefs and our values, economic analysis is beside the point. When economics is involved in environmental policy, it treats our beliefs as if they were mere wants and, thereby, seriously distorts the issue. In an early article, Sagoff claims,

> Economic methods cannot supply the information necessary to justify public policy. Economics can measure the intensity with which we hold our beliefs; it cannot evaluate those beliefs on their merits. Yet such evaluation is essential to political decision making. This is my greatest single criticism of cost-benefit analysis.[36]

What exactly is the distinction between wants and beliefs, and why is it important?

When individuals express a want or personal preference, they are stating something that is purely personal and subjective. Another person has no grounds to challenge, rebut, or support my wants. Wants are neither true nor false. If I express my preference for chocolate ice cream, someone cannot challenge that and claim, "No, you don't." I have a certain privileged status with regard to my wants. In the public sphere, they are taken as a given. Thus do economists treat human interests. Willingness to pay measures the intensity with which I hold my wants (I will not pay more than a few dollars for a dish of chocolate ice cream), but willingness to pay says nothing about the legitimacy or validity of that want.

Beliefs, on the other hand, are subject to rational evaluation. They are objective in the sense that reasons are summoned to support them. Beliefs can be true or false. It would be a serious mistake (a "category mistake" in Sagoff's terms) to judge the validity of a belief by a person's willingness to pay for it. Putting a price on beliefs misunderstands seriously the nature of belief.

Sagoff reminds us that when environmentalists argue that we ought to preserve a national forest for its aesthetic or symbolic meaning, they are not merely expressing a personal want. They are stating a *conviction* about a public good that should be accepted or rejected by others on the basis of reasons, not on the basis of who is most willing to pay for it. Because economics has no way to factor them into its analysis, beliefs and convictions are either ignored or treated as if they were mere wants.

Essentially, O'Toole's marketization solution to environmental problems does exactly this. Remember that O'Toole's goal is to provide all the wilderness and the like that the American people "want." But he equates this goal with what the American people, in their roles as timber users, hikers, hunters, and so forth, are willing to pay. If recreational users are unwilling to pay a user fee that is economically competitive with the fees paid by the timber industry, by definition they must not want recreation as much as timber users want the lumber. Returning to the discussions at the beginning of this chapter, if preservationists in the Sierra Club were not willing to pay as much for Mineral King Valley as Walt Disney Enterprises, they must not want the wilderness area as much as skiers want a new ski resort. Likewise, if a community is unwilling to spend any more tax money to reduce air and water pollution, its residents must not want cleaner air and water as much as they want lower taxes or other public projects.

This tendency to reduce all beliefs and values to wants and preferences also seriously distorts the nature of the human being. That distortion treats people at all times as *consumers*. People, at least insofar as the economist or policymaker is concerned, are simply the locations of a given collection of wants. People care only about satisfying their personal wants, and the role of the economist is to determine how to maximally attain this end.

The alternative that is ignored by economic analysis treats humans as thinking and reasoning beings. The market leaves no room for debate, discussion, or dialogue in which we can defend our beliefs with reasons. It ignores the fact that people are active thinkers, not merely passive "wanters." Most important, by ignoring the distinction between wants and beliefs, economic analysis reduces the most meaningful elements of human life—our beliefs and values—to matters of mere personal taste or opinion. To the degree that they are held with equal intensity, all desires equally deserve to be satisfied, no matter what the desire is.

This leads to a second major challenge to economic analysis. By ignoring the distinction between wants and beliefs, market analysis threatens our democratic political process. By treating us as always and only *consumers,* market analysis ignores our lives as *citizens.* As consumers, we may seek to satisfy personal wants. As citizens, we may have goals and aspirations that give meaning to our lives, determine our nature as a people and culture, and define what we stand for as a people. Ours is a liberal democratic society— liberal in the sense that we value personal liberty to pursue our individual goals but democratic in the sense that collectively we seek agreement about public goods and shared goals. Thus, our political system leaves room for both personal *and* public interests. We are all, at one and the same time, both private individuals and public citizens. Market analysis ignores this public realm and, thereby, undermines our democratic political institutions. According to Sagoff,

> Our environmental goals—cleaner air and water, the preservation of the wilderness and wildlife, and the like—are not to be construed, then, simply as personal wants or preferences; they are not interests to be "priced" by markets or by cost-benefit analysis, but are views or beliefs that may find their way, as public values, into legislation. These goals stem from our character as a people, which is not something we choose, as we might choose a necktie or a cigarette, but something we recognize, something we are. These goals presuppose the reality of public or shared values that we recognize together, values that are discussed and criticized on their merits and are not to be confused with preferences that are appropriately priced in markets. Our democratic political processes allow us to argue our beliefs on their merits.[37]

Economic analysis seems to assume a particular view of democracy wherein representatives passively follow the demands of the electorate, seeking to balance competing demands in a manner that satisfies the majority. The role of the politician in this model is to read the public opinion polls and act accordingly. But this neglects the more participatory nature of democracy in which citizens exchange views, debate their merits, learn from each other, and reach agreement.[38] The model encourages a view of elected officials as active leaders rather than passive followers. We are committed not only to the personal freedom that Baxter's analysis assumes, but also to a system in which we mutually define and pursue a vision of the good life. A healthy, beautiful, undeveloped, and inspiring environment may not benefit me as a consumer, but it may be quite valuable to me as a citizen. This participatory model of democracy would reject the views of the new resource economists that O'Toole approvingly quotes: "It is a common misconception that every citizen benefits from his share of the public lands and resources found thereon."[39]

Many economists reject the notion of a public welfare or public good because they view people solely as consumers. Not every citizen "consumes" Mineral King Valley, for example. But this fails to recognize that we are citizens as well as consumers and that we can benefit from the environment as citizens. Mineral King Valley can be valuable to us as citizens because of what it means to us, because of what it says about our self-image and self-respect. These benefits are not and cannot be priced in the market and, therefore, are ignored by the type of economic analysis offered by O'Toole, the new resource economists, and Baxter.

A final challenge denies that economic analysis has any ethical basis at all. Despite the appearance that markets are committed to utilitarian ends, in actuality the goal of efficiency lacks any coherent and substantive ethical basis at all. Remember the role that economic analysis plays in many contemporary environmental issues. Unquestionably, economic and cost-benefit analyses are the major public policy methodologies used in reaching environmental decisions. Economics tells us as individuals, a society, and a government what we should do. Why should we follow this advice? Presumably because doing so will lead us to a better state of affairs. At first glance, this better state of affairs—economic efficiency—appears to be the utilitarian goal of providing the greatest good for the greatest number. But does economic efficiency provide the greatest good for the greatest number? Again, Sagoff is persuasive in claiming that it does not.

What is the goal of economic efficiency? As suggested earlier, efficiency implies optimal satisfaction of consumer preferences. An efficient market is one in which more people get more of that for which they are most willing to pay. But why should we, as a society and especially when we are concerned with environmental issues, take the satisfaction of individual preferences as our overriding goal? Why should this be the goal of public policy when we recognize the obvious and acknowledge that many individual preferences are silly, foolish, vulgar, dangerous, immoral, criminal, and the like? Why should we think that satisfying the preferences of a racist, criminal, fool, or sadist is a good thing?

What is so good about satisfying preferences? The only options seem to be that satisfying preferences is good in itself or that it is a means to something that is. In terms that we used in describing utilitarianism in Chapter 2, preference satisfaction is either intrinsically good or instrumentally good. Given the wide variety of harmful, decadent, and trivial preferences that exist, surely no one could claim that satisfying preferences is good in itself. Surely it is not good in itself that child molesters or rapists have their preferences satisfied. If not good in itself, what other good is brought about instrumentally by satisfying preferences?

Typically, this economic approach uses such terms as *utility, welfare, well-being,* or *happiness* to explain the goal of satisfying preferences. However, to explain the value of preference satisfaction by simply defining it in these ways is to beg the question by offering a trivially true explanation. On the other hand, if utility, welfare, happiness, or well-being are more thoroughly defined, the claim that preference satisfaction always leads to these goods is false. Satisfying my preference for a cigarette does not always make me happy in a nontrivial sense. Sometimes having my preferences frustrated can be in my best interest by teaching me patience, diligence, or modesty. Sometimes satisfying preferences is disappointing. Sometimes I might have all that the market can supply, but I might still lack what is important ("What good does it benefit a man if he gains a kingdom but loses his soul?"). The economic methodology assumes that all other things being equal, for people to get what they want is a good thing. A more realistic and honest assumption would seem to be that whether what I want is a good thing depends on what it is that I want.

Thus, even if (and it is a big *if*) economic analysis could overcome the measurement problems, all the problems associated with applying market analyses to the real world, and the market succeeded in attaining its goal, we still would have no reason for accepting preference satisfaction as an ethical goal. An efficient allocation of resources is not itself an ethical goal at all.

3.8 SUSTAINABLE ECONOMICS

In recent decades, an alternative to classical, market-based economics has emerged. What we shall call "sustainable economics" offers a different way to think about economics in light of our current environmental challenges and the apparent failure of classical market economics to meet these challenges. Sustainable economics appeals to the same philosophical values for its justification—utility, freedom, and equality—as does classical market economics. It claims, however, to better promote those values, given the current and future environmental reality.

Three points summarize these current and future challenges. First, a large percentage of the world population today lives in abject poverty. Current economic arrangements do not provide for the basic needs of hundreds of millions of people. One-quarter of the world's population lives in industrialized countries and consumes 80 percent of the world's goods. The world would require significant economic growth during the next few decades just to meet the basic needs of the other 75 percent of the planet's population.

Second, the world's population during the next fifty years likely will double, to about 11 billion people. Thus, economic activity to meet the basic needs of the world's population will need to increase significantly.[40]

Finally, the only sources for all this economic activity are the natural resources of the earth itself. Because the world's environment is already under stress from current economic activity, the future looks bleak.

Thus, given these realities, we must create an economic system that can provide for the world's population without destroying the environment in the process. This, according to some, is the role of sustainable economics and sustainable development. A typical statement of the goal of sustainable economics is, in the words of the World Commission on Environment and Development (an agency of the United Nations), to meet the "needs of the present without compromising the ability of future generations to meet their own needs."[41]

Economist Herman Daly is perhaps the best-known champion of sustainable economics. According to Daly, a distinction between *development* and *growth* is at the heart of sustainable economics.

> To *grow* means to "increase naturally in size by the addition of material through assimilation or accretion." To *develop* means "to expand or realize the potentialities of; to bring gradually to a fuller, greater, or better state." When something grows it gets bigger. When something develops it gets different. The earth ecosystem develops (evolves), but it does not grow. Its subsystem, the economy, must eventually stop growing, but can continue to develop. The term "sustainable development" therefore makes sense for the economy, but only if it is understood as "development without growth."[42]

Sustainable economics is best understood in contrast with traditional market economics. The traditional model addresses two fundamental questions: How are resources to be allocated (the production question), and how are the goods and services thus produced to be distributed (the distribution question)? Classical economics, as seen with Baxter and O'Toole, allocates resources to meet the demands of the marketplace. This model of economic activity is linear: resources enter one end, allocation decisions are made to produce various goods, and these are then distributed at the other end in a competitive marketplace. The "law" of supply and demand governs the decisions made at both the allocation and distribution stages.

Sustainable economics is particularly concerned with the rate at which resources flow through this economy. We must first recognize that all the factors that go into production—natural resources, capital, and labor—ultimately originate in the productive capacity of the earth. In light of this, the entire classical model will prove unstable if resources move through this system at a rate that outpaces the productive capacity of the earth or of the earth's capacity to absorb the wastes and by-products of this production. Thus, we need to develop an economic system that uses resources only at a rate that can be sustained over the long term and recycles or reuses both the by-products of the production process and the products themselves. We need to close the loop and pattern the economic system more on a circular ecosystem model than on the linear model of classical economics.

This alternative model would have significant social, economic, and commercial implications. Consumer demand would no longer be the overriding factor in production decisions. Production decisions involving renewable resources, such as those made in forestry and agriculture, would be limited by the rate at which these resources could be replenished. Decisions involving nonrenewable resources would be limited by the rate at which alternatives are developed or lost opportunities compensated. Finally, responsibility for products would extend beyond the life of the product. The "optimal level" of such things as wastes and pollution would be determined not by willingness to pay but by the earth's capacity to assimilate them.

Critics charge that such radical changes are unwarranted. But defenders appeal to the very same values that underlie classical market economics. As this chapter shows, defenders of the market often appeal to utilitarian considerations to justify their proposals. However, given the current level of worldwide poverty, the ever-increasing world population, and the already dangerous levels of environmental stress, the claim that growth-based economies maximize the overall good is doubtful. Sustainable economic institutions, if in fact they do "meet the needs of the present without compromising the ability of future generations to meet their own needs," would appear much more likely to meet the utilitarian goal.

In addition to using this utilitarian defense, market economies appeal to rights of equal respect and liberty for their justification. But here, too, sustainable economics can claim that these rights are better served under an alternative model. Economic activity and growth that prevent many millions of people, specifically those people who will populate the earth during the next few decades, from meeting their basic needs would seem to neither respect them as equals nor protect their liberty. Using the earth's resources at unsustainable rates suggests that the interests of living people have priority over the interests of future people. This seems a clear denial of their equality. Using resources in ways that prevent "as much and as good" from being left for others (to quote John Locke's defense of property rights) would likewise seem to be an unjustified restriction of their freedom.

Sustainable development is a relatively new paradigm in economics. We have provided only the briefest sketch of this model and the directions in which its ethical defense is heading. Much work remains to be done before we can reach any philosophical conclusions, however. One area that will be relevant and that has already received much philosophical attention concerns our responsibilities to future generations, the subject of Chapter 4.

3.9 SUMMARY AND CONCLUSIONS

As we struggle with great environmental controversies, we must look beyond the economic market for a vision to guide policy decisions. Economic analysis cannot answer the fundamental ethical and philosophical questions that these controversies raise. The solution, according to Sagoff, is to

> recognize that utopian capitalism is dead; that the concepts of resource and welfare economics, as a result, are largely obsolete and irrelevant; and that we must look to other concepts and cultural traditions to set priorities in solving environmental and social problems. To set these priorities, we need to distinguish the pure from the polluted, the natural from the artificial, the noble from

the mundane, good from bad, and right from wrong. These are scientific, cultural, aesthetic, historical, and ethical—not primarily economic—distinctions.[43]

Sagoff encourages us to do the hard thinking required to explain and justify environmental policy. We must explain why we value clean air and water, and we must justify why we value the preservation of wilderness areas. We must move beyond simply saying that these are things that we want or prefer and offer reasons that show their value and meaning.

But even Sagoff's alternative is restricted to the important interests of living human beings. The "scientific, cultural, aesthetic, historical, and ethical" values and beliefs tend to keep the environmental debate focused on the claims of the current generation of humans. In Chapter 4, we will see how environmental concerns lead us away from this narrow focus.

Notes

1. See Richard Momeyer, "Philosophers and the Public Policy Process," *Journal of Medical Philosophy* 15 (August 1990): 391–409, and Loretta Kopelman, "What Is Applied About 'Applied Philosophy'?," *Journal of Medical Philosophy* 15 (April 1990): 199–218. Momeyer argues that in addition to simply identifying and clarifying concepts and analyzing arguments, philosophers engaged in applied ethics should become active participants in the public policy debates by arguing for specific normative conclusions. Kopelman argues that whenever principles and theories are applied to specific issues, they are changed in the process. Hence, she argues that applied ethics should not be viewed as derivative of other more theoretical approaches to ethics.

2. For a thorough description of the environmental destruction of the former Soviet Union, see Murray Feshbach and Alfred Friendly, *Ecocide in the U.S.S.R.* (New York: Basic, 1992).

3. Paul Portney et al., *Current Issues in U.S. Environmental Policy* (Baltimore: Johns Hopkins University Press, 1978).

4. Samuel Hays, *Conservation and the Gospel of Efficiency* (Cambridge, Mass.: Harvard University Press, 1959), pp. 41–42.

5. Gifford Pinchot, *The Training of a Forester* (Philadelphia: J. B. Lippincott, 1914), p. 13.

6. See Michael Cohen, *The Pathless Way* (Madison: University of Wisconsin Press, 1984), for a helpful study of John Muir. Chapters 6 and 7 especially provide an insightful introduction to many ethical aspects of Muir's thinking.

7. This may be too simple an interpretation of the conservation movement. An alternative view is defended by Samuel Hays in *Conservation and the Gospel of Efficiency* (Cambridge, Mass.: Harvard University Press, 1959). Hays argues that American business supported the conservation movement, recognizing in it a more enlightened, long-term economic self-interest than fighting it would have provided. Pinchot's writings seem to me to suggest a strong anticorporate sentiment. For an interpretation that supports my reading of Pinchot, see James Bates, "Fulfilling American Democracy: The Conservation Movement, 1907–1921," *Mississippi Valley Historical Review* 44 (June 1957). Whether early twentieth century corporate America supported the conservation movement is irrelevant to the more general point, however. Pinchot's progressivism was

directed against a common nineteenth century view that resources are there for the benefit of immediate economic exploitation. A more pragmatic interpretation, which seeks a common ground for environmentalists, is Bryan Norton, *Toward Unity Among Environmentalists* (New York: Oxford University Press, 1991), especially ch. 2.

8. Pinchot, *Training of a Forester,* pp. 23–25.

9. Department of Agriculture, Forest Service, *1987 Budget Explanatory Notes* (Washington, D.C.: Forest Service, 1986), p. 2.

10. See Department of Agriculture, Forest Service, *National Forest Roads for All Uses* (Milwaukee: U.S. Department of Agriculture, 1985), p. 2, for a defense of the claim that roads support a policy of multiple use.

11. Randal O'Toole, *Reforming the Forest Service* (Washington, D.C.: Island Press, 1988), p. 14.

12. Ibid., xi.

13. Ibid., xii.

14. Ibid., xi, 7.

15. Ibid., 101.

16. O'Toole quotes a more detailed study to support this claim. See Ronald Johnson, "U.S. Forest Service Policy and Its Budget," in *Forestlands: Public and Private,* ed. Robert Deacon and Bruce Johnson (San Francisco: Pacific Institute for Public Policy Research, 1985), pp. 103–33.

17. See especially Richard Stroup and John Baden, *Natural Resources: Bureaucratic Myths and Environmental Management* (San Francisco: Pacific Institute for Public Policy Research, 1983). The new resource economists offer policy analyses and recommendations based on neoclassical economics. They attribute most environmental problems to market failures and recommend policies that would mimic the workings of a competitive free market.

18. Ibid., 7, 29.

19. O'Toole, *Reforming the Forest Service,* p. 190.

20. Baden and Stroup, *Natural Resources: Bureaucratic Myths and Environmental Management,* p. 14.

21. William F. Baxter, *People or Penguins: The Case for Optimal Pollution* (New York: Columbia University Press, 1974).

22. Ibid., 17.

23. Ibid., 5.

24. Ibid.

25. Ibid., 8.

26. Ibid.

27. Ibid., 27.

28. Ibid.

29. Ibid., 2.

30. O'Toole, *Reforming the Forest Service,* p. 189.

31. Ibid., 188–90.

32. Ibid., 190.

33. Baxter, *People or Penguins: The Case for Optimal Pollution,* p. 5.

34. See Bernard Williams, *Morality: An Introduction to Ethics* (New York: Harper Torchbooks, 1972), for a useful introductory evaluation of utilitarianism.

35. Mark Sagoff, *The Economy of the Earth* (New York: Cambridge University Press, 1990).

36. Mark Sagoff, "Economic Theory and Environmental Law," *Michigan Law Review* 79 (1981): 1393–1419.

37. Sagoff, *The Economy of the Earth,* pp. 28–29.

38. For an examination of representative and participatory democracy, see Jane Mansbridge, *Beyond Adversarial Democracy* (New York: Basic, 1980).

39. O'Toole, *Reforming the Forest Service,* p. 189.

40. Economist Herman Daly argues that the doubling of population would require more than a doubling of economic activity, even to meet constant demand. First, significant capital accumulation would be required to transform resources into final products. Second, the mineral and energy resources needed for such growth would have to come from increasingly low-grade and inaccessible deposits because we have already taken much of the readily and inexpensively accessible resources. See Herman Daly, "Sustainable Growth: An Impossibility Theorem," reprinted in *Valuing the Earth,* ed. Herman Daly and Kenneth Townsend (Boston: Massachusetts Institute of Technology Press, 1993), pp. 267–72.

41. World Commission on Environment and Development, *Our Common Future* (New York: Oxford University Press, 1987).

42. Daly, "Sustainable Growth: An Impossibility Theorem," pp. 267–68.

43. Sagoff, *The Economy of the Earth,* p. 22.

Discussion Questions

1. If a Disney-like resort opened in a wilderness area near you, would you be willing to pay money to visit it? If so, would that be evidence that you preferred development to wilderness preservation? Are those things that people are willing to pay for always the things that people most value?

2. Review the distinction between *conservation* and *preservation*. In the debate concerning Hetch Hetchy, would you support Pinchot's conservationist or Muir's preservationist policies? What values underlie your decision?

3. The Rolling Stones once sang, "You can't always get what you want." Is that a bad thing? Should government policy always seek to supply people with what they want? Should government play a role in teaching citizens about what wants are of value and which are not, or should government remain neutral on such questions?

4. Should government agencies such as the U.S. Forest Service aim to make a profit? Why or why not? If you were director of the U.S. Forest Service, how would you understand your role of serving the public?

5. It has been suggested that one way to protect endangered species such as the blue whale would be to sell them to the highest bidder. In this view, only unowned species are threatened with extinction. Species that are owned, such as chickens and cows, seldom face extinction because people (their owners) have a strong incentive (profit) for keeping them around. Property rights would ensure a similar protection for all endangered species. Do you think it would be wise to sell exclusive whaling rights to Norwegian, Russian, or Japanese whalers?

6. Baxter claims that "penguins are important because people enjoy seeing them." Do you agree? Is this the only reason that penguins should be protected?

7. Is human nature "undeniably selfish" as Baxter claims? Can you think of any situations in which people do not act selfishly? In answering this question, be careful to distinguish between a *reason* for acting and the *feelings* that follow from acting.

Further Reading

Garrett Hardin and John Baden, ed., *Managing the Commons* (San Francisco: Freeman, 1977), details the neoclassical economic approach to environmental issues.

A. Freeman, R. Haveman, and A. Kneese, *The Economics of Environmental Policy* (Baltimore: Johns Hopkins University Press, 1973), presents the reform approach of environmental economists.

E. F. Schumacher, *Small is Beautiful* (New York: Harper and Row, 1973), is the well-known defense of "economics as if people mattered."

Herman Daly and John Cobb, *For the Common Good* (Boston: Beacon, 1989), provides a solid introduction to the economics and values of sustainable economics.

4

Responsibilities to Future Generations: Population and Consumption

---

Population and Consumption

Worldwide population was said to have reached 6 billion people on October 12, 1999, having taken thirty-five years to double in size. Demographers estimate that the total world population reached 1 billion in 1804. It then took 123 years to reach 2 billion, 33 years to reach 3 billion, 14 years to reach 4 billion, 13 years to reach 5 billion, and approximately 12 years to reach 6 billion people. Worldwide growth rates appear to be declining slightly, suggesting that the seven billionth person will not be born until 2015, the eight billionth will not be born until 2032, and the nine billionth person will not be born until 2050.

This population growth is not occurring at a random rate across the globe. Population centers are getting more crowded. The number of people living in cities has doubled over the last forty years. In 1900, sixteen cities had a population greater than 1 million residents. By 2000, 326 cities had a population greater than 1 million, and fourteen cities had a population greater than 10 million. Population growth is also occurring at higher rates in less developed countries. According to the United Nations, the top ten countries ranked by population size in 1998 compared to projected 2050 populations are as follows.

1998		2050	
China	1.255 billion	India	1.53 billion
India	976 million	China	1.51 billion
U.S.	274 million	Pakistan	357 million
Indonesia	207 million	U.S.	348 million
Brazil	165 million	Nigeria	339 million
Russia	148 million	Indonesia	318 million
Pakistan	147 million	Brazil	243 million
Japan	126 million	Bangladesh	218 million
Bangladesh	124 million	Ethiopia	213 million
Nigeria	122 million	Iran	170 million

Such trends in both population size and density along with correspon-ding environmental stress have led many observers to conclude that humans are approaching the limits of growth. In the 1972 book, *The Limits of Growth,* Jay Forrester, Donella Meadows, Dennis Meadows, and Jorgen Randers published the results of their computer modeling based on the then current population, resource use, and economic trends. They con-cluded that if these trends remained unchanged, the earth would face envi-ronmental and economic collapse within the next century. While some trends have changed for the better, their twenty-year update, *Beyond the Limits,* suggests that we have already overshot some of the ecological limits for human population size. For example, the United Nations has estimated that in 1996, 1.1 billion people lived without access to clean drinking water, 2.9 billion people lacked sanitation services, and 841 million people, one-sixth of the world population in 1996, were malnourished.

Increased efficiencies in agriculture, fishing, mining, and energy produc-tion seemingly has allowed resource use to keep pace with population growth. Food production has increased as agricultural land use has decreased. Market price for fossil fuels has remained steady, and the price for many minerals and natural resources has declined. Nevertheless, there are other signs of stress.

The United Nations estimated that between 5 to 7 million hectares of agricultural land is lost each year to erosion. Underground aquifers, including the Ogalala Aquifer that underlies much of the American Midwest, are shrinking. Some of the most productive fisheries in the north Atlantic and Pacific Oceans are under stress, with entire population of once-plentiful fish and marine species near collapse. Large areas of the Gulf of Mexico, offshore from the Mississippi delta, are almost devoid of marine life as the result of agricultural and industrial pollution that washes down the Mississippi. Further, while economic price provides one measure of the availability of natural resources, the sheer numbers suggest a different picture. In 1900, worldwide oil use totaled a few thousand bar-rels per day. By 1997, that figure reached 72 million barrels of oil per day. The 1900 total of all metal use was 20 million tons annually. In 1997, that total was 1.2 billion tons. Finally, the increased production of greenhouse gases and the destruction of carbon-absorbing forests threaten the entire planet with shifting climates and global warming.

But resource use, like population size and density, itself is not distributed across the earth equally. Industrialized countries use much higher percentages of natural resources than do less developed countries. One estimate suggests that the United States, with less than 5 percent of the world's population consumes 30 percent of the resources used per year. More generally, the wealthiest 1 billion people consume 80 percent of the world's resources, leaving the remaining 5 billion people to share 20 percent of the resources. The U.S. Geological Survey estimated in 1998, that if the entire world consumed resources at the U.S. rate, per capita consumption of resources would increase by sixfold. This estimate includes an increase by sevenfold in mineral use, a fivefold increase in wood products, and an elevenfold increase in the consumption of synthetics.[1]

4.1 INTRODUCTION

Much of the early philosophical thinking about the environment fit an applied ethics model. As philosophers came to recognize the seriousness of environmental challenges, they tended to turn to standard ethical theories and principles for guidance. "Ethics" was a given, an area where philosophers independently developed their theories and, as the need or interest arose, applied these theories to more practical matters. This implied a negative and conservative function for ethics. The role of theory was to evaluate and analyze issues, with less thought given to constructing a positive environmental ethic. It was conservative in the sense that applying standard theories tended to reinforce the philosophical status quo. The theories applied were those currently accepted and that, by being applied to new issues, tended to define these issues in standard ways.

The next three chapters examine how interaction with environmental issues expands these standard approaches to ethics. Chapter 4 looks at how population and consumption issues raise ethical questions about our responsibilities to future generations. This is a question that did not receive much attention among philosophers until the late twentieth century and required the extension of standard ethical theory in new directions. Chapter 5 considers the question of moral standing and examines early efforts to extend standard ethical theories to include new environmental rights for both humans and nonhumans. Again, philosophers seldom considered these topics. Chapter 6 examines in detail the more systematic attempts to extend moral standing to animals.

4.2 POPULATION, CONSUMPTION, AND ETHICS

Beginning in the late 1960s, population growth became a major focus of environmental concern. *The Population Bomb*, a 1968 best-selling book by Paul Erhlich, argued that exploding population growth was responsible for widespread environmental destruction. Others, for example Barry Commoner in his 1971 book *The Closing Circle,* argued that the consumption-driven lifestyle of industrial societies rather than population size *per se* was more responsible.[2] In most ways, these debates represented a continuation of the applied ethics model. Many debates concerning population involved common issues of individual freedom and social responsibility. Likewise, consumption debates often focused on economic rights and responsibilities to distant peoples. Both areas also focused on issues of social and economic justice to the poor and disenfranchised people living in the developing world. But these debates also began to focus philosophical attention on responsibilities to people living in the future. This shift from geographically distant people to temporally distant people raises philosophical questions seldom previously asked by philosophers. Ethical consideration began to be extended to something other than presently living human beings.

In some obvious ways, overpopulation does increase the environmental damage caused by humans. The more people that exist, the more people will suffer from pollution, global warming, and the like. Even now, at the start of the twenty-first century, environmental problems such as drought, erosion, urban sprawl, loss of farmlands, and pollution have produced ten million "environmental refugees," the world's single largest class of homeless and landless people.[3]

More directly, perhaps, overpopulation places a tremendous strain on the environment. An increasing *number* of people obviously requires providing more energy, homes, food, and jobs and creates more trash, pollution, and development. We need only consider the world's large urban centers like New York, New Delhi, and Mexico City to understand the environmental devastation that follows from human overpopulation.

Further devastation comes when the economic growth and development sought by these populations leads to excessive consumption because of over-population.[4] In industrialized countries like the United States, environmental damage per capita is higher than many less developed countries. For example, with less than 5 percent of the world's population, the United States uses 33 percent of the world's nonrenewable energy and mineral resources. As less developed countries pursue the higher standard of living (as economists might say) attained by the industrialized countries, threats to the environment increase almost unimaginably.[5]

These considerations have wide-ranging ethical implications. Is there some ethically preferable population goal? If so, what are the philosophical grounds for establishing this goal, and what policies should be promoted to attain this goal? Do humans have an obligation to procreate? An obligation to refrain from having babies? Is it ethically responsible for families to have more than two children? Do future generations have a right to be born? Do people in the industrialized countries of the world consume too much? Is it unjust that the richest 5 percent of the world's population consumes 33 per-cent of the world's resources? Do people in the industrialized world have direct ethical obligations to the world's poor? Does the present generation have responsibilities to preserve resources for future people? Let us consider some questions associated with population growth and resource use.

For what, if any, future population goal ought today's generation of humans aim? Do we have a responsibility to bring about a particular size population in the future? To begin to answer these questions, imagine for a moment that scientists determine that certain genes controlling reproduction are particularly susceptible to damage from a contaminate found in drinking water or from increased exposure to ultraviolet radiation that results from ozone depletion. Imagine that, as a result, the entire human race will no longer be capable of reproducing. Within 100 to 125 years, the species Homo sapiens will become extinct. Ignore for now the unhappiness that people today would suffer when they discovered this fact (the mostly psychological harm of not being able to have [more] children, the increasing loneliness of later survivors, and so forth). What, if anything, would be wrong with allowing human beings to become extinct? Is there any ethical reason that future generations should exist? Are there ethical reasons that we should propagate our species?

To avoid questions about the harms done to living humans by such prospects and perhaps to imagine a more idealized scenario, we could change the example. Imagine that the generations decide today, willingly and thoughtfully, to adopt a policy of universal celibacy. Perhaps they recognize the environmental destruction caused by humans and conclude that the world would be better off if this particular species became extinct.

How might we even begin to answer such questions? Perhaps we could begin to sketch answers to these questions by returning to the ethical traditions outlined in Chapter 2. Philosophers in the natural law tradition might well argue that we do have ethical reasons for the continuation of our species. Perhaps arguing from both biological (the natural function of our reproductive organs) and philosophical grounds (the nature of human beings as social beings who live in families and communities), they might make a case that a real moral tragedy would occur if humans became extinct. (When the natural law tradition in philosophy is joined with Christian sources, for example, the biblical injunction to "go forth and multiply," they would have additional arguments.) Utilitarians might suggest that we have a duty to perpetuate our species because doing so will maximize human happiness. Deontologists might argue that future generations have rights and among those rights are the right to life, understood as the right to be conceived and born.

As even this brief thought experiment suggests, thinking about responsibilities to future generations can quickly become puzzling. First, any discussion of future happiness or the rights of people of the future forces us to consider whom those "future people" might be and what they will be like. Yet, because those people do not exist and because we do not know that they will ever exist, it is difficult to understand how we can even talk about responsibilities to them. Yet, it would have to be sensible to talk about such responsibilities if we are to ask present generations to make significant sacrifices for the benefit of future people. Thus, an initial philosophical challenge concerns the plausibility of the very concept of having responsibilities to people who do not and may never exist.

4.3 DO WE HAVE RESPONSIBILITIES TO FUTURE GENERATIONS?

Several arguments have been offered against the view that we do have responsibilities to future generations. We can identify three such arguments as the "argument from ignorance," the "disappearing beneficiaries" argument, and the "argument from temporal location." Because an assumption underlying many environmental issues is that it is meaningful and reasonable to talk about obligations to future generations, it will be helpful to consider these arguments in depth.

The first, what can be called the "argument from ignorance," stresses that we know little about people of the future.[6] We do not know *who* they will be, *that* they will be, *what* they will be like, or what their needs, wants, or interests will be. Thus, because we know so little about them, it makes little sense to try to specify any obligations to them that we might have.

However, it is difficult to see why we should draw this conclusion. Surely we have a fairly good idea about what people of the future will need and what their interests will be if they are to have a reasonably good life. Minimally, this would include an adequate supply of clean air and water, a moderate climate, protection from poisons and disease, and so forth. Further, we already acknowledge responsibilities that parallel those to future generations. In civil law, we hold people responsible for actions that result in unintended but foreseeable harms to others. For example, imagine that someone establishes a toxic waste dump on a piece of property. Imagine that a few years later, escaping toxins poison neighbors of the dump. Imagine that the polluter offers a defense based on the argument from ignorance: "I did not know who would be hurt, I did not even know for certain that anyone would be hurt, and I surely did not know that these people would have a particular interest in health. How can I be said to have had an obligation to them?" Just as in cases of legal negligence, where we hold people liable for unintended but foreseeable and avoidable harms that occur in the future, it is meaningful to talk about foreseeable but unknown harms to future generations.

A second argument against the view that we have responsibilities to future generations has been called the argument from "disappearing beneficiaries." This perspective argues that not only have we no responsibility to bring future generations into existence, but it is also meaningless even to talk about ethical obligations to future generations.[7] The short version of this claim holds that we can have no obligation (based on either the maximum happiness principle or the rights of people of the future) to bring a generation into existence because there are no particular people to whom that responsibility is directed.[8]

Consider the following. In 1997, representatives from 160 of the world's nations met in Kyoto, Japan to consider proposals that would significantly limit the amount of greenhouse gases discharged into the atmosphere. This conference followed a 1992 agreement at the "Earth Summit" in Rio de Janerio in which industrialized countries pledged to reduce greenhouse gas emissions back to 1990 levels. At the Kyoto conference, the United States proposed a plan that would not meet the 1990 levels, arguing that a significant reduction of greenhouse gases would have disastrous economic repercussions. Many environmentalists argued that we ought to accept these short-term consequences in order to protect the interests of future generations. These people argued that we need to reduce our reliance on fossil fuels to ensure a world protected from global warming in the future.

Intuitively, we might say that reducing greenhouse emissions is the ethically preferable decision because those people born into that world will be better off than they would have been had we maintained the status quo and continued our heavy reliance on fossil fuels. "Better off than they would have been" assumes that these very same people would exist if we had chosen the alternative. That is, the moral intuition underlying this decision is that one set of people of the future will either be harmed or benefited by our decisions. But alternative policy decisions, especially those as significant as what would be required to achieve major reductions in carbon dioxide emissions, will surely result in *different* people being born. According to this view, the existence of any one person is dependent on a remarkable number of contingencies. (Imagine all the events that might have prevented your parents or great-grandparents from meeting or caused them to postpone the moment of conception by a year, a month, or even a minute.) Thus, alternative policy decisions will result in two sets, not one, of people of the future: those who will be born if we choose policy A and those who will be born if we choose policy B. (Of course, this simplifies the issue. Alternative policies adopted at Rio de Janerio would be only one of many factors that determine who is born.) Because the group that would be harmed by one choice would not exist unless we made that choice, it makes little sense to say that they would be better off if we had made the other choice (hence the name "disappearing beneficiaries"). Because different policy decisions result in different future generations, there simply is no one future generation that would be made better or worse off by either decision.

Consider the following two responses to the "disappearing beneficiaries" argument. Philosopher Annette Baier developed the first.[9] Baier argues that we can make sense of the claim that someone is made worse off by our actions even if, under the alternative action, that person would not have existed at all. On the one hand, we can acknowledge the significance of a "wrongful life," a life in which the person can say, "I would have been better off not being born."[10] We can imagine a world so polluted and so miserable that a population would acknowledge that its members would have been better off had they not lived and suffered at all. Further, the concept of moral rights provides us with a way to explain "worse off" even when the alternative is nonexistence.

If we acknowledge that all humans have and will continue to have rights to certain goods or to have certain interests protected, our actions today may violate the rights of people of the future. Thus, if we continue to dump massive amounts of pollutants into the atmosphere, we harm people of the future not by making them worse off than they would have been but by violating their rights. That is, we have failed in our duty to provide those people, whomever they turn out to be, with a certain moral minimum. These people can say that they were harmed, not because *they* would have been better off in some other future but because in the future in which they do exist our actions jeopardized certain central interests of theirs (for example, health). In this sense, our obligations are not to any particular people of the future but to the interests those people, whomever they turn out to be, will have. These interests do not disappear with alternative decisions.

Philosopher Mary Anne Warren developed a somewhat different response.[11] Warren distinguishes between "possible people," those people who could but do not necessarily exist, and "future people," those people who will exist in the future. Warren acknowledges that it is absurd to suggest that we have obligations to merely "possible" people. Because the number of possible people is infinite, that view makes little sense. But we can meaningfully compare the happiness or suffering of "future people." We can do this because we can compare "types of human life" and recognize that a life of suffering is worse than a life of happiness. Thus, although any one particular potential beneficiary may "disappear" under alternative decisions, the relative amount of suffering or happiness does not. Our obligations to future generations, in this view, are not obligations to specific possible people but are obligations to "recognize certain *minimal requirements of moral responsibility.*" As Warren sees it, "It is irresponsible, and contemptuous of the welfare of future persons, to deliberately bring into being persons who will almost certainly be unhappy. It is wrong because it results in unnecessary suffering in the future, suffering on the part of individuals [future people] who in the timeless perspective are no less real than we are."[12]

Thus, following Baier and Warren, it can be meaningful to talk about responsibilities to future generations. We have good grounds for believing that our actions today can be restricted by ethical obligations that we owe to people of the future.

A third argument opposing present responsibilities to future generations focuses on the temporal location of future generations and concludes that we cannot have responsibilities in the present to people who will not exist for many years. Responsibility for nuclear wastes is a helpful example for thinking about this claim.

Some of the best ethical analyses of the nuclear issue can be found in the writing of philosophers Richard Sylvan and Val Plumwood.[13] They ask us to imagine a trip on a crowded long-distance train. As the train leaves one station, someone places a package aboard that contains a highly toxic and explosive gas. The gas is packaged in a container that the sender knows is not strong and may well leak before reaching its destination. It will certainly leak if the train is involved in an accident or derails or if some passenger accidentally or intentionally interferes with, mishandles, or attempts to steal the gas. All these events have occurred in the past. Any leak will probably kill those people close by and do serious harm to others. Some but not all the passengers know about the container, and none has consented to its being aboard the train.

The authors suggest that most people would strongly condemn the person who placed the package aboard the train. Even if this sender hopes and believes that no accident will occur or even if the sender had no alternative means of sending the package and cannot afford a safer container, we would condemn this person for jeopardizing the lives and health of many people.

Our policy of creating and storing nuclear wastes is, according to Sylvan and Plumwood, exactly analogous to this example. We are sending extremely toxic wastes on a train ride into the future with the world's future populations, perhaps as many as 40,000 generations, as passengers. We are guilty of a great injustice by placing people of the future at grave risk, all because we wish to avoid making changes in our comfortable consumer lifestyle.

According to Sylvan and Plumwood,

> Like the consignor in the train parable, contemporary industrial society proposes, in order to get itself out of a mess arising from its own life-style—the creation of economies dependent on an abundance of non-renewable energy, which is in limited supply—to pass on costs and risks of serious harm to others who will obtain no corresponding benefits. . . . If we apply to the nuclear situation standards of behavior and moral principles generally acknowledged (in principle if not so often in fact) in the contemporary world, it is not easy to avoid the conclusion that nuclear development involves *injustice with respect to the future* on a grand scale.[14]

The authors suggest that only two paths avoid this conclusion: either we try to deny that we owe future generations any consideration at all, or we must argue that our concerns override our responsibilities to future generations.

As shown, we are usually quite willing to hold people responsible for actions that cause harm at some future date. I am responsible for poisoning you even if the effects of my poison do not occur for some time. Thus, it is not the timing of the harm that has a role in determining our responsibilities. Perhaps the distinction with which we must grapple is that in one case I harm existing people in the future and in the other I harm future people in the future. Does this make a difference?

Philosopher Gregory Kavka argues that it does not. His analysis of what he calls the "futurity problem" rejects three arguments that might be given to support the claim that today's generations have no obligations to people of the future. These arguments are based on temporal location, our ignorance of future people, and the contingency of future people.[15] Because we have seen two of these claims before, we will review only the temporal location argument.

Is our responsibility to future generations that are harmed by our actions excused because they exist in a future time (a different "temporal location")? Kavka offers two reasons for thinking that it is not. First, arguing by analogy to our own future desires, he claims that just as it is unreasonable for any individuals to favor their current desires over their future desires, so it is unreasonable to favor satisfying the desires of people today over those of the future. Consider one example. We normally think it unreasonable for people to sacrifice their future well-being simply to satisfy some current desire. It would be irrational for me to spend my life savings right now simply because the specific desires that I will have during retirement are desires that will occur only in the future. It is because future desires are as important as current desires that the rational person saves for the future. Likewise, we should treat the desires of people of the future as deserving consideration equal to the desires of people today.

Kavka also denies that temporal location is a morally relevant feature of a person. Just as we have good reasons to believe that my dumping of toxic wastes in my yard will harm living people, we have good reasons for thinking that long-term toxic wastes will harm people of the future. The burden of proof is on those who would claim otherwise, and it is a burden not easily dismissed.

Thus, while some real puzzles confront the view that the present generation has responsibilities to future generations, it does seem that we can meaningfully talk about such responsibilities. We have good reason to believe that people will exist in the future and that they will be similar enough to us that we can have a good idea of what their well-being requires. Knowing this and knowing that our present actions can influence their future well-being, it is reasonable to conclude that future people must be given some ethical consideration by presently living humans. But we have not yet considered the content of those responsibilities. Assuming that it is meaningful to recognize ethical standing of future people, what do we owe them?

4.4 RESPONSIBILITIES TO THE FUTURE: UTILITARIAN HAPPINESS

Assuming that we can meaningfully be said to have responsibilities to future generations, how do we decide where those responsibilities lie? What is the ethical basis of these responsibilities? The following sections trace three ethical approaches to answering this question: utilitarian ethics, a rights-based approach, and an ethics of care.

As seen in the discussion of Warren's position, one way to answer these questions is to focus on minimizing suffering. A utilitarian and intuitively plausible view would suggest that minimally we have an obligation to reduce the suffering and optimally to maximize the happiness of future generations. This attempt to further specify this obligation has led to some problems, however.

Suppose we adopt a utilitarian view and argue that we have an obligation to maximize the happiness of future generations. Should that "maximal happiness" commit us to increasing the *total overall* happiness or the *average* happiness?[16] This distinction is not as important when we restrict our concerns to today. Given a constant population, total and average happiness amount to the same thing. However, when we recognize that one of our decisions regarding future generations concerns *how many* future people there will be, we see that the total versus average distinction is quite important.

For example, we might decide that it is preferable to increase future population size, thereby increasing the total overall future happiness, although the average amount of happiness might remain constant. Is it ethically preferable to increase the total overall happiness of the future population or to increase the average happiness of individual people of the future? The answer has significant implications for population and environmental policies.

Suppose we elect the total happiness view and adopt environmental policies aimed at increasing total future happiness. One implication of this view may well commit us to *increasing* future population size. This seems to commit us to what Derek Parfit has called the "repugnant conclusion."[17] So long as overall world happiness is increased, we ought to create as many people as possible. Thus, we might be obligated to create a world with billions and billions of marginally happy people rather than a world with a much smaller population of much happier people. (Or suppose we were committed to a world in which *total* suffering was minimized. Might such a future world contain *no* human beings? Might our obligation under this view be to refrain from having any children?)

The total happiness alternative does not appear to be attractive. It seems to commit us to sacrificing the happiness of individual people of the future to an abstract notion of some total overall happiness. Is it permissible to cause the existence of countless people who will suffer so long as the overall amount of world happiness increases?

On the other hand, suppose we adopt a population policy aimed at increasing the average future happiness. This seems to avoid the problem raised by the total view. Environmental and population policy ought to aim to increase the happiness, on average, of those individual people who will exist in the future. Will the average person living in the future be happier if we reduce carbon dioxide emissions or if we continue the current rate of carbon dioxide emissions?

The average happiness view also has serious problems. It places an unreasonable ethical restriction on the birth of people of the future. In effect, it commits us to saying that people ought not be born unless they will enjoy a life in the future at least as happy as the average person today enjoys. This discounts the happiness of people of the future. Their happiness is important only in comparison to ours. Even if people would be, on balance, happy with their lives, the average happiness view would say that these people ought not be born if they will not be as happy as average people are today.

This view, too, might place us on a slippery slope to a particularly repugnant conclusion. It might be argued that because people living in impoverished, nonindustrialized countries will produce future generations that would likely not increase average happiness, population policy ought to restrict the reproductive freedom of the world's poor. Those countries with relatively high standards of living, with access to plentiful and affordable food, health care, education, resources, and energy, would have an ethical claim to reproductive priority. Those countries in which a person's life prospects are relatively low (even if still moderately happy) should be required to lower birth rates. Minimally, this appears to imply an unfair priority to the status quo. The rich get richer, and the poor get contraception.

It would seem that defenders of the average happiness view need to say more about the *distribution* of both happiness and the resources necessary to achieve happiness. Note that this problem is a version of the justice criticism raised against utilitarianism in Chapter 2. Before turning to this question, let us turn to another issue concerning the utilitarian approach to present responsibilities to future generations.

Might someone now argue on utilitarian grounds that although we do have responsibilities to people of the future, those responsibilities are overridden by more pressing interests today? Because we are concerned with the interests in life and health of people of the future, interests that we normally would not override for reasons of convenience or comfort, this argument assumes a process of *discounting* the interests of those people.

The idea of discounting the interests of people of the future has roots in the classical utilitarianism of Jeremy Bentham. Bentham developed a "hedonistic calculus" as a means of measuring pleasure to aid in calculating the utilitarian consequences of our acts. According to Bentham, the amount of pleasure and pain produced by our actions will vary along several dimensions, including the *certainty* or *uncertainty* that they will occur and their *propinquity* or *remoteness*. Thus, uncertain or remote pleasures count for less than certain and immediate ones. But is it reasonable to do this? We can find reasons for rejecting this practice on both utilitarian and human rights grounds.

The practice of discounting future interests finds a contemporary expression in the economic concept of discounting the present value of future payments. In this view, one dollar held now is worth more than one dollar held at some time in the future because we could invest that dollar today, earn interest on it, and therefore, have more than one dollar at that future date. Thus, future dollars must be discounted to be equivalent to present value. As a result, the practice of discounting future interests is common in economic analyses of environmental issues. As seen in Chapter 3, economic analysis is the methodology most commonly used in deciding public policy. Thus, what may seem like an abstract and arcane concept ends up playing a significant role in environmental policy. One implication of this practice, for example, might require us to maximize the present value of our resources and discount their value to later generations.[18]

Two immediate considerations cast doubt on the logic of discounting future interests. First, no matter how small the discount rate, any discounting eventually reduces future values to nothing. Second, it would seem that some values, such as health and life, should not be discounted at all. A single dollar possessed by my great-great-grandchild may be worth less (in purchasing power) than a single dollar that I possess, but it would be peculiar to claim that my great-great-grandchild's life (assuming that my children and their children's children have children) will be worth less than my life.

Another strong case against the discounting of future interests can be made on utilitarian grounds. Philosopher Mary Williams has developed an interesting version of such an argument.[19] Williams argues that discounting the future value of resources can be consistent with utilitarian goals so long as those resources remain to produce value in the future. In that case, maximizing present value also maximizes the total overall value because in the future these resources will continue to produce value. However, when resources with future value can be removed from production, as happens when current generations deplete nonrenewable resources (or renewable resources at a rate below sustainability), the total overall good is not maximized.

The essential point of this argument, for our purposes, seems to be this: in calculating the future consequences of our current environmental policies, policymakers have a tendency to rely on the economic practice of discounting future values (costs and benefits). As witnessed in Chapter 3, the ethical basis of this approach is a version of utilitarianism. However, Williams claims that even on utilitarian grounds, discounting social value in environmental cases oftentimes frustrates rather than promotes maximum total happiness. This occurs because those resources that would produce the future value are being depleted to the point of extinction by our current policies. Williams' image is that rather than living off the interest of our "investments," we too often are spending our savings so that, eventually, we will have no savings left to generate interest payments.

Her alternative is to defend an environmental policy of "maximum sustainable yield." That is, we should seek to maximize the return on our investments (for example, our environmental and agricultural resources) without jeopardizing the investments themselves. We should, to use the economists' language, live off our interest and not our capital. To use an agricultural image, we should seek to maximize the yield of our croplands in a manner that guarantees that the cropland will continue to be productive for the indefinite future. By discounting future values, we make it easy for the current generation to spend its capital as well as its interest.

4.5 RESPONSIBILITIES TO THE FUTURE: THE RIGHTS OF FUTURE PEOPLE

Perhaps a more direct critical response to both the distributive justice challenge and the practice of discounting future values develops from a deontological approach to the rights of future people. As seen, discounting the interests of future people allows us to override their interests in life and health with our interests in a comfortable lifestyle. Ordinarily, we would think that life and health trump mere comfort. Philosophers who take seriously the rights of future generations (or our obligations to them) deny that we can override the central interests of future people.[20]

We already have seen some of these strategies used by philosophers who would defend the rights of future generations. Many of these strategies attempt to show that no sound argument can be given to deny rights to future generations. Thus, their temporal location, ignorance of them, or their contingency cannot justify denying our obligations to people of the future.

Other philosophers have argued that although we do have obligations to future generations, these obligations extend only into the near future. We have duties to our children's and our grandchildren's generations, perhaps, but we have no duties to the distant future, for example, ten, twenty, or one hundred generations into the future. The defense of these claims rests on a variety of grounds. Some would argue that rights and duties are fundamentally contractual, that they arise from a social contract between people. Although a plausible case can be made for interpreting the relationship between immediate generations on a contractual model (we continue to be bound by the social contract established by the U.S. Constitution), less plausible is thinking that generations separated by thousands of years could be so bound.

A slightly different view argues that rights and responsibilities are relative to our "moral community." Minimally, a moral community consists of those people with a shared moral understanding, a recognition of mutual and reciprocal moral relations and the like. Thus, our rights and responsibilities end at the boundaries of our moral community, be those boundaries conceptual, spatial, or temporal.[21] Still others might argue that our responsibilities are a function of other moral relations such as caring, love, or sympathy. Because these affections can extend into the immediate future but not into the distant future, our responsibilities too extend only into the immediate future.

Chapter 5 considers some of these issues in more depth. Indeed, we will see how some philosophers have pushed the notion of moral considerability well beyond the question of future generations of humans. For now, let us focus on two fundamental philosophical questions. Can future generations be said to have rights? What rights do (would) future generations have?

Is it meaningful to say that future generations have rights *now*? If we tend to think of rights as some sort of attribute that belongs to people and exists in the world to be discovered, it is difficult to see how that claim could be defended. If the rights-holders do not exist, how could they have rights? But if we think of rights in terms of their *function*, assigning rights to future generations becomes more logical. Rights function to limit the behavior of other people. My rights limit your behavior by imposing certain obligations on you. Rights limit behavior in order to protect certain central interests of the rights-holder. Further, some socially recognized means for enforcing my rights should·exist.[22] Thus, the existence of rights depends on what the moral community acknowledges central interests to be. Future generations might be said to have rights to the degree that we acknowledge and accept limitations on our behavior for the sake of their interests.

Do we have good reasons to accept such limitations on our own behavior? It seems to me that we have such good reasons to the degree that we have good reasons for believing that future generations will exist and that they will have central interests that we can now understand and predict. That is, we have extremely strong reasons for attributing rights to future generations. The burden of proof surely rests with those who would claim either that future generations likely will not exist or that their needs and interests will be so different from ours that we cannot predict what they might be.

If we accept something along these lines, the rights we should attribute to future generations will depend on the needs and interests that we assume those future generations will have. Let us return to the question of nuclear energy and nuclear wastes.

We can be fairly certain that future generations will have an interest in being protected from the dangers of nuclear radiation. But what will their energy needs and interests be? If we forgo nuclear energy to protect the interests of future generations, the only plausible alternative for us (at least into the immediate future and assuming the demand remains constant) involves greater reliance on nonrenewable energy sources such as oil, gas, and coal. Ignoring for the moment the pollution problems that follow from burning these fossil fuels, our greater reliance on fossil fuels implies both that less of these resources will be available for future generations and that we are putting them at risk of global warming. How, then, should we balance our responsibilities to future generations regarding limiting nuclear wastes against our interests in and needs for energy and the energy interests and needs of future generations? Do we have obligations to conserve nonrenewable energy resources so that people will have access to these resources in the future? How should we balance the risks of nuclear wastes against the risks of global warming?

Any attempt to specify the rights of people of the future would seem to encounter serious difficulties. By definition, any use of nonrenewable resources means that others will have less available for their use. If we have a duty to conserve out of respect for the rights of the near future generations, ought they not conserve out of respect for the rights of distant future generations? If the near future has the right to use these resources, why do not we?

Philosopher Brian Barry provides an interesting response to these problems.[23] Barry's position is to allow current generations to continue to use nonrenewable energy resources, even if this means placing future generations at a relative disadvantage, so long as we compensate those people for causing them this disadvantage. Barry holds that, at a minimum, justice requires equal treatment. When we use nonrenewable energy resources, we are denying future generations the equal opportunity to use those resources. Justice demands that denials of equality be compensated. We cannot compensate future generations for the loss of energy resources by returning that energy to them, but we can compensate them for the loss of those opportunities and choices that require energy resources. The central human interest lies not in the resources themselves (for example, oil, gas, and coal) but in those uses to which we put energy resources. They and we use energy to produce the goods and services that we need. Barry says it is the loss of an equal opportunity to use these goods (to this "productive capacity") that requires compensation.

> We can now venture a statement of what is required by justice toward future gen-
> erations. As far as natural resources are concerned, depletion should be compen-
> sated for in the sense that later generations should be left no worse off (in terms
> of productive capacity) than they would have been without the depletion.[24]

Barry acknowledges that many practical difficulties are involved in specifying what would be required to offset the loss of productive capacity.
Nevertheless, we can infer some implications. Because the resources that we
are using are relatively accessible, we owe future generations capital and technological investments that will pay future dividends in terms of their ability
to find and extract energy resources. Presumably, we also owe to them an
investment in research and development of alternative energy sources. It
would also seem reasonable to say that we owe them as large an inheritance
of energy resources as is practical. Wasting energy resources is a particularly
callous violation of their rights.

What conclusions might we draw from this discussion of our duties to and
the rights of future generations? I offer three. First, we have the obligation to
make a sincere and serious effort to develop alternative energy sources. The
risks of continued reliance on fossil fuels and nuclear power are real and serious. We can reasonably foresee the dangers that follow from these energy
sources, and it is within our power to minimize them. Failing to take steps to
avoid them is on a par with criminal negligence.

Second, we have the duty to conserve energy resources. At current rates, we
will use up the known reserves of fossil fuels and uranium within two hundred years. Wasting these resources, especially when known technology can
increase efficiency so that we can conserve without significant sacrifice of convenience, denies people of the future a fair opportunity to attain a lifestyle
commensurate with our own.

Finally, we owe these people a reasonable chance for happiness. The earth
cannot continue to support an exploding population. We need to limit population growth so that we do not bring people into the world who will possess little chance for a minimally decent life. Additionally, we need to
recognize that poverty is a major factor that both contributes to and exacer-
bates overpopulation.

4.6 RESPONSIBILITIES TO THE FUTURE: CARING FOR THE FUTURE

If we understand rights as protecting central interests and if we accept the
reasonableness of attributing rights to people of the future, future generations would seem to have strong claims to our use of a variety of resources.
Clean air and water, agricultural lands, and energy are all tied in obvious
ways to the central interests of people of the future. But what about other,
less essential, resources? Do future generations have a right to undeveloped
shorelines, wilderness areas, wetlands, and mountainsides? Do we have a
duty to preserve animal and plant species for future generations? Is the

preservation of these resources more akin to acting out of charity than acting from a duty?

Do future generations have a *right* to such resources? We can understand that future generations, like us, might enjoy such resources. But then again they might not. This issue is even more difficult when we recognize that what future generations will enjoy or desire depends largely on the type of world that they inherit from us. Will a world without the blue whale miss it? Will future generations that have never experienced a wilderness area, rain forest, or grizzly bear care about such things? Do we miss the dodo bird? The passenger pigeon? Would we really miss the snail darter or the California condor?

We can make several arguments that we have a duty to preserve wilderness areas and plant and animal species. We might argue that the biological diversity protected in wilderness areas and represented by plant and animal species has a potential for great benefit to humans. The agricultural and medical potential of biological diversity provides strong and prudent reasons for their preservation.

As will be seen in the chapters that follow, a number of philosophers have argued that animals, plants, and ecosystems should be the direct beneficiaries of our responsibilities. In this view, we should preserve them for their own sake. Before turning to these questions, consider a defense of preservation that has nothing to do with prudence. We should preserve such natural resources because we *care* about future generations. We care about the type of people they will become, and we believe that a life lived in a world in which wilderness areas and rare species are preserved is a better life than the alternative.

Can we care about people who do not exist? To answer this question, we need to say something about what is implied by "caring for" someone. Just a brief consideration suggests that care is a more complex concept than we might initially think. Let us overlook most of the complexity to focus on just a few central ideas. In one sense, care can refer to the responsibility to attend to someone's needs or interests. An elderly parent may be in the care of an adult child, or a nurse may be charged with the care of a patient. This meaning is relevant to our concerns. In part, we are asking whether generations today can be charged with the care of people of the future.

But there is more to care. Just as an adult child may be charged with the care of an elderly parent yet never visit that parent in a nursing home, so too we might be charged with the care of people of the future yet do nothing more than the barest minimum to render that care. A more interesting notion of care involves a motivational or emotional engagement with the subject.

Care is more than a mere feeling or a fleeting recognition of an interest in another person (the way that most of us, when it is brought to our attention, will acknowledge that we care about the victims of some foreign war or natural disaster). If care about future generations involved only this feeling, it would be of little interest for us. For our purposes, care is something closer to love or altruism in that it involves our being engaged with and motivated by the well-being of others. Can our concern for the interests of future people—

for the type of life they will face, the type of people they will become—provide a reason for us to act today? Can it provide a reason that can override our personal interests?

Put in this way, the question would seem easy to answer. Reasonably strong empirical evidence suggests that people are often motivated to act out of a concern for the interests of people of the future. On the political level, decisions to protect wilderness areas, establish national and state parks, forests, and shorelines, build museums and libraries, and fund research and development in medicine, industry, and national defense make sense only if we recognize that the beneficiaries of these decisions will be generations as yet unborn. On a private level, decisions to endow charitable and educational foundations and fund artistic, cultural, and social organizations also seem obviously motivated, at least in part, by a concern to provide people of the future with a decent and humane world. On a personal level, a decision as simple as planting an oak tree, one of countless varieties of plants that mature over long periods of time, suggests that individuals are motivated by a concern for the distant future.

Against this empirical evidence, however, lies a strong philosophical tradition that holds humans are motivated solely by self-interest. This view, called "psychological egoism," is associated with a tradition of thought running from the Sophists of Greece through Hobbes and contemporary economics. That philosophical tradition holds rational people act only when they believe that doing so is in their self-interest. (Remember the economists mentioned in Chapter 3 who suggest that the alternative would require that we rewire human nature.)

Of course, this tradition does not deny that people act in ways that benefit or manifest concern for others. It does not claim that all people are narrowly selfish. It only claims that our ultimate reason for acting to benefit others lies in self-interest. In this view, I help others because I will benefit in turn. When we donate to charity or contribute to posterity, we seek the esteem, status, or tax deduction that follows from such gifts.

Thus, egoism interprets altruism or friendship on a contractual model: "I will benefit you if you will benefit me." Accordingly, because people in the distant future can do nothing that serves my self-interest, it makes little sense to talk about caring for future people.

But surely this is an impoverished understanding of caring for another. If we find that someone cares for us only because doing so is in that person's self-interest, we would be justified in denying that any caring actually exists. Caring for others seems to exclude, rather than be a form of, self-interest. Care requires that we take, as much as possible, the point of view of the other.

In an insightful analysis of the role of caring in ethics and education, philosopher Nel Noddings suggests that

> apprehending the other's reality, feeling what he feels as nearly as possible, is the essential part of caring from the point of view of the one caring. For if I take on

the other's reality as possibility and begin to feel its reality, I feel, also, that I must act accordingly; that is, I am impelled to act as though on my own behalf, but in behalf of the other.[25]

To care for another is to take the other's point of view. It is not to ask "What would *I* do if I were in that position?" but, as far as is possible, "What would be best for this other person from her perspective?" As Noddings says, "When my caring is directed to living things, I must consider their natures, ways of life, needs, and desires. And, although I can never accomplish it entirely, I try to apprehend the reality of the other."[26]

Thus, the question of whether we can care about future generations asks whether we can view the world from their perspective. Can we replace our interests, needs, and desires with the interests, needs, and desires of people of the future?

At first glance, it would seem that we could. Friendship and parenting seem the two most obvious and familiar situations in which people restrain their self-interests for the interests of others. If it were not possible to be motivated by the interests of others, neither friendship nor parenting could exist. "Rational egoism," as we can call it, would make loyalty, love, sacrifice, honesty, and a whole range of other virtues and attitudes rationally impossible.

But friends and children are actual people who have real interests and needs. Future people do not exist, and perhaps this is a relevant difference. But why should this matter? Perhaps we could argue that we could only take the point of view of and care for people who are actually living. Yet many people (this may be more common in other cultures) seem to care deeply about their ancestors. People seem able to act in ways that would make their ancestors proud, honor their ancestors, and show respect for and pay homage to their ancestors.

Perhaps we would argue instead that because the interests and desires of people of the future will depend, in part, on the type of world that they inherit from us, we have no way to know in advance what those interests and desires will be. But if we do not know this, we cannot view the world from their perspective and, hence, would find it impossible to be motivated by their interests and desires. We cannot care about them because we cannot know what would count as their behalf.

However, this argument fails to appreciate the true nature of the motivation to preserve nonessential resources for future people. We do not seek to preserve a wilderness area or an endangered species because we believe people will desire these things in the future. The objection is correct in holding that if people of the future do not know of these things, they cannot desire (or miss) them. But the motivation to preserve for the future does not rest on the content of their desires. It rests with our judgment that a life lived with the possibility of knowing and desiring these things is fuller and more meaningful than one lived without them.

We can make a parallel argument by using the example of distinguished works of art. If we failed to preserve all Renaissance paintings, for example, and all records of this art were lost to future generations, surely they could not be said to miss them. If future generations knew nothing of these paintings, they could not feel their loss. But their lives would nonetheless be impoverished by this loss. It is our concern for this, our caring that they not live an impoverished life, that motivates us to preserve great artwork for the future.

Thus, it does seem meaningful to care about future people. To the degree that we can imagine ourselves in their position, we can recognize that such a life would be missing much were it not to know the wilderness or the rich complexity of biological diversity. We can care about the type of people future generations become and the types of lives they can lead. This care, I suggest, can and does motivate us to act.

4.7 DO WE CONSUME TOO MUCH?

Given this discussion of the moral status of future generations, we should return to questions that were implicit throughout this chapter. Do present population and consumption patterns violate the responsibilities that we have to future generations? Are population or consumption factors more of a threat to the well-being of future people?

As an intellectual exercise it can be helpful to make sharp distinctions and vigorously defend extreme positions. To help our own understanding, it is worth considering and defending that population *or* consumption is *the* major cause of environmental destruction. But surely the truth is that both are responsible. To various degrees in different circumstances, each contributes substantially to environmental distress. For any given finite ecosystem, increased population and increased consumption of resources will each create stress on the ability of that ecosystem to sustain life over the long term.

Nevertheless, into the near future—for the next generation or so—we cannot expect anything other than an increasing world population. While the *rate* of global population growth is slowing, the overall *size* of global population continues to increase and will increase for the foreseeable future. Even at a significantly reduced 1 percent growth rate (the population growth rate during the mid-1990s was approximately 1.7 percent), world population will double in 70 years. Therefore, to the degree that humans will continue to face environmental deterioration in the near future, consumption patterns will prove to be the crucial variable.

Considerations such as these have lead many people to defend the model of sustainable development introduced in the previous chapter. Many environmentalists promote the idea of sustainability as a descriptive and normative framework for understanding an appropriate lifestyle for present generations. The model of sustainable development reminds us that the economy is a subset of the ecosphere and is limited by the productive capacity of that ecosphere. If either population size or economic growth and consumption grow too large, the ecosphere will be unable to support human life. The only defensible public policy, from this perspective, is one that seeks an optimal level of both population and economic activity. Longer term, sustainable development calls for population policies that aim for a stable population size. Shorter term, sustainable development will require a shift away from the consumption patterns of modern industrialized societies. Sustainable development aims for the most productive and efficient use of resources compatible with the ability of the earth's ecosphere to provide consistent, stable, and long-term productivity.

But do we consume too much? Is consumption and economic growth a real threat to environmental health? Do present consumption patterns violate our responsibilities to future generations? Various environmental facts, considered in light of an ethical analysis of our responsibilities to future generations, suggest that they do. Our analysis of utilitarian considerations, for example, suggests that long-term calculations of the greatest overall good requires present generations to conserve the productive capacity of natural resources. Mary Williams' concept of "maximum sustainable yield" advises present generations to refrain from using resources at rates that cannot be sustained over the long term. Similarly, Brian Barry concludes that, at a minimum, future generations have a right to opportunities equal to those enjoyed by present generations. On this view, the present has an obligation to leave the future no worse off in respect to the opportunities provided by natural resources than the present has enjoyed.

Do present consumption and population patterns, in fact, leave future generations a natural environment that is at least as productive as the one we inherited? While air and water quality in some industrialized countries, including the United States, have improved over the last few decades, worldwide air and water quality remains a major problem. A growing consensus of scientists are concluding that global climate change and the possibility of global warming as a result of an increase in atmospheric greenhouse gases mostly due to burning fossil fuels is already underway. Clean drinking water remains a challenge in many parts of the world. Ocean fisheries are in decline due, in large measure, to overconsumption and pollution. Agricultural productivity has increased worldwide, but only with significantly increased reliance on chemical pesticides and fertilizers. The price of many nonrenewable resources has remained low, but little work is being done to encourage alternatives to our heavy reliance on fossil fuels. Loss of habitat due to human economic expansion has caused the greatest extinction event since the extinction of dinosaurs 65 million years ago. It would be difficult indeed to claim that present generations are doing all that they should to fulfill our responsibilities to our descendants.[27]

But with this said, we need to mention three concerns that caution against too quick an acceptance of the sustainability paradigm. First, when we hear talk about "sustainability," we should always be prepared to ask "*What* is being sustained?" The language of sustainability has proven quite popular, even among those who otherwise might not be identified as environmentalists. This should give us pause. It seems clear that sustainability is often assumed to mean "sustaining the present patterns and levels of consumption." In this sense, defending a model of sustainable living means simply sustaining the status quo. But to the degree that present consumption patterns, particularly those found in consumer-driven industrial economies, are causing environmental deterioration, the status quo is exactly what we need to change. Sustainable living and sustainable development will require a changed economy and changed society. It will also require substantially closing the economic gap between wealthy industrialized countries and the poor developing world. We need to be vigilant and not use sustainable development simply as a fashionable way to talk about continued economic growth and consumption.

Mark Sagoff has raised a second concern.[28] Sagoff warns against overreliance on economic, prudential, and scientific arguments to support environmentalism. Sagoff argues that the environmentalist perspective sometimes relies on misconceptions about the depletion and scarcity of natural resources and the danger posed by technology. Some evidence suggest that we are not running out of resources and that environmentally benign technologies may improve rather than harm the ecosphere. If the environmental perspective relies on such claims and if it turns out, as Julian Simon has argued, that natural resources are plentiful and technological ingenuity very innovative, we may be powerless to counter continued environmental destruction. Instead, Sagoff wants to de-emphasize scarcity and overconsumption arguments and rely on a value-based approach that emphasizes spiritual, aesthetic, and ethical values. Consumerism may or may not be depleting natural resources, but it is a lifestyle in which material possessions are taken as a substitute for such goods as self-esteem, beauty, compassion, humility, and worth. Sagoff also warns against overreliance on scarcity arguments because these suggest that the primary value of nature is as a resource. This concern raises a third caveat.

Discussions of sustainable development and sustainable living are criticized by some as overly anthropocentric. Arguing against consumption and overpopulation on the grounds that they are depleting resources and threatening the well-being of present and future generations can ignore harms done to the natural world itself. This shift away from anthropocentric ethics will emerge as the central theme in the following chapters.

Nevertheless, this consideration of present population and consumption patterns and the concept of ethical responsibilities to future generations does provide philosophical support for the concept of sustainable development. Sustainability may not be the complete environmental perspective, but it does offer a plausible model for where present lifestyles ought to be heading.

4.8 CONCLUSION: SUSTAINABLE LIVING— NOW AND IN THE FUTURE

As philosophers turned their attention to environmental issues, it became clear that simply applying standard ethical theories would not produce satisfactory analyses of these issues. As this chapter shows, some of the most pressing environmental challenges force us to consider in detail the ethical effects of our actions on people of the future. Yet this issue was often ignored in much traditional philosophy, and groundbreaking work was required. Philosophical ethics needed to be extended beyond traditional boundaries.

Chapter 5 shows how these boundaries were extended even further. Most of the issues we have considered thus far have focused on the effects that various environmental policies have on humans. Beginning with Chapter 5, a fundamental shift in our philosophical perspective is made. Do we have direct responsibilities to other species? Although many philosophers considered this question, almost all rejected the possibility that anything other than humans, perhaps even humans of the future, had moral standing. Primarily in response to environmental concerns, philosophers have in recent years sought to extend ethical consideration to things other than human beings.

Notes

1. This discussion case was developed with the help of *State of the World 1999*, edited by Lester Brown et. al. (New York: W.W. Norton/Worldwatch Institute, 1999), *Living in the Environment* G. Tyler Miller (Belmont, CA: Wadsworth Publishing, 1993), and the United Nations Population Information Network (www.undp.org/popin) in particular documents from the Commission on Population and Development, Thirty-third session, March 27–31, 2000 (www.undp.org/popin/unpopcom/33rdsess).

2. See Paul Ehrlich's classic *The Population Bomb* (New York: Ballantine, 1968) and the more recent book, *The Population Explosion* (New York: Doubleday, 1990). For a well-known criticism of the view that population growth is the key to environmental devastation, see Barry Commoner, *The Closing Circle* (New York: Alfred A. Knopf, 1971).

3. In examining responsibilities to future generations, philosophers have sometimes distinguished two general issues: What responsibilities do we have to produce or not to produce future generations? What, if anything, do we owe to those future generations that we assume will exist? The first set of issues, what we might call "population policy," is concerned with questions of future population size, population growth, and population control. The second set of issues, sometimes called our "duty to posterity," focuses on the content and type of world that future generations will inherit from us. This is a rough distinction in that there is obvious overlap. For example, ethically responsible decisions about reproduction should take into consideration the state of the world that our descendants will inherit. Nevertheless, this is a helpful way to organize the many ethical and philosophical issues raised by the general topic of our duties to future generations. As far as I can determine, the distinction between population policy and duties to posterity is first made in Jan Narveson, "Future People and Us," in *Obligations to Future Generations*, ed. R. I. Sikora and Brian Barry (Philadelphia: Temple University Press, 1978), pp. 38–60. It is also used in Ernest Partridge, ed., *Responsibilities to Future Generations* (Buffalo, N.Y.: Prometheus, 1980), and Mary Anne Warren, "Future Generations," in *And Justice For All*, ed. Tom Regan and Donald VanDeVeer (Totowa, N.J.: Rowman and Allanheld, 1982), pp. 74–90. All of these books remain very helpful sources for these topics. The Sikora and Barry book, along with Michael Bayles's *Ethics and Population* (Cambridge, Mass.: Schenkman, 1976), focus

primarily on population policy issues. Partridge's book, along with Douglas MacLean and Peter Brown, eds., *Energy and the Future* (Totowa, N.J.: Rowman and Littlefield, 1983), focuses primarily on duties to posterity.

4. As reported in Miller, *Environmental Science*, p. 11, Miller cites, without further reference, the Worldwatch Institute as the source of these figures. Environmental refugees are people who have been displaced or exiled by environmental or ecological emergencies.

5. Ibid., 13–15, refers to these two issues as "people overpopulation" and "consumption overpopulation."

6. For a development of these claims, see Anne Ehrlich and Paul Ehrlich, *The Population Explosion* (New York: Doubleday, 1990).

7. See Gregory Kavka, "The Futurity Problem," in Sikora and Barry, eds., *Obligations to Future Generations*, pp. 180–203, for a full analysis of this argument. Kavka cites Martin Golding, "Obligations to Future Generations," *Monist* 56 (1972): 97–98, as an "interesting variant" of the argument from ignorance.

8. For versions of this argument, see Derek Parfit, "On Doing the Best for Our Children," in Bayles, ed., *Ethics and Population Policy*, pp. 100–15, and Thomas Schwartz, "Obligations to Posterity," in Sikora and Barry, eds., *Obligations to Future Generations*, pp. 3–13.

9. The phrase "disappearing beneficiaries" is from Schwartz, "Obligations to Posterity," p. 3.

10. Annette Baier, "For the Sake of Future Generations," in *Earthbound: New Introductory Essays in Environmental Ethics*, ed. Tom Regan (New York: Random House, 1984), pp. 214–15.

11. Baier compares this with the legal notion of "wrongful life" in, for example, *Curlender v. Bioscience Laboratories* (106 Cal. App. 3d 811 [1980]), in which a California court allowed a tort suit on behalf of a child born with Tay-Sachs disease after the parents had been told that they were not carriers of the Tay-Sachs gene.

12. Warren, "Future Generations."

13. Ibid., 154.

14. Richard and Val Routley, "Nuclear Power," in Regan and VanDeVeer, eds., *And Justice for All*, pp. 116–38.

15. Ibid., 118–19; the emphasis is the Routleys'.

16. Kavka, "The Futurity Problem," pp. 186–203.

17. I rely here primarily on Warren, although further discussion can be found in several papers in the Sikora and Barry collection *Obligations to Future Generations*. See especially the papers by Narveson, Bennett, Scott, Sumner, and Sikora. Warren engages most of these authors in her discussion.

18. Parfit, "On Doing the Best," p. 100.

19. For a discussion of this economic approach, see Colin Clark, *Mathematical Bioeconomics: The Optimal Management of Renewable Resources* (New York: Wiley, 1976).

20. Mary Williams, "Discounting versus Maximum Sustainable Yield," in Sikora and Barry, eds., *Obligations to Future Generations*, pp. 169–85. Another, more general review of criticisms of social discounting can be found in Derek Parfit, "Energy Policy and the Further Future: The Social Discount Rate," in MacLean and Brown, eds., *Energy and the Future*, pp. 31–37.

21. The parenthetic qualification is necessary because some philosophers argue that, although it does not make sense to attribute rights to people who do not exist,

it still makes sense to say that *we* have obligations to the future. See the papers by Richard DeGeorge, "The Environment, Rights, and Future Generations," pp. 157–66, and Ruth Macklin, "Can Future Generations Be Said to Have Rights?," pp. 151–56, in Partridge, ed., *Responsibilities to Future Generations.*

22. See Martin Golding, "Obligations to Future Generations," *Monist* 56 (January 1972): 97–98, reprinted in Partridge, ed., *Responsibilities to Future Generations,* pp. 61–72, for an example of this position.

23. Versions of this familiar understanding are used by Annette Baier, "The Rights of Past and Future Persons," in Partridge, ed., *Responsibilities to Future Generations,* pp. 171–86, and in Joel Feinberg, "The Rights of Animals and Unborn Generations," pp. 43–68, in *Philosophy and the Environmental Crisis,* ed. William Blackstone (Athens: University of Georgia Press, 1974), and elsewhere in Feinberg's writings.

24. Brian Barry, "Intergenerational Justice in Energy Policy" in MacLean and Brown, eds., *Energy and the Future,* pp. 15–30.

25. Ibid., 23.

26. Nel Noddings, *Caring: A Feminine Approach to Ethics and Moral Education* (Berkeley: University of California Press, 1984), p. 16.

27. Ibid., 14.

28. For some who disagree that we are in the midst of an environmental crisis, see Julian Simon, *The Ultimate Resource* (Princeton, N.J.: Princeton University Press, 1981), Gregg Easterbrook, *A Moment on the Earth,* (New York: Viking Penguin Books, 1995), and Joseph Bast, Peter Hill, and Richard Rue, *Eco-Sanity: A Common Sense Guide to Environmentalism* (Palatine, Ill.: The Heartland Institute, 1994).

29. Mark Sagoff, "Do We Consume Too Much?" In the *Atlantic Monthly* 279, no. 6 (June 1997): pp. 80–96. For a response to Sagoff see also "No Middle Way on the Environment," by Paul R. Ehrlich, Gretchen C. Daily, Scott C. Daily, Norman Myers and James Salzman, *Atlantic Monthly* 280, no. 6 (December 1997): pp. 98–104, and Sagoff's answer as a letter to the editor in that same issue.

Discussion Questions

1. Do you believe that overconsumption or overpopulation plays a greater role in environmental destruction? Which problem would you address first?

2. Do you believe that Americans consume too much? Does more material wealth always lead to greater happiness?

3. Population policy raises fundamental ethical questions. Do all people have a right to have children? What restrictions, if any, should society place upon having children? What responsibilities do we have to our (not-yet-conceived) children? What goods are attained by producing a child of one's own that cannot be attained through adoption?

4. Controversies such as those surrounding global warming and ozone depletion involve long-term predictions and therefore are undecidable in the short term. In light of this uncertainty, is there one reasonable course of action? What does reason advise when we must make a decision with only incomplete information?

5. Strong moral relations exist between parents and children, but can moral relations such as love and care exist between people separated by more than one or two generations?

6. Many indigenous cultures were destroyed when Europeans colonized the Americas and Africa. We can only guess at what we have lost as a result of these conquests. Have we been hurt by this loss? Can people be harmed by the loss of

opportunities and the loss of knowledge of which they will never be aware? Will future generations be harmed if they never know about the blue whale or never know of a wilderness area?

Further Reading

The best collections of essays on ethical issues and future generations remain those edited by Sikora and Barry, Partridge, and MacLean and Brown (see note 3).

In addition to the work referenced in note 6, see Anne and Paul Ehrlich, *Earth* (New York: Franklin Watts, 1987), and Paul Ehrlich and John Holdren, eds., *The Cassandra Conference: Resources for the Human Predicament* (Texas Station: Texas A&M University Press, 1988), for discussions of the interplay of population and resource use. A more recent discussion of these issues appears in *Betrayal of Science and Reason*, by Paul Ehrlich and Anne Ehrlich (Washington, D.C.: Island Press, 1996).

See Betsy Hartman, *Reproductive Rights and Wrongs: The Global Politics of Population Control and Contraceptive Choice* (New York: Harper and Row, 1987), and Frances Moore Lappe and Joseph Collins, *World Hunger: Twelve Myths* (New York: Grove, 1986), for instructive critical reflections on population policy and world hunger.

Julian Simon and Herman Kahn, eds., *The Resourceful Earth* (New York: Blackwell, 1984), offers the more optimistic view of resource use and the future. Similar arguments can be found in *A Moment on the Earth* by Greg Easterbrook (New York: Viking Penguin, 1995).

5

Responsibilities to the Natural World: From Anthropocentric to Nonanthropocentric Ethics

Mass Extinctions

In 1914, a passenger pigeon named Martha died at the Cincinnati Zoo. Her stuffed body is displayed at the National Museum of Natural History in Washington, D.C. Martha was the last known surviving member of her species. Only sixty years earlier, one observer had estimated the population of a single flock of passenger pigeons at more than two billion birds.[1]

Before European settlers arrived in North America, more than 125 million bison ranged across the Great Plains from Mexico to Canada. Native Americans enjoyed an ecologically stable and balanced relationship with the bison, relying on these animals for food, clothing, shelter, heat, and tools. As anyone who has ever watched a television or movie western knows, these huge herds were subjected to overhunting, habitat loss, and simply slaughtered for sport by the newly arriving settlers. By 1892, the last remaining bison herd, 85 individual animals, was moved into the protected refuge of Yellowstone National Park. Today, the United States has approximately 75,000 bison.

The blue whale is the world's largest animal, reaching lengths of more than 100 feet and weights of 150 tons. Estimates in the early years of the twentieth century suggested a population of more than 200,000 blue whales in the Antarctic Ocean. Today, the population is estimated at less than 1,000. Because the whales have a low reproduction rate, a population of this size may not be large enough to guarantee the survival of the blue whale.

These three examples, one species extinct, one that has recovered from near extinction, and one still threatened with extinction, symbolize the choices that humans face in the coming decades. We can continue past practices and witness the extinction of millions of plant and animal species, or we can take aggressive steps to preserve and protect other life forms.

Some scientists estimate that 99 percent of the plant and animal species that once existed on Earth are now extinct. Extinction, then, is a common occurrence in nature. All species eventually become extinct. What is uncommon about the extinctions occurring today, however, are its rate and its causes.

The biologist Edward O. Wilson estimates that the naturally occurring "background extinction rate," the rate of extinction that would exist independently of human activity, is approximately one species every few years.[2] He estimates that 4,000 to 6,000 species are now becoming extinct every year. This rate of extinction in the presence of humans, slightly more than ten species a day, is perhaps 10,000 times greater than what would otherwise occur. Without question, human activity is causing the single greatest episode of mass extinction since at least the end of the dinosaur age some 65 million years ago.

These estimates include both plant and animal species. As the three examples suggest, extinctions of animal species tend to be best known. Nevertheless, because humans and other animals depend, directly or indirectly, on plants for oxygen, food, clothing, shelter, medical supplies, and other necessities, we could make a strong case that plant extinctions are the more immediate issue. Some scientists have estimated that by the year 2000, human activity may account for the extinction of as much as 25 percent of all plant species.[3]

Estimates made during the late 1980s calculated the rate of destruction of tropical rain forest at an area the size of two football fields every second of every day. If the burning and clearing of tropical rain forests continue at this rate, almost all will be completely destroyed within the next few decades. Since 1960, about one-half of all the earth's forestlands have been destroyed.[4]

Apart from reasons of prudence, which might show how biodiversity benefits humans, do we have any reason to be concerned with this loss of diverse life-forms? Do we have direct ethical responsibilities to other forms of life?

5.1 INTRODUCTION

As philosophers began to apply various ethical traditions to environmental issues, two fundamental questions guided their work. First, what is the proper ethical relationship between humans and the natural environment? Second, what is the philosophical basis for this relationship? In seeking to answer these questions, many philosophers found that the appeal to standard ethical theories was highly ambiguous. Traditional philosophical (and theological) views on the human relationship with nature seemed in many cases to have contributed to environmental destruction and degradation.

For the most part, the Western philosophical tradition denies that any direct moral relationship exists between humans and the natural environment. According to most ethical theories within this tradition, only human beings have moral standing. All other things have ethical value only insofar as they serve human interests. Thus, when considering some environmental decision, the ethical person needs only to ask how will this decision affect humans? To the degree that it can be said to exist, "environmental ethics" in these views are all *consequentialist* ethics: environmental right or wrong depends on the consequences to humans. Although we have responsibilities regarding the natural world, we have no direct responsibility to the natural world. Environmental responsibility is, at bottom, a matter of prudence: we protect the environment for our own interests. (Of course, sometimes this can include such interests as aesthetic enjoyment or symbolic appreciation.) As seen in Chapter 4, this perspective was later extended to include responsibility to future generations of humans.

With this chapter we begin to see a more radical shift in the philosophical perspective. Paralleling the deontological critique of the utilitarian concern with consequences, some philosophers began to argue that we have direct ethical responsibilities to nature, responsibilities that do not depend on the consequences to humans. This shift can be identified as a shift from anthropocentric to nonanthropocentric theories of ethics.

5.2 MORAL STANDING IN THE WESTERN TRADITION

Setting a historical context for these discussions reminds us how far traditional ethics is being extended. Chapter 2 suggests that the natural law tradition possesses resources that could make it particularly relevant to environmental issues. Nevertheless, the two philosophers most associated with this tradition defended views that exhibited little sympathy to the moral status of natural objects. Aristotle told us,

> Plants exist for the sake of animals . . . all other animals exist for the sake of man, tame animals for the use he can make of them as well as for the food they provide; and as for wild animals, most though not all of these can be used for food and are useful in other ways; clothing and tools can be made out of them. If then we are right in believing that nature makes nothing without some end in view, nothing to no purpose, it must be that nature has made all things specifically for the sake of man.[5]

Sixteen centuries later, Thomas Aquinas picked up this issue and placed it in a theological context.

> We refute the error of those who claim that it is a sin for man to kill brute animals. For animals are ordered to man's use in the natural course of things, according to divine providence. Consequently, man uses them without any injustice, either by killing them or employing them in any other way. For this reason, God said to Noah: "As the green herbs, I have delivered all flesh to you."[6]

Aristotle and Aquinas could hold these positions because they believed that only human beings (and perhaps angels and gods) have moral standing. Human beings have moral standing because they possess an intellect (or "soul") capable of thinking and choosing. Because animals and other living beings lack this capacity, they cannot be considered morally relevant in themselves. Any duties that we have regarding nature are explainable in terms of the needs or interests of human beings.

Kantian ethical theory is only a little less restricted. We have some evidence that Kant was sympathetic to duties to future generations, and the categorical imperative seems relevant to several environmental issues.[7] Nonetheless, in his *Lectures on Ethics,* Kant was quite clear in saying that our duties regarding nature are indirect, that is, they are duties to other humans. More generally, the Kantian analysis—which limits rights and moral standing to "subjects" and "ends," as distinct from "objects" and "means"—strongly reinforces the view that only humans have moral standing. In this view, only autonomous beings, capable of free and rational action, are moral beings. Again, because eighteenth century Europeans believed that other living things lacked this capacity, they could exclude them from moral consideration. Nonhuman animals and plants were the clearest examples of objects.

Another view that proved quite influential is traceable to the seventeenth century philosopher René Descartes. Descartes argued that all reality is reducible to two fundamental types of substances, "minds" and "bodies." The realm of the mental includes all thinking, sensation, and consciousness. The realm of the body includes all things physical and spatial. This physical realm is the domain of physics, seen as purely mechanistic and devoid of consciousness. Although not denying the animals and plants are alive, Descartes nonetheless denied that they are anything other than machines or "thoughtless brutes." In the Cartesian view, therefore, the criterion for moral standing is consciousness. Anything not conscious is a mere physical thing and can be treated without concern for its well-being.

One of the few philosophers who did not unquestioningly exclude animals from moral consideration was Jeremy Bentham. In a passage that is famous because it is such an exception to the mainstream of Western philosophy, Bentham suggested that

> the day *may come,* when the rest of the animal creation may acquire those rights which never could have been withholden from them but by the hand of tyranny.

The French have already discovered that the blackness of the skin is no reason why a human being should be abandoned without redress to the caprice of a tormentor. It may come one day to be recognized that the number of the legs, the villosity of the skin, or the termination of the *os sacrum*, are reasons equally insufficient for abandoning a sensitive being to the same fate. What else is it that could trace the insuperable line? Is it the faculty of reason, or perhaps the faculty of discourse? But a full-grown horse or dog is beyond comparison a more rational, as well as more conversable animal, than an infant of a day, or a week, or even a month old. But suppose they were otherwise, what would it avail? The question is not, Can they *reason*? nor Can they *talk*? but Can they *suffer*?[8]

True to his utilitarian views, Bentham expanded the realm of moral considerability to include all things that have the capacity to feel pleasure and pain. We will see a view similar to Bentham's developed and defended when we consider the writing of Peter Singer.

To summarize, for most philosophers in the Western tradition, human beings and only human beings have moral standing. Few philosophers ever considered the question of whether other beings have moral standing, and most of those who did denied any moral status to natural objects. Most often, the criteria used to draw the boundaries of the moral realm are in some sense intellectual, for example, the ability to think or reason in some particular way. As a result, two strategies are available to critics. We could reject the philosophical basis for the exclusion of animals by arguing, for example, that rationality is an inappropriate criterion for moral standing. We might argue instead, following Bentham's suggestion, that sensation should be the criterion for moral standing. On the other hand, we could accept the philosophical basis but deny the conclusions drawn from it. With this approach, we could argue that rationality is an appropriate criterion, but that animals, at least certain "higher" mammals, do in fact possess this capacity.

Thus, we can make a case that much of the Western philosophical tradition is unsympathetic to the idea of a direct ethical responsibility to the natural world. Indeed, a plausible case can be made that this tradition provides a rationale for the exploitation and dominance of the natural world and, thus, has been partly responsible for our present environmental predicament. But philosophers are not alone here. Some scholars have suggested that the Western religious traditions are equally culpable in this regard. One of the first people to make this claim was the historian Lynn White, Jr.

These religious traditions are represented symbolically by the passage from Genesis, in which the Judeo-Christian God creates all living creatures and says,

Let us make man in our image and likeness to rule the fish in the sea, the birds in the sky, the cattle, all the wild animals on earth and all the reptiles that crawl upon the earth. So God created them in his own image and blessed them and said to them "be fruitful and multiply, and fill the earth and subdue it; and have dominion over the fish of the sea and over the birds of the air and over every living thing that moves upon the earth.[9]

The possibility that our Western theological traditions are at the root of our current environmental crisis is the focus of White's classic essay "The Historical Roots of Our Ecological Crisis."[10] White argues that many of our modern scientific and technological approaches to nature began in a particular Judeo-Christian perspective. That perspective, developing from biblical sources like the passage taken from Genesis, is especially anthropocentric. In this view, humans occupy a privileged position in all creation. Being created in the "image and likeness of God," they have a moral and metaphysical uniqueness. Humans are separate from and transcend nature. God has created a moral hierarchy in which humans are superior to nature and have been commanded by God to subdue and dominate it.

White's claim is not that this is the only or the most reasonable interpretation of Christian theology. Indeed, he goes on to suggest an "alternative Christian view" that would support a much more harmonious relationship with nature. What is crucial is that this is the interpretation that many Jews and Christians have given to the biblical story of the Creation. Much of contemporary science and technology developed in a context in which this anthropocentric view of nature held sway. This, according to White, lies at the root of our current ecological crisis.

5.3 EARLY ENVIRONMENTAL ETHICS: PASSMORE AND BLACKSTONE

Thus, we find in Western philosophical and religious traditions the ideas that encourage viewing humans as superior to and, therefore, justified in dominating nature. At the same time, these very traditions contribute much to philosophical theories that were being applied to solve environmental problems. In a very real sense, the tension between these two developments of mainstream Western philosophy creates the biggest challenge to traditional ethical theories. Can the dominant ethical traditions provide the resources to resolve environmental controversies? A good example of this ambiguity appears in one of the first philosophical examinations of environmental issues, John Passmore's *Man's Responsibility for Nature* (1974).

Using an image that characterizes much of applied ethics, Passmore understands his own philosophical role in terms first used by John Locke. In identifying issues and clarifying and analyzing arguments, the ethicist is "employed as an under-labourer in clearing ground a little and removing some of the rubbish that lies in the way to knowledge." The first role of the philosopher is to dispose of unhelpful, unreasonable, or dangerous alternatives. Passmore places all views that call for the abandonment of the "Western tradition," including "mysticism," the "nature-as-sacred" view, and animal rights among the "rubbish" to be removed.

Nevertheless, Passmore recognizes the paradoxical character of his appeal to Western traditions. On the one hand, he acknowledges that the dominant Western tradition "denied that man's relationship with nature is governed by any moral considerations whatsoever."[11] In this tradition, the human being is the "despot" who rules over nature with arrogance and hubris and treats nature as mere wax to be molded in whatever manner humans desire. On the other hand, Passmore believes that the Western tradition contains the seeds for an ethically appropriate relationship with nature.

> The traditional moral teaching of the west, Christian or utilitarian, has always taught men, however, that they ought not so to act as to injure their neighbors. And we have now discovered that the disposal of wastes into sea or air, the destruction of ecosystems, the procreation of large families, the depletion of resources, constitute injury to fellow-men, present and future. To that extent, conventional morality, without any supplementation whatsoever, suffices to justify our ecological concern.[12]

Thus, the call for a "new set of moral principles" is "not entirely wrongheaded." However, what is needed is "not so much a 'new ethic' as a more general adherence to a perfectly familiar ethic." For example, Passmore concludes that the ethical problems associated with pollution are not overwhelming but involve applying the generally accepted principle that "nobody ought to poison his neighbor." He also believes that the primary causes of our ecological disasters are "greed and short-sightedness," problems that can be overcome with an "old-fashioned procedure, thoughtful action."[13]

For the most part, Passmore's work follows the standard applied ethics model. Careful philosophical analysis has much to offer to environmental controversies. However, one aspect of his analysis calls for an extension of modern Western ethics. Lamenting the materialistic greed of consumerist societies, Passmore calls for a more "sensuous" attitude toward the world. The "puritan attack" on sensuousness, which he traces from Plato through Augustine and the Protestant Church to the modern Western world, leads to a denial of the beauty and love of nature. The "new ethic" that the environmental crisis demands must be one in which aesthetic value plays a prominent role. The denial of sensuousness contributes to the environmental threats caused by the population explosion by "restricting the publicizing of birth control methods and condemning all sexual relationships which do not have procreation as their aim."[14] It also fosters an easy acceptance of environmental degradation.

> A more sensuous society could never have endured the desolate towns, the dreary and dirty houses, the uniquely ugly chapels, the slag heaps, the filthy rivers, the junk yards which constitute the "scenery" of the post-industrial West. . . . Only if men can first learn to look sensuously at the world will they learn to care for it.[15]

Thus, Passmore is willing to criticize much of the Western philosophical and religious traditions for encouraging "man to think of himself as nature's absolute master, for whom everything that exists was designed."[16]

Nevertheless, like much of that tradition, his ethics remains anthropocentric. The natural world has no value in its own right. It is valuable because humans care for it, love it, find it beautiful. We have responsibilities regarding the natural world, but the basis of these responsibilities lies in human interests.[17]

For many philosophers like Passmore, standard ethical theory does contain the resources for articulating new environmental rights. Another early attempt at extending standard ethical theories was developed by William Blackstone.[18] Contrasting those things that we merely *desire* with those things to which we have *rights,* Blackstone argues for recognition of a new human right, the "right to a livable environment."

To provide a context for this discussion, return to the framework presented in Chapter 3. One way to look at environmental problems is to view them as involving conflicting interests. One side (for example, Walt Disney Enterprises) prefers one thing, where another side (for example, the Sierra Club) prefers something else. The challenge to public policymakers is to resolve these conflicts in fair and impartial ways.

The economic model resolves the conflict by treating all competing preferences as equally deserving of satisfaction. The goal, therefore, is to satisfy an optimal number of these preferences. That is, the resolution of conflict is accomplished on quantitative grounds: more is better.

On the other hand, someone like Mark Sagoff would argue that environmental conflicts should be settled on qualitative grounds. We need to make a political and ethical judgment that some preferences are more worthy of being satisfied than others. Not all interests are equal, and some deserve special consideration.

Unfortunately, as Sagoff acknowledges, articulating and defending such value judgments is notoriously difficult. The relativist challenge remains in the background: Who are you to say that what you want is more valuable than what I want?

Traditionally, the concept of a moral right functions to protect certain important interests from being sacrificed for a net increase in the overall good. As defended in the Kantian tradition, our strong moral obligation to respect the dignity of people has meaning only when we protect central human interests by granting them a status ethically superior to mere wants. When my wants conflict with your wants, the market goal of seeking the optimal satisfaction of wants is attractive so long as the conflict does not involve rights. For example, if you want to dump toxic wastes on your property, which is adjacent to my home, we have more than merely a conflict of wants. In this case, what you *want* conflicts with my *rights.* In this view, rights trump mere desires and should not be sacrificed, even if doing so would maximize the overall good.

In Passmore's view, standard ethical theory has the resources to handle such situations. But to other philosophers, the changing environmental conditions of our world make crucially important certain interests that were not previously recognized as such. The interest in clean air and water or in preserving dwindling wilderness areas may be important today in ways that they were not a generation ago. They may have become so important that they now deserve protection by moral rights.

Blackstone's approach adopts a standard deontological defense of human rights, similar to the Kantian view described in Chapter 2. Blackstone defends the general view that there are universal and inalienable human rights. These rights entail a "correlative duty or obligation" on the part of other people to either act or refrain from acting in certain ways. Our moral duties in turn limit our liberties and the exercise of certain other rights. Thus, to use a well-worn example, the liberties that follow from my property rights to a hunting knife are restricted by those duties that I owe to you as a result of your right to live, that is, I cannot stab you with this knife.

The question that arises from this general framework is whether humans have a right to a livable environment. Blackstone argues that they do. In this view, each person possesses human rights

> in virtue of the fact that he is human and in virtue of the fact that those rights are essential in permitting him to live a human life (that is, in permitting him to fulfill his capacities as a rational and free being).[19]

Blackstone further argues that we can realize none of those basic human rights that follow from our nature as free and rational beings—equality, liberty, happiness, life, and property—without a safe, healthy, and livable environment. Thus, a right to a livable environment can be defended as necessary to fulfilling a human life. Because a livable environment is equally necessary to all humans, there is "no relevant grounds for excluding any human the opportunity" to live this life.[20]

Accordingly, we have a fairly standard philosophical framework. Human rights follow from basic interests that we have by virtue of our nature as free and rational agents. They are defended as being necessary for fulfilling our natural human capacities and on the ground that no relevant basis exists for denying these rights to anyone, that is, they can be universalized. But how is this a new human right? Blackstone reasons that "changing environmental conditions" require us to restrict traditional freedoms and rights, especially property rights, in the name of both the public welfare and equality. Thus, "what in the past had been properly regarded as freedoms and rights (given what seemed to be unlimited natural resources and no serious pollution problems) can no longer be so construed."[21] When the traditional ethical and political framework of natural rights is applied to the new environmental reality, some traditional rights must be modified and some new ones created.

Critics can raise several challenges to Blackstone's position, however. They might argue that talk of a new right is not useful and is true only in a trivial sense. At best, this right to a livable environment is a shorthand way of talking about more fundamental rights such as life, liberty, or property. If I dump toxic wastes into a river, I have caused harm to or violated the rights of people living downstream from me. Standard property rights would seem sufficient to handle this issue. If I pollute the groundwater you drink or the air you breathe, I have harmed you in fairly standard sorts of ways. The generally accepted principle of which Passmore speaks, that "nobody ought to be allowed to poison his neighbor," suggests that talk of a right to a livable environment is unnecessary. In fact, this new right might even be detrimental to the environmental cause by creating a new layer of rights that hides the real harms caused by pollution and environmental destruction. An expansion of the number of rights might make it more, rather than less, difficult to specify the ethical and legal harms of pollution.

Another criticism holds that, when properly understood, rights entail only *negative* and not *positive* duties. My duty that follows from your right to live involves only the negative duty not to kill you. It does not entail the positive duty that I supply you with all that you need to live, for example. From this perspective, the right to a livable environment is either unnecessary or it requires too much of others. If it is understood as a *negative* right, for example, the right not to be harmed by pollution or more generally the right not to have my well-being threatened by your environmental actions, it does nothing ethically or legally that is not already done by standard ethical and legal concepts. If it is understood as a *positive* right, implying a duty on the part of others to provide or produce a clean environment, then, like education or health care perhaps, it is a desirable state of affairs but not a right. Serious challenges could be raised about the extent of other people's duties that would follow from the positive right to a livable environment. Are my rights violated whenever anyone drives a car and, thereby, pollutes the air, for example? Or whenever anyone uses pesticides to grow vegetables? Or disposes of sewage sludge in the ocean? Surely this would result in a proliferation of rights and duties so great as to paralyze much of modern life.

There are, of course, responses to these concerns. A defender of the right to a livable environment might argue that this right involves only certain minimal and basic duties on the part of others. A parallel might be drawn to education or health care, for example. The right to health care need not imply a universal right to any and all medical procedures, such as cosmetic surgery, but it should include a right to emergency care. A right to education need not imply a right to free tuition for a graduate degree at a private university, but it might imply free public education through high school. So, too, a right to a livable environment need not imply a right to pristine and pure air and water, but it would prohibit a laissez-faire policy in regard to dumping of toxic wastes, polluting the oceans with municipal garbage and sewage, the burning of high sulfur coal, and so forth.

A deeper criticism of this approach is reflected in the work of some philosophers who reject as meaningless the very notion of rights. Jeremy Bentham, for example, claimed that talk of rights is nonsense and talk of natural rights is "nonsense on stilts." The contemporary philosopher Alasdair MacIntyre suggests that we have as little reason for believing in rights as we have for believing in witches and unicorns.[22] Examining this debate is far beyond our concerns here. Nevertheless, these challenges can provide the opportunity to reflect on the implications of claiming new environmental rights.

Critics who reject rights seem to miss one of the most important functions that rights perform. By identifying something as a right, we are giving it a status as a centrally important human interest. Rights are distinct from merely desirable states of affairs in that they are more central and more important to human well-being. We should not think of rights, even "natural rights," as something to be figured out or recognized (as self-evident). Rights are human creations that function to protect certain human interests from being sacrificed too easily, if at all.[23] In this way, Blackstone's call for a new right is a summons for us to recognize how important a clean environment is to human well-being. It is a proclamation that past practices that pollute, exploit, and degrade the environment can no longer be tolerated if we value human well-being. In this sense, environmental challenges have extended ethics into new areas.

5.4 MORAL STANDING: THE RECENT DEBATE

As witnessed in Chapter 4, environmental issues provoked philosophers to extend ethical concepts beyond their traditional boundaries. Developing a philosophically adequate account of energy or population policy, for example, required that philosophers consider the moral status of something other than living human beings. The remainder of this chapter examines further extensions of ethics that require consideration not only of our duties *regarding* objects in our natural environment, but also our duties *to* these objects.

Consider carbon dioxide pollution. In standard ethical views, such pollution would be wrong if it harmed other human beings, perhaps by threatening their health or property. If standard ethical practice does not adequately address the harms caused by pollution, we could argue, as William Blackstone does, for a recognition of some new environmental rights. When we learn that some harmful effects of carbon dioxide pollution might not occur for generations, we extend our ethical concepts such as duties and rights to include future generations. This extension gives future generations a moral standing that they do not possess under more traditional ethical theories. We can identify the practice of extending moral standing to include future humans or to develop new human rights as *anthropocentric extensionism*. Ethics is extended beyond traditional boundaries, but only human beings continue to possess moral standing. Our duties, such as not to pollute, are duties *regarding* the environment, but they are not duties to the environment. As this brief survey of representative philosophers suggests, mainstream Western philosophy and theology hold an anthropocentric view of moral standing. Human beings and only human beings have moral standing.

We now consider *nonanthropocentric extensions* of ethics. That is, we will examine attempts to extend ethics and give moral standing to things other than human beings. Candidates for moral standing include animals, plants, species, natural objects like mountains, rivers, and wilderness areas, and even the earth itself. Throughout these debates two fundamental positions emerge:

those who extend moral standing to include animals and other natural objects and those who believe that these extensions are too outlandish and that traditional ethical concepts are sufficient to address environmental concerns.

The general concern in this chapter is with our duties *to* the natural environment. Much of the discussion will be in terms of the rights of animals, trees, wilderness, and so forth. However, not every philosopher is willing to attribute rights in every case in which we have duties. For example, we have seen that some philosophers are willing to say that although we have duties to future generations, it makes little sense to say of people who do not exist that they possess rights or anything else for that matter. More generally, utilitarians reject talk of rights, although they too are willing to talk about duties. For this reason, although many philosophers speak in terms of rights, it is preferable to think in terms of moral standing and moral considerability when we examine our duties to the natural environment. These more general terms include, but are not limited to, cases in which animals or trees are said to have rights. The general philosophical question is what things have a moral claim on us such that we have a duty to consider them in our moral deliberations. Who and what count morally? On what grounds do we recognize (or attribute) moral standing?

Phrased in this way, we can recognize that many other contemporary moral problems and public policy debates are located at the boundaries of moral standing. The abortion debate often focuses on the moral status of the fetus: Is a fetus a moral person? Does it have rights? Many debates in medical ethics concern euthanasia and treatment of seriously impaired patients. These issues force us to consider the moral status of patients in irreversible comas and those who are brain-dead, frozen embryos, and severely impaired infants. We also have seen how concerns for future generations further stretch these boundaries. Thus, in pursuing the question of our duties to the natural environment, it is helpful to begin by examining a more fundamental philosophical issue: Where do we draw the boundaries of moral consideration? Who and what should have moral standing? On what grounds do we make these decisions?

What, then, is the proper relationship between humans and other living things? One of the earliest contemporary discussions of the moral standing of animals and other living beings is Joel Feinberg's "The Rights of Animals and Unborn Generations."[24] Feinberg's 1974 essay was quite influential, and a brief review of his argument provides a valuable introduction to the more recent debates.

Feinberg begins with a common understanding of rights as involving a claim *to* some good, *against* some other person (who would therefore have some duty), that is socially recognized in some way, for example, by legal rules or an "enlightened conscience." Feinberg's strategy is to begin with clear and unproblematic cases of moral standing and attempt to pull from them a criterion that best explains our intuitions. We then can apply this criterion to more problematic cases.

In the familiar cases of rights, the claimant is a competent adult human being. . . . Normal adult human beings, then, are obviously the sorts of beings of whom rights can meaningfully be predicated. . . . On the other hand, it is absurd to say that rocks can have rights, not because rocks are morally inferior things unworthy of rights (that statement makes no sense either), but because rocks belong to a category of entities of whom rights cannot be meaningfully predicated. . . . In between the clear cases of rocks and normal human beings, however, is a spectrum of less obvious cases, including some bewildering borderline ones. Is it meaningful or conceptually possible to ascribe rights to our dead ancestors? to individual animals? to whole species of animals? to planets? to idiots and madmen? to fetuses? to generations yet unborn?[25]

Turning to the case of individual animals, Feinberg recognizes that most people acknowledge that we have a duty not to mistreat or be cruel to animals. Some might argue that this duty derives from a duty to other humans, that is, those who are offended by the mistreatment of animals. Others might argue that this duty is derived from a duty to ourselves, for example, to avoid situations in which we might develop character traits like callousness or cruelty. Feinberg argues that these explanations are disingenuous, that surely animals are the direct beneficiaries of this duty. We can owe a duty *to* animals, according to Feinberg, because animals have interests that can be promoted or harmed by our actions. In order to say that something has rights, this thing must have interests or a "sake" or a good of its own to be protected by rights. A mere thing, even a precious thing like the Taj Mahal or a beautiful natural wilderness, cannot be said to have rights because it cannot be said to have any interests of its own.

Feinberg focuses on the question of rights, rather than on the more general question of moral standing. But the point is significant. In order to meaningfully say that we have an obligation *to* some object, rather than merely an obligation *regarding* that object, the object of our obligations must have some welfare or good of its own. If I have a duty to something, my fulfilling my duty to this thing must be good for this thing. But to say that something has a good or a "bad" is to say that it has interests. For example, it is in a dog's interest not to be tortured. I can have a duty not to torture animals if it can be said that it is good *for the dog* not to be tortured. But what things can have interests? In Feinberg's view, only things with a "conative life," with "conscious wishes, desires, hopes; or urges or impulses; or unconscious drives, aims, or goals; or latent tendencies, direction of growth, and natural fulfillments," can be said to have interests.[26]

Feinberg then applies this criterion to various objects of environmental concern. Individual animals, at least those higher animals, can be said to have rights, although those of lower orders can be treated as mere pests. Plants cannot be said to have rights because they lack the "rudimentary cognitive equipment" necessary to possess interests. Neither can we say that species have rights, although we might attribute rights to individual members of that species.

Thus, for example, we might say that an individual dolphin has an interest in not being drowned in fishing nets and, therefore, might be said to have a right not to be killed in a fishing net. But dolphins as a species have no corresponding right to survive. We might have a duty not to kill an individual animal, but we have no duty to a species to protect it from extinction. Our duties can only be to individual beings that possess the appropriate "cognitive equipment."

Finally, because we can say that future generations will have interests with as much certainty as we can say that they will exist, it makes sense for us to talk about their rights as well.

Feinberg's essay was groundbreaking in many ways. Read narrowly, it offers merely a conceptual or "metaethical" analysis of what can and cannot meaningfully be said about rights. Yet this essay also symbolizes a liberation of sorts for philosophical ethics. Environmental concerns encouraged philosophers to expand greatly the realm of moral considerability. Essentially, for the first time philosophers considered the possibility that beings other than humans deserve moral consideration for their own sake, not merely because humans happen to be interested in them.

5.5 DO TREES HAVE STANDING?

Before turning to more systematic attempts to extend ethical consideration to animals, we should consider another early attempt at moral extensionism. Law professor Christopher Stone argues to extend legal, if not moral, rights to "forests, oceans, rivers and other so-called 'natural objects' in the environment—indeed, to the natural environment as a whole."[27] Unlike many defenders of animal rights, Stone bases his claim for standing less on the characteristics of humans and more on the nature of legal rights.

The occasion for Stone's defense of the rights of natural objects was the legal dispute concerning Mineral King Valley. The Sierra Club had filed suit to prevent Walt Disney Enterprises from building a large ski resort in the Sierra Mountains. This suit was rejected in California courts because the Sierra Club lacked standing. That is, members of the Sierra Club could not show that they would suffer any legally recognized harm by the development of Mineral King Valley. As this case made its way on appeal to the U.S. Supreme Court, Stone wrote an essay titled "Should Trees Have Standing?" Stone hoped to support the Sierra Club's case by arguing that the natural objects like trees and mountainsides that would be destroyed in this development should be given legal standing. The Sierra Club could then be seen as a legal guardian of these rights.[28]

Stone's analysis begins with an examination of the nature of legal rights. Implicitly rejecting the view that rights are somehow there in nature to be discovered, Stone emphasizes the evolutionary development of rights. Rights exist when they are recognized by "some public authoritative body [that] is prepared to give some amount of review" to violations of that right. Citing Darwin's observation that "the history of man's moral development has been a continual extension in the objects of his social instincts and sympathies," Stone shows how the recognition of legal rights is witness to a parallel development.[29] Rights function to protect rights-holders from injury, and the list of rights-holders has been continually expanded. He reminds us that at one time only landowning white adult males enjoyed full legal rights. Legal standing now includes people who do not own land, women, blacks, Native Americans, and such things as corporations, trusts, cities, and nations. It is time to extend this protection to natural objects.

Stone argues that recognition by some authoritative body alone is not enough to establish the existence of rights.

> As I shall use the term, "holder of legal rights," each of three additional criteria must be satisfied. All three, one will observe, go towards making a thing *count* jurally—to have a legally recognized worth and dignity of its own right, and not merely to serve as a means to benefit "us." They are, first, that the thing can institute legal actions *at its behest*; second, that in determining the granting of legal relief, the court must take *injury to it* into account; and, third, that relief must run to the *benefit of it*.[30]

The proposal to give legal rights to trees and other natural objects satisfies all three criteria.

How can natural objects "institute legal actions" on their own behalf? Noting that corporations and mentally incompetent humans have legal standing, Stone argues that a guardian or conservator or trustee could be appointed to represent the interests of natural objects. Just as a comatose person has a legal guardian, for example, or a corporation a board of trustees, forests, streams, and mountains could be legally represented by humans who are charged with representing their interests.

But do natural objects have interests that (1) we can agree on and (2) can be harmed in a legally recognizable way? Stone thinks that they do. Again noting the parallel with corporations, Stone believes that we can "know" the interests of and acknowledge the injuries to natural objects with at least as much certainty as we do in corporate cases.

> The guardian-attorney for a smog-endangered stand of pine could venture with more confidence that his client wants the smog stopped, than the directors of a corporation can assert that "the corporation" wants dividends declared.[31]

Similarly, Stone believes that we can give meaning to the concept of a legal remedy that can provide relief to the injured natural object. As a guiding principle, we could adopt a common legal standard and aim to make the environment whole. Just as when a person is injured in an automobile accident and is compensated for medical costs to return that person to health, so we could require the responsible party to compensate the natural object by returning it to health. In this sense, "environmental health" would be the state in which the environment existed before the injury.

Consider how this proposal might work. During the summer of 1991, a train derailment dumped 20,000 gallons of pesticide into the Sacramento

River in California. This resulted in the death of virtually all living things along a forty-mile stretch of the river. Unlike the lingering effects of an oil spill, however, the river flushed itself clean and was soon capable of supporting life again.

Under current legal guidelines, the door is open for injured humans to file for damages against the Southern Pacific Railroad, which was responsible for the train that derailed. Landowners downriver or businesses that depend on tourism and fishing, for example, might argue that they deserve to be compensated for certain losses. Under Stone's proposal, representatives of the river and the fish killed by the pesticide could also sue for damages. Thus, not only would humans be compensated for their injuries, but also the river itself should be "made whole," that is, returned to its prederailment state.

There are, of course, challenges for this proposal to overcome. First, despite Stone's suggestions, it is not at all clear that we can agree on the interests of natural objects. For example, some believe that the Sacramento River should immediately be restocked with fish from hatcheries. Others argue that the river should be allowed to restock itself with wild fish swimming in from tributaries. Good reasons can be given to support both options. Which is in the best interest of the river?

A second challenge follows from this. Perhaps Stone's response would allow the river's guardians to make that decision in the same way that a legal guardian might decide what is best for an orphaned child. But who should this guardian be? The Wilderness Society would have one view of the river's interests, and a local fishing club would have another view. Choosing the guardian would also be to choose the theory of interests that is ascribed to natural objects. Should the Sierra Club represent the interests of Mineral King Valley? Should a lumber company? Perhaps, as Mark Sagoff suggests, the mountain is tired of being undeveloped and would prefer to be represented by Walt Disney Enterprises.

None of this suggests that Stone's approach cannot work. But it does suggest that more work needs to be done to articulate and defend a view of nature's interests. Stone's proposal essentially relies on society's reaching a consensus about the extension of legal standing to natural objects. It is, after all, something that needs to be "recognized" by a public body. But it would seem that this consensus can only be reached after the public has already reached a consensus about the nature and value of natural objects. This consensus, regrettably, is still to be achieved.

5.6 SUMMARY AND CONCLUSIONS

This chapter examined a number of early debates concerning responsibilities regarding and to the natural world. Many of these attempts challenge the mainstream approach to ethics, but they remain more suggestive than completely developed principles. By far the most sophisticated treatment of this question appears in the works of those philosophers who focus their attention to the ethical status of animals. Those debates are presented in Chapter 6.

Notes

1. These estimates are given in G. Tyler Miller, *Environmental Science*, 3d ed. (Belmont, Calif.: Wadsworth, 1991), p. 354. Although the particular estimate may seem fanciful, it no doubt testifies to an extremely large population.

2. Edward O. Wilson, "Threats to Biodiversity," *Scientific American* 261 (September 1989): 108–16. See also E. O. Wilson and Frances M. Peter, eds., *Biodiversity* (Washington, D.C.: National Academy Press, 1988).

3. Miller, *Environmental Science*, p. 356.

4. Ibid., ch. 15.

5. Aristotle, *The Politics*, book 1, ch. 8, p. 1256b, in *Basic Works of Aristotle*, ed. Richard McKeon (New York: Random House, 1941).

6. Thomas Aquinas, *Summa Contra Gentiles*, ed. English Dominion Friars (London: Burns and Oates, 1924), book 3, pt. 2. See Gen. 9:2–3, for the command to Noah. See also John Passmore, *Man's Responsibility for Nature* (New York: Scribner's, 1974), p. 6, for a brief discussion of Aquinas's views on this passage from Genesis. Passmore remains an excellent source for understanding the philosophical roots of the "man-as-despot" view.

7. See Passmore, *Man's Responsibility for Nature*, ch. 4, for a discussion of Kant's concern for future generations, and Annette Baier, "For the Sake of Future Generations," in *Earthbound: New Introductory Essays in Environmental Ethics*, ed. Tom Regan (New York: Random House, 1984), pp. 214–46, for further discussion of this issue.

8. The italics are Bentham's. This passage appears in *The Principles of Morals and Legislation* (Oxford, England: Oxford University Press, 1907), ch. 17, sec. 1, footnote to paragraph 4.

9. Gen. 1:26–29.

10. Lynn White, Jr., "The Historical Roots of Our Ecological Crisis," *Science* 155 (March 10, 1967): 1203–1207.

11. Passmore, *Man's Responsibility for Nature*, pp. 186–87.

12. Ibid.

13. Ibid.

14. Ibid., 189.

15. Ibid.

16. Ibid., 13.

17. For insightful critical appraisals of Passmore, see Robin Attfield, "Western Traditions and Environmental Ethics," in *Environmental Philosophy*, ed. Robert Elliot and Arran Gare (University Park: Pennsylvania State University Press, 1983), pp. 201–30, and Richard and Val Routley, "Human Chauvinism and Environmental Ethics," in *Environmental Philosophy*, ed. Don Mannison, Michael McRobbie, and Richard Routley (Canberra: Research School of Social Sciences, Australian National University, 1980), pp. 109–34.

18. William Blackstone, ed., *Philosophy and Environmental Crisis* (Athens: University of Georgia Press, 1974). See Blackstone's contribution, "Ethics and Ecology," pp. 16–42.

19. Ibid., 31.

20. Ibid., 32.

21. Ibid.

22. Alasdair MacIntyre, *After Virtue* (South Bend: University of Notre Dame Press, 1981), p. 67.

23. For a more adequate treatment of how rights trump utilitarian benefits, see Ronald Dworkin, *Taking Rights Seriously* (Cambridge, Mass.: Harvard University Press, 1977).

24. Joel Feinberg, "The Rights of Animals and Unborn Generations," in Blackstone, ed., *Philosophy and Environmental Crisis*, pp. 43–68.

25. Ibid., 44.

26. Ibid., 49.

27. Christopher Stone, *Should Trees Have Standing? Toward Legal Rights for Natural Objects* (Los Altos, Calif.: William Kaufmann, 1974), p. 9.

28. For a brief account of this history, see Roderick Nash, *The Rights of Nature* (Madison: University of Wisconsin Press, 1989), pp. 128–31.

29. Stone, *Should Trees Have Standing?*, p. 11.

30. Ibid.; the emphasis is Stone's.

31. Ibid., 24.

Discussion Questions

1. The biblical story of creation speaks of a God who creates humans "to rule the fish in the sea, the birds in the sky, the cattle, all the wild animals on earth and all the reptiles that crawl upon the earth" and grants humans "dominion over" all other living things. Some have interpreted this to mean that humans may rightfully "dominate" and control the natural world. Others have argued that humans should act as stewards or caretakers for what is, after all, God's creation. What reasons do you see for either view?

2. Throughout the world many laws prohibit abuse of animals. List as many reasons for these prohibitions as you can. Do any of these reasons commit you to holding that animals have a moral standing in their own right?

3. Can natural objects be said to have interests? What are the interests of Mineral King Valley? Of the Sacramento River? Can certain things be said to be good for rivers, mountains, and forests? Is this the same meaning of good that we use when we talk about the moral good for humans?

4. Christopher Stone argues that trees should be granted legal standing. If this happens, how should their interests be represented? In the well-known Dr. Seuss book, *The Lorax*, it is the Lorax who "speaks for the trees." Can anyone truly speak for the trees?

5. Try the following mental experiment concerning what objects have moral standing. Assume that competent adult human beings are placed at one end of a continuum and a rock at the other. Where along that continuum would you place the following: a child, a brain-dead adult, a fetus, a dolphin, a dog, an insect, an alien, a bird, a species, and a tree? Have you used a single criterion either implicitly or explicitly?

Further Reading

Roderick Nash, *The Rights of Nature* (Madison: University of Wisconsin Press, 1989), offers a historically informed argument for attributing rights to natural objects.

Eugene Hargrove, *Foundations of Environmental Ethics* (New York: Prentice Hall, 1989), presents an aesthetic accounting of environmental values.

Theological writing on the environment has developed substantially in recent years. Jay McDaniel, *Of God and Pelicans: A Theology of Reverence for Life* (Louisville, Ky.: Westminister Press, 1989), is a good start. David Kinsley, *Ecology and Religion* (Englewood Cliffs, N.J.: Prentice-Hall, 1995), offers an introductory and cross-cultural survey of ecological spirituality. Roger Gottlieb, ed., *This Sacred Earth* (New York: Routledge, 1996), is a comprehensive anthology of traditional religious perspectives on ecology and nature.

6

Responsibilities to the Natural World: The Case for Animals

DISCUSSION

Animal Research and Factory Farming

The U.S. Environmental Protection Agency (EPA) is charged with regulating such things as smokestack emissions and the use of pesticides and many other potentially toxic chemicals. Likewise, the Food and Drug Administration (FDA) must regulate consumer products to ensure that they will not harm the people who use them.

To set standards and determine whether some chemical is toxic, the EPA and the FDA must rely on scientific research. Perhaps the most infamous procedure used in conducting toxicity research is the LD50, "lethal dose 50 percent." In a 1987 report, the director of the EPA's toxicology branch said that the EPA had records of more than 16,000 LD50 tests in its files.[1]

In LD50 tests, the substance being examined is administered to research animals in increasing doses to determine the level at which 50 percent of the animals will die from exposure to the substance. In most cases, before 50 percent die, all will be poisoned, and all will suffer. In the case of particularly toxic chemicals, the 50 percent level is reached with relatively low doses. Of course, this increases the poison levels in the remaining 50 percent. In the case of less toxic chemicals, like food additives and cosmetics, scientists must use enormous quantities of the substance before 50 percent of the animals die. These animals are force-fed and injected via feeding tubes or needles. Because the scientific validity of the tests requires that death be caused solely by the substance being tested, dying and suffering animals cannot be euthanized.

Largely as a result of the protests of animals rights activists, some countries have banned the LD50 test. Many companies involved in such research have suspended use of LD50 while they develop alternative research methods. Nevertheless, we do not have far to look to find many other cases in which animals are systematically mistreated and abused. We need only look at how food animals like calves, pigs, and chickens are raised. In the words of Peter Singer, "It is here, on our dinner table and in our neighborhood supermarket or butcher's shop, that we are brought into direct touch with the most extensive exploitation of other species that has ever existed."[2] Singer's book, *Animal Liberation,* has done much to publicize the nature of modern factory farming. Singer's ethical analysis of these practices is examined in some detail in this chapter. Let us review briefly one well-known example, veal production.

Veal is the flesh of young calves. It tends to be an expensive cut of meat and, therefore, more likely to be found in expensive restaurants and gourmet cooking than on the dinner tables of middle-class families. Veal is especially prized when it is tender and pink. How does a farmer produce animal flesh that is tender and pink?

First, the calves are taken from their mothers when they are just a few days old. To prevent exercise, which would develop muscles and therefore make the flesh less tender, these young calves are confined in small wooden stalls. The stalls are so small that the calf typically is unable to turn around or even lie down. The calf will spend its entire life, perhaps sixteen weeks, confined to this stall.

Normal flesh is red because of the iron in the blood. A cow gets iron from the grass and hay that it eats. Veal calves are systematically deprived of a diet containing iron. They are, in other words, intentionally made anemic. Of course, if they become too anemic they die, so they receive a dietary balance—just enough iron to keep them alive but not enough that their flesh and blood are red. All this is done even though pinkness adds nothing to the taste of veal.

To speed up the calves' growth and control their diet, they typically are fed a liquid diet of powdered milk, vitamins, and growth-producing drugs. This may be all that they eat in their entire lives. To ensure that the calves take in as much of this formula as possible, calves are denied water and kept in warm buildings. Their only alternative is to turn to the formula to quench their thirst. Singer concludes his description of this process as follows. "If the reader will recall that this whole laborious, wasteful, and painful process of veal raising exists for the sole purpose of pandering to people who insist on pale, soft veal, no further comment should be needed."[3]

6.1 INTRODUCTION

We could discuss many different arguments for why it is wrong to torture and kill animals for cosmetic research or for reasons of gourmet tastes. We can find many anthropocentric reasons to defend the position that we have ethical duties regarding animals. After all, many people own animals and, thus, have property rights over them. Many people care about animals and, thus, would be affected by the mistreatment of them. Further, mistreating animals can have an adverse effect on the person doing the mistreating. Such actions make us callous and insensitive to suffering.

In short, people value animals for a variety of reasons. But can we say that we owe any moral consideration directly to the animals themselves? Do animals have moral standing. Do they deserve moral consideration? These questions are among the first ethical issues raised in connection with environmental concerns to receive close and developed philosophical attention.

6.2 PETER SINGER AND THE ANIMAL LIBERATION MOVEMENT

Perhaps the person most associated with the extension of philosophical ethics to animals is Peter Singer. Since the 1970s, Singer has argued that our exclusion of animals from moral considerability is on a par with the earlier exclusions of blacks and women. Singer popularized the term *speciesism* to draw a parallel with racism and sexism.[4] Just as it is morally wrong to deny equal moral standing on the basis of race or sex, Singer argues that it is wrong to deny equal moral standing on the basis of species membership.

Singer begins his argument with a "fundamental presupposition" of moral theory, the "basic moral principle," that all interests should receive equal consideration. Essentially, this is the formal principle that any being that qualifies for moral standing "counts for one and none for more than one." Even racists and sexists can accept this principle, although they would deny that blacks or women have equal moral standing. Singer must, therefore, explain the criterion for inclusion. What characteristic qualifies a being for equal moral standing? Here Singer cites the passage from Bentham referred to earlier: The question is not can they *reason*, nor can they *talk*, but can they *suffer*? Singer goes on to say,

> The capacity for suffering and enjoyment is a *prerequisite for having interests at all*, a condition that must be satisfied before we can speak of interests in a meaningful way. It would be nonsense to say that it was not in the interests of a stone to be kicked along the road by a schoolboy. A stone does not have interests because it cannot suffer. Nothing that we can do to it could possibly make any difference to its welfare. The capacity for suffering and enjoyment is, however, not only necessary, but also sufficient for us to say that a being has interests—at an absolute minimum, an interest in not suffering. A mouse, for example, does have an interest in not being kicked along the road because it will suffer if it is.[5]

Like Joel Feinberg and Christopher Stone, discussed in the last chapter, Singer focuses on the concept of interests to explain moral standing. Unlike

Feinberg and Stone, Singer is not concerned with using interests as a basis for attributing rights to animals. He is sympathetic to Bentham's dismissal of rights as nonsense or at least as only a shorthand way of speaking about moral protections. Nor does he turn to cognitive elements as the essential aspect of interests. In Singer's view, the capacity for suffering (and enjoyment) is all that is needed to establish that a being has interests.

Singer uses the term *sentience* to refer to the capacity to suffer and/or experience enjoyment. Sentience is *necessary* for having interests, in that an object without sentience, a rock, for example, cannot be said to have interests. But Singer also believes that sentience is *sufficient* for having interests. A being that is sentient has at least minimal interests, that is, the interest in not suffering.

Because any and only sentient beings have interests, any and only sentient beings have moral standing. We are required to treat all sentient beings with equal moral consideration. This does not mean that we are required to make no distinctions between humans and other animals. Humans are different from other animals. They have different interests. A "hard slap across the rump" of a horse will cause relatively little pain and, therefore, is not particularly unethical. But this does not mean that the principle of equal consideration would justify an equally hard slap across the face of a child. A horse's rump is solid and broad, usually muscled or fat, whereas a child's face is bony and small. Certain human mental capacities might cause humans to suffer more from certain actions and in different ways than would other animals. Beings with sophisticated mental capabilities and the capacity for complex emotional and affective states have a greater range of interests and, thus, a different moral standing than creatures with simple cognitive and emotional capacities. But the essential point is that the capacity to suffer and amount of suffering are what determine specific moral requirements. Because all animals above a certain neurological threshold are sentient, all such animals deserve direct moral consideration.

What are the implications of these views? Singer acknowledges that making comparisons of sufferings can be difficult, especially when these comparisons are made between species. Nevertheless, if we were to restrict ourselves to only those cases in which severe animal suffering was condoned for the sake of mere human convenience,

> we would be forced to make radical changes in our treatment of animals that would involve our diet, the farming methods we use, experimental procedures in many fields of science, our approach to wildlife and to hunting, trapping and the wearing of furs, and areas of entertainment like circuses, rodeos, and zoos. As a result, a vast amount of suffering would be avoided.[6]

As the references to Bentham and the emphasis on minimizing suffering suggest, Singer's approach is basically utilitarian. He provides an account of intrinsic good (enjoyment and the absence of suffering) and says that our ethical responsibility is to minimize the overall amount of suffering. Before examining the implications of Singer's views, let us turn to an alternative, nonutilitarian defense of animal rights.

6.3 TOM REGAN AND ANIMAL RIGHTS

As Peter Singer has defended the moral standing of animals on utilitarian grounds, Tom Regan has developed a rights-based defense of animals. Regan explicitly argues that some animals have rights and that these rights imply strong moral obligations on our part. Like Singer, Regan condemns on ethical grounds a wide variety of human activities that affect animals. These activities include the use of animals in scientific and commercial research, use of animals as food, and recreational uses of animals that include sport hunting, zoos, and pets. Regan believes that these practices are wrong in principle but not because of the pain and suffering they cause. They violate animal rights by denying the intrinsic ethical value that some animals possess.

Imagine that Singer's criticisms convince veal producers to change their methods so as to minimize suffering. The calves get some exercise, fresh air, a balanced diet, and perhaps are even groomed regularly. Like the cows in the old advertisements, these are contented calves. Imagine also that human taste for veal increases so that many consumers have a real desire for veal. Consumers suffer, not much but many do, when they are denied veal.

In such a situation, we could argue that Singer's utilitarian position allows veal production to continue. With these imagined changes in the farming practices of the veal industry, the calves suffer minimally while human enjoyment increases notably.

A defender of Singer's position could dispute this example, of course. However, the dispute would likely involve specific calculations of relative suffering, pain, and enjoyments. That is, we would need to measure and dispute the consequences of the alternative practices. In this view, raising, slaughtering, and eating the calf for food is not wrong in principle. It is only wrong when the suffering that it causes outweighs the resultant enjoyment. Regan picks up at this point.

> The forlornness of the veal calf is pathetic, heart wrenching. . . . But the fundamental wrong isn't the pain, isn't the suffering, isn't the deprivation. These compound what's wrong. Sometimes, often, they make it much worse. But they are not the fundamental wrong. The fundamental wrong is the system that allows us to view animals as our resources, here for us, to be eaten, or surgically manipulated, or put in our cross hairs for sport or money.[7]

How does Regan explain the principle that underlies this view? To understand this, we should consider why it would be wrong to subject humans to similar treatment. Suppose someone were to follow Jonathan Swift's satirical "Modest Proposal" and treat disadvantaged young children as food. These children would be raised in a manner that kept them content and relatively free from suffering. However, at a certain point in their lives (Swift proposed

a well-nursed one-year-old), these humans were slaughtered, albeit pain-
lessly, and "stewed, roasted, baked, or boiled." Presumably, we would all
acknowledge the moral evil of these activities even if the overall balance of
enjoyment over suffering were increased. Why?

Regan argues that the answer lies in our belief that humans possess a certain type of value, what he calls "inherent value." We have seen this concept
before in our discussion of ethical theories. Essentially, to have inherent value
is to have value independent of the interests, needs, or uses of anyone else.
Inherent value is to have value in and of oneself. It is to be contrasted with
instrumental value, in which a thing's value is a function of how it might be
used by or what it might mean to others. Objects with inherent value are ends
in themselves, goals, not merely means to some other end. It is wrong to treat
humans (and, as it will turn out, some animals) as mere means to other ends,
even if this includes as an end maximizing the net amount of enjoyment over
suffering, because to do so denies to these humans the inherent value that
they possess.

So far, this approach sounds similar to the Kantian tradition in ethics, and
clearly it is greatly influenced by that tradition. But Regan denies that the
basis for inherent value lies in the capacity for autonomous action. To see why,
we need to introduce a distinction between *moral agents* and *moral patients*.[8]
Thus far in our discussion of moral standing, we have taken competent adult
human beings as the clearest example of things with standing. As discussed,
philosophers have disagreed about the criterion used to establish standing,
but they all agree that competent adult humans meet it. These adults are full
moral agents because they are free and rational. As such, they can understand
their duties, choose whether to act on them, and can be held responsible for
those choices.

This characterization raises familiar problems with incompetent or immature humans, however. Infants and mentally incapacitated or comatose individuals lack the ability to understand and choose. Therefore, they cannot be
said to be moral agents. They have no duties and cannot be held responsible
for what they do or fail to do. Indeed, they are *moral patients*. This means that
they have moral standing—we cannot do just anything to or with them—
even though they are not full moral agents. They cannot *act* morally or otherwise, but they can be *acted on* morally or immorally.

When we understand this distinction and recognize that many things that
are not full moral agents but have moral standing, we can figure out what is
missing from much of the standard discussions of moral standing. Too many
philosophers have focused exclusively on moral agents in establishing the criterion of moral standing. The class of all things with moral standing includes
both agents and patients. We need to ask what it is about moral agents and
moral patients that explains their inherent value. Why is it wrong, in principle, to treat either agents or patients as food, targets, entertainment, or slaves?

Regan's answer is that they are *subjects-of-a-life*. Having a life, as opposed to
merely being alive, involves a fairly complex set of characteristics.

To be the subject-of-a-life . . . involves more than merely being alive and more than merely being conscious. To be the subject-of-a-life is to . . . have beliefs and desires; perception, memory, and a sense of the future, including their own future; an emotional life together with feelings of pleasure and pain; preference and welfare-interests; the ability to initiate action in pursuit of their desires and goals; a psychophysical identity over time; and an individual welfare in the sense that their experiential life fares well or ill for them, independently of their utility for others.[9]

Regan argues that justice demands that we treat all individuals with inherent value in ways that respect that value. This "respect principle" identifies Regan's views as an *egalitarian* theory of justice. Justice demands that we treat individuals with respect. Because inherent value is not reducible to any other type of value, we fail to treat individuals who have inherent value with the respect they deserve when we treat them as if they are valuable only as a means to some other end. Individuals with inherent value thus have the *right* to be treated with the same respect due to all individuals with inherent value.

It remains for Regan to conclude that animals can be subjects-of-a-life. At least some mammals possess the characteristics required for "having a life." These animals therefore have inherent value, and justice demands that we treat them with respect. Minimally, this means that we have a strong prima facie obligation not to harm them. (Regan acknowledges that this obligation can sometimes be overridden. But it can be overridden only in the same sorts of cases in which we would override the rights of an innocent human being.)

6.4 ETHICAL IMPLICATIONS OF ANIMAL WELFARE

Both Singer and Regan have written extensively on the ethical implications of their views. Although each has written on a variety of specific issues, we will limit ourselves to four topics.[10] First, both would argue that we have a responsibility as a society to end most commercial animal farming. None of the considerations that might be used to defend animal farming—taste, nutrition, convenience, efficiency, and property rights—can justify treating animals as food. Similar arguments would not suffice to justify eating humans, and they cannot suffice to defend eating animals. Individually, we have an ethical responsibility to be vegetarians. As citizens, we should outlaw these practices.

Likewise, sport hunting and trapping are unjust. Killing and often torturing animals for sport and entertainment is more than cruel. It is a serious injustice. Likewise, abusing and mistreating animals for any form of human entertainment is wrong. Just as it was cruel and vicious for Romans to use Christians for a particularly brutal form of entertainment, it is wrong for us to use animals in zoos, rodeos, and the like.

A third issue concerns the use of animals in science and research. As seen in the discussion of LD50, experimentation on animal subjects can be especially harsh. We ordinarily would conclude that experimenting on human subjects who have not given their consent is unjust at best and barbarous at worst.

People have been convicted as war criminals for such behavior. So, too, should we judge experimentation on animals.

Finally, like Feinberg, Regan and Singer do not support moral standing for species. Regan's view protects individual animals from harm but does not recognize species as having rights. An individual animal can be a subject-of-a-life, but a species cannot. Likewise, for Singer, although individual animals can suffer pain, a species cannot. Thus, although these views support efforts to save endangered species, they do so only because the remaining members of that species, as individuals, have a moral standing that we must respect. In this context, Regan raises an issue that will become the focus of important discussions later in this textbook. Let us introduce this issue within a general review of philosophical challenges to the views of Singer and Regan.

6.5 CRITICISMS

Let us step back at this point and consider some criticisms raised against the animal liberation/animal rights view. The work of Singer and Regan generated a significant response among philosophers, much of it critical. Many of these criticisms followed familiar lines.

For example, some philosophers, including Regan, challenge the utilitarian basis of Singer's program. Singer, after all, makes no *in principle* case against causing animals to suffer. Other philosophers develop the debate about attributing rights to nonhumans. Some argue that the concept of interests is so vague that it would allow tractors and buildings to have moral standing.[11] Although a complete review of these debates would take us too far afield, several challenges help make the transition to later chapters.

One type of criticism directed against Singer calls to mind the measurement problems discussed in the introduction to utilitarianism. On one level, the equal consideration of interests principle defended by Singer does suggest a helpful decision process. It directs us to take all suffering into consideration when deciding among alternative policies. However, this directive soon confronts enormous complexity in application. As Singer acknowledges, humans are different from animals, and therefore, equal consideration does not entail equal (or identical) treatment. Further, interests and suffering admit of degrees. Not all interests deserve to be treated equally, and not all suffering is created equal. For example, some philosophers distinguish between *basic* and *peripheral* interests.[12] Life, food, water, clothing, and freedom from intense pain might be thought of as basic interests. Indoor plumbing, automobiles, fur coats, air conditioning, and gourmet cooking might be considered peripheral interests.

But how are we to sift through these diverse and competing interests? Would a human's interest in fencing off prairie for agricultural purposes (something that might be necessary if we follow Singer's and Regan's advice and become vegetarians) override a wild animal's interest in unobstructed habitat? How does the spotted owl's interest in old-growth forests in the Pacific Northwest compare with human interest in lumber? Would

the lumber's use make a difference? As moral agents, do we have a responsibility to interfere with the life of animals in the wild? Should we protect
predators or prey?[13] Are the interests of a starving wolf equal to the interests of a single member of a large herd of caribou? Are the interests of pets
equal to the interests of farm animals? Of wild animals? Do we really want
to give the interests of a rat *any* consideration when they conflict with the
interests of a poor child it might bite?[14]

These questions suggest problems for any view that gives the interests of
individual animals serious moral weight. The relationships of humans and animals, animals of different species, animals and their habitat, and humans, animals, and the land are many and diverse. Establishing equal moral standing for
individual animals is really only the beginning of the debate. Indeed, it frames
the debate as a conflict, as fundamentally adversarial. Without a clear and
determinate decision procedure, the question that began this entire debate—
what is the proper relation between humans and other animals?—remains
unanswered, if not unanswerable. Although "minimizing suffering" seems
clear and simple, it does not seem a practical guide in light of complex realities.

Other challenges, usually aimed at Regan, suggest that the boundary of
moral considerability is too restrictive. (Similar criticisms of Singer, who has
suggested that the boundary of considerability be drawn somewhere
"between shrimp and oysters," charge that his line is too inclusive) Although
Regan most often speaks in general terms of "animals," the subject-of-a-life
criterion most clearly applies to "mentally normal mammals of a year or
more."[15] According to many environmentalists, this neglects important members of the ecological community.

The influence of ecology underlies other important criticisms of the animal
welfare movement. For example, Regan acknowledges that his rights-based
ethics, like most traditional ethical theories, is *individualistic*. That is, ethics is
concerned with protecting and promoting the well-being of individuals, not
communities or societies or some one "common good." This puts him at odds
with much environmental and ecological thinking, which is *holistic*. Many
environmentalists emphasize "biotic communities" or "ecosystems" rather
than individual members (including humans) of those communities.
Alluding to a parallel issue in political philosophy, Regan warns us of "environmental fascism" in which individual rights are willingly sacrificed to the
greater good of the whole. "Environmental fascism and the rights view are
like oil and water: they don't mix."[16]

Further, as mentioned earlier, Regan is unwilling to attribute rights to
species. He acknowledges that his view is individualistic. Only individual
animals can be said to have moral standing or, more specifically, can be said
to have rights. This is a controversial claim even within the ethical tradition
of which Regan is a part. Corporations and nations are but two examples of
collections of individuals that are taken to have rights (albeit legal rights) that
are not reducible to the rights of individual members. But beyond this issue,

the individualistic bias of both Regan and Singer seems to imply other consequences that many environmentalists find unacceptable.

In Regan's view, an animal that is a member of an endangered species has
no special moral status. The last remaining pair of bald eagles or spotted owls
have less of a moral claim on us than a single whitetail deer. Preservation of
the endangered blue whales is ethically no more important than preserving
cows. We have no greater duty to mountain gorillas and black rhinos than to
a stray cat, and we certainly have no direct ethical obligation to the millions
of species of plants and animals that are not subjects-of-a-life.

Similarly, Singer's views would also suggest counterintuitive conclusions
to many environmentalists. Given the amount of suffering that can take place
with intensive farming techniques, any one of literally billions of chickens
would have a stronger moral claim against us (to relieve its suffering) than
would the last remaining members of a plant or invertebrate species. Thus,
according to critics, whatever else it might be, the animal welfare movement
is not a central part of the environmental movement.

The emphasis on individuals also leads to controversial suggestions for
wildlife management. Singer, for example, recognizes that it is conceivable
that human interference could improve the conditions of wild animals.
Nevertheless, based in part on past failures, he recommends a policy of leaving wild animals alone as much as possible. We do enough, he tells us, "if we
eliminate our own unnecessary killing and cruelty toward other animals."[17]
This is consistent with a standard utilitarian belief that we have a greater
responsibility to reduce suffering than to increase happiness. Regan apparently endorses a similar laissez-faire attitude. So long as we protect the rights
of animals (or again, at least mammals), other ecological concerns will take
care of themselves. In his rights view,

> assuming this could be successfully extended to inanimate natural objects [which
> he thinks is unlikely at best], our general policy regarding wilderness would be
> precisely what the preservationists want—namely, let it be! . . . Were we to show
> proper respect for the rights of the individuals who make up the biotic commu-
> nity, would not the *community* be preserved?[18]

But there are problems with this laissez-faire approach. First, we would
need to reverse the long history of destruction and habitat loss before we
could preserve biotic communities. Next, complete noninterference with the
environment is impossible. The idea that some "untamed wilderness,"
untouched by human activity, can exist is a mirage. No place on earth, no animal on earth, and no period on earth has escaped human influence for quite
some time. If only through the pollutants that we dump into the air and water
(and our influence is much greater than that), humans affect every corner of
the earth. The question is not *should* we actively influence the wilderness but
how should we?

Second, the answer to Regan's question would seem, in many cases, to be no. Showing proper respect for the rights of deer, for example, can have disastrous consequences for its ecological community.[19] As is the case in many areas, the population of these deer can often overwhelm the carrying capacity of their habitat. With abundant food, protective hunting laws, and loss of natural predators, deer populations wreak havoc on their habitat and with many other species that populate that habitat. The result is destruction of many other life-forms in that ecological community.

Similar consequences face wildlife managers in parts of Africa. In some protected refuges in East Africa, the elephant population grew so large that it threatened to outpace its food supply. Left alone, many elephants would die a slow death of starvation but not before destroying much of the surrounding vegetation. One alternative seems to be selective killing ("thinning the herd" or "culling the herd," in less offensive terms).[20]

The point of these examples is that animals, like humans, are part of a complex ecological community. Although constantly changing, this community seems to involve a delicate balance of interdependencies. For many environmentalists, the equilibrium of natural ecosystems should be the goal of an environmental ethics. Giving special ethical protection to individual animals threatens to upset that balance and cause damage elsewhere within that system. A laissez-faire attitude in conjunction with animal rights may well lead to serious ecological harms. There simply is no guarantee that a species—or, more generally, an ecological community—would be preserved if only we "show proper respect for the rights of the individuals who make up the biotic community."[21]

Many challenges to animal welfare ethics arise from the individualistic approach characteristic of Regan and Singer. Defending individual animals may not be the most appropriate environmental strategy. Other criticisms suggest that the extension of moral standing to animals has remained, in a peculiar sort of way and despite its intentions, anthropocentric.

How could moral standing for animals remain anthropocentric? Consider the philosophical method used by Feinberg, Singer, and Regan. They all begin by taking human beings as the paradigm of beings with moral standing. They all then ask what is it about humans that give them moral standing? Feinberg answers with interests, Singer answers with the capacity to suffer, and Regan answers with being a subject-of-a-life. But why draw the line here? In effect, Feinberg, Singer, and Regan all seem to say that the paradigms of holders of moral value are human beings. Thus, only animals that are enough like us can have (or we can "give them") moral standing. Moral standing seems a benefit that is derived from human nature and that living beings receive only if they are enough like humans.

Consider the case of invertebrates, the "little things that run the world," in the words of biologist Edward O. Wilson.[22] In the views of many environmentalists, preservation of invertebrates (animals that lack a backbone such as insects, jellyfish, and mollusks) should be an ethical concern. Yet in the most obvious reading of Singer and Regan, these animals lack the necessary criteria for moral standing. Singer suggests that sentience is both necessary and sufficient for moral standing. That is, without sentience a being does not have moral standing (the necessary condition), and sentience alone is enough (sufficient) to qualify for moral standing. Regan argues that moral standing derives from the inherent value found in subjects-of-a-life. But although it may be plausible to say that sentience and subjectivity are sufficient, why must we say that they are necessary? Why restrict inherent value to pleasure-pain or subjectivity?

One early challenge to this view was developed by philosopher Kenneth Goodpaster. Goodpaster argues,

> Neither rationality nor the capacity to experience pleasure and pain seem to me necessary (even though they may be sufficient) conditions on moral consider-ability. And only our hedonistic and concentric forms of ethical reflection keep us from acknowledging this fact. Nothing short of the condition of being alive seems to me to be a plausible and nonarbitrary criterion.[23]

Further, Goodpaster reasons that sentience seems to be an adaptive charac-teristic that contributes to the survival of the organism. Presumably, the same could be said for subjectivity. This, according to Goodpaster, "at least sug-gests, though of course it does not prove, that the capacities to suffer and to enjoy are ancillary to something more important rather than tickets to con-siderability in their own right."[24] This "something more important" is life itself. When we restrict the range of moral standing among all living things to only those sentient or conscious beings, we are, in fact if not logically, restrict-ing moral standing to those beings most like us. Without further argument (and, in fairness, both Singer and Regan have answers), this would be an arbi-trary restriction with significant environmental costs.

Thus, some critics have come to believe that the animal welfare movement is not an adequate environmental philosophy. At best, it addresses only some environmental issues. In their view, an adequate environmental ethics must reject both the individualism and the narrowness of philosophers like Singer and Regan.

6.6 SUMMARY AND CONCLUSIONS

Whether Singer or Regan fall victim to these challenges or not, an important point has been established. Environmental ethics requires more than a simple concern for individual animals of a certain type. At a minimum, we need to consider questions about the moral status of a diversity of plant and animal life, ecological communities, and our role in those communities. A shift to such holistic and truly nonanthropocentric ethics, however, would require a radical break from tradition.

Toward the end of *Animal Liberation*, Peter Singer tells us,

> Philosophy ought to question the basic assumptions of the age. Thinking
> through, critically and carefully, what most of us take for granted is, I believe, the
> chief task of philosophy, and the task that makes philosophy worthwhile.
> Regrettably, philosophy does not always live up to its historic role.[25]

In the view of many environmentalists, Singer himself, along with Tom Regan,
is guilty of exactly this failure. All of what follows in this textbook implicitly
takes up this challenge to "question the basic assumptions of the age."

Notes

1. As described in Peter Singer, *Animal Liberation*, 2d ed. (New York: New York
Review of Books Press, 1990), p. 60; much of this discussion of LD50 comes from
Singer.

2. Ibid., 95; the emphasis is Singer's.

3. Ibid., 136.

4. Singer attributes the term speciesism to Richard Ryder's essay, "Victims of
Science," in *Animals, Men, and Morals,* ed. Stanley Godlovitch, Roslind Godlovitch,
and John Harris (New York: Grove Press, 1973). This book was the subject of a 1973
review by Singer, "Animal Liberation," *New York Review of Books,* April, pp. 17–21.

5. Singer, *Animal Liberation*, pp. 7–8; the emphasis is Singer's.

6. Ibid., 16–17.

7. Tom Regan, "The Case for Animal Rights," in *In Defense of Animals,* ed. Peter
Singer (Oxford, England: Basil Blackwell, 1985), p. 13; the emphasis is Regan's.

8. See Gary Varner, "The Schopenhauerian Challenge in Environmental Ethics,"
Environmental Ethics 7 (Fall 1985): 209–30, for a more detailed analysis of the
distinction between moral agents and moral patients. Varner argues that Regan's
account of agents and patients is flawed because he fails to distinguish moral
patients, which have a good of their own, from those objects that are merely
intrinsically valuable but are not patients. Varner acknowledges that this second
class nonetheless is morally considerable.

9. Tom Regan, *The Case for Animal Rights* (Berkeley: University of California Press,
1983), p. 243.

10. These are the four that Regan considers in *The Case for Animal Rights.* For other
discussions, see especially Tom Regan, *All That Dwell Therein* (Berkeley: University
of California Press, 1982). Singer's *Animal Liberation* remains the best single source
for his views.

11. See, for example, R. G. Frey, "Rights, Interests, Desires, and Beliefs," *American
Philosophical Quarterly* 16 (July 1979): 233–39.

12. See Donald VanDeVeer, "Interspecific Justice," *Inquiry* 22 (summer 1979):
55–70.

13. For a detailed response to some of these questions, see S. F. Sapontzis, *Morals,
Reason, and Animals* (Philadelphia: Temple University Press, 1989), especially ch. 13,
"Saving the Rabbit from the Fox," pp. 229–48.

14. This example is from Singer's *New York Review* essay, "Animal Liberation," p. 21.

15. See Regan, *The Case for Animal Rights,* especially pp. 77–78. Regan later
expands this a bit, suggesting that although it is always difficult to draw such

lines, it would not be unreasonable to give the benefit of the doubt to any animal that shares the "relevant anatomical and physiological properties" with mammals. His example of such a relevant property is the central nervous system.

16. Ibid., 361–62.

17. Singer, *Animal Liberation*, p. 226.

18. Regan, *The Case for Animal Rights*, p. 363; the emphasis is Regan's.

19. For a review of these and similar challenges, see J. Baird Callicott's "Review of Tom Regan's The Case for Animal Rights," *Environmental Ethics* 7 (winter 1985): 365–72. Callicott also cites Mark Sagoff, "Animal Liberation and Environmental Ethics: Bad Marriage, Quick Divorce," *Osgoode Hall Law Journal* 22 (1984): 306, as a reference for this particular point.

20. For a good discussion of the Tsavo National Park dispute, see Daniel Botkin, *Discordant Harmonies* (New York: Oxford University Press, 1990), ch. 2.

21. For development of this claim, see Mark Sagoff, "Animal Liberation and Environmental Ethics," p. 26; J. Baird Callicott, "Review of Tom Regan"; and "Animal Liberation: A Triangular Affair," *Environmental Ethics* 2 (1980): 311–28.

22. E. O. Wilson, "The Little Things That Run the World," *Conservation Biology* 1 (December 1987): 344–46. Wilson gave this as an address at the opening of the invertebrate exhibit at the National Zoological Park in Washington, D.C., in 1987; it is reprinted in *The Environmental Ethics and Policy Book*, ed. Donald VanDeVeer and Christine Pierce (Belmont, Calif.: Wadsworth, 1994), pp. 84–86.

23. Kenneth Goodpaster, "On Being Morally Considerable," *Journal of Philosophy* 75 (1978): 308–25.

24. Ibid., 31.

25. Singer, *Animal Liberation*, p. 236.

Discussion Questions

1. How exactly would you distinguish Jonathan Swift's "Modest Proposal" and modern factory farming of veal, cows, chicken, and pigs? What are the relevant similarities, if any? Relevant differences?

2. Do you see any morally relevant differences between domesticated and wild animals? Would Singer? Would Regan? Do you see any morally relevant differences between animals threatened with extinction and those that are not?

3. What kinds of arguments can you give for vegetarianism? Which are moral arguments? Are you convinced by any of them? Why or why not?

4. During a particularly harsh winter recently, the state of Minnesota delivered tons of feed to wild deer faced with starvation. Do humans have such responsibilities to wild animals, particularly those that are in no danger of extinction? Does it matter to you that this state's action was supported mostly by hunters who feared a dwindling deer population?

5. Does hunting or fishing raise any moral issues? If people eat the animals they kill, does that make a difference?

6. In many areas, deer are overpopulating local habitats. Destruction of the habitat as well as mass starvation can occur in such circumstances. Would you favor selective hunting to thin overpopulated herds?

Further Reading

The already classic positions of Singer and Regan can be found in Peter Singer, *Animal Liberation*, 2d ed. (New York: New York Review of Books Press, 1990), and

Tom Regan, *The Case for Animal Rights* (Berkeley: University of California Press, 1983).

Two solid anthologies on the moral status of animals are Peter Singer and Tom Regan, *Animal Rights and Human Obligations* (Englewood Cliffs, N.J.: Prentice-Hall, 1989) and Eugene Hargrove, *The Animal Rights/Environmental Ethics Debate* (Albany: State University of New York Press, 1992).

Between the Species is an ethics journal focusing on issues concerning animals and ethics.

III

THEORIES OF ENVIRONMENTAL ETHICS

7

Biocentric Ethics and the Inherent Value of Life

Biodiversity

The diversity of life on earth is amazingly complex. Biological science has been categorizing animal and plant species since before Aristotle began his taxonomy of living organisms more than 2,000 years ago. Current estimates suggest that more than 1.4 million different species have been scientifically categorized.[1] But the categorized species represent only a small percentage of the actual number of species that exist. Based on research conducted in tropical forests in Brazil and Peru, some estimates place the number at more than 30 or 40 million species. Biologist E. O. Wilson estimates that invertebrate species alone may number as many as 30 million.

Each species contains from a few members (for example, the California condor) to many billions of members (such as bacteria). Each species exists in an ecological niche in which its members interact with their environment to maintain life. Wilson tells of many highly specialized life forms.

> One of my favorite examples of such specialists living in microniches are the mites that live on the bodies of army ants: one kind is found only on the mandibles of the soldier caste, where it sits and feeds from the mouth of its host; another kind is found only on the hind foot of the soldier caste, where it sucks blood for a living and so on through various bizarre configurations.[2]

Each organism must take in nutrition from its environment to sustain its life and propagate its species. The ability to do this has evolved through millions of years of changing environments, mutations, and natural selection. This ability is stored in the genetic code of each organism. Each organism contains one million to ten billion bits of information in its genetic code. This represents an enormous genetic library of information developed over billions of years.

This diversity and complexity of life has inspired scientists, philosophers, and poets for millennia. It is a remarkable phenomena. But that diversity is being threatened at astonishing rates. Some scientists, including E.O. Wilson, estimate that over one hundred species per day, almost 50,000 species each year, become extinct. Fossil records show that extinction has been a fact of life. But these very same fossil records show that the rate of extinction independent of human factors, what scientists call the "background extinction rate," is significantly smaller than present extinction rates. Mammals, for example, are becoming extinct at 100 times the background rate. The present extinction rates for rain forest species and freshwater species are even higher. Without question, the earth is in the midst of the greatest single extinction episode since the one associated with the extinction of dinosaurs 65 million years ago. The difference, unfortunately, is that this episode is largely due to human factors. Further, estimates suggest that it may take more than 10 million years for life on earth to recover from human-caused extinctions.

But what, exactly, is wrong with the loss of such life. What does it matter that a mite living only on the mandible of the soldier caste of army ants becomes extinct? What is the value of life? Many instrumental justifications can be given to support the preservation of this biodiversity. Tremendous medicinal, agricultural, economic, aesthetic, recreational, and scientific potential lies in the variety and diversity of life. Indeed, we depend on other life-forms for our existence. But does the simple fact that they are alive imply that we have any ethical relationship to them? Is it reasonable to speak of a life-centered or *biocentric* ethics?

7.1 INTRODUCTION

Chapters 3, 4, 5, and 6 showed how standard ethical principles and concepts can be applied to environmental issues. Beginning with this chapter, our focus changes as we consider more systematic attempts at developing comprehensive environmental philosophies. These approaches question the wisdom of simply *extending* traditional ethics, or what we can call "ethical extensionism," in favor of more dramatic and radical shifts in our ethical perspective.

The problems with ethical extensionism center around three issues. First, despite the work of philosophers like Singer and Regan, the principles and concepts used in their application often remain narrowly focused. The criteria for moral considerability defended by many philosophers are most clearly found in adult human beings. Critics charge that ethical extensionism gives moral standing only to those animals that most closely resemble adult humans. As a result, these extensions remain fundamentally hierarchical and, according to critics, beg the question about the moral status of other living things. For example, both Singer and Regan attribute moral standing only to higher animals. Other living things remain outside the range of moral consideration. This omission strikes many environmentalists as both an ethical and logical mistake.

Second, these extensions remain thoroughly individualistic. Individual animals have standing, but plants, species, habitat, and relations have no standing in their own right. Yet so much of the science of ecology stresses the interconnectedness of nature. Ecology emphasizes such wholes as species, biotic diversity, ecological communities, ecosystems, and biological, chemical, and geological cycles. Relations, communities, systems, and processes play a major role in the science of ecology. Unfortunately, standard ethical theories have little room for such concerns. Indeed, we need only remember Regan's dismissal of the ethical focus on communities as environmental fascism to see how unreceptive these standard ethical views can be. To some environmentalists, this is the perfect example of a perspective caught in the grasp of a philosophical theory and ignoring the facts of science.

Finally, these extensions are not, nor were they intended as, comprehensive environmental ethics. Philosophers applied ethics to specific problems as they arose and as they were perceived, with little or no attempt at building a coherent and comprehensive theory of environmental ethics. This focus has had two unhappy results. First, the extension of ethics to cover, for example, the rights of animals can provide no guidance for many other environmental issues like global warming or pollution. Second, extensionism tends to remain critical and negative. It often tells us what is wrong with various policies and actions but seldom offers much about what the alternative "good life" should be.

The chapters that follow present a survey of attempts to develop more systematic environmental ethics. Much of the recent philosophical work on the environment breaks with standard ethical theory and strives to rethink the human-nature relationship. Indeed, some of these emerging schools of thought might more appropriately be described as environmental philosophies rather than as ethics. As philosophers seek a comprehensive account of the place of human beings in their natural environment, they must address more than merely ethical questions. Topics in metaphysics (nature and the natural, the ontological status of systems, relations, species, and so forth), epistemology (the logical relation between descriptive and normative claims), aesthetics (beauty and intrinsic value), and political philosophy (civil disobedience and environmental justice) become important issues when we begin to rethink ethics in this way.

Let us, then, put aside the role of the philosopher who approaches environmental problems with a previously articulated ethical theory. Instead, let us adopt the point of view of an environmentalist (or, more simply, of a concerned citizen) seeking to articulate, develop, and defend a coherent and comprehensive environmental philosophy.

To understand what is involved with such a task, we need only review the opening paragraph of the introduction to Chapter 1. It is helpful to repeat it here.

Upon entering the twenty-first century, it is fair to say that human beings face environmental challenges unprecedented in the history of this planet. Largely through human activity, life on Earth faces the greatest mass extinctions since the end of the dinosaur age 65 million years ago. Some estimates suggest more than 100 species are becoming extinct every day and that this rate could double or triple within the next few decades.[2] The natural resources that sustain life on this planet—air, water, and soil—are being polluted or depleted at alarming rates. Human population growth is increasing exponentially. In 1999, world population reached 6 billion people. While it was not until 1804 that world population first reached 1 billion people, the most recent 1 billion increase took just twelve years. The rate of population increase is slowing somewhat. Estimates are that it may take 15 years to add another 1 billion people. The prospects for continued degradation and depletion of natural resources multiply with this population growth. Toxic wastes that will plague future generations continue to accumulate worldwide. The world's wilderness areas, its forests, wetlands, mountains, and grasslands, are being developed, paved, drained, burned, and overgrazed out of existence. With destruction of the ozone layer and the potential that the "greenhouse effect" will lead to global warming, human activity threatens the very atmosphere and climate of the planet Earth.

No rational person can reflect on these developments without some concern and distress. But to understand the goals of an environmental philosophy, we need to go beyond the stage of merely reacting to these sins. We need to examine the source of this concern. Why exactly are we troubled by these facts? Why *should* we be troubled by these facts?

These questions seem to have no single answer. In some cases, our reasoning lies in the environmental destruction that poses a clear danger to human beings and, thus, raises familiar ethical concerns. In other cases, the way we treat the environment offends spiritual, aesthetic, or cultural values. In still other cases, we seem to be causing direct moral harm to natural objects themselves. The goal of many environmental philosophers is to provide a single systematic principle or theory that can account for these various concerns. Achieving such a goal would require work not only in ethics, but also in metaphysics, epistemology, aesthetics, and political philosophy. Still other philosophers conclude that no such systematic account is possible and argue instead for a position called "moral pluralism."[3]

7.2 INSTRUMENTAL VALUE AND INTRINSIC VALUE

One way to understand the philosophical shift that is occurring at this point is to contrast questions of morality with more general questions of value. Morality, narrowly understood, has always taken human well-being and the relationship between humans as its focus. Morality seeks to understand our responsibilities to others and the rights we have against others. Therefore, it is perhaps not surprising that philosophers have difficulty granting environmental concerns moral consideration. Environmental concerns simply do not fit within the traditional domain of morality.

But understood more broadly, philosophical ethics asks more general questions about the good life and about human flourishing. These questions involve wider concerns of *value*. From this perspective, environmental concerns are more legitimately ethical concerns because they raise a wide variety of value questions that establish norms for how we ought to live. Not all value questions concern moral value (narrowly understood). We also recognize aesthetic, spiritual, scientific, and cultural values as worthy and deserving of respect.[4]

Thus, central to a comprehensive environmental philosophy is a consideration of the nature and scope of value. A full account of value determines the ethical domain by helping to define what objects have moral relevance or what objects deserve consideration. Ethics is concerned with how we should live, how we should act, and the kind of persons we should be. Defining the full scope of these "shoulds" is to give an account of all that has value or worth.

Consider the example described in the preceding discussion case. Uncounted species of insects are becoming extinct as the result of the destruction of the rain forest. Many people find the wanton destruction of diverse life-forms offensive. But what exactly is wrong with causing the extinction of millions of insects? Insects do not feel pain, are not conscious, and are not subjects-of-a-life. They are not, in any obvious way, moral beings. What seems to be wrong is that something of value is lost, indeed perhaps wantonly destroyed, by human activity. Too often these values are lost for the sake of greed or out of sheer ignorance. A similar explanation might be given for the destruction of the rain forest itself, as well as for the loss of wilderness areas, wetlands, trees, lakes, oceans, fish, and plants. The shift from an ethics of animal welfare to a more holistic environmental philosophy can perhaps best be understood as a shift from a narrow conception of morality and moral value to a broader concern with value itself.

Philosophers often have discussed this moral value in terms of interests. Among the philosophers considered in the last two chapters, Joel Feinberg, Christopher Stone, Peter Singer, Tom Regan, and Kenneth Goodpaster all use the concept of interests to decide what sorts of things deserve moral consideration. To say that an object has interests is to say that it has a "sake of its own" (Feinberg), a "worth" in its own right (Stone), a "welfare" of its own (Bentham and Singer), "inherent value" (Regan), or its own "well-being" (Goodpaster). All this is to say that these objects have a value or worth that is independent of the value and worth ascribed to them by human beings. This implies that we do something wrong when we treat an object that has a value in itself and of its own as if it has value only in relation to us. This difference is typically expressed in the important distinction between instrumental and intrinsic value.

Instrumental value is a function of usefulness. An object with instrumental value possesses that value because it can be used to attain something else of value. A pencil is valuable because I can write with it. A dollar bill is valuable because I can use it to buy something. The instrumental value of an object lies not in the object itself but in the uses to which that object can be put. When such an object no longer has use or when it can be replaced by something of more effective or greater use, it has lost its value and can be ignored or discarded.

Thinking of natural objects in terms of "resources" is to treat them as having instrumental value. For example, Gifford Pinchot's conservation movement emphasized the instrumental value of forests and wilderness areas. We should protect and conserve the wilderness because it is the home of vast resources that humans can use. Pinchot and other progressives argued that the value of national resources was too often unfairly distributed or wasted, which is to say, improperly used. Many other environmental concerns rest on the instrumental value of the environment. Clean air and water are valued because without them human health and well-being are jeopardized. The preservation of plant and animal species is valued by many because of the vast potential for medical and agricultural uses. Virtually any utilitarian or economic proposal is based on the instrumental value of nature.

Appealing to the instrumental value of the environment can be an effective political strategy. Public opinion is often most responsive to claims of lost opportunities, wasted resources, and the like. Yet an environmental ethics that is based solely on the instrumental value of the environment may prove unstable. As human interests and needs change, so too would human uses for the environment. The instrumental value of the Colorado River as a water and hydroelectric power source for southern California will quickly override its instrumental value as a scenic wilderness or recreation area. Emphasizing only the instrumental value of nature effectively means that the environment is held hostage by the interests and needs of humans, and it immediately evokes the necessity to make tradeoffs among competing human interests.

An object has *intrinsic value*, on the other hand, when it is valuable in itself and is not valued simply for its uses.[5] The value of such things is intrinsic to them. To say that an object is intrinsically valuable is to say that it has a good of its own and what is good for it does not depend on outside factors. In this sense, it would be a value found or recognized rather than given. Not all things that we value are valued instrumentally. Some things we value because we recognize in them a moral, spiritual, symbolic, aesthetic, or cultural importance. We value them for themselves, for what they mean, for what they stand for, for what they are, and not for how they are used.

Some examples can help explain this distinction. Think of friendships. If you value a friend only for her usefulness, you have seriously misunderstood

friendship (and you would not be a very good friend). Consider also historical monuments or cultural and aesthetic objects. The Liberty Bell, Taj Mahal,
and Michelangelo's *David* possess a value far beyond their usefulness.

Clearly, many of our environmental concerns rest on the intrinsic value that
we recognize in nature. Life itself, in the view of many, is intrinsically valuable, no matter what form it takes. Wilderness areas, scenic landscapes, and
national parks are valued by many people because, like the Liberty Bell, they
are a part of our national heritage and history. (This essentially is the argument Mark Sagoff made in Chapter 3.) Grizzly bears may have little instrumental value, but many people value knowing that the bears still exist in
Yellowstone National Park. The symbolic value of the bald eagle transcends
any instrumental value that it might have. Undeveloped and unexplored
wilderness areas are highly valued, even by people who will never visit,
explore, or use these areas. John Muir's disagreement with Gifford Pinchot
was a disagreement between one who saw an intrinsic value in wilderness
(Muir) and one who did not (Pinchot). Muir spoke of the great sequoia groves
as a cathedral, suggesting that they possess a spiritual and religious value far
above their economic usefulness.

When we say that human activity degrades the environment, we are
often expressing the loss of or disrespect for intrinsic value. When sections
of the Grand Canyon are eroded by flooding caused by water released
from hydroelectric dams upriver, when acid rain eats away at ancient archi-
tecture in Greece and Rome, or when shorelines are replaced by board-
walks and casinos, human activity destroys some of the intrinsic goods that
we find in nature.

For a number of philosophers working in environmental ethics, the biggest
challenge is to develop an account of intrinsic value that can counter arguments based on instrumental values. As presented in Chapter 5, John
Passmore calls for an emphasis on the sensuous to offset the materialism and
greed dominant in modern culture. After criticizing the dominant economic
model (which sees all value as instrumental), Mark Sagoff summons philosophers to articulate the cultural, aesthetic, historical, and ethical values that
underlie our environmental commitments. These values, Sagoff tells us,
determine not just what we *want* as a people but what we *are*.

Thus, development of a more systematic environmental philosophy often
involves a shift from a narrow focus on moral standing or moral rights and
responsibilities to a more general discussion of value, especially intrinsic
value. Unfortunately, appeals to intrinsic value often meet with skepticism.
We seem to lack the language for expressing intrinsic value. Many people
think that such value is merely subjective, a matter of personal opinion:
"Beauty is in the eye of the beholder." Thus, when a measurable instrumental
value (such as profit) conflicts with intangible and elusive intrinsic value
(such as the beauty of a wilderness), the instrumental value too often wins by
default. The remainder of this chapter considers views that hold that life itself
possesses intrinsic value and, thus, humans have some responsibilities to it.

7.3 BIOCENTRIC ETHICS
AND THE REVERENCE FOR LIFE

Biocentric ethics refers to any theory that views all life as possessing intrinsic value. (The word *biocentric* means life-centered.) Thus, although someone like Tom Regan is willing to attribute an inherent worth to some animals, his view is not biocentric because it does not include all living things. Kenneth Goodpaster's focus on life itself as sufficient for moral considerability is biocentric.

An early version of a biocentric ethics is Albert Schweitzer's "reverence for life" principle. Schweitzer (1875–1965) wrote extensively about religion, music, ethics, history, and philosophy. He also, of course, devoted much of his life to bringing medical care to remote and isolated communities in Africa. His ethics, captured in the phrase "reverence for life," is an extremely interesting precursor of contemporary biocentric ethics.

Schweitzer's was an active and full life committed to caring and concern for others. Yet he was also a prolific writer, devoting many volumes to diagnosing the ethical ills of modern society and seeking a cure for them. Reverence for life was the attitude that he believed offered hope to a world beset with conflict. It is worth our while to examine briefly Schweitzer's diagnosis and cure.[6]

Modern industrial society had moved away from a worldview that connected the goodness of life with the goodness of nature. This belief, what Schweitzer called "world-and-life-affirmation," is reminiscent of the natural law tradition in ethics. The rise of science and technology and the industrialized society that accompanied them split the connection between ethics and nature by viewing nature as an indifferent, value-free, mechanical force. Modern science often views nature as a machine, governed by physical and mechanical laws. There is no good (nor, for that matter, evil) intrinsic to nature itself. Set adrift in such a world, human ethics is left without foundation. Ethical value becomes no more than personal opinion or sentiment. Modern industrial society with its wars, impersonal bureaucracies, meaningless work, and cultural decay is the result of this separation.

Schweitzer's ethical thinking sought to reestablish the bond between nature and ethics. Yet, having spent time traveling in the most remote sections of Africa, Schweitzer did not deceive himself into thinking of nature as benign and gentle. He had been made more than aware of the destructive and arbitrary force of nature. He was convinced nonetheless that there was good in nature, an intrinsic value, that could help provide a basis for human ethics. The idea that Schweitzer developed to solve this issue is captured by his phrase "reverence for life."

Schweitzer describes in almost mystical terms the moment that this idea came to him. While riding on a barge traveling upriver in Africa, "at the very moment when, at sunset, we were making our way through a herd of hippopotamuses, there flashed upon my mind, unforeseen and unsought, the phrase *Reverence for Life*."[7]

What does reverence for life mean? Schweitzer's original German phrase was *ehrfurcht vor dem leben. Ehrfurcht* implies an attitude of awe and wonder. Although *reverence* perhaps connotes a religious tone that is missing in *ehrfurcht*, it seems clear that Schweitzer had something like this in mind. The etymological roots of *ehrfurcht* suggest a combined attitude of honor and fear. It would not be misleading to think of the attitude often inspired by majestic vistas seen from atop high mountains or the attitude inspired by violent storms.

Schweitzer held that the most fundamental fact of human consciousness is the realization that "I am life which wills to live, in the midst of life which wills to live."[8] Ethics begins when we become fully aware and fully in awe of that fact.

> The man who has become a thinking being feels a compulsion to give to every will-to-live the same reverence for life that he gives to his own. He experiences that other life in his own. He accepts as being good: to preserve life, to promote life, to raise to its highest value life which is capable of development; and as being evil: to destroy life, to injure life, to repress life which is capable of development. This is the absolute, fundamental principle of the moral.[9]

In our terms, Schweitzer is claiming that all living things have an intrinsic value, a value that commands our awe and reverence. Life is not a neutral, value-free "fact" of the universe. Life is good in itself. It is inspiring and deserving of respect.

Critics are quick to caricature the reverence for life ethic. Is Schweitzer suggesting that the life of a virus or of bacteria is as worthy as human life? Does he suggest that we treat the life of an ant with as much respect as we treat human life? If not, does he offer any formula for resolving conflicts between human life and the life of, for example, the HIV virus?

Schweitzer lived his life in a manner that many people would find overly demanding. He would go to great lengths to avoid killing even mosquitoes, going so far as to carry them out of the room rather than kill them. Even when fighting disease-carrying mosquitoes, he was reluctant to kill. He resisted using DDT, for example, because he mistrusted the way it killed indiscriminately. Nevertheless, Schweitzer was not naive about the necessity of sometimes taking lives, especially out of reverence for other lives. To maintain life, other life must be sacrificed as food. He was also willing to take an animal's life to end its suffering.[10]

But this does not mean that Schweitzer defended some formula or rule to be applied in cases of conflict to establish priorities. Such a hierarchy would undermine the foundation of the reverence for life ethic by suggesting that some rule or criterion is more fundamental than reverence itself. It would also downplay the serious dilemma that we often face when we must take life. A principle or rule that unequivocally resolves conflict would suggest that any ethical conflict is only apparent and not real.

Schweitzer did not envision reverence for life merely as some rule that we could apply to specific situations and, as it were, simply read off the recommended decision. Reverence for life is more an attitude that determines who we are rather than a rule for determining what we should do. It describes a character trait or a moral virtue rather than a rule of action. A morally good person stands in awe of the inherent worth of each life.

But what does this say about those circumstances in which the good person must choose to kill? What about the doctor who kills a virus? The butcher who kills a pig? The farmer who cuts down a tree? Schweitzer denies that we can escape responsibility for these decisions. They must be made, but they should be made responsibly and consciously. Reverence for life is that character trait that sensitizes us to the responsibility of these decisions. It is an attitude that makes us aware of the full implications of these decisions. It makes us reluctant to take a life randomly, callously, or without remorse. In doing this, it helps us live an authentic and moral life.

Schweitzer's ethical views are richly textured and firmly based in the experiences of many years in the African wilderness. Yet these views never attained wide popularity among either the public or philosophers. Perhaps the tendency to see such a perspective as overly romantic or naive is too common and too strong an obstacle. Schweitzer also never developed the type of scholarly defense of this position that professional philosophers demand. However, recent biocentric theories may be more persuasive.

7.4 ETHICS AND CHARACTER

Before moving to more recent biocentric views, it is helpful to reflect for a moment on a philosophical issue that underlies this discussion. In the opening section of this chapter, we suggested that recent environmental philosophies represent a break with many traditional theories. We have seen hints in recent pages of what this might involve, and developing these hints at this point will prove useful.

For many defenders of traditional ethical theories like utilitarianism, deontology, and natural law, the fundamental question for ethics is what should I do? The goal of ethics is to articulate and defend rules or principles that can guide our behavior. The philosopher's job, then, is to justify that rule by demonstrating why all rational people should act in accord with it. For most philosophers in these traditions, this task ultimately requires showing that obeying the rule is in a person's rational self-interest.[11]

Given this approach to ethics, we can understand why many people would have difficulty accepting Schweitzer's views on the reverence for life. If we do treat Schweitzer's view as a rule for guiding our actions, reverence for life might well commit us to the type of counterintuitive positions we have just mentioned.

But as suggested, Schweitzer did not offer reverence for life as an ethical *rule*. Reverence for life would be a fundamental *attitude* that we would take toward the world. In this sense, Schweitzer's ethics focused not on the question of what I should do but on what type of person I should be. His was not an ethics solely of rules as much as it was an ethics of character, seeking first to describe morally good people in terms of their *character*, dispositions, and values rather than in terms of their actions.

This shift represents a return to a tradition of philosophical ethics that goes back to Plato and Aristotle. An *ethics of virtue* emphasizes moral character or virtues rather than rules or principles. Ethical systems like utilitarianism, deontology, and natural law focus on human *actions* and seek to defend some rule or principle that we use to judge whether those actions are right or wrong. Virtue-based ethics constructs a philosophical account of the morally good person, describing and defending certain character traits of that good person. Like Aristotle, most virtue-based theories are teleological. Virtues are distinguished from vices (the opposite of a virtue) by their connection with attainment of some human *telos*, or goal. For Aristotle, the virtues were those character traits and dispositions that enable people to live a meaningful and fulfilling human life.

Keep this distinction in mind as we examine more recent environmental philosophies. Many of these emerging philosophies are not simply proposing alternative rules or principles to utilitarianism or deontology. Instead, they require us to make a shift in our philosophical perspective, a shift away from a concern with rules of behavior toward a concern with moral character. These shifts require not only a different view of the environment but, at least as important, a different view of ourselves.

Recollect an earlier discussion by Mark Sagoff. Sagoff tells us that a satisfactory environmental ethics must address not only those values that determine what we *want*, but also those values that determine what we *are*. Implicit in this distinction is the recognition that our identity as a person is constituted in part by our values and attitudes. A person's character, those dispositions, relationships, attitudes, values, and beliefs that popularly might be called a "personality," is not some feature that remains independent of that person's identity. Character is not like a suit of clothes that the self steps into and out of at will. Rather, the self is identical to a person's most fundamental and enduring dispositions, attitudes, values, and beliefs. Thus, when an environmental philosophy requires that we change our fundamental attitude toward nature, it is requiring quite literally that we change ourselves.

Note how this shift changes the nature of justification in ethics. If, as seems true in many traditional ethical theories, justification of some rule requires that it be tied to self-interest, we should not be surprised to find that this justification often fails. Ethical controversies often involve a conflict between self-interest and ethical values. Consider how we would "justify" the reverence for life. For a self that does not already include a disposition to treat life with reverence, the only avenue open for justification would involve showing how the disposition serves some other interest of the self. Why should I who does not already treat life with reverence do so now? The only way to answer this question appears to be to show how it is in your self-interest to adopt this attitude. But this means connecting the attitude to, in Sagoff's terms, those values that determine what we want instead of those that determine what we are. But this is to say that reverence for life must be reducible to some instrumental value. We should adopt the attitude of reverence because it, in some way, serves our purposes or satisfies our wants. Of course, this is exactly what the reverence for life ethic denies. Life has *intrinsic value*. It is much more than merely *instrumentally* valuable.

On the other hand, for the person already characterized by a reverence for life, the question of justification is less relevant. If one of my fundamental attitudes is a reverence for life, the question of why I should revere life ordinarily would not arise.[12] Thus, justification for an ethics that requires a fundamental shift in moral attitude involves something other than an appeal to self-interest.

7.5 TAYLOR'S BIOCENTRIC ETHICS

Paul Taylor's 1986 book *Respect for Nature* is one of the most fully developed and philosophically sophisticated contemporary defenses of a biocentric ethics. Although Schweitzer tried to explain what reverence for life meant and what practical implications follow from this attitude, he never provided an adequate justification for adopting that attitude. Part of the strength of Taylor's view lies in his careful defense of why it is reasonable to adopt the attitude of respect for nature. For this reason, we will concentrate on his view as our example of biocentric ethics.

As a biocentric theorist, Taylor seeks a systematic and comprehensive account of the moral relations that exist between humans and other living things. Taylor sees this relationship as being based on the inherent worth of all life.

> The central tenet of the theory of environmental ethics that I am defending is that actions are right and character traits are morally good in virtue of their expressing or embodying a certain ultimate moral attitude, which I call respect for nature.[13]

Taylor's explanation and defense of this theory proceed through a number of steps. He first argues that it is meaningful to say that all living things have a good of their own. All living things can be said to have a good of their own because all living things are, in Taylor's phrase, "teleological centers of life." Taylor believes that this "good" is a simple fact that follows from living beings have a life. Having a good of itself is necessary, but not sufficient, for attributing any human responsibility to that entity.[14] To say that an entity has inherent worth is to go beyond the factual claim that they have a good and make the normative claim that this entity deserves moral consideration and that moral agents have duties toward it. We move from the descriptive claim that a being has a good of its own to the normative claim that it possesses inherent worth when we come to understand and accept what Taylor calls "the biocentric outlook on nature." Accepting this outlook and recognizing the inherent worth of all living things is to adopt respect for nature as our "ultimate moral attitude." In turn, adopting this attitude means that we will act in morally responsible ways toward the natural environment.

To understand Taylor's views, we first need to distinguish things that have a good of their own from things that do not. Taylor cites a child as a being with a good of its own and a pile of sand as something about which it makes no sense to ascribe goodness. Parental decisions aim to promote the child's good. The child is benefited when that good is furthered and harmed when that good is frustrated. On the other hand, it is meaningless to talk of the sand's own good, as if the sand itself can be harmed or benefited in any way.

Taylor next relies on a traditional philosophical distinction between *real* and *apparent* good or between what he calls *objective* and *subjective* value concepts. A thing's good is not always identical with what that being *believes* is its good. What *appears* to me to be good for me (subjectively) may not *really* (objectively) be good for me. This distinction allows Taylor to include in his biocentric ethics any being that has an objective good of its own. By ignoring the concept of apparent or subjective goods, he is not limited to including only those beings that possess the beliefs, interests, or desires presupposed in any account of subjective good.

What entities have an objective good of their own? Taylor's answer is to be found in the concept of a teleological center of a life. To understand this, it is helpful to draw some parallels with Schweitzer's reverence for life ethics and the natural law tradition of Aristotle. It also is informative to contrast what Taylor says with the concept of a subject-of-a-life as Regan uses it in animal rights ethics.

Let us begin with an example from Taylor.

> Concerning a butterfly, for example, we may hesitate to speak of its interests or preferences, and we would probably deny outright that it values anything in the sense of considering it good or desirable. But once we come to understand its life cycle and know the environmental conditions it needs to survive in a healthy state, we have no difficulty in speaking about what is beneficial to it and what might be harmful to it. . . . Even when we consider such simple animal organisms as one-celled protozoa, it makes perfectly good sense to a biologically informed person to speak of what benefits or harms them, what environmental changes are to their advantage or disadvantage, and what physical circumstances are favorable or unfavorable to them. The more knowledge we gain concerning these organisms, the better are we able to make sound judgments about what is in their interest or contrary to their interest.[15]

This is something that most of us, at least when we are not caught in the grips of a philosophical theory, would accept. It makes perfect sense to talk about the good of any living thing. This good is objective in the sense that it does not depend on anyone's beliefs or opinions. It is a claim that biological evidence can support. It is something that we can come to *know*. When we know an entity's good, we know what would be in that entity's interests, even if the being itself, like a plant, has no conscious interests of its own. Thus, even the weekend gardener can meaningfully talk about compost being good for tomatoes, pruning being good for an apple tree, drought being bad for vegetables, aphids being bad for beans, and ladybugs being bad for aphids.

All living things have a good because living beings are teleological-centers-of-life. Remember from the discussion of natural law ethics in Chapter 2 that the Greek word *telos* is translated as "purpose," or "goal," or "end." Aristotle was led by his biological observations to claim that all living things act toward some distinctive goal, or telos. Like Aristotle, Taylor claims that each species has a distinctive nature that determines the specific good for that species. Unlike Aristotle, this nature need not be identified with the organism's essence or soul. For Taylor, this nature is more like the ecological niche or function fulfilled by that species.

As the aphid and ladybug examples suggest, however, the good of one species may not be good for another species. Each species has its specific end, but all living things do have ends. In general, that end is growth, development, sustenance, and propagation. Life itself is directional in the sense that it tends toward this end. Each living thing is the center of this purposive activity. Each living thing is the teleological center of a life.

Schweitzer's phrase in this context was "I am life which wills to live in the midst of life which wills to live." So long as we do not assume that all things that "will to live" must do so consciously, Schweitzer's thinking is similar to Taylor's on this point. Each living thing has its own good because, as a living thing, each life has direction, a goal, a telos. This is true whether the being itself is consciously aware of that fact or not. The will to live is manifested in the biological processes of growth, development, propagation, and sustaining life.

This view can be contrasted with Tom Regan's defense of animal rights. In Chapter 6, Regan argued that all beings that are subjects-of-a-life have the inherent value that qualifies that being for moral standing. (Regan's use of "inherent value" functions for him as "inherent worth" does in this chapter.) To be a subject-of-a-life involves a complex set of characteristics that go beyond merely being alive and merely being conscious. In this way, Regan defends moral standing only for "mentally normal mammals of a year or more." Taylor's concept of a teleological center of a life is more inclusive than Regan's subject-of-a-life. According to Taylor,

> To say it is a teleological center of a life is to say that its internal functioning as well as its external activities are all goal-oriented, having the constant tendency to maintain the organism's existence through time and to enable it successfully to perform those biological operations whereby it reproduces its kind and continually adapts to changing environmental events and conditions. It is the coherence

and unity of these functions of an organism, all directed toward the realization of its good, that make it one teleological center of activity.[16]

Like Regan, unlike Aristotle and Schweitzer perhaps, Taylor is especially careful in moving from the *descriptive* claim that some being has a good of its own to the *normative* claim that we have ethical duties toward that being.[17] According to Taylor, it is a matter of biological fact that living things have a good of their own. But this is not an ethical good in the sense that this fact alone does not commit us to any particular ethical stance toward living things. Having a good of its own does not by itself confer moral standing on a being.

Taylor's perspective explains the normative claims that all living things have moral standing and that we have duties toward them by reference to the concept of inherent worth. As he uses this phrase, inherent worth commits us to making two further normative judgments: entities with inherent worth deserve moral consideration and all moral agents have duties to respect that entity's own good.[18] What is the connection between a thing's having a good of its own and its possessing inherent worth?

Having a good of its own makes it possible for a living thing to be the object of human duties. That is, we can have duties to promote or preserve a being's good only if it does, in fact, have a good of its own to be promoted. Having a good of its own is, therefore, necessary for a being to possess inherent worth. But it is not sufficient. The normative claim that living things have an inherent worth is to be explained and justified by reference to what Taylor calls the "biocentric outlook."

The biocentric outlook is a system of beliefs that conceptualizes our relationship to other living things. It is a system of beliefs that provides a fundamental worldview of the natural world and our relationship to it. Once we adopt this worldview, we see that treating all living things as possessing inherent worth is the only way of treating them that makes sense. Only this way of understanding them is consistent with the biocentric outlook.

The biocentric outlook on nature centers around four central beliefs. First, humans are seen as members of Earth's community of life in the same sense and on the same terms as all other living things. Second, all species, including humans, are part of a system of interdependence. Third, all living things pursue their own good in their own ways (the teleological center of life belief). Finally, humans are understood as not inherently superior to other living things.[19]

Taylor goes on to explain that the biocentric outlook is a way of conceiving nature that all rational and factually informed people should adopt. It is an outlook that is firmly based on reasonable scientific evidence. Rejecting this outlook would require us to give up or significantly revise a good deal of what the science of ecology has learned. Once a person adopts this view, such a person would see that recognizing the inherent worth of all living things is the only perspective on life that is consistent with this outlook.

To regard living things as possessing inherent worth is to adopt the attitude of respect for nature. It is to adopt a fundamental attitude toward nature that establishes certain basic motivations and dispositions. To adopt this attitude is to be disposed to promoting and protecting the good of other living things simply *because* it is their own good. It is to accept the good of other beings as a reason for one's own action.

Taylor's biocentric ethics addresses a number of philosophical issues that were missing in Schweitzer's reverence for life ethics. His account of how the biocentric outlook makes the attribution of inherent worth to all living things reasonable offers a rational basis for this belief that is missing in Schweitzer. Likewise, his description of inherent worth and a good of one's own adds much to the philosophical debate. It remains for Taylor to turn to issues of normative ethics and offer more practical advice.

7.6 PRACTICAL IMPLICATIONS

Taylor's normative ethics focuses on two basic issues: the general rules or duties that follow from the attitude of respect for nature and priority rules for resolving conflicts between the ethical claims of humans and other living things. Let us briefly review these normative implications as an example of how more recent ethical thinking might be applied to environmental practice.

Taylor develops four general duties that follow from the attitude of respect for nature. They are the rules of *nonmaleficence, noninterference, fidelity,* and *restitutive justice.*[20] As the term suggests, the duty of nonmaleficence requires that we do no harm to any organism. Taylor understands this as a negative duty. That is, we have the duty to refrain from any act that would harm an organism with a good of its own. We do not, however, have the positive duty to prevent any harms that we are not causing. Nor do we have the duty to reduce suffering or aid the organism in attaining its own good. Finally, like all duties, this requirement applies only to moral agents. For example, except for humans, predatory animals cannot be required to refrain from harming their prey.

The rule of noninterference also establishes negative duties. By this rule, we are required not to interfere with the freedom of individual organisms or, in general, with ecosystems or biotic communities. Because humans can interfere with individual organisms in a variety of ways, a variety of specific duties follows from this general rule. We should neither actively prevent organisms from freely pursuing their good, nor should we act so as to deny them the necessities required to attain that goal. Thus, we should not trap or enslave organisms or do anything that would deny them health or nutrition. The duty of noninterference requires that we "not try to manipulate, control, modify, or 'manage' natural ecosystems or otherwise intervene in their normal functioning."[21] Finally, because this is a negative duty, we have no positive obligation to help such organisms fulfill their telos, *except* where our own actions are the cause of the harm.

Taylor applies the rule of fidelity only to animals that live in the wild. Respect for nature requires that we not deceive or betray wild animals. Most hunting, fishing, and trapping—and much of the enjoyment and challenge of these activities—involve the attempt to deceive and then betray wild animals. As in any case of deception, the deceiver assumes a superiority over the deceived. The deceived, whether an animal or another human, is taken to have a lower worth than the deceiver. Although hunting, fishing, and trapping also typically involve violating the duties of nonmaleficence and noninterference, breaking the rule of fidelity is yet another means of showing disrespect for nature.

The fourth rule, the duty of restitutive justice, requires that humans who harm other living organisms make restitution to those organisms. Justice demands that when a moral subject has been harmed that the agent responsible for that harm make reparations for the harm. In general, the first three duties establish the basic moral relationship between humans and other living organisms. When any of these rules is violated, the rule of restitutive justice requires that the moral balance between the two be restored. Thus, if we destroy an animal's habitat, justice demands that we restore it. If we capture or trap an animal or a plant, justice demands that we return it to its natural environment.

Finally, Taylor argues for a priority relation for these four rules. He believes that the duty of nonmaleficence is our "most fundamental duty to nature." He also believes that with careful attention, we can minimize conflicts involving the other three. However, when conflicts cannot be avoided and when significant good can result without permanent harm, restitutive justice outweighs fidelity, which outweighs noninterference.

Perhaps the biggest challenge to any biocentric ethics arises when human interests conflict with the interests of nonhumans. In many ways, this is the primary test of any environmental philosophy, and it is typically the major motivation behind any attempt to develop an environmental philosophy. What is to be done when important human interests come into conflict with the welfare of nonhuman organisms?

We need to recognize that in order to remain consistent with the fundamental principle of biocentric ethics, any resolution of such conflicts must not privilege human interests. That is, we cannot accept as a solution any decision that grants an in-principle advantage to humans. Any solution to conflict must respect the inherent moral worth of nonhumans.

We thus recognize that many moral conflicts and dilemmas would not arise within an anthropocentric framework. It is only after we acknowledge the inherent worth of other living things that a wide variety of conflicts can arise. Taylor mentions several as examples: filling in a wetland to build a marina, bulldozing a meadow of wildflowers to build a shopping mall, plowing a prairie to plant wheat or corn, and strip-mining a mountainside.

These activities raise moral problems only when we acknowledge that they create significant harm to other living organisms. But how do we resolve these conflicts without automatically favoring humans?

Following a long tradition in liberal political philosophy, Taylor argues for several formal or procedural rules to provide fair and impartial resolution of these conflicts. These rules are (1) self-defense, (2) proportionality, (3) minimum wrong, (4) distributive justice, and (5) restitutive justice.

Self-defense would justify favoring human interests when the conflicting interests of nonhuman organisms threaten or endanger human health or life. Thus, we would be justified in killing an attacking grizzly bear or exterminating an infectious organism or insect. As in the case of human self-defense, this principle holds only as a last resort.

The other four principles come into play when no serious harm to humans is threatened. They all rely on a distinction between *basic* and *nonbasic interests*. The principles of proportionality and minimum wrong govern those cases in which the basic interests of nonhumans conflict with the nonbasic interests of humans. In this case, if the nonbasic human interest is incompatible with the basic interests of nonhumans, the principle of proportionality prohibits us from satisfying the human interests at the expense of the (basic) nonhuman interests. Thus, for example, human interest in killing reptiles to make fashionable shoes and handbags is prohibited, via the principle of proportionality, by the respect for nature.

When nonbasic human interests can be made compatible with the basic interests of nonhumans, even though they threaten or endanger the nonhumans, the principle of minimum wrong sets the conditions for satisfying human interests. Thus, the respect for nature might allow damming a river for a hydroelectric power plant even when this will adversely affect other living things.

The principle of distributive justice sets the conditions for resolving conflicts between the basic interests of humans and nonhumans. In general, fairness demands that burdens be shared equally and that the distribution of benefits and burdens be accomplished impartially.

Finally, restitutive justice demands that restitution be made whenever a resolution of conflict fails to meet the conditions established by the principles of minimum wrong or distributive justice.

7.7 CHALLENGES AND DEVELOPMENTS

Even Taylor's careful defense of biocentric ethics faces serious challenges. First, the emphasis on noninterference as a major normative principle suggests a view of humans and nature that is questionable at best. To say that we ought not "interfere with" nature implies that humans are somehow outside of or distinct from nature: humans are separate from nature and, thus, we should leave natural processes alone. Thus, the claim is that environmental change—or even environmental destruction—is allowable (good?) if it results from natural processes. Change or destruction is wrong if it results from human interference. But surely humans are as much a part of natural processes as any other organism. Thus, the fact that change is brought about by humans should not in itself have any ethical implications.

More important, a number of challenges center on Taylor's emphasis on individual organisms. Inherent worth resides only in individual organisms. We have no *direct* duty to ecosystems, nonliving objects, or species, for example. Thus, although Taylor's biocentrism is nonanthropocentric, it remains individualistic. Several problems follow from this.

First, Taylor's ethics tends to assume an *adversarial* relationship between individuals. By focusing on individuals, each pursuing their own telos, Taylor assumes that conflict and competition are the natural state of life. The challenge for biocentric ethics, on this model, is to find a procedure for resolving these conflicts impartially. We will see other philosophers suggest that a more holistic philosophy would emphasize cooperation and mutual dependencies rather than conflict.

Further, the focus on individuals seems to place Taylor in a serious dilemma. Consider one example. I am planning to dig up a small section of my front yard and replace the lawn with a concrete and brick patio. In the process, I will be destroying countless living things, from the individual blades of grass to millions of microbiotic organisms. Does this action raise a serious moral conflict?

As discussed, Taylor cannot simply grant the human interest a priority without abandoning his biocentric egalitarianism. Thus, he would rely on the distinction between basic and nonbasic interests and the principles of proportionality, minimum wrong, and restitutive justice to resolve this conflict. Ultimately, I will either be allowed to build the patio, or I will not.

If I am not allowed to build the patio, Taylor's ethics may require too much of us. This is more than simply saying that it is counterintuitive. (Taylor argues that we have no reason to reject a conclusion solely because it is counterintuitive.) Rather, Taylor's standard would require a level of attention and care far beyond the abilities of most people. (Should I refrain from often walking across my lawn, lest I create a path and thereby destroy countless blades of grass? Do I really need to provide an ethical justification for eating vegetables?) It is difficult to see how we could ever be justified in doing much of anything if we did treat all nonhuman life-forms as deserving moral consideration.

On the other hand, if I am allowed to build the patio, Taylor must show exactly why such a nonbasic interest as this can override the basic interests of the grass and microorganisms. Clearly, we could never allow the mass killing of humans for the sake of a patio. So, in order to maintain the nonanthropocentrism, we need strong justification for why patio construction is allowed in the case of plants. Taylor seems to suggest that, finally, the principle of restitutive justice comes into play. I can build the patio so long as I "restore the balance of justice between us and them."

Unfortunately, because I cannot restore the balance with those organisms that I have destroyed, this option seems to imply that my duty is to the organism's species. Perhaps I ought to replant some grass elsewhere in my yard.

But, of course, this requires us to abandon the individualism on which Taylor's ethics rests.

In recent years philosopher James Sterba has attempted a revision and defense of the biocentric ethics. Sterba refers to his approach as "biocentric pluralism" to emphasize his attempt to bring ecological wholes such as species and ecosystems into the biocentric perspective. Sterba's biocentric pluralism offers several advances over Taylor's earlier views.[22] Sterba provides a simpler normative argument that seeks to avoid the complexities of Taylor's concern with reacting normative ethical conclusions from factual premises. Sterba claims that his practical principles require neither too much nor too little of humans. Finally, he argues that species and perhaps ecosystems can meaningfully be said to have a good of their own and, hence, can be incorporated into the biocentric perspective.

Sterba's argument can be summarized in five steps.

1. Some object, X, has a good of its own if it can be harmed or benefited.

2. If an object has a good of its own, then it would be wrong to harm it unless we have a good reason for doing so.

3. There are no nonquestion-begging reasons to assume that human interests always override the good of X.

4. Xs have moral standing. That is, Xs are subjects to the same fundamental principles of justice that govern human relationships.

5. Liberal justice, a balancing of liberty and equality, is the most defensible principle of social justice to guide human-nonhuman relationships.

Sterba takes Premise 1 to be a definitional explanation of what it means to have a good of one's own. What fits in for X is taken to be a factual question to be determined by science. Premise 2 is an assumed premise of morality. Premise 3 is to be established by logical argumentation. Statement 4 is claimed to follow from the previous three. Statement 5 is also to be established by philosophical argument.

This argument is an advance over Taylor in that it simplifies the move from objects having a good of their own to the conclusion that we have ethical responsibilities to them. Sterba thinks that we can avoid the complexities of the "biocentric outlook" by recognizing that, unless we have good reason to do otherwise, any object with a good of its own must be left alone in pursuit of that good. Like Taylor, he argues that we have no nonquestion-begging reasons to assume that human interests always trump the goods of other living beings.

Further, stating the argument without reference to "teleological centers of life" makes it more apparent that ecological wholes such as species and perhaps ecosystems count morally. Species can be harmed and benefited in ways that are independent of harms and benefits to individual members of the species (for example, it is good for a species that some members of the species be preyed on by predators). Thus species have a good of their own. Evidence from ecology (as presented in the following chapter) is inconclusive on whether ecosystems have a good of their own. If, in fact, they do, then ecosystems will have moral standing.

Sterba's practical principles differ slightly from Taylor. Rejecting the stricter equality found in Taylor, Sterba argues that liberal justice provides a better framework for all moral relationships, including those between humans and nonhuman living beings. This justice allows aggression against others in self-defense and in order to meet basic needs for preservation. However, humans are not required positive duties of care to the natural world, for doing so would require unreasonable sacrifices and too great a loss of individual liberty. Rather, we have a general obligation to leave objects with a good of their own alone. Left alone, living things will naturally get on with their lives, that is, move toward their own good.

But the major challenge to any biocentric theory remains. Are we justified in attributing a good to all living beings? Clearly some things, Taylor's example was a pile of sand, have no good of their own. Clearly, other things do. Autonomous human beings, who form and pursue their own purposes and goals, surely have independent goods of their own. But do all living things have an independent good? What distinguishes life from random change, such that interference with one is a harm and with the other is not? It seems that unless we retrieve an Aristotelian teleological biology in which living beings naturally move to fulfill some natural end or purpose, it is not obvious that life left alone is good. Some life, those beings with their own purposes for example, qualify, but others may not. The challenge remains for biocentrists to explain and defend the sense that all living things have a good intrinsic to their own life.

7.8 SUMMARY AND CONCLUSIONS

The biocentric approach pushes the bounds of moral standing about as far as they might ever go. All living beings, simply by virtue of being alive, have moral standing. Biocentrists are surely right to focus attention on the value of all living things. But the question is whether the value of life is moral value in the sense of full moral standing or a different, perhaps still anthropocentric, meaning of value. Reflecting on Schweitzer's reverence for life calls to mind the spiritual, symbolic, and aesthetic values discussed by Mark Sagoff in Chapter 3. Perhaps not every object with noninstrumental, intrinsic value should be included in the category of moral standing.

Biocentrists also face the challenge arising from a more ecological point of view. Even in Sterba's revised biocentric pluralism, serious questions remain. It is not at all clear that species or ecosystems can be incorporated into the biocentric theory since neither is alive in any straightforward sense. According to many environmentalists, such ecological wholes should be the primary focus of environmental ethics. We turn to these concerns in the following chapters.

Notes

1. See, for example, E. O. Wilson, "Threats to Biodiversity," *Scientific American* 261 (September 1989): 108–16; E. O. Wilson, "The Current State of Biological Diversity," in *Biodiversity,* ed. E. O. Wilson and Frances Peters (Washington, D.C.: National Academy Press, 1988); and John C. Ryan, "Conserving Biological Diversity," in *State of the World 1992,* ed. Lester Brown (New York: Worldwatch Institute, 1992), pp. 9–26. For estimates of extinction rates besides Wilson, see Dick Bryany, Daniel Neilsen, and Laura Tangley, *The Last Frontier Forests* (Washington, D.C.: World Resources Institute, 1997), and *Global Biodiversity Assessment*, United Nation Environmental Program (New York: Cambridge University Press, 1995). The statement on recovery rates is taken from the work of James Kirchner, University of California—Berkeley press release, March 3, 2000, "New Study Suggests Human Will Not Live Long Enough to See Earth Recover from Mass Extinction."

2. E. O. Wilson, "The Little Things That Run the World," address given at the opening of the invertebrate exhibit, National Zoological Park, Washington, D.C., May 7, 1987. Reprinted in *The Environmental Ethics and Policy Book,* ed. Donald VanDeVeer and Christine Pierce (Belmont, Calif.: Wadsworth, 1994), p. 84.

3. See Christopher Stone, *Earth and Other Ethics: The Case for Moral Pluralism* (New York: Harper and Row, 1987). Moral pluralism is discussed further in the epilogue to *Environmental Ethics.*

4. Perhaps the best philosophical account of the values that support a comprehensive environmental ethics can be found in the writings of Holmes Rolston. See especially *Environmental Ethics* (Philadelphia: Temple University Press, 1988).

5. The philosophical debate over the meaning and legitimacy of instrumental, intrinsic, and inherent value continues. The understanding of instrumental value is relatively trouble free. In what follows, I adopt Susan Armstrong and Richard Botzler's suggestion that an "emerging consensus" is settling on the meaning of intrinsic and inherent value. In this view, intrinsic value is independent of the presence of a valuer. An object has intrinsic value when it has value both in and for itself. Inherent value, on the other hand, requires the presence of a valuer who confers the value on the object. Thus, while it may be valued for its own sake (its value does not come from its usefulness), it does not have value in itself (if there were no one around to value it, it would be without value). For example, children have intrinsic value (they are valued in and for themselves), whereas a family heirloom has inherent value (it is valued for itself and not for its economic worth) but would be valueless were no family around to value it.

If we accept this distinction as meaningful, the major question becomes whether natural objects and nonhuman living beings have intrinsic or inherent value. For the emerging consensus claim, see Susan Armstrong and Richard Botzler, *Environmental Ethics: Divergence and Convergence* (New York: McGraw-Hill, 1993), p. 53. For a defense of intrinsic value, see Holmes Rolston, *Environmental Ethics* (Philadelphia: Temple University Press, 1988). For a defense of inherent value, identified as intrinsic value in a "truncated sense," see J. Baird Callicott, "The Intrinsic Value of Nonhuman Species," in *The Preservation of Species,* ed. Bryan Norton (Princeton, N.J.: Princeton University Press, 1986), ch. 6.

6. The most complete statement of Schweitzer's ethical views is found in his *Civilization and Ethics* (London: A. & C. Black, 1946). His autobiographical *Out of My Life and Thought,* trans. A. B. Lemke (New York: Holt, 1990), is also quite

helpful. James Brabazon's biography, *Albert Schweitzer: A Biography* (New York: Putnam, 1975) is a good secondary source.

7. Schweitzer, *Out of My Life and Thought*, p. 130.

8. Ibid., 130.

9. Ibid., 131.

10. Brabazon, *Albert Schweitzer: A Biography*, p. 257, reports that Schweitzer was willing to kill his pelican when he recognized that its injuries were untreatable. The other anecdotes reported in this paragraph are also from Brabazon.

11. See Kenneth Goodpaster, "From Egoism to Environmentalism," in *Ethics and Problems of the Twenty-First Century*, ed. Kenneth Goodpaster and Kenneth Sayre (Notre Dame, Ind.: University of Notre Dame Press, 1979), pp. 21–35.

12. Of course, people do have moments in which their fundamental attitudes are questioned. Such moments of existential crisis, however, tend to reinforce rather than counter the view that no further justification can be given.

13. Paul Taylor, *Respect for Nature* (Princeton, N.J.: Princeton University Press, 1986), p. 80.

14. Here Taylor uses the phrase "inherent worth" in roughly the same sense that I have been using "intrinsic value." An object with inherent worth possesses a value that is independent of any (other) valuer. It is to be valued both in and for its own sake.

15. Taylor, *Respect for Nature*, pp. 66–67.

16. Ibid., 121–22.

17. For Tom Regan's views on this "naturalistic fallacy," see *The Case For Animal Rights* (Berkeley: University of California Press, 1983), pp. 247–48.

18. Taylor, *Respect for Nature*, p. 75.

19. Taylor, *Respect for Nature*, especially ch. 3, fully develops the biocentric outlook.

20. Ibid., ch. 4, for the full presentation of these duties.

21. Ibid., 175.

22. Sterba's views can be found in "From Biocentric Individualism to Biocentric Pluralism" *Environmental Ethics* vol. 17, pp. 191–207, "A Biocentrist Strikes Back" *Environmental Ethics* vol. 20, pp. 361–376, and "The Environmental Challenge to Traditional Ethics" paper delivered at the American Philosophical Association, Central Division meetings, April 22, 2000 and forthcoming in *Three Challenges to Ethics* (New York: Oxford University Press, 2001).

Discussion Questions

1. We use the word value both as a noun and as a verb. Certain objects are said to possess value and humans value numerous objects. If no humans were around to do the valuing, would anything of value remain?

2. Compose a list of things that you value. Distinguish those things that you value instrumentally from things valued for their own sake. How many different types of value can you think of?

3. Like Aristotle, Taylor suggests that each species has a distinctive nature that can best be identified in terms of a characteristic activity. How else might you distinguish between species?

4. Taylor relies on a distinction between basic and nonbasic interests to mediate conflicting interests. Do you find this distinction helpful? What might some basic human interests be? Nonbasic human interests? Do basic interests always override nonbasic interests?

5. In Taylor's account, does it make sense to attribute interests or goods to a wilderness area, river, or other ecosystems? Can such things be teleological centers of life?

Further Reading

James Brabazon, *Albert Schweitzer: A Biography* (New York: Putnam, 1975), is an excellent biography.

Holmes Rolston, *Environmental Ethics* (Philadelphia: Temple University Press, 1988), as well as other writing by Rolston, offers a well-considered account of the varieties of value at work in environmental ethics.

In addition to the works by E. O. Wilson mentioned in note 1 to this chapter, useful discussions of biodiversity and environmental policy can be found in R. Edward Grumbine, ed., *Environmental Policy and Biodiversity* (Washington, D.C.: Island Press, 1994).

8

Wilderness, Ecology, and Ethics

Fires and Wilderness Management: The Cases of Yellowstone and the Boundary Waters Canoe Area Wilderness

The Greater Yellowstone Area (GYA) encompasses nearly 5 million hectares (approximately 12 million acres) of mostly public land surrounding Yellowstone National Park and Grand Teton National Park. The GYA includes two national wildlife refuges and six national forests in Idaho, Wyoming, and Montana. The summer of 1988 was the driest in Yellowstone's recorded history, with virtually no rain during June, July, and August.

Each year, dozens of fires burn within the GYA. Many result from lightning, and most extinguish naturally after burning little more than an acre or two. But the summer of 1988 was different. Through May and June, rangers routinely allowed numerous small fires to burn, and most soon extinguished naturally. But by mid-July, high winds and continued drought conditions had led to a growing intensity of the fires. By late July, the National Park Service declared all the fires "wildfires" and began a major effort to suppress them. Despite the efforts of nearly 25,000 fire fighters, hundreds of fire-fighting vehicles and airplanes, personnel from the U.S.

Army, Air Force, Marines, and National Guard and more than $120 million, the fires continued to burn out of control throughout August and into September. For nearly two months, Americans watched and read news accounts of the fire as it burned through Yellowstone Park.

Only a snowstorm in September finally brought the fires under control. By that time, nearly 1 million acres inside Yellowstone Park and an additional one-half million acres outside the park had burned. Wild landscapes that had appeared as lush green forest in the spring had become blackened devastated terrain by early fall.

For one hundred years after the creation of Yellowstone National Park in 1872, fire suppression was the guiding policy of wilderness management, both in national parks and national forests. Smokey Bear was the well-known symbol of the effort to fight fires wherever possible. This policy had almost universal support. Timber interests saw it as a means for preserving valuable resources. Recreationists saw it as protecting their varied uses of the land. Preservationists saw it as a means for preserving the natural beauty of the wilderness.

As early as the 1940s, the U.S. Forest Service had begun to use fire as a tool for managing some forests. Through the 1950s and 1960s, the National Park Service experimented with controlled burns in certain areas. But the people charged with managing national forests and parks began to recognize the natural and beneficial function that fires can play within an ecosystem. Fires contribute to biotic diversity and natural plant succession. Seeds of some species, the giant sequoia and the jack pine, for example, can germinate only after exposure to the intense heat of fires. Some animal species, like the Kirtland's warbler, in turn depend on such "fire species" of trees for habitat.[1] Fire can help litter decompose and aid in recycling soil nutrients. Fires also help maintain habitat for larger species and allow access to food sources that sprout after a burn.

By the early 1970s, many parks, including Yellowstone, had adopted a fire policy that would allow certain naturally occurring fires to burn unchecked, as long as they did not threaten lives and property. Between 1972 and 1988, hundreds of these so-called prescribed fires were allowed to burn within Yellowstone Park. (When a fire does not meet these prescriptions, it is designated as a wildfire, and efforts are made to suppress it.) Most prescribed fires extinguish naturally after burning small areas. Most observers considered this prescribed natural burn policy a success.

Two more recent events have challenged those who manage natural wild areas to reexamine policy regarding the use of fire as a management tool. On May 4, 2000, the National Park Service was conducting a prescribed burn to clear underbrush at Bandelier National Monument. High winds quickly whipped it into a wildfire that spread over the town of Los Alamos, New Mexico. The fire burned out of control for over two weeks, burning almost 50,000 acres and destroying 260 homes. Over 25,000 people were required to evacuate their homes. The fire damaged buildings at the Los Alamos Nuclear Weapons Laboratory, birthplace of the atom bomb and now the nation's major nuclear weapons plant. A report conducted by the U.S. Department of Interior criticized the National Park Service for failing to follow guidelines for such controlled burns. However, Interior Secretary Bruce Babbitt reiterated the Department of Interior's commitment to controlled burns as a management tool for wilderness areas. Secretary Babbitt emphasized that prescribed fires are an important management tool. "We have no choice but to manage these forests to get the fuel loads down. We can't abandon this program." Babbitt said that the U.S. forests are healthier and safer as a result of controlled burns. According to Babbitt, Western forests are becoming more "dangerous and explosive" each year because "the natural fire cycle is no longer present. We've used this prescribed fire program for many years. The fire management agencies have successfully reduced the fuel load, reduced the fire hazard, by burning literally millions of acres every year." This policy will face an immediate challenge in managing the Boundary Waters Canoe Area (BWCA) wilderness following a destructive windstorm during the summer of 1999.

On July 4, 1999, a devastating storm moved through the BWCA in northern Minnesota. In a short time, the storm damaged over 400,000 acres of forestland in and around the BWCA. Most trees in a path 30 miles long and 12 miles wide were downed or damaged. The BWCA is a strictly controlled wilderness area in which no motorized vehicles or boats are allowed. Entrance is restricted by a permit system that controls the number of visitors allowed in each day. Travel is by hiking or canoe only. By law, these dead and damaged trees within the wilderness area must be left alone and timber harvesting outside the BWCA in the Superior National Forest is tightly regulated. As a result, millions of dead trees now litter the forest floor. Many observers believe that a major fire throughout the BWCA is inevitable unless significant steps are taken to reduce the buildup of dead timber. Two options have been mentioned as means for doing this: a series of controlled burns within the BWCA to burn off excess deadwood and create firebreaks or allowing motorized vehicles, in the form of chainsaws, bulldozers, and trucks, into the wilderness to harvest the downed trees as lumber.

Beyond the fire issue, BWCA authorities recognize that the postblowdown region will be very different from what existed previously. Many of the trees lost to the storm were red and white pine, some 100 feet tall or more. The most likely species to regenerate will be aspen, a relatively short-lived deciduous tree. It would take many decades, if ever, for a pine-dominated coniferous ecosystem to return. Should the U.S. Forest Service actively replant pine, or should it "let nature takes its course"? What exactly is the natural course of things?

8.1 INTRODUCTION

As described in Chapter 7, biocentric ethics represents a significant departure from traditional ethical thinking in several ways. By making life itself, and not any particular characteristic of living things, the criterion of moral standing, biocentric ethics greatly expands the moral domain while avoiding the moral hierarchy implicit in traditional theories. It, thus, involves a radical shift in ethical thinking by extending moral standing to much of the natural world.

But for many environmentalists, biocentric ethics has not gone far enough in breaking with tradition. Biocentric ethics seems inadequate for addressing a wide variety of environmental issues. According to a variety of approaches that we can identify as *ecocentric*, an adequate environmental ethics must also give serious consideration to nonliving natural objects (for example, rivers and mountains), and it must give due consideration to ecological systems. *Ecological ethics* should be holistic in the sense that ecological wholes, such as ecosystems or species, as well as nonliving natural objects and the relationships that exist among natural objects are seen as deserving ethical consideration. Ecocentric thinkers argue that biocentric approaches literally fail to see the forest for the trees. They claim that environmental concerns for ecosystems and wilderness areas are not the same as a concern for the individual trees, plants, and animals that live within them. Wilderness areas, forests, wetlands, prairies, and lakes are valuable in their own right and deserve moral consideration. According to these critics, biocentric ethics does not or cannot account for the value that we attribute to these ecological wholes. Since ecosystems, species, mountains, rivers, and so forth are not alive in any obvious sense, biocentric approaches seem unable to account for the ethical value that ecocentrists want to attribute to ecological wholes.

Ecocentric ethics owes much to the science of ecology, the study of the interactions of living organisms with each other and with their nonliving environments. *Ecosystems*—forests, wetlands, lakes, grasslands, and deserts—are areas in which a variety of living organisms interact in mutually beneficial ways with their living and nonliving environment. Ecologists seek to understand and explain these systematic interactions and dependencies. Unlike traditional botanists and zoologists, ecologists focus more on interdependencies and relationships than on individual organisms.

Ecocentric philosophies likewise focus more on the ecological communities formed by these interdependencies than on individual organisms. Ecocentric ethics is thus a holistic rather than an individualistic ethics. Ecology plays a major role in each of the ecocentric philosophies examined in the chapters that follow. Each of these philosophies appeals to ecology for help in explaining and defending its conclusions. Unfortunately, challenges arise whenever anyone attempts to use the science of ecology in philosophical and ethical reasoning. First, ecologists do not completely agree on proper scientific methods, models, and conclusions. Ecology has not become a single, unified science. Second, it is unclear what, if any, ethical conclusions can be drawn from scientific observations. It is possible to reason from similar ecological facts to widely different normative conclusions and from different ecological observations to identical normative conclusions. Thus, the relevance of ecology to ethics is always an open question.

This chapter offers a general introduction to some important ecological concepts and the ways in which philosophical implications can be drawn from science. Particular attention will be paid to the ethical and philosophical issues raised by a focus on the value of wilderness areas. As we begin to widen our philosophical and ethical focus to include value questions beyond moral ones, an understanding of the ways in which earlier traditions have thought about and valued the natural world will also prove useful. A good place to start is the various understandings of the term *wilderness*.

Wilderness areas are prominent examples of natural ecosystems, and the preservation of wilderness areas is at the forefront of many environmental disputes. Biocentric approaches seem unable to give direct consideration to wilderness areas. Indeed, any ethical extensionism—arguing for a moral standing for the wilderness, for example—seems unlikely to account for the variety of ways in which we value the wilderness. How we understand the wilderness, how and why we value it, and how we relate to and manage wilderness areas, therefore, are central concerns of ecocentric ethics.

But what principles should guide human interaction with the wilderness? On what ethical basis should we protect the wilderness? Should we actively *manage* the wilderness (if so, how?), or should we be more passive and merely seek to *preserve* or *protect* it? Do we have a responsibility to *restore* wilderness areas that have been developed? If so, what exactly would count as restoration? The Yellowstone fires of 1988 and the resultant controversies regarding fire suppression policy provide a prime example of such debate. Preserving such areas as Yellowstone and the BWCA requires active management—allowing some fires to burn but not others, for example. How should the U.S. Forest Service manage the BWCA after the major blowdown? The postblowdown wilderness area will be very different from the earlier one. Will it be better, worse, or just different? Would a pine ecosystem restored by human activity be better than an aspen-dominated ecosystem or just different?

8.2 THE WILDERNESS IDEAL

The *Wilderness Act of 1964* defines wilderness as those areas "where the earth and its community of life are untrammeled by man, where man himself is a visitor who does not remain." The wilderness denotes an area unspoiled and undisturbed by human activity. The *Wilderness Act of 1964* allowed the federal government to set aside large tracts of public land to protect them from development. Wilderness areas are set aside "for the use and enjoyment of the American people in such a manner as will leave them unimpaired for future use and enjoyment as wilderness."[2] Typically, this means that activities like hiking, camping, nonmotorized boating, and some hunting and fishing are allowed. Commercial activities like mining and timber harvesting and permanent buildings or road construction are prohibited.

The idea of the wilderness is much more complex than it might at first appear. At first glance, a wilderness is much like a river or mountain range. It is a natural object that is just "out there" to be observed. But the *idea* of the wilderness is a much richer concept than this simple example suggests. Wilderness as a natural area set over and against human-inhabited areas such as cities and towns presupposes concepts and values that are far from universal. Indigenous peoples, for example, are unlikely to have a concept of wilderness like the one implied by the Wilderness Act. Agricultural and nomadic people would likely not make as distinct a contrast between inhabited and uninhabited areas as might urban dwellers. There are reasons for thinking that the idea of a wilderness is a relatively modern invention.

Taken literally, few wilderness areas "untrammeled by man" remain on Earth, although many areas where humans are only visitors remain. Humans inhabit much of the globe, and human activity affects the entire earth. The climatic and atmospheric effects of pollution is just one example of human activity that reaches every area of Earth. Most wilderness areas are human constructs in that constant human activity is necessary to preserve and manage them. Thus, even the decision to set aside and preserve a wilderness area involves the active management of the wilderness. A wilderness may be less something that we discover than something that we create. The decision to create, preserve, and manage a wilderness area, therefore, involves ethical questions of how we *should* manage wilderness ecosystems. Should forest fires be suppressed or allowed to burn? Should species be reintroduced to areas in which they once lived? Are these policies for the benefit of humans or to preserve some natural state?

Policy decisions about wilderness management depend greatly on how we conceive of and value the wilderness. Part of this understanding, in the minds of many contemporary observers, can be derived from the science of ecology. Part of this understanding also derives from our own history and culture. As suggested in Chapter 1 a primary role of descriptive ethics is to make explicit the models and metaphors that shape our understanding of the world. This section describes several traditional ways in which recent generations, especially Euro-Americans, have conceived of the wilderness.

As the word sometimes suggests, the wilderness is often taken to refer to a wild or untamed area. In this model, the wilderness is a threat to human survival. It is cruel, harsh, and perilous. This is an ancient view, common to many Judeo-Christian traditions that trace it to biblical discussions of the wilderness.

Both the Old and New Testaments describe the wilderness as a barren and desolate place. In truth, the arid desert surrounding the ancient settlements of the Middle East was an exceptionally inhospitable place. Humans truly were only visitors there because prospects for long-term survival outside a settlement were bleak. But the wilderness also has a deeper symbolic meaning.

The Bible states that Adam and Eve were banished from the Garden of Eden into an "accursed" wilderness that "will grow thorns and thistles for you and none but wild plants for you to eat."[3] Moses later leads his people out of slavery and wanders in the wilderness for forty years before entering the Promised Land. In the New Testament, Jesus enters the wilderness to fast for forty days, only to be tempted by Satan.[4] The symbolism is clear. The wilderness not only is dangerous, but it is also home to the devil. It is the antithesis of Eden and the Promised Land.

The views of other cultures provide an interesting contrast. Nomadic cultures, for example, rely too heavily on the wilderness to consider it an enemy. Chief Luther Standing Bear, an Ogallala Sioux, illustrated this point in his 1933 book.

> We do not think of the great open plains, the beautiful rolling hills, and the winding streams with tangled growth as "wild." Only to the white man was nature a "wilderness" and only to him was the land "infested" with "wild" animals and "savage" people. To us it was tame. . . . Not until the hairy man from the East came and with brutal frenzy heaped injustices upon us and the families we loved was it "wild" for us.[5]

To a large degree, the "hairy man from the East," the European settlers and pioneers, shared the biblical view of the wilderness.

When the *Mayflower* arrived at Plymouth in 1620, the new settlers confronted a "hideous and desolate wilderness," according to William Bradford.[6] Two years later, Michael Wigglesworth described it as:

> A waste and howling wilderness
> Where none inhabited
> But hellish fiends and brutish men
> That devils worshiped.[7]

Time and again, Puritan writing and preaching noted the biblical parallels to the Europeans' experiences. Like the Israelites, they had escaped persecution, only to be led into the wilderness where God would test their faith. The wilderness was indeed the "Devil's den," home to "savages" trapped in "the snare of the Devil," "men transformed into beasts," serving as "slaves of Satan."[8]

This *Puritan model* gave rise to an ambiguous attitude toward the wilderness. On one hand, the wilderness was an area to be avoided and feared. It was the area forsaken by God and home to the devil. Cities and towns were where humans could flourish. Bradford's hideous and desolate wilderness was where they suffered and died.

On the other hand, the wilderness represented an escape from oppression and, if not exactly the Promised Land itself, provided at least a temporary haven in which they could build the Promised Land. The Puritans believed that their faith was being tested in the New England wilderness. The wilderness, after all, was where their God had entered into a covenant with the Israelites. Proof that the Puritans were indeed the new "chosen people" would come from how well they fared in this wilderness. In this way, the wilderness also represented a challenge to be overcome, an enemy to be dominated, and a threat to be conquered.

The Puritan model encouraged an aggressive and even antagonistic attitude toward the wilderness. The wilderness must be tamed. New land must be conquered, and a new Eden must be established. Humans are called to subdue and master the wilderness. The land is developed and improved and its value enhanced when woodlands are cleared, wetlands drained, soil tilled, and permanent settlements established. Like some of the native inhabitants, the Puritans relied on fire as a tool for controlling and conquering the wilderness. Eradication of "pests," "varmints," and "predators" such as wolves, coyote, and bears is a moral imperative that follows from the perspective.

As these European settlers succeeded in this mission, the early Puritan model gave way to a different understanding of the wilderness. The wilderness could now be seen as a potential source for supplying the material resources for building the good life. Once conquered, nature becomes identified with natural resources, and wilderness is simply the undeveloped stockpile of resources. Until it is transformed into resources, the wilderness is a vast wasteland. Once human mastery is assured, the wilderness is less of a threat and more of a promise. We are reminded of John Locke's image (see Chapter 2) of a great unowned frontier being transformed by human labor into productive and valuable property. This *Lockean model* sees the wilderness as given by God to all people in common, waiting for an individual with initiative and ambition to go out and work it and in the process convert it into private personal property.

Thus, the Lockean model sees the wilderness as real estate, a commodity to be owned and used. Its value is a function of the human labor with which it is mixed. No longer something to be feared, the wilderness represents great potential for serving human ends. The wilderness is relatively passive. It is "just there," serving no purposes other than those of its owners. Unowned and, therefore, unused land literally is a wasteland. Unless and until put to human use, it is wasted potential.

It is fair to say that much of the early conservation movement embraced the Lockean model of the wilderness. Gifford Pinchot and other conservationists identified the wilderness with resources and valued it primarily for the commodities it produced. Of course, the Lockean model also was shared by those who opposed the conservation movement. Those who sought to control and exploit the wilderness in pursuit of personal fortune shared the Lockean assumption that the value of the wilderness is a function of human use. They agreed with the conservationists that the wilderness should be controlled and managed for human use. They disagreed over the range of beneficiaries of these resources.

Unlike the Puritan model, the Lockean model would tend to support a fire suppression policy. Although fires could be used to clear land for some uses, forest fires represented a loss of resources and potential. The early conservationists guided the fire suppression policy in national forests and national parks. Smokey Bear was a product of the conservation movement. Conservationists could also use the Lockean model to justify eradication of predators because they competed with humans for "game" and eliminating them would increase the resources available for human use.

A third model of the wilderness, influential among many people in the environmental movement, can also be traced to early European-American roots. The *romantic model* views the wilderness as a symbol of innocence and purity. In this model, the wilderness is the last remaining area of unspoiled and uncorrupted nature. In contrast to the Puritan model, the romantic model identifies the wilderness with Paradise, the Garden of Eden. This is the place to which humans can turn to escape the corrupting influences of civilization. Where the Puritans saw threats and satanic temptations, the romantic sees a sacred purity. Where the Puritans saw the city as home to human flourishing, the romantics see the city as the genuine wasteland.

The philosophical roots of this view can be found in Jean-Jacques Rousseau and in the Americans Ralph Waldo Emerson and Henry David Thoreau. Like Locke, Rousseau spoke in general terms about a "state of nature" that contrasted with the state of life within a society. For Rousseau, nature represented what was genuine, authentic, and virtuous about human existence. Society imposes artificial desires, selfishness, and inequality on human life. Although he did not propose a return to nature, Rousseau did believe that education and politics should be guided by principles derived from an understanding of the natural and intrinsic goodness of human beings. He proposed as a model a life lived in harmony with nature, characterized by self-sufficiency, simplicity of desires, independence from culture and technology, and tranquility. In this view, the innate goodness of human nature is inseparable from the innate goodness of nature itself, a nature Rousseau often identified with the unspoiled wilderness of the Swiss Alps.

But it was the writings of Emerson and especially of Thoreau that had the earliest philosophical influence on the romantic view of the wilderness. Emerson was influenced by the European romantic movement of the eighteenth and nineteenth centuries. This outlook rejected scientific empiricism and rational analysis as the primary modes for understanding nature. The world of our ordinary experience, the world observed and analyzed by science, is largely a product of human creation and cultural conventions. We see and experience what we are taught to see and experience by our culture. At best, that world only mirrors a deeper reality, a reality unconditioned by human beliefs and values. True understanding comes only when we grasp this deeper or "transcendent" reality.

The American philosophical movement associated with European romanticism is called "New England transcendentalism." Transcendentalists, of whom Emerson and Thoreau are the best known, held that we grasp this deeper reality not by scientific and technological analysis but through intuition and imagination and through poetry and literature. Unspoiled by human activity, the wilderness is the most authentic instance of transcendent reality. It is the purest example of God's creation. The wilderness represents a retreat from the corrupting influences of civilization. The wilderness is the environment in which humans may attain their closest contact with the highest truths and spiritual excellence.

Thus, Thoreau retreats to his cabin on Walden Pond. Walking in the wilderness had a tonic effect on his spirit, where "my nerves are steadied, my senses and my mind do their office." The wilderness provides the opportunity to "settle ourselves, and work and wedge our feet downward through the mud and slush of opinion, and prejudice, and tradition, and delusion . . . till we come to a hard bottom and rocks in place, which we call *reality*."[9]

Perhaps nowhere is this romantic vision of the American frontier more fully observed than in James Fenimore Cooper's "Leatherstocking Tales." In a series of novels beginning with *The Pioneers* and followed by *The Last of the Mohicans, The Prairie, The Pathfinder,* and *The Deerslayer,* Cooper traced the life of Natty Bumpo. Natty—known variously as the Deerslayer, Hawkeye, and Leatherstocking—was the ideal romantic hero. He was raised among the Native Americans of upstate New York and from them learned the ways of the wilderness. He was a simple man, innocent yet wise, honorable, forthright, and virtuous. He was totally without pretense or any of the other vices conditioned by social life. He was at home in the wilderness, living in harmony with it.

As Natty's life unfolded through these novels, he was continuously being pushed farther westward by advancing civilization. He lived always on the border between civilization and the wilderness, a border located in central New York early in his life and on the Great Plains by the end of his life. From this perspective, we can see how the demands and expectations of society turn natural innocence and virtue into greed, destructiveness, and vice. With Natty, we lament the loss of wilderness and with it the loss of a simpler life of authenticity and integrity.

8.3 THE WILDERNESS "MYTH": THE CONTEMPORARY DEBATE

These various models for understanding and valuing the wilderness have had a significant influence on contemporary environmentalism. Obviously, Pinchot's conservationism and its view of the wilderness as a vast warehouse of natural resources has greatly influenced much of twentieth century environmental policy. But the romantic model has had, in all likelihood, a more pervasive and pivotal influence on contemporary environmentalism. As early as the mid-1800s, the romantic appreciation of the wilderness and the corollary regret over its destruction led to calls for the preservation of wilderness areas. Thus, the lines between conservationists and preservationists described in Chapter 3 were drawn six decades before the public debates over Hetch Hetchy. During the first decades of the nineteenth century, John James Audubon, for whom the Audubon Society is named, mourned the "destruction of the forest." He witnessed the "woods fast disappearing under the axe" and concluded that the "greedy mills told the sad tale, that in a century the noble forests should exist no more."[10] In an 1858 essay, Thoreau explicitly called for the creation of wilderness preserves. "Why should not we have . . . our national preserves . . . in which the bear and the panther, and some even of the hunter race, may still exist and not be 'civilized off the face of the earth'—our forests . . . not for idle sport or food, but for inspiration and for our own true recreation?"[11]

This transcendentalist conviction that wilderness areas could be the source of inspiration if not divine revelation was shared by perhaps the most influential preservationist, John Muir. Muir's writing and organizing contributed significantly to the creation of national and state parks and wilderness preserves. Although the earliest parks like Yellowstone were not established solely for preservationist reasons, Muir's defense of the wilderness clearly underlies much of the contemporary understanding of parks and preserves. To a large extent, this defense is based on the romantic wilderness model as described by Emerson and Thoreau.

If this romantic model of the wilderness underlies many environmental values, it is important to proceed cautiously. We need to be clear about how much this model is based on an accurate description of wilderness areas. We also need to be clear in articulating exactly where the value of wilderness areas lies. Finally, we need to be clear about the reasoning that leads us from a description of wilderness to value-based ethical and policy prescriptions.

Does the romantic model provide an accurate description of wilderness areas? Certainly, many wilderness areas match the beautiful and awe-inspiring images captured by romantic observers. We need only compare the scenic beauty of Glacier National Park with the urban decay of many industrial cities or the tackiness of suburban strip malls to recognize the attractiveness of the romantic model. Nevertheless, the model is not without problems. In recent years many observers, most of whom are sympathetic to the environmental movement, have challenged this "received view" of the wilderness.[12] These critics claim that this view of the wilderness is seriously flawed on scientific, historical, and ethical grounds. A flawed understanding of wilderness, they argue, can lead to misguided and dangerous environmental policies.

On first consideration, the claim that the wilderness is a "myth" might seem bizarre. The wilderness is a place, a natural object. It is "out there," a part of nature. How can a natural place be a myth?

The new critics of this received view of wilderness argue that "wilderness" is a concept best understood within a particular historical and cultural context. Environmental historian William Cronon identifies two primary sources for this idea.[13] Cronon claims that the eighteenth and nineteenth century

European-American concept of the sublime, a concept central to romanticism, and the particularly American notion of the frontier go a long way toward explaining the modern understanding of the wilderness. For the romantics, a sublime experience was that rare opportunity on this earth to "glimpse the face of God." The sublime implied a sacred, spiritual, otherworldly experience. Such experiences were most likely to be had in situations away from human contrivances and artifacts, mostly likely to occur in places where one was overwhelmed by the recognition of one's own mortality and insignificance. Such magnificent places as Yellowstone, Yosemite, and the Grand Canyon come to mind as paradigm cases of sublime environments.

The particularly American experience of the frontier also contributed to the creation of the wilderness myth. The frontier myth of the rugged individual, that independent, creative man of integrity who tested himself against nature, was a powerful force in shaping the American self-image. But as historian Frederick Jackson Turner wrote at the turn of the twentieth century, that frontier was over. It was no accident, according to Cronon, that a culture seeking to hang on to this powerful image would seek to protect the few remaining undeveloped wild areas within its borders.[14]

What are we to make of such claims? It would appear that a society that does not make as sharp a distinction between nature and culture and one for whom individualism, geographical expansion, and conquest played a small role would be a society for whom the idea of preserving a wilderness area from human encroachment would mean little.

While historical explanations of the origins of the idea of wilderness can situate this concept in a historical context, they do not show that the concept is misguided or mistaken. Defenders of wilderness preservation can accept the historical explanation of how the idea developed but continue to argue that wilderness areas deserve strong protection from human development. The new critics of the wilderness idea, while often defenders of wilderness protection themselves, doubt that the traditional understanding of the wilderness can provide sufficient rationale for its protection. Their criticisms of the wilderness *idea* fall into three general categories. Critics charge that the received view of the wilderness is factually and scientifically unsound, that it is ethically suspect, and that it is likely to have unacceptable political and practical implications.

The received view of the wilderness may in fact be an inaccurate model of the world. First, it has a tendency to view the unspoiled wilderness as a relatively benign and temperate place. Many romantic landscape portraits suggest a lush green forest with open meadows, no underbrush, spectacular sunsets, plentiful sources of food and shelter, docile animals, and temperate climate. In reality, of course, the wilderness can be a harsh place. Deserts, Arctic tundra, and rain forests are not at all like the romanticized image of nature that a person forms while walking around Walden Pond. Even the relatively welcoming areas within national parks and forests can be quite inhospitable places in the absence of modern conveniences or within the depth of

winter. All too often, we appreciate the sublime wilderness only from a perspective distant and apart from nature—standing on a ridge looking down on
the Grand Canyon, for example, rather than on the canyon floor on a dusty,
hot summer day.

Further, the received view can encourage thinking that might be called
"pre-Darwinian." This model can see humans as separate from nature, perhaps drawing inspiration from it but nevertheless radically different from it.
The human spirit is "transcendent," and although unspoiled nature is our
closest contact with transcendent reality, it remains part of a lower physical
reality. Many ecocentric ethics stress the Darwinian understanding that
humans are much a part of nature, neither transcendent to nor radically different from it. From that perspective, acceptance of a dualism ("man and
nature") can encourage moral hierarchies ("man above nature") and conflict
("man against nature").

The received view also has a tendency to identify the wilderness with an
idealized image as it existed at one particular point in time. For example,
North American and Australian environmentalists sometimes romanticize
the land before the arrival of the first European settlers. But many areas "discovered" by the Europeans were of course much used by the native inhabitants. Large human populations were already living in these forests and
grasslands when the first Europeans arrived. Thus, this view has more than a
small amount of cultural bias, if not racism, from systematically ignoring or
distorting that fact.[15]

Finally, the received view is inclined to see the wilderness as a static
unchanging place. The suggestion is that if we simply leave it alone, the
wilderness will be preserved in its natural unspoiled state. This view is
expressed by George Perkins Marsh, a nineteenth century environmentalist,
whose writings influenced both conservationists and preservationists. In his
1864 book *Man and Nature*, Marsh claimed,

> In countries untrodden by man, the proportions and relative positions of land
> and water, the atmospheric precipitation and evaporation, the thermometric
> mean, and the distribution of vegetable and animal life, are subject to change
> only from geologic influences so slow in their operation that the geographical
> conditions may be regarded as constant and immutable.[16]

But this assumption has some problems. Few areas on Earth are unaffected
by human activity. Even the decision to protect an area as a wilderness preserve makes the wilderness dependent on human actions. But more to the
point, as the controversies over the Yellowstone fires imply, the image of an
unspoiled "constant and immutable" wilderness is incompatible with the ecological reality of natural processes. Does the commitment to preserving
Yellowstone as a wilderness area require that we allow it to be devastated by
a fire started by natural events? Lightning fires occur by the dozens every
year in Yellowstone. Yet, a charred, blackened, treeless landscape might not be

the sublime and romantic wilderness envisioned by many environmentalists. But to prevent this from happening and, therefore, to "preserve" the wilderness would require substantial human interference with nature. On the other hand, allowing natural processes to unfold may result in a wilderness unlikely to inspire the sort of unity with a transcendent reality suggested by the romantic images of Yosemite and Yellowstone.

Imagine, for example, that you sought to preserve the Boundary Waters Canoe Area wilderness of northern Minnesota in its natural state. What would that look like? Are snowmobiles and canoes part of this natural state? Are Native Americans? Would hunting, fishing, and rice harvesting by native peoples be consistent with an unspoiled wilderness? Should Native Americans be allowed to pursue these traditional activities only in the traditional manner, or would they be allowed to use motorized boats? Is the ideal an image of what this area was like before Europeans arrived? Should we seek to reinstate the tundra that characterized this area many centuries ago? Perhaps its natural state is as it was during the last ice age. Is its natural state the coniferous forest of pine, cedar, and spruce, or is it the deciduous forests of aspen and birch that will likely flourish after the July 4, 1999 blowdown? Questions like these challenge the view of nature as constant and immutable.

Many contemporary ecologists reject the view of an unspoiled and unchanging nature. The wilderness must be understood as more dynamic than static. Change and evolution are often the norm, and uniformity and constancy are the exception. Ecologist Daniel Botkin makes this point in *Discordant Harmonies* (1990).

> George Perkins Marsh's idea of nature as undisturbed by human influence is the one generally advocated; this point of view is dominant in textbooks on ecology and in the popular environmental literature. Perhaps even more significant, this idea of nature forms the foundation of twentieth-century scientific theory about populations and ecosystems. . . . Until the past few years, the predominant theories in ecology either presumed or had as a necessary consequence a very strict concept of a highly structured, ordered, and regulated, steady-state ecological system. Scientists know now that this view is wrong at local and regional levels—whether for the condor and whooping crane, or for the farm and the forest woodlot—that is, at the levels of populations and ecosystems. Change now appears to be intrinsic and natural at many scales of time and space in the biosphere. . . . In at least some cases these changes are necessary for the persistence of life, because life is adapted to them and depends on them.[17]

The challenge for an ecocentric approach is to develop a coherent philosophical ethics that is consistent with ecology's emphasis on biotic wholes and yet recognizes that change is as normal as constancy. Thus, we need an explanation of the relationship between parts and the whole and an explanation of the dynamics of change that govern this whole. Again, any ethics that takes ecology seriously must provide a philosophically adequate account of these topics.

Critics also suggest that the received view can encourage an ethnocentric perspective that is ethically suspect. As mentioned previously, this view often ignores the native people who populated the wilderness before white settlers and colonialists arrived. Once a wilderness is set aside to be preserved, traditional indigenous activities such as hunting and food gathering may no longer be allowed. Such a perspective marginalizes native peoples not only to the point where they can be ignored, but it also has reinforced policies that have lead to the dispossession and worse destruction of the people and their cultures.[18]

Finally, according to critics, the received view can have undesirable political consequences. If environmentalists base their defense of wilderness protection on a faulty understanding of the wilderness, then there is a danger that the rationale will no longer convince when those faults are exposed. If wilderness areas are "untrodden by man" and if few such areas exist, then the wilderness preservation movement is pursuing an impossible, albeit perhaps, noble dream. This exact argument was used, for example, during debates about the original founding of the BWCA wilderness. Wilderness advocates sought to designate over one million acres in Northern Minnesota as a wilderness area. Critics pointed to the homes, cabins, and fishing camps located within the proposed boundary. If a wilderness is an area "where man is a visitor who does not remain" and if there are long-time residents in this area, then it follows that this area is not a wilderness.

Of course, defenders of the wilderness idea have responses to these challenges. Holmes Rolston, for example, argues that such criticisms can gloss over important differences between the wilderness and inhabited regions and between nature and culture.[19] While humans are part of the natural world, the extent and rate of change due to human activities is significantly different from natural change. This is particularly true of modern, technological societies with their bulldozers, chainsaws, and machinery. Even when natural change is dramatic and extensive as with the BWCA blowdown, it is still significantly different from human change. Human change is intentional and purposive. Natural change has its own history and causes. The BWCA storm is different—scientifically, historically, biologically, and aesthetically—from a comparably sized clear-cut. Further, even though native peoples populated much of the Americas and Australia before European settlers arrived, the scale and type of habitation changed noticeable with the arrival of European culture. Even though native peoples had complex cultures, they did not have the technology and machinery that could destroy and disrupt entire ecosystems. To say that humans are a part of nature should not imply that all human activities are equally compatible with natural processes. Critics of the wilderness idea are simply not discriminating enough in distinguishing between wild nature and human culture. Defenders claim that there is much to the idea of wilderness that justifies protecting wilderness areas from further human manipulation and habitation.

What are we to make of this debate? Two editors of a major anthology on the wilderness debate, J. Baird Callicott and Michael Nelson, conclude that "the received wilderness idea has been mortally wounded by the withering critique to which it has been lately subjected." Nevertheless, they believe that the wilderness idea is too important to be abandoned. Instead, we must look to a reformed idea of wilderness that can continue to guide environmental policy.[20] These editors offer two alternatives to this received view.

One alternative de-emphasizes the human-centered aspects of the received view. Much of the rationale for the received view was connected to human values, often as a resource reserve but also for aesthetic, spiritual, and recreational values. Instead, we might focus on the nonhuman values associated with wild areas, particularly their value as habitat for other, often rare and endangered, life-forms. Such "biodiversity reserves" should have a valued place as a refuge for diverse life-forms in a world of increasing human population. This alternative understanding can meet the challenges raised against the received view. They are scientifically defensible, as the science of conservation biology can provide solid ground for identifying and managing wilderness as habitat. They are also compatible with some human uses, especially the sustainable lifestyles of traditional cultures. They would also broaden our understanding of wild areas by focusing on biodiversity and habitat rather than scenery and recreation. Thus, biodiversity reserves are compatible with the nature-culture distinction that Rolston, for example, defends.

Alternatively, we might reconceive wilderness areas are providing opportunities for humans to live within a natural, sustainable, and symbiotic relationship with wild nature. The preservation of a wilderness area provides humans with their only and perhaps last opportunity to live, learn, or relearn to live in harmony with the natural world. However this debate develops, it seems that a romantic and simple understanding of "the" wilderness is no longer an valid option for environmental policy or ethics.

8.4 FROM ECOLOGY TO PHILOSOPHY

Wilderness areas were examined as a paradigm case of the importance of ecological concepts for environmental ethics. The moral standing debates examined in Chapters 4 through 7 lacked the ecological perspective that many believe lies at the heart of environmental ethics. A central notion for understanding ecocentric ethics is the nature and implications of the biological science of ecology. Because many environmentalists and all of the ecocentric approaches to environmental philosophy that will be examined in the remaining chapters appeal to ecology to explain or justify their conclusions, we must be familiar with some of the models that have guided ecological research. Not only do philosophers disagree about the lessons to be drawn from ecology, but the ecological models of nature from which these lessons are drawn vary widely.

As a distinct science, ecology is little more than one hundred years old. The first use of the term *ecology* is usually attributed to the German biologist

Ernst Haeckel in the 1860s. Haeckel combined two Greek words: *oikos* meaning "household" or "home" and *logos* meaning "study of." Ecology is the science that studies living organisms in their home or environment. (*Economics* has similar Greek roots: *oikos* plus *nomos* meaning the "rules of the household.")

One of the earliest models to guide ecological science was the *organic model*. In this view, individual species were related to their environment as organs were related to the body. Just as an organism grows through developmental stages toward a mature level, so too do ecological "households" grow, develop, and mature. Ecological environments can, therefore, be described as healthy, diseased, young, mature, and the like, according to a normal and natural developmental standard. Thus, this model explains the parts-to-whole relationship in terms of an organism and the nature of change in terms of development or maturity.

This model provides an attractive foundation for many environmental policy recommendations and ethical conclusions. If the natural world goes through a normal and natural developmental process that has evolved over millions of years, we at least ought to proceed cautiously when we interfere with it. With reasoning that is reminiscent of the Aristotelian tradition, we might argue that because ecological systems have a natural telos that we can determine in a scientifically objective manner what is good and proper for that system. Using this organic model as a guide, some environmentalists reason from the objective facts of ecology to policy and ethical conclusions. Just as we speak of the health and well-being of individual organisms, we can speak of the health and well-being of ecosystems.

This organic model appears in the pioneering work of two late nineteenth century American ecologists, Henry Cowles and Frederick Clements. These scientists focused their research on the process of plant succession within a particular geographical area. Working from the University of Chicago, Cowles studied the plant succession along the sand dunes of Lake Michigan. He found that in moving away from the shore, plants are replaced by other species in a determinate and well-defined progression. Thus, the ecologist could describe the normal or natural sequence of plant succession at any given location along the shore.

At the University of Nebraska, Frederick Clements was pursuing similar research on the prairies and grasslands of the western plains. Clements was also taken with the dynamic process of biological change that occurs within a particular habitat. He recognized that through time various species are introduced into an area and become increasingly prevalent before eventually declining and disappearing. But Clements denied that this plant succession is random or arbitrary. He believed that for any given location and climate plant succession develops toward a stable and relatively permanent population, what came to be called the "climax community." Thus, for any particular location or habitat, ecologists could determine the specific climax community that would be most at home in this area. This community could itself be thought of as a "superorganism," which provides the end point or telos for any given location.

In this organic model, the ecologist is like a physician. Just as the physician studies anatomy and physiology to determine the normal and proper function of the body, the ecologist studies a habitat—temperature range, rainfall, soil conditions, and so forth—to determine the normal and proper functioning of that area. The ecologist can then diagnose problems and prescribe treatment to ensure a healthy and balanced organism.

For Clements, this climax community can be understood as itself a "complex organism." It is

> of a higher order than an individual geranium, robin or chimpanzee. . . . Like them it is a unified mechanism in which the whole is greater than a sum of its parts and hence it constitutes a new kind of organic being with novel properties.[21]

Later, Clements claimed that

> the unit of vegetation, the climax formation, is an organic entity. As an organism, the formation arises, grows, matures, and dies. . . . The climax formation is an adult organism, the fully developed community, of which all initial and medial stages are but stages of development. Succession is the process of the reproduction of a formation.[22]

According to the organic model, ecosystems strive toward a natural equilibrium, a stable and unified state of balance and harmony. For environmentalists eager to prevent destruction of wilderness areas, the organic model can prove helpful. It provides a seemingly scientific basis for identifying and diagnosing problems and offering advice for solving environmental problems. Not surprisingly, this advice typically faults human intervention and defends preservationist policies.

By the early twentieth century, the organic model had begun to fall out of favor among ecologists. Many ecologists came to believe that the organic model is mistaken on both scientific and philosophical grounds. Natural biotic communities do not always develop toward some one single organic whole. Ecologists began to see that the interaction among species, among plants and animals, and among the biotic and abiotic elements—soil, nutrients, and climate—is more complex and variable than the organic model suggests. The type of unity and stability observed by Clements and Cowles might be true in some locales and over the short term, but it is not true for other locales and over the long term. The organic model also tends to treat the abiotic elements of a habitat as simply the location or the passive environment in which the superorganism grows and lives. Instead, critics wanted to emphasize how this abiotic environment plays a more active role in the functioning of ecological processes.

In the mid-1930s, British ecologist Arthur Tansley introduced the concept that would replace the organic model in mainstream ecological thinking. In a

1935 article, Tansley defends the concept of an ecosystem as a more appropriate model for ecological research.

> But the more fundamental conception is, as it seems to me, the whole *system* (in the sense of physics), including not only the organisms-complex, but also the whole complex of physical factors forming what we call the environment of the biome—the habitat factors in the widest sense.
>
> It is the systems so formed which, from the point of view of the ecologist, are the basic units of nature on the face of the earth.
>
> These *ecosystems*, as we may call them, are of the most various kinds and sizes. They form one category of the multitudinous physical systems of the universe, which range from the universe as a whole down to the atom.[23]

The concept of an ecosystem remains a central scientific concept to this day.

Tansley was seeking to establish ecology as a legitimate scientific discipline. Talk of biotic communities as superorganisms with a life of their own struck many as unscientific and too metaphorical. Tansley wanted to keep ecology connected with the more legitimate physical sciences by replacing the language of complex organisms with the language of physical systems. In this view, ecosystems are no more mysterious than any other physical system and can be understood in the same terms and with the same categories used to describe other physical systems ranging from atoms to the solar system.

The concept of an ecosystem has several advantages over the organic concept. First, it eliminates any reference to a superorganism or complex organism, which implies an independent being that is alive. In the 1930s, these ideas seemed to be based more on philosophical or metaphorical thinking than on careful scientific observation. Second, the system concept is well grounded in more mainstream science with analogues in physics, chemistry, and mathematics. Third, the ecosystem concept is open to the important role that abiotic elements play in ecological processes. These elements contribute much to the structure and function of ecological wholes. This concept unites the physiochemical processes of the abiotic elements with the biological processes of the living elements. Finally, the ecosystem concept preserves the key ecological idea that ecological wholes are a fundamental part of nature. The individualism that characterizes much of zoology and botany cannot tell the entire story of the biological sciences. Ecology contributes by observing and explaining the integration, connections, and dependencies within and among ecological wholes. The ecosystem concept can be used to explain that nature is not reducible to a collection of independent and isolated parts. Nevertheless, this whole is not itself a being or organism with an independent life but simply a collection of living and nonliving elements organized in a determinate way.

Beginning with Tansley, ecologists began to focus on the structure and function of ecosystems. A system's structure would refer to how the many parts are related. A key concept introduced with the ecosystem idea was the notion of a "feedback loop." Elements within an ecosystem are related not simply in linear and causal ways but in more complex ways characterized as feedback loops. Essentially, this means that the elements within a system not only are affected by other elements, but they in turn also produce effects on other elements in a dynamic network of interconnections. This feedback is not random but works to maintain a balance or equilibrium within the entire system. The standard example of a feedback loop is the thermostat on a home heating system. Falling room temperature triggers a reaction by the thermostat, which in turn changes the room temperature by turning on the heating system. The change in room temperature affects the thermostat, which shuts off the heating system until, yet again, room temperature falls and the cycle begins anew.

Thus, this approach holds that nature is organized into ecosystems—grasslands, lakes, prairies, and forests—that are structured in such a way that through the normal functioning of the individual members the systems maintain a relatively stable equilibrium, much like a heating system maintains room temperature. Both the structure—the network of relationships—and the function—the activities of feedback loops working to maintain an equilibrium—can be explained in scientific and mathematical terms. Thus, the holism of ecology is incorporated in the prevailing physical scientific paradigm.

More specifically, the structure of ecosystems can be explained in terms of the feeding relationships among species within the ecosystem. The network of relationships within an ecosystem is a network of food chains. Species are located at different "trophic levels" (from the Greek work *trophikos* meaning "nourishment") along the network that corresponds to what they eat and what eats them. We can further specify the activity among the trophic levels in terms of the energy and biochemical nutrients exchanged by them. In this way, ecology is further tied to the physical sciences.

By the mid-twentieth century, the ecosystem had become the standard model for ecological science. The idea of an ecosystem—a structured and identifiable whole that acts to maintain a reasonably unified and stable equilibrium—became an important influence for many environmentalists. We can further identify two strands within this tradition that might suggest different philosophical and ethical implications. We can call one the "community model" and the other the "energy model."

According to the community model, nature is understood as a community or society in which parts are related to the whole as citizens are related to a community or as individuals are related to their family. Change is viewed less as development or growth and more in terms of food exchanges. Members of a community fill different roles or "professions" that contribute to the overall functioning of the community. In the community model, ecology truly does study nature's household.

Some early defenders of the community model were motivated by a desire to refute the Darwinian (and, to them, irreligious) emphasis on competition and conflict among species.[24] Nature is designed as a household, with each member cooperating and contributing to the whole. Many of these defenders were more comfortable identifying their project with a phrase older than ecology. Studying nature's household is to study "nature's economy."

One of the most influential and respected scientists associated with the community model was the English zoologist Charles Elton. Elton described his zoology as "the sociology and economics of animals." His goal was to present a description of nature as an integrated and mutually dependent economy.

Elton's community model, therefore, was a *functional* model: individual members are identified by the food function that they perform in the system. The system is seen in economic terms. Some members function as producers, and some members function as consumers. The commodity is food, and ecological communities can be described as "food chains" in which individual members fill various occupations. The laws of ecology, thus, describe the processes of producing, distributing, and consuming food. Accordingly, an individual species' function or role within a food chain—its ecological *niche*, in Elton's terms—is determined by what it eats and what eats it.

The idea of a food chain is perhaps the most familiar concept of the community model. Some organisms, called "producers," manufacture their food by producing organic compounds (sugars, starches, and cellulose) from inorganic molecules (carbon dioxide and water) and energy. Photosynthesis is the primary process through which producers manufacture food.

Other organisms, called "consumers," depend on producers directly or indirectly for their food source. Herbivores or primary consumers feed directly and exclusively on plants (producers). Carnivores feed either on plant-eating animals (called "secondary consumers") or on other animal-eating animals (called "tertiary consumers"). Omnivores such as pigs, rats, and humans eat plants and animals.

At the far end of the food chain, decomposers (mostly fungi and bacteria) feed on dead organic material, breaking it down into simpler inorganic molecules. The inorganic molecules can again be used by producers, whereas the decomposers are in turn eaten by worms, insects, and other organisms.

Although this community model continues to influence both ecologists and others, it competes with a less metaphorical and anthropomorphic version. Consistent with Tansley's desire to legitimize ecology by connecting it with the physical sciences, some ecologists de-emphasize such qualitative terms as food, producers, consumers, communities, and occupations and replace them with the seemingly more objective language of ecosystems and energy.

In this *energy model*, the focus of ecological research is on the ecosystem as an energy system or circuit. Just as the physicist studies the flow of energy through a physical system, the ecologist studies the flow of energy through an ecosystem. The language of a food chain is replaced with the mathematically more precise language of chemistry and physics. The ecosystem appears as just another physical, mechanical system.

Further, the energy model breaks down the distinction between living (biotic) and nonliving (abiotic) components of the system. The abiotic components like solar energy, temperature, water, chemical molecules, and the like are equally important elements in the system. We can trace the flow of energy through an ecosystem in a way that parallels the flow of food through the food chain but without using economic or household metaphors. Photosynthesis is the process through which solar energy breaks the chemical bonds of carbon dioxide and water molecules, forming new molecules of carbohydrates and oxygen. Respiration transforms carbohydrates and oxygen back into carbon dioxide, water, and energy. The energy released in this process powers the chemical and physical processes of life, growth, reproduction, and so forth. Photosynthesis and respiration are the principles of the carbon and oxygen cycles in ecosystems.

Living organisms also need nitrogen, which provides the chemical basis of proteins, DNA, and other essential molecules. Nitrogen can also be traced through an ecological cycle. Atmospheric nitrogen, which makes up 78 percent of the atmosphere, is converted into water-soluble nitrate ions by various biological and physical processes. Bacteria living in the soil and in the roots of various plants, algae living in water, and even lightning contribute to this conversion. Plants in turn convert nitrates obtained from the soil to the more complex nitrogen-based molecules like proteins and DNA. Animals obtain the nitrogen-based molecules that they need by eating plants or other animals. Finally, when plants and animals die, decomposers eventually break these nitrogen molecules back down into nitrogen gas and nitrate ions. Thus, the cycle begins again.

Because the carbon, oxygen, and nitrogen cycles—as well as a similar cycle for phosphorus and the more familiar water cycle—are all ultimately driven by solar energy, ecologists can account for ecosystems in terms of the energy that flows through various chemical, biological, and climatic cycles.[25]

The focus on "community" or "energy" is more a matter of emphasis within the ecosystem model than the separate models. Obviously, not just any energy system is an ecosystem. The energy cycles of interest to the ecologist are cycles that support life and are a part of life cycles. Nevertheless, the different emphases can suggest different normative conclusions.

For the most part, all the ecological research mentioned to this point shares a common assumption. Natural ecosystems tend toward a point of relative stability or equilibrium. When the system is disturbed, natural forces work to return to a point of equilibrium. A system in equilibrium tends to resist change and stay in equilibrium. Recently, however, some ecologists have challenged this conclusion, arguing instead that natural systems are more chaotic than previously thought.[26] This view suggests that ecosystems are constantly changing and perhaps more important that this change occurs without direction or any sense of "development." Influenced by chaos theory in mathematics and science and emphasizing the complex interconnections within ecosystems, this view holds that even small random changes within an ecosystem can have major and unpredictable results. Ultimately, the chaos model denies that any balance or long-term equilibrium exists within natural systems.

8.5 FROM ECOLOGY TO ETHICS

When we consider the ethical and policy implications that many environmentalists wish to draw from ecology, we can see the relevance of the different models. For people interested in bringing holism into the ethical domain,
the organic model offers an intriguing option. The organic model suggests
that ecosystems are or at least can be understood as independent living organisms. Thus, we can reason to evaluative conclusions concerning ecosystems
with the same scientific confidence that we use in making, for example, medical judgments. These value judgments—healthy, diseased, immature, and
developed—are particularly useful if we are seeking to restore an ecosystem,
preserve it in its natural form, or manage it for sustainable yields. The organic
model would also be useful for those who want to argue for moral standing
for ecosystems. If the ecosystem is in fact an organism, it might well possess
minimal criteria for moral standing.

In recent years, some observers, led by the British scientist James Lovelock
and American biologist Lynn Margulis, have suggested that the earth itself
can be understood as a living organism.[27] Much of Lovelock's writing uses
the ecosystemic concepts of feedback loops and equilibrium, but by giving the
entire system a name, *Gaia* (after the Greek goddess of the earth), this view
suggests a sympathy for the organic model. Lovelock and other defenders of
the Gaia hypothesis use this view to criticize human activities that degrade
and pollute the living planet. Whether intended metaphorically or literally,
the Gaia hypothesis is a powerful source of ethical arguments in favor of protecting the natural environment.

However, a central challenge to any attempt to ground ethical values in natural facts is the claim that a gap in logic lies between statements of fact and
judgments of value, between what is and what ought to be. Identified in
recent decades as the "naturalistic fallacy," many philosophers reject as fallacious the conclusion that something is good or right based solely on a description of what is natural.

Since at least the time of Plato, philosophers have recognized the problem
with such reasoning. In Book I of *The Republic,* Plato showed many of the con-
fusions that underlie the view that identifies justice with the natural property:
"advantage of the stronger." More recent discussions have focused on the
eighteenth century philosopher David Hume's distinction between *is* and
ought.[28] The point of these challenges is that grounds for proving that "this is
the way things *are*" are logically distinct from the grounds for proving that
"this is the way things *ought* to be." Even after something has been established as natural, whether it is good always remains an open question.[29]

Chapter 2 related how the natural law—teleological tradition in ethics
makes much of the connection between natural activities and the good. From
a description of the normal and natural activity of the heart, for example, we
reason to an account of a good or healthy heart. From a description of a normal progression of growth from birth through maturity and eventually to
death, we also can reason to an account of a good healthy life. Living systems

can be described in teleological terms, and they seem open to evaluations based on this naturalistic description.

If we adopt the organic ecological model and view an ecosystem as an organic whole, teleological reasoning would seem fitting. From a natural science description of the normal development of the system (its equilibrium and stability), we could reason about what is good or bad, right or wrong, and healthy or unhealthy for elements of that system. Predators are good and ought to be protected, for example, because they contribute to stable populations within the system.

But note that one question always remains: Why *should* we value the overall health of the system itself? If the organism in question is an individual human, we would have fairly standard ways of explaining the value of a healthy heart. But why should we value the integrity and stability of a wetland, desert, or prairie? The teleological model of value is attractive when we are concerned with the relation of parts to whole (the heart) or with the growth and development of a single organism. If, however, ecologists reject the organic model, we seem to be faced with an even greater gap between ecological facts and environmental values.

Perhaps this gap between the natural facts described by ecologists and the values of environmentalists is clearer when we consider the implications of more recent ecological models. For example, the ecosystems approach often concludes that ecosystems have a natural equilibrium and stability. For many environmentalists, this suggests a policy of preservation or protection. Left alone, nature will find its own best way to stability, balance, and harmony. The natural harmony and cooperation within ecosystems guide us toward a policy of respect for nature's way and the preservation of natural systems.

But consider an alternative argument. We might just as well conclude that because nature does work toward balance, we humans can be much more sanguine about our interactions with nature. Further, because we know the mechanisms through which this balance is maintained—specifically the physiochemical cycles of energy and nutrients—we are in an even better position to manage and control the ecosystem. We can learn to create and manage the harmony of natural processes—perhaps by adding nutrients and fertilizers to the soil, perhaps by killing nonnative species of goats, or perhaps by introducing new predators to prey on the goats.

Similar ambiguity characterizes the implications drawn from a more chaotic view of ecosystems. Imagine that we do conclude that the governing principle of ecology is change rather than stability, that the natural state of things is chaos and flux rather than harmony and equilibrium. What follows? We could use this as evidence to argue against wilderness preservation and restoration because there is no natural order to preserve or restore. Paralleling the social Darwinists of the nineteenth century, chaos theorists might argue that because all species struggle to survive in a chaotic world, humans also have a natural inclination to manage their environment for their own self-interest.[30] On the other hand, we might argue that the very complexity and chaos of nature mean that we should be even more cautious of our activities rather than less cautious. This complexity is more rather than less of a reason to stand in awe of and respect the natural world and to be much more modest about our understanding of and ability to manage nature.

The point of this exercise is to demonstrate that we can draw diverse ethical conclusions from even the most uncontroversial facts of science. Thus, despite the importance of ecology to environmental concerns, this science alone is not sufficient to decide among competing environmental policies. We will need to be careful whenever anyone appeals to ecology in defense of some environmental evaluation, ethical judgment, or policy prescription.

8.6 VARIETIES OF HOLISM

At the beginning of this chapter, it was suggested that holism is the unifying idea for ecocentric theories. But this concept, like so many philosophical abstractions, is elusive. At one level, we can grasp it easily enough. The common expression that "the whole is more than the sum of its parts" seems to get at the essence of holism. Yet just below the surface of this ordinary insight lies deep philosophical complexity.

What does it mean to say that the whole is more than the sum of its parts? In one sense—what might be called "metaphysical holism"—this claim can mean that wholes *exist* apart from or as real as their parts. Metaphysical holism claims that wholes are real, perhaps more real than their constituent parts. For our purposes, this would involve the claim that ecosystems have an independent existence beyond the existence of their individual elements. If this were so, the door would be open for arguing that they qualify for moral standing in their own right.

We have seen hints of this before. The organic model, for example, seems to suggest a metaphysical holism. We noted that Frederick Clements referred to the "climax community" itself a complex organism that "constitutes a new kind of organic being." A similar point is made by J. Baird Callicott, the leading philosophical interpreter of Aldo Leopold's land ethic.

> Ecology is the study of relationships of organisms to one another and to the elemental environment. . . . The ontological primacy of objects and the ontological subordination of relationships characteristic of classical western science is, in fact, reversed in ecology. Ecological relationships determine the nature of organisms rather than the other way around. A species is what it is because it has adapted to a niche in the ecosystem. The whole, the system itself, thus, literally and quite straightforwardly shapes and forms its component parts.[31]
>
> From the perspective of modern biology, species adapt to a niche in the ecosystem. Their actual relationships to other organisms (to predators, to prey, to parasites and disease organisms) and to the physical and chemical conditions (to temperature, radiation, salinity, wind, soil and water [acidity]) literally sculpt their outward forms, their metabolic, physiological, and reproductive processes, and even their psychological and mental capacities.[32]

This seems to suggest that individual organisms do not comprise their ecosystems, but that ecosystems create individuals. Callicott's "ontological primacy" would seem equivalent to metaphysical holism.

A second sense of holism might be called "methodological or epistemological holism." Unlike metaphysical holism, this version is not concerned with claims about what exists or what is real. Methodological holism focuses instead on how best to understand or come to know various phenomena. In this view, we would have an inadequate and incomplete understanding of an ecosystem even if we knew everything about its constituent parts.

In some ways, we could see the ecosystem model as suggesting methodological holism. In offering *functional* explanations for individual organisms, the ecosystem model implies that an adequate understanding comes only when we view individuals relative to the system of interdependencies in which they exist. The food chain, for example, identifies individuals in terms of the role they play in the chain.

Finally, what we can call "ethical holism" would suggest that moral considerability should be extended to wholes. Just as we recognize that corporations, for example, have a legal standing independent of the legal standing of their individual members, the ethical holist argues that ethical standing can also be extended to relevant kinds of nonindividuals.

There is perhaps no better example of such a view than Aldo Leopold's statement.

A thing is right when it tends to preserve the integrity, stability, and beauty of the biotic community. It is wrong when it tends otherwise.[33]

Right and wrong are functions of what is good or bad for the whole community, not for its constituent members.

This is not the place to review the philosophical debates concerning holism. Serious philosophical challenges can be raised against each type of holism. Indeed, we will see specific versions of these criticisms raised in what follows. But this should indicate the challenges that lie ahead for ecocentric environmental philosophies.

8.7 SUMMARY AND CONCLUSIONS

Ecocentric approaches to environmental ethics develop from the conviction that ecology must play a primary role in our understanding and valuing of nature. The primary shift of the ecocentric approach involves an emphasis on ecological wholes and moves away from individual plants and animals. However, as presented in this brief survey, the science of ecology is evolving. Thus, we need to recognize that with ecocentric philosophies we are dealing with environmental approaches that are not yet fully formed. We need to pay particular attention to what specific ecological facts are being used in these philosophies and how well that use is explained and justified.

Notes

1. For a discussion of the Kirtland's warbler and its dependence on the jack pine, see Daniel Botkin, *Discordant Harmonies* (New York: Oxford University Press, 1990), pp. 68–71.

2. *Wilderness Act of 1964,* 16 U.S.C. 1131(a).

3. Gen. 3:17–19.

4. Matt. 4:1.

5. Luther Standing Bear, *Land of the Spotted Eagle* (Boston: Houghton Mifflin, 1933), as quoted in T. C. McLuhan, ed., *Touch the Earth: A Self-Portrait of Indian Existence* (New York: Promontory Press, 1971), p. 45.

6. William Bradford, *Of Plymouth Plantation, 1620–1647* (Boston: Wright and Potter, 1899), p. 62, as quoted in Roderick Nash, *Wilderness and the American Mind* (New Haven, Conn.: Yale University Press, 1967), p. 24. Much of this section relies on Nash's superb history of the notion of wilderness.

7. Massachusetts Historical Society, *Proceedings of the Massachusetts Historical Society* 83 (1871–1873), as quoted in Mark Sagoff, *Economy of the Earth* (New York: Cambridge University Press, 1990), p. 125.

8. John White, *The Planter's Plea* (1630), quoted in Peter Carroll, *Puritanism and the Wilderness* (New York: Columbia University Press, 1969), p. 11.

9. Henry David Thoreau, *Walden* (1854; New York: Library of America, 1985), as quoted in Nash, *Wilderness and the American Mind*, pp. 89–90; the emphasis is in the original.

10. John James Audubon, *Delineations of American Scenery and Character,* ed. Francis Hobart Herrick (New York: Baker, 1926), pp. 9–10, as quoted in Nash, *Wilderness and the American Mind*, p. 97.

11. Henry David Thoreau, *The Maine Woods,* in *The Writings of Henry David Thoreau,* vol. 3 (Boston: Houghton Mifflin, 1894), pp. 212–13, as quoted in Nash, *Wilderness and the American Mind*, p. 102.

12. *The Great New Wilderness Debate,* J. Baird Callicott and Michael P. Nelson, eds., (Athens, Ga.: University of Georgia Press, 1998) provides the best single resource for central writings of this debate. I follow Callicott and Nelson in adopting the language of the "received view" here.

13. "The Trouble with Wilderness, or Getting Back to the Wrong Nature" by William Cronon, in *Uncommon Ground: Toward Reinventing Nature,* William Cronon, ed. (New York: Norton and Co., 1995).

14. Ibid.

15. James Fenimore Cooper's "Leatherstocking Tales" are a perfect example of the connection between the romantic wilderness myth and culturally biased and racist attitudes toward Native Americans. Throughout these books, natives are described as fitting one of two stereotypes. Either they are heroic and noble or they are dangerous savages.

16. G. P. Marsh, *Man and Nature,* ed. D. Lowenthal (1864; Cambridge, Mass.: Harvard University Press, 1967), pp. 29–30, as quoted in Botkin, *Discordant Harmonies*, p. 8.

17. Botkin, *Discordant Harmonies*, p. 9.

18. One of the first contemporary authors to call attention to the bias implicit in American understandings of the wilderness was Ramachandra Guha, "Radical American Environmentalism and Wilderness Preservation: A Third World Critique" *Environmental Ethics* 11: 71–83. See also "Indian Wisdom," in *Land of the*

Spotted Eagle by Chief Luther Standing Bear (Boston: Houghton Mifflin, 1933). A fine collection of similar critiques of the wilderness idea can be found in Part Two of *The Great New Wilderness Debate*, edited by J. Baird Callicott and Michael Nelson (Athens, GA. University of Georgia Press, 1998).

19. "The Wilderness Idea Reaffirmed" by Holmes Rolston, originally published in *The Environmental Professional* 13 (1991): 370–77.

20. "Introduction" by J. Baird Callicott and Michael Nelson, pp. 1–20 of *The Great New Wilderness Debate*, op. cit.

21. As quoted in Donald Worster, *Nature's Economy* (Cambridge, England: Cambridge University Press, 1985), p. 211.

22. Ibid.

23. Alfred Tansley, "The Use and Abuse of Vegetational Concepts and Terms," *Ecologist* 16 (1935): 284–307, quoted in Frank Golley, *A History of the Ecosystem Concept in Ecology* (New Haven, Conn.: Yale University Press, 1993), p. 8; the emphasis is Tansley's. I rely on Golley's book for much of the section that follows.

24. See Worster, *Nature's Economy*, ch. 14.

25. A very readable summary of these topics can be found in David Gates, "The Flow of Energy in the Biosphere," *Scientific American* 224 (September 1971): 89–100.

26. For an excellent review of this more chaotic approach to ecology, see Donald Worster, "The Ecology of Order and Chaos," in *The Wealth of Nature* (New York: Oxford University Press, 1993), ch. 13.

27. James Lovelock, *Gaia: A New Look at Life on Earth* (Oxford, England: Oxford University Press, 1979); *The Ages of Gaia: A Biography of Our Living Planet* (Oxford, England: Oxford University Press, 1988); and Dorian Sagan and Lynn Margulis, "The Gaia Perspective of Ecology," *Ecologist* 13 (March–April): 160–67.

28. David Hume, *A Treatise on Human Nature* (London: Oxford University Press, 1740), book 3, pt. 1, sec. 1.

29. The classic twentieth century discussion of the naturalistic fallacy appears in G. E. Moore, *Principia Ethica* (London: Cambridge University Press, 1903). Perhaps the best critical commentary on Moore is William Frankena, "The Naturalistic Fallacy," *Mind* 48 (1939): 464–77. A helpful collection of analytic essays on this topic is W. D. Hudson, *The Is/Ought Question* (New York: St. Martin's, 1970).

30. Donald Worster discusses this "ideological" attribution of social Darwinism to chaos theory in "Ecology of Order and Chaos," pp. 165–70.

31. J. Baird Callicott, "The Conceptual Foundations of the Land Ethic," in *In Defense of the Land Ethic* (Albany: State University of New York Press, 1989), p. 87.

32. J. Baird Callicott, "The Metaphysical Implications of Ecology," in *In Defense of the Land Ethic*, p. 110.

33. Aldo Leopold, "The Land Ethic," in *A Sand County Almanac* (New York: Oxford University Press, 1949), p. 262.

Discussion Questions

1. If you were responsible for managing a national park such as Yellowstone, would you support or oppose road-building plans to provide more people with access to the backcountry? Should national parks be made more accessible to RVs and campers? To elderly and disabled people?

2. Should the U.S. Forest Service take steps to prevent a major fire within the Boundary Waters Canoe Area wilderness? Should the U.S. Forest Service replant the red and white pine trees that were destroyed in the blowdown, or should they

"let nature takes its course" even if the results would be a forest of short-lived aspen and birch?

3. What images come to mind when you think of wilderness? What is the origin of those images? What adjectives would you use to describe the wilderness?

4. Can aesthetic appreciation and value be taught? Could you persuade someone that a mountain vista is beautiful if he or she did not already appreciate it? What considerations would you cite in your argument?

5. What model should guide policies aimed at restoring a wilderness area? Should it be restored to the point at which it was found by the first white settlers? Should it simply be left alone, even if this means that nonnative species will populate the area?

6. What role should the science of ecology play in managing wilderness areas? What decisions are not appropriate to ecological answers?

7. Is the good for some collective such as a team or country identical to the good of its individual members? Can the good for an individual become identical to the good of the group? Are there any rules to follow to resolve conflicts between collective goods and individual goods?

Further Reading

In addition to Roderick Nash's excellent history of the wilderness idea in America (see note 6), see Max Oelschlaeger, *The Idea of Wilderness from Prehistory to the Present* (New Haven, Conn.: Yale University Press, 1990), and Max Oelschlaeger, ed., *The Wilderness Condition* (Washington, D.C.: Island Press, 1992), for a more general and diverse discussion of these topics. *The Great New Wilderness Debate*, J. Baird Callicott and Michael P. Nelson, eds., (Athens, Ga.: University of Georgia Press, 1998) provides the best single resource for central writings of the debate concerning the wilderness.

Michael Cohen, *The Pathless Way* (Madison: University of Wisconsin Press, 1984), provides an excellent intellectual biography of John Muir.

Donald Worster's *Nature's Economy* (Cambridge, England: Cambridge University Press, 1985) and *The Wealth of Nature* (New York: Oxford University Press, 1993) are scholarly and readable environmental histories.

9

The Land Ethic

A Place for Predators

In its most direct meaning, the "predator-prey relationship" simply refers to the fact that some species feed on members of other species. When the member of the feeding species lives in or on its food, it is called a *parasite*, and its food is called a *host*. When the feeding species does not live in or on its food, it is called a *predator*, and its food is called the *prey*. Thus, most non-microscopic life-forms, including all the familiar herbivores and carnivores, are predators. Further, as suggested by the image of a food chain, most predators turn out to be prey for another species.

Beyond this neutral description of predators and prey, however, lies a more value-laden and provocative connotation. Predator suggests malevolence and cruelty. A predator is a menacing presence, secretly stalking its prey. Thus, we never think to call a songbird, deer, or squirrel a predator. We usually reserve this name for the larger carnivores, those animals with sharp claws or teeth that just might have humans as their prey. Bears, wolves, coyote, mountain lions, and sharks are the classic predators. It is not surprising, then, that humans have hunted and poisoned many of these animals to near extinction.

But something other than fear of being attacked must account for the vengeance with which humans have hunted these animals. In fact, even before these populations were devastated, few humans actually became prey to large carnivores. Certainly, the Puritan tradition of viewing the wilderness as evil and threatening reinforced the fear of wild animals. Perhaps the biggest factor is that large carnivores compete with humans for food. Ranchers, farmers, hunters, and government-sponsored programs working in their behalf are the single greatest factor in the near extinction of wolves, grizzly bears, and mountain lions in North America. These animals threatened livestock and game—our food—and thus had to be eliminated.

Government policy regarding predators parallels, in many ways, policy toward forest fires. By the first decades of the twentieth century, federal policy was guided by the progressive conservation movement associated with people like Gifford Pinchot. The conservation movement aimed to guarantee a steady supply of natural resources, whether these were trees, livestock, or crops. By later in the century, the growing influence of ecology had introduced a more tempered approach to threats to these resources, whether from fire or predators.

The conservationists of the early twentieth century fought the greed and exploitation that characterized almost all previous attitudes toward natural resources. They fought to conserve these resources and manage them in the public interest. Scientific forestry and, later, scientific game management pursued the most efficient use of natural resources. They also involved the commitment to protect these resources from predators.

The conservation movement adopted a Lockean view of the wilderness and wild animals. Both were understood as property, private or public, that should serve as a resource for human use. Game conservationists would manage wildlife the way Pinchot's foresters managed the forests, in a way that guaranteed a long-term stable supply of resources.

Unfortunately, from this perspective predators could be viewed as a threat to natural resources. Like a cancer growing within an organic body, predators eat away at resources, jeopardizing the continued health and well-being of the supply and, thereby, jeopardizing the efficient management of natural resources. Large carnivores were on a par with locusts and other pests that threatened crops. They would be eradicated to protect human interests.

Through the first half of the twentieth century, various government agencies aggressively pursued policies aimed at exterminating predators. In the beginning, these policies carried on the centuries-old bounty system that rewarded private individuals for killing predators. By 1920, the bounty system was supplemented by government-trained and government-paid hunters, trappers, and poisoners. For decades, the United States spent millions of dollars per year to kill bears, wolves, coyote, and mountain lions. By the 1970s, all but the coyote were nearly extinct in the lower forty-eight states.

A minority perspective began to emerge among scientists and wildlife managers during the 1920s and 1930s. Emerging ecological perspectives indicated a natural balance or equilibrium in nature, suggesting that ecosystems normally develop toward a stable community. Influenced in part by ecology's growing focus on interdependent communities, this new perspective pointed out the functional role that predators play in the "economy of nature." Paralleling foresters who saw a beneficial role for fire in forest man-agement, these people believed that predators acted as a natural check on the populations of other wild animals. Like all other members of the ecological community, predators filled a role and contributed to the overall balance of nature. Thus, guided by ecological science, experts could manage wildlife so as to ensure the natural stability of a local ecosystem.

Specifically, predators were seen as nature's way of maintaining stable and healthy populations. Unchecked, populations would increase expo-nentially. In reality, various factors work together to keep populations in check. This idea can be expressed mathematically in terms of an S-shaped curve called a "logistic." A population increases until it reaches a point at which it exceeds the capacity of its habitat to support that number of organ-isms (the habitat's "carrying capacity"). The population then decreases through starvation, for example, below the level that its habitat can sup-port. Once a population falls below the habitat's carrying capacity, the pop-ulation is free to resume its growth. Over time, this growth rate oscillates across the line that represents a population's equilibrium with its habitat's carrying capacity.

Predators serve as one ecological factor that keeps a population in check. When a prey's population increases, predators find food plentiful. They also tend to eat the least fit organisms within a population. This helps main-tain the genetic strength and fitness of a population. The abundance of prey leads to an increase in the predator population, which in turn leads to a decrease in the prey population. Over time, this decrease in prey leads to a decrease in predators, which once again leads to an increase in prey. Thus, the population size of predators and prey can be pictured as a set of sym-metrical S-curves, mathematically known as the Lotka-Volterra equations.[1]

By the middle of the twentieth century, most ecologists subscribed to this predator-prey model, resulting in a reversal of earlier environmental senti-ment in regard to predators. Recent attempts to restore large carnivores to some of their original habitats within the lower forty-eight states, such as the reintroduction of wolves into the Yellowstone ecosystem, are the direct result of this reversal.

In the early 1980s, the U.S. Fish and Wildlife Service began considering plans to reintroduce gray wolves into Yellowstone. The plan involves trap-ping Canadian wolves and transporting as many as fifteen per year into Yellowstone beginning in 1995. The hope is to establish ten breeding pairs or as many as one hundred wolves in the park by the year 2002.

Like the grizzly bear, mountain lion, and other large predators, the wolf was aggressively hunted and killed during the early decades of this cen-tury. Ranchers and farmers viewed these predators as threats to their stock as well as a danger to humans. By the 1940s, wolves had been eradicated from Yellowstone and other areas throughout the American West.

The plan to reintroduce wolves into Yellowstone met with fierce opposi-tion. In response to criticism, the U.S. Fish and Wildlife Service conducted the most exhaustive review process in the history of federal regulation, including holding eighty-three public hearings, before proceeding with the reintroduction plan. In late 1994, the American Farm Bureau Federation, representing the interests of ranchers, filed a lawsuit and temporarily blocked the plan. In January 1995, a court lifted the ban and the U.S. Fish and Wildlife Service proceeded to transport the trapped wolves from Canada to the United States. After a period of being held in cages at Yellowstone to acclimate them to the area, the wolves were released into Yellowstone in early 1995. A similar process was followed with a second group one year later.

The U.S. Endangered Species Act requires federal agencies not only to prevent the loss of endangered species, but also to work to recover viable populations of threatened species whenever possible. But with over 50,000 wolves in Canada, 6,000 to 7,000 in Alaska, and more than 3,000 in the lower 48 United States, wolves as a species are not in any immediate danger of extinction. They are "extinct" or threatened only in particular areas. Indeed, we have some confirmed reports of solitary wolves making their way back into Yellowstone without human intervention. This possibility raises questions about the reintroduction plan.

Federal law treats threatened species that reestablish themselves differently than it treats a species that is reintroduced with human intervention. A "reestablished" species (without human aid) receives full protection, which includes a ban on any hunting or other activities that threaten the breeding population. Further, the law would prohibit reintroduction plans as a means of protecting the genetic integrity of the reestablished population. If a species is reintroduced by human intervention, the animals receive less protection. In the wolf reintroduction plan, authorities allow the killing of animals that roam outside the park's boundaries and threaten livestock. In addition, compensation is paid to ranchers who lose livestock to the wolves. Further, the mortality rate for reintroduced animals is estimated to exceed 50 percent, often the result of illegal hunting and other human activities. As of the spring of 1996, estimated survival rates suggest that the reintroduction plan is enjoying reasonable success in establishing a wolf population in Yellowstone.

9.1 INTRODUCTION

Aldo Leopold (1887–1948) is the single most influential figure in the development of an ecocentric environmental ethics. The science of ecology developed during his lifetime, and he was the first person to call for a radical rethinking of ethics in light of this new science. His life's work sought to integrate ecology and ethics. Leopold was an eloquent and prolific writer, and the collection of essays published posthumously as *A Sand County Almanac* (1949) is a classic text of the environmental movement. The definitive essay of this book, "The Land Ethic," is the first systematic presentation of an ecocentric ethics.

This chapter focuses on Leopold's land ethic as the best example of an eco-centric ethics.

The development of Leopold's thinking parallels the change in thinking about predators. In many ways, Leopold is the person most responsible for this change. In his early research, Leopold was to game management what Pinchot was to forestry. He introduced scientific techniques and principles to the management of natural resources, in this case to the management of game. Leopold was trained at the Yale Forest School, and his book, *Game Management*, published in 1933, became the classic text in the field. It was also a classic conservationist text: game species like deer and quail were "resources" or "crops" that should be managed to increase their harvest. "Like all other agricultural arts, game management produces a crop by controlling the environmental factors which hold down natural increase, or productivity, of the seed stock."[2] One environmental factor that "holds down" game resources, of course, is the existence of predators.

In an early essay published in 1915, Leopold set out the conservationist position regarding predators or, as they were labeled, "varmints." Regretting the antagonism that seemed to exist between ranchers and hunters, Leopold advises in "The Varmint Question" that ranchers, hunters, and game protectionists are "mutually and vitally interested in a common problem. This is the reduction of predatory animals." In a passage that today would outrage most ecologists and environmentalists, Leopold explains,

> It is well known that predatory animals are continuing to eat the cream off the grower's profits, and it hardly needs to be argued that, with our game supply as low as it is, a reduction in the predatory animal population is bound to help the situation. If the wolves, lions, coyotes, bob-cats, foxes, skunks, and other varmints were only decreasing at the same rate as our game is decreasing, it might at least be said that there was no serious occasion for worry.... Whatever may have been the value of the work accomplished by bounty systems, poisoning, and trapping, individual or governmental, the fact remains that varmints continue to thrive and their reduction can be accomplished only by means of a practical, vigorous, and comprehensive plan of action.[3]

But as his own ecological understanding developed as a result of his field experiences and research, Leopold began to see problems with this conservationist approach to nature. Specifically, the conservationist approach tends to view nature mechanically, as a mere object that can be manipulated for human ends without repercussions. Leopold recognized that this conflicts with a more ecological perspective in at least two ways. First, it seriously underestimates the interconnectedness of nature. Manipulating one part of nature by exterminating predators, for example, surely has significant implications elsewhere, for example, the overpopulation of deer herds. Further, unlike a mechanistic model, ecology teaches us that we never know with any certainty what consequences will follow from these manipulations. Second, the mechanistic approach treats the earth as "dead" when, in fact, ecology recognizes that even a handful of dirt contains an abundance of living organisms. Less than ten years after writing "The Varmint Question," Leopold discussed conservation as a "moral issue" that transcends the utilitarian-economic calculations of earlier conservationism.

> Many of the world's most penetrating minds have regarded our so-called "inanimate nature" as a living thing, and many of us . . . have felt intuitively that there existed between man and the earth a closer and deeper relation than would necessarily follow the mechanistic conception of the earth. . . .
>   Philosophy, then, suggests one reason why we cannot destroy the earth with moral impunity; namely that the "dead" earth is an organism possessing a certain kind of degree of life, which we intuitively respect as such.[4]

This new perspective, what we might call an "ecological conscience," developed over decades and was presented most fully in the late 1940s as the land ethic. This ecological conscience represents a shift from a view of nature as having only instrumental value to one that recognizes an intrinsic worth in natural systems. We can see this shift in Leopold's own thinking in his short essay "Thinking Like a Mountain," published in *A Sand County Almanac*. Leopold recalls a time when, "young and full of trigger-itch," he shot a wolf and reached it in time to watch it die, "to watch the fierce green fire dying in her eyes."[5] At the time, he believed that fewer wolves meant more game. But on seeing the wolf die, he began to recognize that from a broader, what we would call ecological, perspective that this was not true. In fact, our short-sightedness was more likely to harm rather than help the balance of nature. Until we learn to "think like a mountain" and understand nature from a wider and longer-term perspective, we are doomed to mismanage natural ecosystems. It is likely that Leopold would support reintroducing wolves into the Yellowstone Park area. In this respect, the U.S. Fish and Wildlife Service approaches the ideal of thinking like a mountain.

9.2 THE LAND ETHIC

Leopold opens "The Land Ethic" by retelling the story of Odysseus who, on returning from the Trojan War, hanged a dozen of his women slaves for misbehavior. Because slaves were understood as property, Odysseus's action was not seen as unethical or inappropriate. Since that time, ethics has evolved so that moral standing now is extended to all human beings. "The Land Ethic" is Leopold's call to continue this extension of ethics to include land, plants, and animals. At mid-century, land, like Odysseus's slaves, was understood as mere property. We had privileges in respect to the land but no obligations to it.

An ecological understanding of land rebuts the Lockean view of land as property. We can no longer treat the land as a mere object, as dead matter that can be used and shaped in any way that humans desire. Land should be viewed as a living organism that can be healthy or unhealthy, injured or killed. "Land, then, is not merely soil; it is a fountain of energy flowing through a circuit of soils, plants, and animals,"[6] Leopold writes.

Thus, Leopold opens "The Land Ethic" by suggesting the sort of moral extensionism presented in earlier chapters. He speaks of the "extension of ethics" and tells us that "the land ethic simply enlarges the boundaries of the community to include soils, waters, plants, and animals, or collectively, the land." Although "we have no land ethic yet, we have at least drawn nearer the point of admitting that birds should continue as a matter of biotic right."[7] His suggestion seems to be that we should extend moral consideration, what he termed "biotic rights," to birds, soils, waters, plants, and animals.

However, Leopold never abandons his belief that these natural objects can and should be used as "resources" that can be managed for human benefit. As a result, it would be difficult to read Leopold as a defender of animal and plant rights, in the style of Singer, Regan, or Stone.[8] It is difficult to reconcile granting moral rights to animals while being willing to treat them as resources. Leopold's own long-standing practice of hunting also suggests that he cannot be placed in the animal rights camp.

This apparent inconsistency is resolved when we view the land ethic *holistically*. It is the "land community" that is granted moral standing. Individual members of that community can still be treated as resources as long as the community itself is respected. The "ecological conscience" teaches that humans are but members of the biotic community, "biotic citizens," rather than conquerors of nature. Ecology shifts the focus of moral consideration away from individuals and onto biotic wholes.

Accordingly, the moral extensionism that is at work in Leopold's writing does not ask that we simply make room in our moral deliberations for yet another type of individual moral subject. Leopold asks that we make a radical category shift away from individuals. We now ought to grant moral standing to communities, symbolically represented as the land.

This aspect of the land ethic is concisely summarized in Leopold's most celebrated and controversial statement.

> A thing is right when it tends to preserve the integrity, stability, and beauty of the biotic community. It is wrong when it tends otherwise.[9]

When combined with some basic ecological observations, this principle can be used to generate specific normative conclusions.

Leopold uses the image of a "biotic pyramid" or "land pyramid" to help us understand the nature of the biotic community. This is an important image for it shows how Leopold has adopted many elements of Tansley's ecosystem approach to ecology. The land pyramid is a "highly organized structure" of biotic and abiotic elements through which solar energy flows. This structure can be represented as a pyramid, with soil on the bottom, followed by a plant layer, an insect layer, a bird and rodent layer, "and so on up through the various animal groups to the apex layer, which consists of the larger carnivores."[10]

Thus, species are arranged in layers or "trophic levels" according to the food that they eat. Because there must exist numerically more members of a prey species than its predators (otherwise the predators would soon starve), "each successive layer decreases in numerical abundance," forming the pyramidal shape of the system. The "lines of dependency for food and other services are called food chains."

> Each species, including ourselves, is a link in many chains. The deer eats a hundred plants other than oak, and the cow a hundred plants other than corn. Both, then, are links in a hundred chains. The pyramid is a tangle of chains so complex as to seem disorderly, yet the stability of the system proves it to be a highly organized structure. Its functioning depends on the co-operation and competition of its diverse parts.[11]

With this, we can begin to reach some general normative prescriptions. Given the complexity of this "highly organized structure," only a "fool would discard seemingly useless parts." Preservation of life-forms in all their diversity is the first general rule that we ought to follow, because not even ecologists understand how this complex system operates.

Because this complex structure has developed through millions of years of evolution, human interference with it ought to always be humble and constrained. Any change in the system requires that many other elements adjust themselves to it. When this occurs slowly, as it does through evolution, the system is self-regulating. When change is introduced abruptly and violently, as it typically is through human intervention, the potential for disaster is genuine. Thus, we should tread lightly on the ecosystem. It is also wise to assume that native plants and animals are best suited for a particular locale. We can speculate that Leopold would support reintroducing wolves into Yellowstone. On the other hand, introducing nonnative species is courting disaster. It is likely that Leopold would favor removing mountain goats from Olympic National Park. So, too, we can speculate that he would warn against reliance on chemical pesticides, herbicides, and fertilizers.

More generally, a portrait of a stable and harmonious ecological relationship emerges from *A Sand County Almanac*. The many images of Leopold living on his Sand County farm depict a healthy relationship with the land. We feel that if only we could generalize from life on a small self-sustaining farm, we would be close to the ideal ecological and environmental lifestyle.

Just one of the many images that is particularly moving is the almanac entry for February.

> There are two spiritual dangers in not owning a farm. One is the danger of supposing that breakfast comes from the grocery, and the other that heat comes from the furnace. To avoid the first danger, one should plant a garden, preferably

where there is no grocer to confuse the issue. To avoid the second, he should lay a split of good oak on the andirons, preferably where there is no furnace, and let it warm his shins while a February blizzard tosses the trees outside. If one has cut, split, hauled, and piled his own good oak, and let his mind work the while, he will remember much of where the heat comes from, and with a wealth of detail denied to those who spend the weekend in town astride a radiator.[12]

Leopold then lets his mind work as he traces the life cycle of an oak tree. The oak now used as firewood was killed by lightning during a July storm. The lightning "put an end to woodmaking by this particular oak" and "bequeathed to us three cords of prospective fuel wood." Leopold mourns the loss of the old tree but is satisfied to know that a dozen of its progeny have already set down roots in the nearby woods. After a year of drying, he cut the oak by hand, each pull of the saw cutting through years of the oak's life as captured in its annual rings. Leopold traces the life of the oak with each pull, rehearsing the changes in the local environment back through the years to the time around the Civil War when the oak first sprouted from an acorn. At the other end of the cycle, the oak is reduced to ashes in the fireplace while providing heat for the farmhouse. Eventually, the ashes will be returned to the land as compost, only to reappear, in time, as a red apple or a "fat squirrel bent on planting acorns."[13]

Thus, the death of a single magnificent oak tree, while sad in itself, can be viewed from a broader perspective. All living things, including humans, must be viewed as members of the ecological community. The oak is honored as a member, even as it is used as firewood. One oak dies and other species benefit by consuming it. Yet in a harmonious and stable relationship, each member of the community is a resource for the continuation of the lives of others. An oak dies, but oaks live on. Resources are used but never without being recycled into the system. The community is characterized by countless of these interdependencies. Its health is characterized by its long-term integrity and stability.

At this point, there are several elements of the land ethic that make it an attractive philosophical option. First, the land ethic offers a fairly comprehensive perspective. At first sight, it appears to offer a decision process for most, if not all, environmental and ecological issues. Unlike the animal welfare movement, it can offer normative guidance for issues as diverse as wilderness preservation, pollution, conservation, energy, resource depletion, and so forth.

Second, it also can avoid many of the counterintuitive conclusions that burden the individualistic biocentric approach. We do not need to be overly concerned with such seemingly insignificant issues as killing a mosquito, cutting a tree, or tearing up a lawn. The continued healthy functioning of the system is the primary concern.

Finally, the land ethic is thoroughly nonanthropocentric. Humans are said to have no privileged status in the ecological community. They are reduced from conquerors to mere members. Not only does this shift accord natural objects and systems moral standing, but it also is more consistent with the teachings of ecology. For many environmentalists, this is the single most important prerequisite for a sound environmental perspective.

9.3 LEOPOLD'S HOLISM

Before assessing the land ethic, it is important to have an understanding of the nature of Leopold's version of holism. The summary statement quoted earlier clearly suggests that Leopold is committed to a form of *ethical holism*. Right and wrong are a function of the well-being of the community, not of its constituent members.

In this view, we could argue that it is ethically permissible to kill individual deer as long as the "integrity, stability, and beauty" of the deer population were preserved. In fact, in the many cases in which an overpopulation threatens the stability of the herd or the integrity of an entire ecosystem within which the deer live, we might well have an obligation to selectively kill individual deer.

But why is it reasonable to adopt ethical holism in regard to ecological communities? We can find traces of three answers in Leopold's writings. First, ethical holism is the most *practical* approach to take when making decisions concerning resource management. Second, ethical holism is implied by an *epistemological* holism implicit in ecology. Finally, ethical holism acknowledges the *metaphysical reality* of ecological wholes.

A practical reason for adopting ethical holism stems in part from the failure of more individualistic thinking. History supplies ample evidence that when we think only in terms of individual plants and animals, we adopt misinformed and risky land management policies. We have more than ample evidence for the abuse and destruction that follow from ignoring the interdependencies within an ecosystem. As an example, Leopold cites the effects that the destruction of predators can have on the population of deer. Therefore, treating ecosystems as if they had moral standing, "thinking like a mountain" in Leopold's words, would be a significant corrective to these errors. When Leopold writes to ranchers, farmers, hunters, and policymakers, he tends to adopt this more pragmatic approach to ethical holism.

Epistemological holism follows from the claim that an adequate understanding of ecology can come only from holistic or functional explanations. A full understanding of a wolf, for example, must include an account of how that species functions within the ecosystem. As a member of the biotic community, the wolf plays a role in the overall stability and integrity of the system. This functional community model of the ecosystem, in turn, provides a basis for ethical holism. The value of an individual organism is derived in part by its function, role, operation, relationships, and the like. Ecological understanding, thus, gives reasons for adopting an ethical perspective that grants moral consideration to factors other than individual organisms.

We have also seen Leopold, in passages quoted here, suggest that the land might be regarded as a living thing. The metaphysical holism that is implied by the organic model provides further reasons for accepting ethical holism. Quoting the Russian philosopher Ouspensky, Leopold tells us that it is possible "to regard the earth's parts—soil, mountains, rivers, atmosphere, etc.—as organs, or parts, of a coordinated whole." Our belief that the earth is dead matter arises in part from our inability to recognize the "enormously slow, intricate, and interrelated functions" of its life processes. In a passage that makes the connection between metaphysical and ethical holism explicit, Leopold says,

> Philosophy, then, suggests one reason why we cannot destroy the earth with moral impunity; namely that the "dead" earth is an organism possessing a certain kind and degree of life, which we intuitively respect as such.[14]

If the earth itself is alive and if we can attribute to it such attributes as health, sickness, growth, and death, we can argue along familiar lines that the earth itself deserves moral consideration.

But to say that there are various reasons for adopting ethical holism is not yet to explain the nature of the biotic wholes in question. As seen in Chapter 8, ecologists have relied on several different models of ecological systems, and each of these models can have different ethical implications. How exactly should the biotic community be understood? Which model best describes the activities of ecosystems?

Because Leopold's life spanned the early years of ecology, we should not be surprised to find various ecological emphases in his writing. We have already seen quotes in which Leopold refers to the earth as a living organism. Throughout much of "The Land Ethic," Leopold relies on the community model of ecology. The crucial image of the food pyramid has strong ties to Elton's functional community model. But even in the midst of this, Leopold also emphasizes the language of the energy model: "Plants absorb energy from the sun. This energy flows through a circuit called the biota which may be represented by a pyramid consisting of layers."[15] Whether we are concerned with food flowing through food chains of producers and consumers or energy flowing through circuits may make an ethical difference.

Take, for example, the images of land health and death. Leopold often emphasizes our duty to preserve the health of the land and often laments those cases in which the land has died. But whereas *health* and *death* can straightforwardly be applied to organisms, they can be applied only metaphorically to communities and energy circuits. Most of us would be willing to defend the intrinsic value of health, but what is its value when used metaphorically? Again, the "integrity and stability" of an organism may mean one thing, and the integrity and stability of a community or energy circuit may mean quite another. These are crucial questions for the land ethic. Clearly, Leopold reasons from ecological factors to normative ethical conclusions. Those conclusions attribute "integrity, stability, and beauty" to ecosystems. Two major challenges emerge: Can such properties be attributed to ecosystems, and how do ecological facts support the ethical conclusions?

What, exactly, was Leopold's model for understanding ecological wholes? The honest answer likely is that he was not as finely attuned to the nuances of these various models and perhaps especially to the ethical nuances as we might like. Leopold seems mostly to abandon the organic model in his later writings.[16] But if we take "The Land Ethic" as his most mature work, we must conclude that he either did not see or did not think it important to make a clear and constant distinction in the various models.

9.4 CRITICISMS OF THE LAND ETHIC: FACTS AND VALUES

We will separate challenges to Leopold's land ethic into two general sections: the move from the facts of ecology to the values of ethics and the ethical implications of Leopold's holism. The first topic focuses on what philosophers have called the "naturalistic fallacy," and the second topic focuses on the nature of ecological wholes.

As outlined in Chapter 8, a central challenge to any attempt to ground ethical values in natural facts is the claim that a logical gap exists between statements of fact and judgments of value, between is and ought. Identified in recent decades as the naturalistic fallacy, the conclusion that something is good or right based solely on a description of what is natural is rejected by many philosophers as fallacious. Leopold's famous dictum, "A thing is right when it tends to preserve the integrity, stability, and beauty of the biotic community. It is wrong when it tends otherwise," would seem to be an example of exactly this type of reasoning.

At first glance, if Leopold adopts the organic model, one way to bridge this gap might be the type of teleological reasoning defended by the Aristotelian tradition. The organic model presents a view of ecosystems as distinct wholes and develops toward a point of stable equilibrium. From such a natural scientific description of the normal development of an organic whole, with its own identifiable integrity and stability, we could reason about what is good or bad, right or wrong, and healthy or unhealthy for elements of that system. Predators are good and ought to be protected, for example, because they contribute to stable populations within the system and, thus, to its health. Eliminating exotic species (such as the mountain goat in Olympic National Park) or reintroducing native species (such as the Yellowstone wolves) is right because it maintains the natural integrity of the ecosystem.

But note that one question, described in Chapter 8, always remains: Why *should* we value the overall integrity or stability of the system itself? We could appeal to the role that particular ecosystems play in the overall stability and integrity of some larger organic whole. Thus, like a heart, a wetland performs a function for some organic whole. Accordingly, we ought to preserve the integrity and stability of an ecosystem because, in doing so, we are promoting the good of some larger whole of which the ecosystem is a part. Following this line, we would eventually argue, as Leopold sometimes does, that the earth itself should be considered an organic whole. But even if this were scientifically valid (and as we have seen in our survey of ecological models, that is far from clear), this line of reasoning simply pushes the open question back a step. Why value the integrity and stability of this larger organic whole? Because instrumental and individualistic reasons (for example, that the larger whole should be valued because it preserves the well-being of its constituent parts such as human beings) are not part of the land ethic, we would have to argue that some teleological goal exists for the entire system. Here the teleological model seems to break down. Neither ecology nor philosophy has produced a plausible account of what the earth's telos might be.

The other option is for the land ethic to argue that an ecosystem, like an individual organism, goes through developmental stages. The normal developmental progression would thereby provide a basis, as it does in human medicine, for evaluating the health and well-being of that system. Unfortunately, this is logical only if we assume the validity of the organic model, wherein every locale has a single climax stage toward which ecological succession aims and each ecosystem is separate and unique. But given that most ecologists have moved away from the organic model, use of this option is weak. There may well not be a single ecosystem that develops through time. For example, over time the populations of a field might go through a series of ecological transformations from weeds to perennials and grasses, to shrubs, to pine forests, to oak forests. What would the "integrity and stability" of this system be? Should we seek to preserve the field as home to prairie grasses and shrubs, as a pine forest, or stay out altogether and let whatever happens happen? The important point is that we can meaningfully ask these questions. Hence, the leap from ecological fact to ethical value remains an open question.

Abandoning the organic model in favor of the more mainstream ecosystem model also does not resolve this problem. In the community model, individuals are related to each other functionally (as members of a food chain), but there is little reason to assume a function for the chain itself. We might be able to give a functional evaluation of the roles of individual organisms and species in the food chain, for example, that my garden's abundance of aphids is good for ladybugs. But why any particular food chain or, more to the point, any particular arrangement of the food chain should be valued in itself is yet to be answered. We have even less reason to assume a normative account of energy circuits. Why is the preservation of the integrity and stability of a food chain or energy circuit good or right?

We can summarize the philosophical point of these challenges. Leopold's normative conclusion ("a thing is right when it tends to preserve the integrity, stability, and beauty of the biotic community") seems to be derived, in some way, from the facts of ecology. Even assuming that a factual and meaningful basis exists for attributing integrity, stability, and beauty to ecosystems (and as we have seen in the discussion on ecological models, that is far from established), how these facts are connected to the value conclusion remains an open question.[17]

If we speak of ecological functions in an Aristotelian teleological sense as aiming toward some goal, either as parts within a larger whole or as a whole with its own goals, we might have some basis for reaching normative conclusions. But, again as witnessed in Chapter 2, the Darwinian account of natural selection casts serious doubts on the meaningfulness of teleological explanations in biology. In this account, members of an ecosystem do not function the way they do because of some forward-looking goal or purpose toward which they are aiming. Components of an ecosystem function the way they do because functioning in this way has, in the past, proved adaptive.

Consider the example of large predators such as wolves within an ecosystem such as Yellowstone. When we speak of how predators function within an ecosystem, it is easy to think that wolves exist in order to prey on elk and other species and maintain a natural stability and equilibrium. But the Darwinian explanation suggests that wolves prey on elk and other species because in the past this behavior has proved adaptive and wolves that have done it have survived to reproduce. Note that this backward-looking explanation of ecosystem function gives us much less reason to conclude that this functional activity is right or good. In the phrase used in Chapter 2, "nature is neither good nor bad; it just is."

We should be careful to avoid overstating the force of these criticisms. The point is not that we cannot support ethical judgments by appeal to naturalistic facts. The point is that in defending something as right or wrong, we need to do more than simply say that it is normal or natural. Ecological facts, in themselves, do not "prove" that ecological integrity and stability are ethical values.

We can find indications in "The Land Ethic" for how Leopold might respond to these challenges. Leopold suggests that the ethical revolution implicit in his extension of ethics to the land can come about only alongside a radical change in human psychology. This change in psychology, brought about through moral and ecological education, might bridge the gap between is and ought.

> It is inconceivable to me that an ethical relation to land can exist without love, respect, and admiration for land, and a high regard for its value. By value, I of course mean something far broader than mere economic value; I mean value in the philosophical sense.[18]

This passage suggests that ethical holism, extending direct ethical consideration (the "philosophical sense" of value) to ecological wholes, can come about only when humans change their attitudes toward the land. Only when humans come to love, respect, and admire the land will they have reasons to act in ways that benefit it. But how will humans come to love, respect, and admire the land? "One of the requisites" for an ecological valuing of land "is an understanding of ecology."[19] Thus, the natural facts of ecology do not lead directly to ethical conclusions but instead to a change of attitude that can in turn lead to a change in ethical evaluations. Accordingly, we value the preservation of an ecosystem not simply because it is natural or normal but because, given what we have learned of it from ecology, we love it, respect it, and admire it.[20] In this interpretation, the role of ecology is focused more toward moral education than on normative ethics.

Unfortunately, if we take this approach, the "integrity and stability" principle loses some of its force. In this view, the principle is not a straightforward normative principle, "Act in ways that tend to preserve the integrity, stability, and beauty . . ." Rather, it is an exhortation to get people to think in a certain way, "Stop thinking solely in economic and instrumental terms; try thinking this way: a thing is right when . . ." The principle becomes, as Leopold suggests, a challenge to the logjam preventing the "evolutionary process" from extending ethical consideration to land. It provides an alternative and a challenge to the economic way of thinking. But it provides no independent reason for acting on behalf of the land.

9.5 CRITICISMS OF THE LAND ETHIC: HOLISTIC ETHICS

A second group of challenges to the land ethic centers on its holism. Two general concerns underlie these challenges: Can a meaningful account of ecological wholes be defended, and are its ethical implications acceptable?

The most serious ethical criticism of the land ethic's holism is that it condones sacrificing the good of individuals to the good of the whole. If we do define right and wrong in terms of the biotic community, it would seem possible to sacrifice individual members—for example, individual human beings—for the good of the community. For example, Leopold seems willing to condone hunting individual animals to preserve the integrity and stability of the biotic community. But because he also describes humans as equal members of that community, he would seem to be committed to the permissibility of hunting humans if doing so would preserve the integrity, stability, and beauty of that community.

Various critics have offered versions of this challenge. Marti Kheel, a writer and activist, has called ethical holism totalitarian, and philosopher Eric Katz has claimed that it subverts respect for individuals.[21] Another criticism was voiced by Tom Regan, who labeled Leopold's approach "environmental fascism."

> The difficulties and implications of developing a rights-based environmental ethic . . . include reconciling the *individualistic* nature of moral rights with the more *holistic* view of nature. . . . Aldo Leopold is illustrative of this latter tendency. . . . The implications of this view include the clear prospect that the

individual may be sacrificed for the greater biotic good, in the name of "the integrity, stability and beauty of the biotic community." It is difficult to see how the notion of the rights of the individual could find a home within a view that . . . might be fairly dubbed "environmental fascism."[22]

These are serious charges. If they cannot be answered by defenders of the land ethic, we will have good reason to look elsewhere for a satisfactory environmental ethic.

One approach might develop the suggestion concerning practical holism. Given the history of human destruction of natural environments, we are well advised to act as if ecosystems had moral standing. The problem with this approach is that it merely postpones the question of fascism. What ought we to do when the good of an ecological community conflicts with the good of an individual human? Either we act as if the community itself has standing and override the interests of the human, or we abandon the pretense and allow the human interest to take precedence. With the first option, we face the fascism charge, and with the second, we abandon holism.

Philosopher Don Marietta suggests another response.[23] He points out that ethical holism can have a variety of implications. A statement like Leopold's integrity and stability claim might imply that the *only* source of right and wrong is the good of the biotic community. It might imply that the *most important* source lies with the good of the community, or it might imply simply that *one* source of right and wrong lies with the good of the community.

Marietta goes on to argue that we cannot justify treating the good of the biotic community as the only or necessarily the most important source of right and wrong. These extreme positions are reductionistic in that they treat human beings as if they were *only* biological entities. Humans are more than that, of course, and a satisfactory ethics must take into account the wide range of morally relevant factors about humans. This includes, but is not limited to, humans' biological role in nature.

Thus, Marietta concludes that ethical holism should be seen as introducing one new source of right and wrong into ethics. Only if we assume that it introduces the only or the most important source does holism fall victim to the fascism charge. As it stands, we should recognize that we face complex moral situations with few specific and overriding rules that determine exactly what we should do. Holism calls our attention to some complexity that we may have missed otherwise. It does not necessarily commit us to environmental fascism.

But can Leopold's holism be defended in this way? At first glance, it cannot. Leopold's principle that "a thing is right when . . . it is wrong when it tends otherwise" would seem to suggest exactly the sort of overriding rule that Marietta rejects. This principle suggests that something is either right or wrong and, hence, leaves no room for the type of moral pluralism that Marietta accepts. But perhaps there is a way to synthesize these two views.

First, we can follow Marietta's suggestion and recognize that in a morally complex world certain acts might be both right in one way and wrong in another way. Thus, it might be both right and wrong for a farmer to fill in a wetland in order to increase the land available for agriculture. From the eco-centric point of view, it might be wrong. From the point of view of the farm family that is facing bankruptcy, it might be right. In this case, right or wrong would simply mean that good and plausible reasons can be given for both sides.

Philosopher Jon Moline suggests yet another approach.[24] Moline's inter-pretation focuses on the word *thing* in Leopold's account of right and wrong. If by thing we mean an individual *action,* Leopold would be open to the fas-cism charge. But if we interpret thing to mean a *type* of action, rule, or attitude, the fascism charge is less plausible. Moline calls the first option "direct holism" and the second option "indirect holism" and suggests that Leopold ought to be read as an indirect holist.

> I argue that Leopold, by contrast, is an *indirect* holist, i.e., one who applies holis-tic criteria not directly to acts, but only indirectly to these through criticisms of practices, rules, predilections, and attitudes. He criticizes above all our manner of thinking and wishing, seeing that all our actions flow from this.[25]

We can integrate Moline's suggestion with the discussion of an ethics of character discussed in Chapter 7. Leopold's integrity and stability principle should be viewed as normative for human character: our attitudes, disposi-tions, and "our manner of thinking and wishing." It proposes the type of per-son we should be, a trait of character, not the specific acts we should perform.

Moline acknowledges that some critics will charge that direct and indirect holism ultimately are indistinguishable.[26] In any particular instance, either the indirect principle will have exactly the same prescription as the direct ver-sion, or it will not. If it does, there is no practical difference between the two (if the direct holism is fascistic, so is the indirect version). If it does not, the indirect version is not, after all, holistic (because in tough cases, it abandons the holistic conclusion).

But this criticism is valid only if we assume that any particular case always has one unambiguous and knowable prescription. But time and again, Leopold points out that even the ecologist does not know exactly what will preserve the integrity and stability of the biotic community.

> The ordinary citizen today assumes that science knows what makes the com-munity clock tick; the scientist is equally sure that he does not. He knows that the biotic mechanism is so complex that its workings may never be fully understood.[27]

Given the complexity of ecosystems and given the realization that they undergo constant change, we should not presume that we ever know with certainty what will or will not preserve integrity or stability in any particular case. Thus, as a direct guide for action, Leopold's principle would be empty and irrelevant.

We now can see a way to integrate Leopold's appreciation of the ecological complexity of nature, Marietta's appreciation of the moral complexity of our world, and Moline's indirect holism. Ecology teaches that natural biotic systems are extremely complex. We need to abandon the mechanistic view of nature and be suspicious of any abrupt and human-wrought changes to it. Marietta cautions us to be sensitive to moral complexity as well. Combine these two perspectives, and we would conclude that ecological ethics is fundamentally indeterminate. That is, we just might never be able to know, in any particular case, what the ethically correct act is. We often will not know enough about an ecosystem to understand the consequences of our actions, and competing values might be pulling us in different directions. But it is exactly in such a situation that a second-order principle of the type Moline describes can help us.

In these situations, we should be guided by those attitudes, dispositions, and practices that have tended to preserve the integrity and stability of ecosystems. In general, these are attitudes of love, respect, and admiration. In practice, this would imply a relatively conservative approach to natural systems: presumptions in favor of natural evolutionary changes (rather than human-wrought changes), native plants and animals, slow rather than rapid change, and biological rather than mechanical, artificial, and manufactured solutions to environmental problems.

In this view, Leopold's ethics is focused less on rules that guide action and more on moral dispositions or virtues. We may be unable to specify in any detail what the correct act or decision is, but we can determine whether a person is acting responsibly. If a person acts out of a "loving and respectful" character, the decision will be a responsible one. Both the world of ecology and the world of morality make it unlikely that any specific moral rule will be able to offer us unambiguous practical advice. In such a situation, the best we can do is to rely on the best judgment of a particular type of person. This would be a person who loves, respects, and admires the biotic community. Whatever this person decides will be the ethically responsible thing, even though we have no way of independently and antecedently specifying what that ought to be.

Before turning to a final consideration of Leopold's holism, consider one further point. Philosophical critics may not find the foregoing line of reasoning persuasive. After all, they might charge that implicit in whatever act the virtuous person performs will be a rule (or maxim) that could be made explicit. Either that maxim should be followed in relevantly similar situations, or it should not. If it should, then we do after all have a rule to guide our actions, and we can proceed with the philosophical examination of that rule. If it should not, we have abandoned ethics completely in favor of an arbitrary decision process.

Perhaps an example arising in medical ethics can help illustrate the alternative. We have all become familiar with cases in which individuals who are suffering from major physiological damage are kept alive (or at least their bodies are kept functioning) only by complex technological devices. Many states have responded to these tragedies by enacting legislation that recognizes the validity of "living wills." In such cases, an individual can specify while they are competent the conditions under which they would choose to have life-support technology removed. We seem, as a society, to have accepted the principle of self-determination. Competent individuals may decline any medical procedures.

The problem confronting living wills is not unlike that facing the ecologist. Science, in this case medicine, is often indeterminate. Given the complexity of the human organism, physicians simply never know with certainty a patient's prognosis. When writing a living will, therefore, a person is faced with extreme uncertainty about what their condition might be, their prognosis, the technology that might be available in the future, and so forth. But they are also faced with moral uncertainty. Strong reasons can be given for and against the decision to discontinue life support.

In the face of this deep complexity, we might argue that a living will should be an *indirect*, not a *direct*, guide. The will should specify *who* should be empowered to make the decision, not the conditions under which a specific decision should be made. Thus, we might decide that a loved one—spouse, parent, or child—should have the authority to decide for us. The view is that whatever such a person decides will be the correct decision. Our justification for this judgment lies in the character of this person. While writing the living will, I might reason as follows. Because this person loves me and is generally a reasonable, thoughtful, and sensitive person, this person will make the best decision in a complex situation. I recognize that this is a decision that even I cannot make in the abstract, and I also recognize that good reasons can be given for and against whatever that decision turns out to be.

This interpretation makes Leopold sound like a modern Aristotelian. Like Aristotle's ethics, the land ethic would focus on the formation of an ethical character rather than on the defense of some ultimate moral rule or principle. Like Aristotle, moral education and moral psychology have an important role to play in the development (evolution?) of ethics. Whether this is a plausible reading can be left for another time. At this point, we should acknowledge that the land ethic faces serious challenges but is not without resources for answering these challenges.

We now turn to a final challenge to Leopold's holistic ethics. Is a meaningful account of ecological wholes defensible? We have seen that ecologists have defended different models of an ecosystem: organic, community, and energy circuit. Which, if any, can be made compatible with the land ethic?

We have seen Leopold at times adopt an organic model of ecosystems. The land itself is seen as a living organism. In some ways, this is the model best suited for the land ethic. We seem most able to move between the facts of ecology and the values implicit in such concepts as integrity and stability, health, and well-being when we treat ecosystems as organic wholes.

Human and veterinary medicine provide a powerful example of how this reasoning could develop. Given a scientific understanding of the normal growth and development of an individual organism, medical science has proved capable of diagnosing ills and promoting health. If it turns out that ecosystems are relevantly similar to these individual organisms, the potential exists for a similar synthesis of science and values.

But we have already seen that ecologists have moved beyond this organic model. The very science that Leopold relied on to present the holism of ecosystems has concluded that the organic model of ecological systems is inadequate. The classical refutation of the organic model is found in the writings of Arthur Tansley.[28]

Tansley argued that ecosystems could be viewed as organisms only in a metaphorical way. They were not literally organisms because individuals within an ecosystem, unlike the individual organs of a body, could exist outside the organism. Ecosystems do not have the "unity and definiteness" of real organisms, and their constituent parts are quite capable of moving into other systems and becoming full members of them. This independence means that members of an ecosystem are quite unlike the organs of a body.

Perhaps, then, Leopold's holism should be understood within the functional community model. Here, members of an ecosystem are not understood as parts to a whole or as organs to a body but as functionally dependent on each other. An individual organism is identified as part of the biotic community or the food chain by reference to what it eats and what eats it. The arrangement of individual organisms and their relations to one another are what constitute the system.

But can this account of an ecosystem provide what is required of it in Leopold's ethics? Leopold is clear that at least one object of our moral consideration (our love, respect, and admiration) is the community itself, not its constituent members. The well-being of this community consists of its integrity and stability. But what can integrity and stability mean if we are talking about food chains and not organisms?

Consider what is being asked. In the reading of Leopold offered so far, human beings are encouraged to act out of a love, respect, and admiration for the biotic community. But this seems possible only insofar as this community has some good or interests of its own. (Otherwise, we would be acting for the good of the community only as a means for attaining the good of its constituent members. This would be to abandon the holistic perspective.) But is it reasonable to hold that we can love and respect a biotic community? Leopold's principle suggests that it is. A community can be loved and respected because it has interests and its interests rest on its integrity and stability. But are biotic communities the kinds of things that possess integrity and stability?

At any given time, it might appear that they do. A small pond, for example, can be said to possess integrity and stability if it is not drained, its various biotic populations remain stationary, the climate remains constant, artificial or nonnative elements are not added, and so forth, in short, if its structure and functional relationships can be maintained. But as shown, ecosystems do not remain stable over time. Through natural biological, chemical, geological, and climatic forces, biotic communities evolve into different types of ecosystems. Thus, we are faced with a choice: either interfere with these natural processes in order to preserve a particular integrity and stability or allow these natural processes to continue and abandon the most obvious sense of integrity and stability. The examples of Olympic mountain goats and Yellowstone wolves raise these questions rather dramatically.

But perhaps biotic community can be understood to refer not to the particular members of the community or to a particular arrangement of those members but to the conditions under which the biological processes and relationships can be preserved. Thus, an ecosystem, now meaning something more akin to a locale, has integrity and stability to the degree that it is capable of sustaining biological processes. Thus, a healthy community has topsoil that is rich in nutrients and not eroded, has rain that is not acidified, is pesticide and herbicide free, does not suffer from an overpopulation of any species, and so forth.

Unfortunately, this answer has several problems. First, this concept of ecosystem health may be too open-ended. Certain biological processes have shown themselves quite capable of surviving in the most ecologically blighted areas. For example, the HIV, bubonic plague, and polio agents seem to thrive in conditions of something less than the ecological ideal. We would need some further standard to decide which biological processes contribute to a system's health and which do not.

More important, this answer also seems to base the land ethic on instrumental and nonholistic values. In effect, this answer says that we ought to preserve the integrity and stability of a system or community not because it has value in itself but because it contributes to the well-being of other things that have intrinsic value.

9.6 CALLICOTT'S REVISIONS

Since the mid-1970s, the American philosopher J. Baird Callicott has written extensively in defense of Leopold's land ethic.[29] Callicott's work offers valuable insights into Leopold's thinking and provides a creative interpretation of the land ethic. Callicott's work demonstrates that Leopold's approach remains a rich resource for continued work in environmental ethics.

Underlying the challenge identified as the naturalistic fallacy is the assumption that a gap in logic exists between statements of fact (is) and statements of value (oughts). Facts are independent of human judgment. They are objective. Values are subjective and are dependent on human judgments. A primary goal for normative ethics, in this view, is to reason from facts to values. But the facts themselves are never sufficient for drawing normative conclusions.

Callicott seeks to bridge this gap by locating Leopold within an ethical tradition extending from David Hume and Adam Smith through Charles
Darwin. According to Callicott, this tradition places moral sentiments at the
center of ethics. In this view, ethics arises out of human sentiments, what we
might variously call feelings, attitudes, dispositions, or affections. For David
Hume, sympathy is one of the most fundamental human sentiments. Human
beings can identify with and feel sympathy for other human beings. This feeling for the other is at the origins of ethics. Thus, the oughts of ethics arise not
from simple facts about the world (it was, after all, Hume who so clearly identified the gap between is and ought) but from facts about us. To figure out the
moral wrong with willful murder, for example, Hume tells us to look within
ourselves and we will find a "sentiment of disapprobation." The evil is a matter of fact, but "it lies in yourself, not in the object."

Consider an example of how moral sentiments help bridge the gap from is
to ought. We can begin with purely descriptive factual "is" statements. In the
yard is a young child who has fallen and scraped his knee. He is crying. He is
my son. From these statements, I conclude that I ought to rush outside to comfort and care for this child. To the question of why I ought to rush to that child
Hume would answer, "Because he is your son, and you love him." The fact
that he is my son, in and of itself, does not logically lead to the ought statement according to Hume. It does so only when conjoined with additional
(also factual) statements about my own and more generally human psychology: parents love their children. Thus, judgments of value are rooted in fundamental elements of human psychology.

Callicott believes that this approach is further developed in Darwin and
later picked up by Leopold and incorporated into the land ethic.

> Darwin's account, to which Leopold unmistakably (if elliptically) alludes in "The
> Land Ethic," begins with the parental and filial affections common, perhaps, to
> all mammals. Bonds of affection and sympathy between parents and offspring
> permitted the formation of small, closely kin social groups, Darwin argued.
> Should the parental and filial affections bonding family members chance to
> extend to less closely related individuals, that would permit the enlargement of
> the family group. And should the newly extended community more successfully
> defend itself and/or more efficiently provision itself, the inclusive fitness of its
> members severally would be increased, Darwin reasoned. Thus the more diffuse
> familial affections, which Darwin (echoing Hume and Smith) calls the "social
> sentiments," would be spread throughout a population.[30]

Thus, the sentiments of affection and sympathy, sentiments that bridge the
gap between facts and values, can be extended from the individual to include
a wider social universe. In Leopold's words, "The land ethic simply enlarges
the boundaries of the community to include soils, waters, plants, and animals,
or collectively: the land."[31]

In Callicott's interpretation, Leopold is part of this Hume-Darwin tradition.
Leopold encourages us to extend our recognition of family and community

bonds to include all other members of the biotic community. Thus, reasoning from is to ought, from the facts of ecological destruction to the oughts of environmental activism, is logically the same as reasoning from the facts of a child's suffering to the conclusion that I ought to help. According to Callicott, the logic of the land ethic

> is that natural selection has endowed human beings with an affective moral response to perceived bonds of kinship and community membership and identity; that today the natural environment, the land, is represented as a community, the biotic community; and that, therefore, an environment or land ethic is both possible, the biopsychological and cognitive conditions are in place, and necessary, since human beings collectively have acquired the power to destroy the integrity, diversity, and stability of the environing and supporting economy of nature.[32]

Although this interpretation may place Leopold within a distinguished intellectual tradition, it is not without problems. Perhaps the most serious challenge is that sentiments are a notoriously unstable foundation on which to build an ethics. It would seem that for every case in which humans act out of sympathy, affection, or cooperation, we can find a case of someone acting out of selfishness, hatred, or competition. Human psychology seems just as capable of building barriers between people as it is of building bonds. Thus, the open question remains: Why should I extend my sympathy rather than my animosity to the land? We still need reasons to develop positive rather than negative sentiments.

This challenge may gain some practical weight when we recognize that at least some environmental issues arise from cases in which humans destroy the integrity, stability, and beauty of an ecosystem in the name of family or community well-being. For example, in many areas of the world, people destroy rain forests, wilderness areas, and endangered species so that they can provide a basic living for their families. In such cases, moral sentiments would seem to provide an incentive to destroy rather than protect the ecosystem. If we base the land ethic on moral sentiments, we have little moral answer to those who would destroy the land in the name of those very sentiments.

This problem echoes the challenge that Immanuel Kant raised against Hume's ethics. Human psychology is an insufficient basis for ethics because it can offer only hypothetical imperatives. If you care about others, you should not harm them. Ethics, for Kant, must supply categorical imperatives, normative judgments that are inescapable for any rational person. Oughts should not depend on the feelings, attitudes, or sentiments of the individual.

It may well be unfair to ask more of Leopold than what we ask of philosophers. Despite Kant's best efforts, philosophers still much debate this point. Callicott has offered a thoughtful and provocative account of the ethical foundations of the land ethic. Mainstream Western philosophy has no doubt

judged that foundation to be unstable, at least when compared to the possibility of a more categorical imperative. Perhaps Western philosophy has
asked too much of ethics. Perhaps the best we can hope for is an ethics based
on sympathy, compassion, and love.

Callicott also offers an interpretation of Leopold that responds to the challenge raised against holism. In this interpretation, the land ethic adopts a
metaphysical holism, with ethical implications following from this. Callicott's
interpretation of Leopold's metaphysical holism was encountered in
Chapter 8. Using the functional energy language of ecosystems ecology to
explain Leopold's food pyramid, Callicott argues for the metaphysical primacy of relations and wholes.

> Ecology is the study of relationships of organisms to one another and to the ele-
> mental environment. . . . The ontological primacy of objects and the ontological
> subordination of relationships characteristic of classical western science is, in fact,
> reversed in ecology. Ecological relationships determine the nature of organisms
> rather than the other way around. A species is what it is because it has adapted
> to a niche in the ecosystem. The whole, the system itself, thus, literally and quite
> straightforwardly shapes and forms its component parts.[33]

In another place, Callicott tells us that

> from the perspective of modern biology, species adapt to a niche in the ecosys-
> tem. Their actual relationships to other organisms (to predators, to prey, to para-
> sites and disease organisms) and to the physical and chemical conditions (to
> temperature, radiation, salinity, wind, soil and water [acidity]) literally sculpt
> their outward forms, their metabolic, physiological, and reproductive processes,
> and even their psychological and mental capacities.[34]

Guided by modern ecological science, Callicott reasons that relationships are
"prior to" the things related, and "ecosystemic wholes are logically prior to
their component species because the nature of the part is determined by its
relationship to the whole."[35] Thus, ecological holism points us toward the
underlying nature of reality. Callicott believes the ecology not only has implications for metaphysics but that it leads to ethical conclusions as well.

> Since individual organisms, from an ecological point of view, are less discrete
> objects than modes of a continuous, albeit differentiated, whole, the distinction
> between self and other is blurred. . . . As one moves, in imagination, outwardly
> from the core of one's organism, it is impossible to find a clear demarcation
> between oneself and one's environment. . . . The world is, indeed, one's extended
> body.[36]

Thus, "the relational view of self . . . transforms egoism into environmentalism." Because we are one with nature, it is in our self-interest (egoism) to preserve and protect the natural world (environmentalism). Accordingly,

Callicott reasons from ecology to metaphysics to ethics, once again providing a bridge from ecological facts to ethical value.

We are left with two questions: Does ecology provide reasons to adopt the type of holism Callicott defends, and does that holism commit us to a defensible environmental ethics?

Both issues confront serious problems. First, as the review of ecological models in Chapter 8 suggests, ecologists have not agreed that the functional energy model that Callicott attributes to the land ethic offers the most accurate description of nature. More important, we need to be careful with any attempt to draw metaphysical conclusions from scientific observations. Indeed, most philosophers would likely argue that metaphysics and epistemology precede science, not the other way around. Scientific claims and observations presuppose a set of assumptions about what is real and what can be known. It begs the question to derive philosophical conclusions from science because science cannot begin without philosophical assumptions.[37]

More relevant to our present concerns, perhaps, is the move from metaphysical holism to an ethics of environmentalism. Callicott reminds us that the intrinsic value of individuals is taken as a given in much Western philosophy. Earlier chapters noted that the question of intrinsic value is a key question in the move away from animal welfare rights and a more general ethical extensionism toward a broader environmental ethics. Callicott answers this question by telling us that ecological holism outflanks the problem of attributing intrinsic value to natural objects other than humans. Because humans are assumed to possess intrinsic value (and if they do not, what does?) and we cannot make a clear distinction between self and nature, we are justified in attributing intrinsic value to nature.

But this (alleged) synthesis of self and nature is a metaphysical one, not a psychological one. Whatever Callicott claims to be true metaphysically, it nevertheless remains true that for most of us the distinction between self and nature is an obvious, immediate, and lived one. I certainly do not believe (or feel, if we wish to remain consistent with the Humean ethics of Leopold/Callicott) that I am one with nature. The claim that no firm divide (metaphysical or natural) exists between self and other is not in itself enough to establish what we ought to do. In effect, the naturalistic fallacy challenge has risen again.

Consider an alternative conclusion that might be drawn from Callicott's metaphysical holism. Assume that the self does become merged psychologically as well as metaphysically with the natural world. What ought "I" to do? Callicott suggests that, driven by a new "enlightened self-interest," I ought to extend the intrinsic value previously reserved for the self to the natural world. But why do this rather than extend the mere instrumental value previously reserved for nature to the self? Why should I not always be willing to sacrifice the self for the good of the whole? More generally, might we lose the intrinsic value of humans in the name of the greater good? The specter of fascism has returned.

Remember that a major challenge to ethical holism is that in service to the well-being of the whole, one will sacrifice the well-being of individuals. As the intrinsic value originally reserved for the individual gets transferred to the whole, the possibility arises that the individual would be left without intrinsic value. As we begin to extend our affections from the self to the land, the self might get totally merged into the whole and deprived of its moral standing.

Callicott surely has resources to answer this challenge. At times, he speaks of our existing within "nested and overlapping communities," suggesting a model of concentric circles in which our affections are extended first to self and family and later to more extended communities.[38] In this model, we extend membership for moral considerability to the land without disavowing an initial and prior value that characterizes the inner circles. But, again, what do we do in cases in which conflict exists between responsibility to the innermost circle, that is, to myself and my family, and responsibility to outer circles, which include ecosystems and wilderness areas? If we favor the objects in the outermost circles, we are open to charges of fascism. If we favor ourselves and families, holism seems not to have advanced the ethical standing of the nonhuman natural world.

What are we to make of these debates? It seems that we have gone far afield from the elegance of Leopold's inspiring and original work. Seeking to defend it from challenges, we find ourselves deep within philosophical debates that seem quite removed from environmental and ecological concerns. But this is testimony perhaps to the continued need for philosophy. As seen throughout this textbook, environmental concerns do raise fundamental questions about how we ought to live. We should not expect that these fundamental questions will be easily answered.

9.7 SUMMARY AND CONCLUSIONS

Thus, serious philosophical challenges to the land ethic remain. Nevertheless, Leopold's work holds promise for philosophical reflection on the environment. Without question, his writing provides inspiration for everyone concerned with environmental ethics. Perhaps his greatest contribution lies in focusing attention on ecosystems and relationships—in short, to take ecological wholes as worthy of serious moral consideration. Whether this consideration turns out to be in the form of direct or indirect moral standing, after Aldo Leopold this issue can no longer be ignored.

Notes

1. For a helpful critical discussion of this model, see Daniel Botkin, *Discordant Harmonies* (New York: Oxford University Press, 1990), ch. 3.
2. Aldo Leopold, *Game Management* (New York: Scribner's, 1933), p. 179.
3. Aldo Leopold, "The Varmint Question," reprinted in *The River of the Mother of God and Other Essays* by Aldo Leopold, ed. Susan Flader and J. Baird Callicott (Madison: University of Wisconsin Press, 1991), pp. 47–48.

4. Aldo Leopold, "Some Fundamentals of Conservation in the Southwest" (1923), reprinted in Flader and Callicott, eds., *River of the Mother of God and Other Essays*, pp. 47–48.

5. Aldo Leopold, "Thinking Like a Mountain," in *A Sand County Almanac* (1949; New York: Ballantine, 1970), p. 138.

6. Leopold, "The Land Ethic," in *A Sand County Almanac*, p. 253.

7. Ibid., pp. 253, 239, 247.

8. Callicott argues this point forcefully in "Animal Liberation: A Triangular Affair," *Environmental Ethics* 2 (fall 1980): 311–38. Callicott tempers his claims a bit in later essays, but he does not abandon the essential point that Leopold's views are incompatible with the animal rights movement. See J. Baird Callicott, *In Defense of the Land Ethic* (Albany: State University of New York Press, 1989). Jon Moline makes a similar point in "Aldo Leopold and the Moral Community," *Environmental Ethics* 8 (summer 1986): 99–120.

9. Leopold, "The Land Ethic," p. 262.

10. Ibid., 252.

11. Ibid., 252–53.

12. Leopold, *A Sand County Almanac*, pp. 6–7.

13. Ibid., 6–19.

14. Leopold, "Some Fundamentals of Conservation in the Southwest," p. 95.

15. Leopold, *A Sand County Almanac*, p. 252.

16. For a discussion of this point, see J. Baird Callicott, "The Conceptual Foundations of the Land Ethic," in *In Defense of the Land Ethic*, pp. 87–90.

17. For a sustained and sophisticated defense of the use of integrity in this context, see Laura Westra, *An Environmental Proposal for Ethics: The Principle of Integrity* (Lanham, Md.: Rowman and Littlefield, 1994).

18. Leopold, "The Land Ethic," p. 261.

19. Leopold, *A Sand County Almanac*, p. 262.

20. Callicott develops this defense in greater detail in "Hume's Is/Ought Dichotomy and the Relation of Ecology to Leopold's Land Ethic," reprinted in *In Defense of the Land Ethic*, pp. 117–27. Callicott's interpretation and defense of the land ethic are always worth reading, even if it is not always clear where Leopold's work leaves off and Callicott's begins.

21. Marti Kheel, "The Liberation of Nature: A Circular Affair," *Environmental Ethics* 7 (summer 1985): 135–49, and Eric Katz, "Organicism, Community, and the 'Substitution Problem,'" *Environmental Ethics* 7 (fall 1985): 241–56.

22. Tom Regan, *The Case for Animal Rights* (Berkeley: University of California Press, 1983), pp. 361–62; the emphasis is Regan's.

23. Don E. Marietta Jr., "Environmental Holism and Individuals," *Environmental Ethics* 10 (fall 1988): 251–58.

24. Jon Moline, "Aldo Leopold and the Moral Community," *Environmental Ethics* 8 (summer 1986): 99–120.

25. Ibid., 105.

26. Ibid., 106. This criticism is best known when directed against act-and-rule utilitarianism. See, for example, David Lyons, *Forms and Limits of Utilitarianism* (Oxford, England: Clarendon, 1965), p. 118.

27. Leopold, "The Land Ethic," pp. 240–41.

28. Arthur Tansley, "The Use and Abuse of Vegetational Concepts and Terms," *Ecology* 16 (1935): 284–307. See also an earlier Tansley article, "The Classification of

Vegetation and the Concept of Development," *Journal of Ecology* 8 (1920): 118–49.
For a general history of ecology, see Donald Worster, *Nature's Economy* (Cambridge, England: Cambridge University Press, 1985).

29. Many of Callicott's most important essays are collected in *In Defense of the Land Ethic*.

30. Callicott, "Conceptual Foundations of the Land Ethic," p. 79. Callicott cites Darwin's *Descent of Man*, especially ch. 4, as the source for these claims.

31. Leopold, "The Land Ethic," p. 239.

32. Callicott, "Conceptual Foundations of the Land Ethic," p. 83.

33. Ibid., 87.

34. Callicott, "The Metaphysical Implications of Ecology," in *In Defense of the Land Ethic*, p. 110.

35. Ibid., 110–11.

36. Ibid., 112–13.

37. Two insightful and convincing sources that advance this claim are Andrew Brennan, *Thinking About Nature: An Investigation of Nature, Value, and Ecology* (Athens: University of Georgia Press, 1988), and Karen Warren and Jim Cheney, "Ecosystem Ecology and Metaphysical Ecology: A Case Study," in *Environmental Ethics* 15 (summer 1993): 99–116.

38. This view is seen most clearly in Callicott's "Animal Liberation and Environmental Ethics: Back Together Again," in *In Defense of the Land Ethic*, ch. 3.

Discussion Questions

1. Should farmers and ranchers be allowed to kill wild predators such as coyote and wolves in order to protect their herds? How should government balance these competing interests?

2. Do you support reintroducing wolves into the Yellowstone ecosystem? Respond to those who would oppose your conclusions.

3. How might Singer and Regan differ from Leopold on the question of hunting deer? How relevant would such factors as herd size and ecosystem condition be? Would these thinkers have different views on the value of domestic versus wild animals?

4. Do you support the view that humans are equal moral citizens of the biotic community? Is there a middle ground between humans as masters of nature and humans as equal biotic citizens?

5. Leopold suggests that the "dead earth" is an organism that does possess a certain kind of life. What exactly is the difference between a living organism and a nonliving object? Is the earth itself alive?

6. Can land or an ecosystem really be characterized as healthy or unhealthy in anything other than a metaphorical way? What exactly would a healthy ecosystem be?

7. Return to a question asked at the end of Chapter 1. Are all things that are "natural" also good? Has your thinking on this question changed since you read Chapter 1?

Further Reading

Aldo Leopold's writings are eminently readable. *The River of the Mother of God and Other Essays*, ed. Susan Flader and J. Baird Callicott (Madison: University of

Wisconsin Press, 1991), is a collection of more than fifty of Leopold's essays span-
ning more than forty years of writing.

Susan Flader, *Thinking Like a Mountain* (Columbia: University of Missouri Press,
1974), and Curt Meine, *Aldo Leopold: His Life and His Work* (Madison: University of
Wisconsin Press, 1988), are both solid biographical studies of Leopold.

J. Baird Callicott, *In Defense of the Land Ethic* (Albany: State University of New
York Press, 1989), develops a contemporary philosophical defense of the land ethic.
Callicott's work offers the best and most developed interpretation of Leopold.

10

Deep Ecology

Environmental Activism: Legal and Illegal

Faced with environmental and ecological destruction, we soon realize that science and philosophy can take us only so far. No matter what conclusions we reach from scientific and philosophical analysis, we still face the further political question of how best to influence and direct public policy.

We might be convinced by scientific and philosophical reasoning that the most justified course of action involves, for example, preserving a wilderness area or protecting an endangered species. But the question remains: What is the best way, practically and ethically, to get these decisions made at the level of public policy? These questions are particularly challenging when we recognize that a decision to protect ecological interests can often have high economic and political costs. Quite often, environmental interests are pitted against entrenched and influential corporate and government interests.

Mineral King Valley was such a case. That case involved corporate and government interests in the form of the agreement between Walt Disney Enterprises and the U.S. Forest Service going against the environmental interests represented by the Sierra Club. In pursuit of its environmental goals, the Sierra Club relied on a traditional course of action. Its members filed a lawsuit to block development of the valley. Since the early 1970s, litigation has been a primary political strategy to effect environmental change.

Environmental activism also occurs within both the legislative and executive branches of government, as well as within the private sector.

Lobbying for legislation, writing letters, supporting political candidates, attending Earth Day rallies and celebrations, holding protest marches, and staging economic boycotts have all, to various degrees, influenced contemporary environmental policy. Underlying these actions is the shared assumption that change can effectively be brought about by working within existing political and economic systems.

But what happens if you believe that a political and economic system is responsible for environmental problems? The economic and political influence of polluters and developers, lax enforcement of the law, biased or deficient media coverage, an economic system that rewards selfishness, competition, and consumption, and a system of private property rights that allows private owners almost total control over their property are just some of the factors that diminish the effectiveness of working within the system. In light of this, are illegal means ever justified in the pursuit of environmental and ecological goals?

We can distinguish between two extralegal strategies for environmental protection. The first is a variation on a long tradition of civil disobedience, and the second has been called "ecosabotage" or "ecoterrorism."[1]

The history of conscientious acts of civil disobedience can be traced from Socrates and Jesus through Thoreau, Gandhi, and Martin Luther King, Jr. In this tradition, civil disobedience involves choosing to disobey the law on moral grounds as a means of protesting or thwarting government policy. The leading defenders of civil disobedience typically are committed to nonviolence and accept public responsibility (and punishment) for the act.

In this vein, we recognize that numerous actions of environmental activists can be classified as acts of civil disobedience. The environmental group Greenpeace is perhaps best known for its activities that fit the civil disobedience model. Some Greenpeace members have been known to sail their ships into restricted nuclear testing zones, climb smokestacks to hang banners denouncing pollution, harass and ram whaling and fishing vessels, and the like. Typically, these acts involve criminal trespass and other minor offenses but pose little or no danger to humans or property. Defenders of these acts argue that they can be justified in the same ways that civil rights activists in twentieth century America have justified their civil disobedience.

Essentially, we could argue that we live in a culture and at a time in which people are slow to recognize the serious wrongs being committed. The normal political and legal processes are unlikely to change things because much of the public is unaware of or has failed to appreciate the extent of the harms. Public acts of civil disobedience, especially if they are covered in the media and result in well-publicized arrests and trials, can be an effective means for focusing public attention and stimulating public action. If done in such a way as to minimize the detrimental effects that can accompany breaking the law, which often means if done respectfully and nonviolently, the beneficial consequences can justify civil disobedience.

Might the dire environmental consequences of political inaction justify something more than civil disobedience? Might illegal acts directed against private citizens or private businesses be justified? Are acts of sabotage against property, what is often called "monkey wrenching," morally justified? Could violence against individuals, what we might call "ecoterrorism," ever be justified?

Monkey wrenching was popularized in a series of publications originating with Edward Abbey's novel *The Monkey Wrench Gang*. The publications of the radical environmental group Earth First! have described and encouraged, if not advocated, monkey wrenching. As defined by sociologist Bill Devall, monkey wrenching is the "purposeful dismantling or disabling of artifacts used in environmentally destructive practices at a specific site— dismantling fishing gear or logging equipment, for example." Devall goes on to define *ecosabotage* or *ecotage* as "disabling a technological or bureaucratic operation in defense of one's place."[2] Typical examples of monkey wrenching include tree spiking (driving large metal spikes into trees to discourage logging), pouring sand into the gas tanks of construction and logging vehicles, pulling up survey stakes, and cutting down power lines. Similarly destructive acts against property are performed by animal liberation groups that break into and sometimes destroy laboratories to save animals from experimentation.

Unlike classic instances of civil disobedience, monkey wrenching and ecosabotage are often performed under the cover of darkness with the intent of escaping detection. For example, a group called the Sea Shepherd Conservation Society sank two Icelandic whaling boats while they anchored in harbor in 1986. These saboteurs secretly entered the boats at night and opened seacocks to flood and sink the ships. Unlike wellestablished cases of civil disobedience, these activities usually involve destruction of property and, if not themselves acts of violence, hold the potential of injuring or killing people. Loggers have been injured when their saws hit a spike driven into a tree.

The Sea Shepherd Conservation Society refused to sink a third ship when they found a night watchman aboard. They had pledged not to injure human beings. This decision stands in contrast to the actions of the French government against Greenpeace protesters in 1985. Greenpeace members intended to sail their vessel, *Rainbow Warrior*, into restricted waters where the French were planning to conduct nuclear weapons testing. The French government sent intelligence agents into New Zealand with false passports to sink the *Rainbow Warrior*. A crew member aboard the ship at the time of the sinking was killed. In the fall of 1995, the French military again forcibly seized several Greenpeace ships that were protesting French nuclear tests in international waters.

Throughout much of the Western tradition, governments have often justified violence and killing in pursuit of important social goals. The just war theory and self-defense are two ways that violence has been ethically justified. Sometimes, our culture has accepted violence, if it is a last resort and a way to protect innocent life. Might violence against individuals ever be justified in order to protect nonhuman life? Could rationales like the just war or self-defense arguments be extended to ecological issues?

10.1 INTRODUCTION

This chapter examines the *Deep Ecology* movement. Unlike the land ethic, Deep Ecology has not developed out of one primary source, nor does it refer to one systematic philosophy. Deep ecology has been used in a variety of ways, ranging from a general description of all nonanthropocentric theories to the highly technical "ecosophy T" developed by the Norwegian philosopher Arne Naess.[3] In recent years, the phrase "Deep Ecology" has come to refer primarily to the approach to environmental issues developed in the writings of academics Naess, Devall, and George Sessions, which is how it is used in this chapter.[4]

Arne Naess first introduced a distinction between deep and shallow environmental perspectives in 1973.[5] Naess characterizes the shallow ecology movement as committed to the "fight against pollution and resource depletion." It is an anthropocentric approach with a central objective to protect the "health and affluence of the people in developed countries." Deep Ecology, on the other hand, takes a "relational, total-field" perspective, rejecting the anthropocentric "man-in-environment image" in favor of a more holistic and nonanthropocentric approach.

Perhaps a simpler characterization that is still faithful to Naess's basic point could be made in terms of symptoms and underlying causes. By focusing on issues like pollution and resource depletion, the shallow approach looks only at the immediate effects of the environmental crisis. Just as a sneeze or a cough can disrupt a person's daily routine, pollution and resource depletion disrupt the lifestyle of modern industrial societies. However, it would be a mistake for medicine to treat only sneezing and coughing and not investigate their underlying causes. So, too, it is a mistake for environmentalists to be concerned only with pollution and resource depletion without investigating their social and human causes.

Seen in this way, of course, Deep Ecology would refer to a wide variety of approaches. What distinguishes Deep Ecology as a philosophical approach is its tenet that the current environmental crisis can be traced to deep philosophical causes. Thus, a cure for the crisis can come only with a radical change in our philosophical outlook. This change involves both personal and cultural transformations and would "affect basic economic and ideological structures."[6] In short, we need to change ourselves as individuals and as a culture. But this change, according to Devall and Sessions, is not the creation of something new but a "reawakening of something very old." It involves the cultivation of an "ecological consciousness," an "ecological, philosophical, and spiritual approach" to the crisis that recognizes the "unity of humans, plants, animals, the Earth."[7]

Deep Ecologists trace their philosophical roots to many of the people and positions that this textbook has already examined. The debate between Gifford Pinchot and John Muir examined in Chapter 3 was an early version of the tension between shallow (Pinchot) and deep (Muir) thinkers. Rachel Carson's critique of anthropocentrism in *Silent Spring* and Lynn White's critique of *Western Christianity*, along with the nineteenth century romanticism of Thoreau, were precursors of Deep Ecology.[8]

As a philosophical movement, Deep Ecology presents a critique of what is called the "dominant worldview" as being responsible for environmental destruction. This critique is based on two positions seen previously: ecocentrism and nonanthropocentrism. Deep Ecologists attempt to work out an alternative philosophical worldview that is holistic and not human-centered. For many people involved in radical environmentalism as a political movement, members of Earth First!, for example, Deep Ecology provides the philosophy that legitimizes their form of activism.

But any call for a radical change in people's philosophical worldview immediately faces a major challenge. How do we even begin to explain the alternative if, by definition, it is radically different from the starting point? How do we step outside our personal and cultural worldview or ideology to compare it with something radically different?

Deep Ecologists use a variety of strategies to meet these challenges, including reliance on poetry, Buddhism, spiritualism, and political activism using acts of civil disobedience and ecosabotage. Perhaps the most helpful strategy involves seeking common agreement first on a platform of general principles. This platform serves as a core around which the diverse Deep Ecology movement can be unified.

10.2 THE DEEP ECOLOGY PLATFORM

Deep Ecologists are committed to the view that solutions to grave environmental crisis require more than mere reform of our personal and social practices. They believe it requires a radical transformation in our worldview. Thus, Deep Ecologists proceed in two directions. On one hand, they are committed to work for the types of changes needed. Many people who can be identified as Deep Ecologists dedicate their work as scientists, artists, and political activists to bring about these changes. On the other hand, Deep Ecologists also seek to develop and articulate an alternative philosophy to replace the dominant worldview that is responsible for the crisis. Naess calls the field that considers such questions and seeks alternative worldviews "ecophilosophy" and any particular working out of an alternative worldview an "ecosophy." Just as a variety of strategies for bringing about the necessary changes is possible, so, too, is it possible for a variety of ecosophies to be developed.

In light of this diversity of aims and formulations, Naess and Sessions developed the Deep Ecology platform as a statement of common principles. The principles provide reasons that can explain and justify the movement's activism. They also provide a less abstract focus for philosophical speculation. The platform is intended to be general enough to allow for a diversity of philosophical interpretations and specific enough to distinguish the deep from the shallow approach to practical matters.[9]

As developed by Naess and Sessions, the platform includes these principles:

(1) The flourishing of human and nonhuman life on Earth has intrinsic value. The value of nonhuman life-forms is independent of the usefulness these may have for narrow human purposes.

(2) Richness and diversity of life-forms are values in themselves and contribute to the flourishing of human and nonhuman life on Earth.

(3 Humans have no right to reduce this richness and diversity except to satisfy vital needs.

(4) Present human interference with the nonhuman world is excessive, and the situation is rapidly worsening.

(5) The flourishing of human life and cultures is compatible with a substantial decrease of the human population. The flourishing of nonhuman life requires such a decrease.

(6) Significant change of life conditions for the better requires change in policies. These affect basic economic, technological, and ideological structures.

(7) The ideological change is mainly that of appreciating *life quality* (dwelling in situations of intrinsic value) rather than adhering to a high standard of living. There will be a profound awareness of the difference between *big* and *great*.

(8) Those who subscribe to the foregoing points have an obligation directly or indirectly to participate in the attempt to implement the necessary changes.[10]

We can see how these principles could serve to explain and support a wide range of specific positions on practical environmental controversies. In working against the continued destruction of rain forests, for example, we could appeal to the first three principles. Principles 5 and 7 would be important in developing an energy policy that would address such issues as resource conservation, population growth, consumer demand, and nuclear energy.

An important point is that the platform also reflects the ways in which the science of ecology influences Deep Ecology. In some sense, ecological science would provide direct support for principles 4 and 5. Ecology would also be relevant in explaining and defending principles 1 and 2. But ecology is also important for ecophilosophy in that it provides a model for a nonreductionist, holistic worldview.

10.3 ECOLOGY AND ECOPHILOSOPHY

Like the land ethic, Deep Ecology relies on the science of ecology for a variety of purposes. Ecology provides a good deal of information about how natural ecosystems function. Ecology helps us to diagnose environmental disorders and prescribe policies that can resolve these disorders. Thus, in general, ecology provides us with an understanding of natural ecosystems, and this understanding in turn is the basis from which we can make evaluations and recommendations.

More specifically, ecology also cautions against any quick fix technological solution to environmental problems. Echoing a theme found in Leopold, Naess argues for a humble and constrained approach to environmental change. The conclusions reached in ecology and conservation biology are often "statements of ignorance." "Only rarely can scientists predict with any certainty the effect of a new chemical on even a single small ecosystem," Naess writes. Faced with this scientific ignorance, the burden of proof should rest with anyone who proposes a policy that intervenes in the natural environment.

> Why does the burden of proof rest with the encroachers? The ecosystems in which we intervene are generally in a particular state of balance which there are grounds to assume to be of more service to mankind than states of disturbance and their resultant unpredictable and far-reaching changes. In general, it is not possible to regain the original state after an intervention has wrought serious, undesired consequences.[11]

Accordingly, ecology contributes to ecophilosophy in the same ways that scientific understanding has often contributed to ethical analysis. We gain a better understanding of the world, and based on this understanding, we are in a better position to offer ethical evaluations and prescriptions. Because ecological understanding offers new insights, an ethics that relies on ecology can be expected to offer new evaluations and prescriptions.

But Naess also is aware of the limits of science and warns against too great a reliance on ecology. Although scientific ecology can contribute to the goals of Deep Ecologists, it should not be mistaken for the final authority on environmental disputes. There are dangers in what Naess calls "ecologism," the view that takes ecology as the ultimate science.

Essentially, two related dangers follow from raising ecology to a position of final authority. First, we should avoid the danger of turning ecology into an "all-encompassing worldview." This occurs when the science of ecology is treated as if it can provide resolutions to all environmental issues. Naess is aware of the problems raised in Chapter 9 in regard to Leopold and Callicott's reliance on ecology. Ecologism overgeneralizes and universalizes ecological concepts.[12] As a science, ecology can make significant contributions to our understanding of the natural world. But we must recognize that many problems are traced to epistemological and philosophical sources. Ecology is not a substitute for philosophical analysis.

Naess believes that ecology can provide a model for thinking about the deep philosophical questions that need to be addressed. These would include the following questions: What is an individual? What things have intrinsic value and moral standing? What is the most reasonable model for understanding nature? Ecology might suggest insightful and new ways for approaching these questions, and these approaches might well prove helpful in developing alternative ecophilosophies. But we must remember that the model does not prove the validity of the philosophical position developed with its help. We cannot simply reason from the *is* of ecology to the *oughts* of ethics and politics, nor can science alone establish epistemological and metaphysical conclusions.

A second danger arises when we rely too heavily on ecology for solutions to specific problems. Treating ecology as just another science that can offer scientific answers to specific problems is to be tempted by the standard shallow hope for a technological quick fix. Consistent with the Deep Ecology commitment, Naess believes that environmental issues like wilderness destruction and species extinction point to fundamental questions about how we ought to live. These are philosophical questions that have political implications that the institutions and individuals who defend the status quo wish to avoid asking.

The fear is that the recent development of an "ecological conscience" that shifts attention away from models based in physics and mechanics and onto ecological models will be used simply to substitute one shallow quick fix approach for another. In this view, ecology would simply be a new means for treating the symptoms. Thus, it would subvert attempts to probe deeper into the underlying causes of the environmental crisis. Ecology might then become a diversion from these more fundamental issues. The risk is that ecology will be used as part of a political strategy to derail movements that question the fundamental assumptions of a culture. In Naess's words, we need to "fight against depoliticization" to stay focused on the political nature of the Deep Ecology movement.[13] For example, reliance on ecology could encourage citizens to remain passive and leave decision making to the experts, or some models in ecology might reinforce a laissez-faire attitude similar to the social Darwinism of the nineteenth century.

10.4 METAPHYSICAL ECOLOGY

Thus, scientific ecology provides a model for thinking about the deep fundamental issues that underlie the environmental crisis. Inspired by ecology, Deep Ecologists seek to develop alternative worldviews that echo ecological insights into such issues as diversity, holism, interdependencies, and relations. Deep Ecology traces the roots of our environmental crisis to fundamental philosophical causes. Solutions can come only from a transformation of our fundamental worldview and practices. These fundamental questions include what is human nature? What is the relation of humans to the rest of nature? What is the nature of reality? These questions are traditionally identified as *metaphysical* questions. Deep Ecology, therefore, is as concerned with questions of metaphysics and ontology (the study of what is) as it is with questions of ethics.

Deep Ecologists trace the cause of many of our problems to the metaphysics presupposed by the dominant philosophy of modern industrial society. The transformation that we have mentioned involves a shift away from the dominant model and onto an alternative worldview that takes its inspiration from ecology. Deep Ecology is concerned with a *metaphysical ecology* rather than a scientific one.

The dominant metaphysics that underlies modern industrial society is fundamentally *individualistic* and *reductionistic*.[14] This view holds that only individuals are real and that we approach a more fundamental level of reality by reducing objects to their more basic elements. These most basic elements, whatever they turn out to be, are related according to strict physical laws. But this dominant worldview also sees humans as fundamentally different from the rest of nature. Individual human beings possess a "mind" or "free will" or "soul" that exempts them from the strict mechanical determinism characteristic of the rest of nature. Thus, the dominant worldview rejects the position identified in Chapter 8 as metaphysical holism.

Rejection of these dominant beliefs is central to the metaphysics of Deep Ecology. Taking its cue from ecology, the metaphysics of Deep Ecology denies that individual humans are separate from nature, the so-called man-in-nature perspective. Instead, Deep Ecologists are committed to a version of metaphysical holism. Humans are fundamentally a part of their surroundings, not distinct from them. Humans are constituted by their relations to other elements in the environment. In an important sense, the environment—by which the Deep Ecologists mean both the biotic and abiotic constituents—determines what human beings are.

When Naess speaks of the "relational, total-field image," he is alluding to a recognition that humans are formed by their relationships. Without the relationships that exist among humans and between humans and nature, human beings would literally become different sorts of beings. A philosophy that "reduces" humans to "individuals" that are somehow distinct from their social and natural environment is radically misguided.

This point has been expressed by Warwick Fox, an Australian philosopher and Deep Ecologist.

> It is the idea that we can make no firm ontological divide in the field of existence: that there is no bifurcation in reality between the human and the non-human realms . . . to the extent that we perceive boundaries, we fall short of Deep Ecological consciousness.[15]

Thus, echoing the metaphysical holism that Callicott described in Chapter 9, Deep Ecologists deny the reality of individuals—at least as they are typically understood in Western philosophy. There are no individuals apart from or distinct from relationships within a system, a "total field."

Human "nature" is inseparable from nature. Viewing human beings as individuals is how the dominant worldview has understood humans and has broken up reality, but it is a dangerous and misleading metaphysics.

No doubt, thinking like this can tempt many people to place Deep Ecologists on the fringe of environmental philosophy. This certainly is a radical shift from mainstream Western thinking. But, as suggested, any call for a radical shift in perspective faces difficulties in being understood. We can, perhaps, approach this outlook in a variety of ways in the hope that we can begin to understand the alternative.

In the spirit of Deep Ecology, we might begin by taking a hint from scientific ecology. If we think of ecosystems as energy circuits through which solar and chemical energy flow, we might begin to think of individual organisms as less permanent and less real than the chemical and biological processes themselves. Individual organisms come and go, but the process goes on as long as the environmental conditions permit. Individual organisms can be thought of as the location at which these chemical processes occur. In Naess's terms, scientific ecology "suggested, inspired, and fortified" the metaphysical conclusion that individual organisms are constituted by their relations to other entities.

Another way of approaching this conclusion is to consider what it means to say that an individual organism is alive. Minimally, an individual organism is alive only if certain chemical and biological processes are occurring. When these processes cease to occur, the organism ceases to live. Thus, the processes are necessary for the existence of the organism. On the other hand, when the processes are occurring, life exists. Thus, the processes are sufficient for life. Because chemical and biological processes are both necessary and sufficient for the existence of life, we have some reasons for saying that the processes are at least as, if not more, real than individual living organisms.

Biophysicist Harold Morowitz makes a similar point.

> Viewed from the point of view of modern [ecology], each living thing is a dissipative structure, that is, it does not endure in and of itself but only as a result of the continual flow of energy in the system . . . From this point of view, the reality of individuals is problematic because they do not exist per se but only as local perturbations in this universal energy flow . . . An example might be instructive. Consider a vortex in a stream of flowing water. The vortex is a structure made of an ever-changing group of water molecules. It does not exist as an entity in the classic Western sense; it exists only because of the flow of water through the stream. If the flow ceases the vortex disappears. In the same sense the structures out of which the biological entities are made are transient, unstable entities with constantly changing molecules dependent on a constant flow of energy to maintain form and structure.[16]

Finally, we might better appreciate metaphysical ecology by considering the language of "individualism." Ordinarily, we seem confident that we know what we refer to when we speak of individuals. But although we often use *individual* as a noun (*an* individual, *the* individual), the word is perhaps more precisely used as an adjective (an individual person, an individual tree, and the like).

Imagine being asked to go out and count the individuals that you see. We might assume that the assignment involves individual humans, or we would be well advised to ask, "Individual what?" This suggests that when we speak of individuals, we have already adopted a worldview or metaphysics that has divided our experiences up in one way rather than another way. Our ordinary language seems to presuppose a metaphysics in which separate and isolated organisms are most real. But recognize that we might just as well refer to individual communities, individual ecosystems, individual species, and individual chemical cycles. We might just as well refer to individual body parts, individual organs, individual cells, individual molecules, individual atoms, and so forth. The individual human person can be seen either as a part of some larger individual (such as a species or ecosystem) or as a collection of other individuals (such as organ systems, cells, and the like).

The implication of this is that the world does not come already broken down into categories like individuals and wholes. Rather, particular ways of understanding the world and particular needs in so understanding it determine what is to count as an individual and what is to count as a whole. Deep Ecology argues that the dominant worldview assumes an artificial distinction between individuals and their surroundings. The ecological and environmental devastation that has followed from this particular metaphysics has proved it to be dangerous. An alternative metaphysics, one inspired by scientific ecology, can offer an opportunity for reversing this devastation.

10.5 FROM METAPHYSICS TO ETHICS

Perhaps the most philosophically challenging aspect of Deep Ecology involves connecting the metaphysical views to the normative prescriptions derived from them. The early chapters of this textbook examined a variety of ways in which standard ethical theories were extended and applied to environmental problems. At the time, we mentioned recent critics who claim that traditional ethics has been stretched beyond the breaking point by environmental challenges. With Deep Ecology, we now see how radically different the alternatives can be.

Environmental challenges require not just new ethics but a new metaphysics as well. This section considers how Deep Ecologists move from metaphysical ecology to ethical and political concerns. The goal of ecophilosophy is to provide a philosophical account of the metaphysics, epistemology, and ethics of this alternative view of reality.

One of the most common and fundamental distinctions made within the Western philosophical tradition is between *objectivity* and *subjectivity*. Mainstream Western metaphysics, particularly the field of ontology, investigates the nature of reality. The *real* world is taken to be that which exists independently of human beings and human understanding. This is the objective world, and it is the goal of science to comprehend this reality. Insofar as it does this, scientific claims are "true" and "objective" because they correspond to reality. On the other hand, human beings ("subjects") interpret the world, make judgments about it, perceive it, value it, and have feelings about it. These human factors are *subjective* because they depend on the human subject. Because they depend on human subjects, they should not be mistaken as objective "truths" about the real world.

In general terms, this distinction has had significant implications for mainstream epistemology and ethics. Deep Ecologists believe that it has had a detrimental influence both on how we understand and how we value nature.

Epistemologically, objective descriptions of nature could be measured, tested, verified, and the like. Subjective judgments about nature, on the other hand, are arbitrary, unpredictable, biased, and unverifiable. Objective descriptions could be rational and true. Subjective judgments could not. In ethics, subjective judgments of value ("oughts") cannot be derived from objective descriptions of fact ("is").

To elaborate this distinction, philosophers in the seventeenth century relied on a contrast between the *primary* and *secondary* qualities of physical objects. An object's primary qualities exist in the object and are taken to represent what the object truly and really is. Size, shape, mass, extension, and movement were understood as examples of an object's primary qualities. They existed in the object itself. On the other hand, secondary qualities were said to exist as a result of the interaction between an object and an observer. An object's color, texture, taste, and smell were secondary qualities in that they exist only insofar as there exists a perceiver who experiences them. Because secondary qualities depend on a perceiver, they are subjective and not really a part of the object itself.

Continuing this seventeenth century perspective, the role of science is to fully describe an object's primary qualities. Because all these primary qualities could be fully described in mathematical terms, the real world turns out to be the world of mathematical physics and mechanics. Real trees, for example, have no color. They merely reflect light waves. If our eyes were constituted differently, they would appear differently. Trees are not heavy. They have mass that is subject to the force of gravity. Were we larger, stronger beings, trees would be less heavy than they now appear. Thus, descriptions of natural objects that refer to secondary qualities like color, weight, and taste are scientifically irrelevant. They are not really true, rational, or objective.

Further, more complex descriptions of natural objects, called *tertiary* qualities, are even less objective and true than judgments about secondary qualities. For example, to describe a tree as "majestic," "beautiful," or "awe inspiring" is to say something that is merely personal opinion. Although color may exist as an interaction between object and subject (reflected light waves reacting with nerve cells), beauty is totally in the eye of the beholder.

Notice how these distinctions and the value conclusions that flow from them depend greatly on a clear distinction between subject and object. When the human subject is viewed as essentially one with the natural world, as Deep Ecologists argue it should, the rationale for clinging to a strict distinction between objective and subjective, between real and perceived and between fact and value is weakened. We can still make these distinctions and they can be useful for us, but they lose their metaphysical priority. The real world ceases to exist "out there," separate and apart from us. We exist in the real world. Our perceptions, judgments, and evaluations are as real as the abstract judgments of science. Just as important, these judgments and evaluations can be as rational, true, and objective as the judgments of science.

Note also how these distinctions can play a significant role in debating environmental controversies. Often, environmentalists are dismissed as sentimentalists who allow their emotions to cloud their reason. A stand of oak really is only a collection of primarily carbon and water molecules that play a role in cycling carbon, oxygen, nitrogen, and other elements through the ecosystem. Rationally, we might just as well put the carbon to a more useful purpose like furniture or firewood, especially if we can find the technological means for replacing the oaks' function in the carbon, oxygen, or nitrogen cycles. To fight against development for the sake of a "majestic" stand of oak trees is mere emotion and sentiment. When environmental positions are cast as emotional and sentimental, they can be dismissed as irrelevant. According to the dominant worldview, they are not rational, objective, or scientific.

Naess makes a similar point.

> Confrontations between developers and conservers reveal difficulties in experiencing what is *real*. What a conservationist sees and experiences *as reality*, the developer typically does not see, and vice versa. A conservationist sees and experiences a forest as a unity, a gestalt, and when speaking of the *heart of the forest*, he or she does not speak about the geometrical centre. A developer see quantities of trees and argues that a road through the forest covers very few square kilometers compared to the whole area of trees, so why make so much fuss? And if the conservers insist, he will propose that the road does not touch the centre of the forest. The heart is saved, he may think. *The difference between the antagonists is one rather of ontology than of ethics. . . .* To the conservationist, the developer seems to suffer from a kind of radical blindness. But one's ethics in environmental questions are based largely on how one sees reality.[17]

According to many Deep Ecologists, as long as we maintain a strict distinction between individuals and nature, we can make an equally strict distinction between objective and subjective judgments. This distinction provides a rationale for taking the judgments of science and technology as epistemologically justified while dismissing the evaluative judgments of ethics and aesthetics. But when Deep Ecologists challenge the distinction between individual and nature, they also are challenging the strict distinction between objective and subjective. This leaves open the possibility that evaluative judgments about the value and beauty of a wilderness, for example, can be shown to be as rationally justified as the judgments of science.

Naess is careful to recognize that mere spontaneous feelings or emotional reactions and outbursts are not rational arguments. The mere expression of a feeling does not advance rational dialogue and debate. However, we need to be equally clear in recognizing that evaluative judgments "motivated by strong feelings" do have "a clear cognitive function." The *feeling* of anger produced by the destruction of a forest or the imperative to "stop that destruction" is neither true nor false in itself. But the judgment that "this mountainside has been destroyed and ruined" is open to rational assessment and might well be true.

The challenge to ecophilosophers is to specify the conditions under which such environmental judgments can be demonstrated as true and rational. Naess phrases his approach to such challenges in terms of relational properties and gestalts. Properties like "being destroyed" and "being ruined" can be understood only within a context, what Naess calls a "gestalt" or "totality." The conservationist and the developer experience different realities. Their concepts and perceptions occur within different contexts and are related to many different concepts and perceptions. Given these contexts, and each of their judgments makes sense, each is in that way "rational." At the same time, neither can claim a privileged status as better reflecting reality.

But the point remains that conservationists and developers disagree radically about what we should do. Their respective practical recommendations are embedded in their different gestalts. However, if each gestalt makes sense and if neither enjoys a privileged status, we are left without means for deciding which course of action, if either, is more reasonable. In general terms, how do we judge between the conservationist's and the developer's worldviews?

In some sense, rational discourse breaks down at this point. Each worldview has its standards of rationality, values, and reality. But Naess believes that continued discussion is possible and that we eventually can attain substantiation of one side or the other. Naess suggests that this is possible if we avoid "absolutism" and take care in clarifying our norms while remaining open to honest and nonviolent communication with our opponents.

> If a speaker's norm pronouncement, "It is right to deny X," is answered from the audience, "It is not right to deny X," there is nothing to get in a fuss about. The situation begs to be debated. A debate requires clarification of value priorities.[18]

At this point, other Deep Ecologists rely on stories, poetry, narrative, myths, and ritual. The goal is to make the Deep Ecology worldview understandable to people who do not yet view reality in this way. Because, by definition, these people do not share the concepts, norms, values, and metaphysics of Deep Ecology, straightforward linguistic explanation typically is unsuccessful. The epistemology of Deep Ecology involves the search for ways to encourage people to make radical shifts in their worldviews. In addition to poetry and ritual, the religious concept of "bearing witness" in the way that we live our lives along with the "forceful announcement" of our values and living in accord with those values are other methods for communicating the Deep Ecology worldview.

10.6 SELF-REALIZATION AND BIOCENTRIC EQUALITY

The practical ethics of Deep Ecology is best seen in the platform discussed earlier. These are the principles we can directly apply to concrete situations to explain and justify environmental activism. But at a more abstract and philosophical level, the ethics of Deep Ecology focuses on two "ultimate norms." These norms are ultimate in the sense that they are not derived from any further or more basic principles or values. They are the point at which ethical justification ends. We can perhaps best think of them as connecting Deep Ecology's abstract metaphysics with its more specific ethical platform.

The two ultimate norms of Deep Ecology are *self-realization* and *biocentric equality.* Self-realization is a process through which people come to understand themselves as existing in a thorough interconnectedness with the rest of nature. Biocentric equality is the recognition that all organisms and beings are equally members of an interrelated whole and, therefore, have equal intrinsic worth.

Although self-realization grows out of a tradition that is as old as philosophy itself, the particular version developed within Deep Ecology represents perhaps its most original insight. The ancient Greek directive to "know thyself" and Socrates's claim that "the unexamined life is not worth living" imply that the good life involves a process of self-examination and self-fulfillment. The teleological understanding of the good as the actualization of internal potentialities provides a similar insight. The suggestion from these traditions is that as we go through a process of self-examination, we become able to separate trivial, superficial, and temporary interests from deeper, more central, and lasting interests.

To understand the concept of self-realization, we can start with a general distinction that we used earlier in this textbook for *needs, interests,* and *wants.* Needs can be understood as those elements that are necessary for survival. Food, clothing, shelter, and nontoxic air and water would be obvious examples of needs. A person's interests are those factors that contribute to well-being. It is in a person's interest to have friendships, education, and good health. Wants are the immediate desires and goals toward which a person is inclined. I want a vacation, glass of juice, or free lunch.

Note that these categories can overlap. Nutritious food and clean air are things that I need, have an interest in getting, and in fact want. But there can also be tensions and conflicts between these categories. Although it is in my interest to improve my education and therefore stay home and read, I want to go out to a party with my friends.

Wants seem to be a matter of individual psychology. They are those factors that provide a motive for acting. Wants come to be developed, chosen, learned, created by advertising, and the like. Interests are not a matter of immediate psychological states. They are connected to what is good for a person and, therefore, are not a matter of choice. (Even if being free is in a person's interest, that freedom is in that person's interest is not a matter of individual choice.) Interests can be understood and determined but not chosen.

Wants are typically seen as a product of individual choice, culture, or society. They are superficial and temporary in the sense that they are dependent on an individual's personal background, history, and culture. Various ethical traditions encourage humans to separate these transitory wants from their basic interests as rational beings. The good life is a life spent in pursuit of basic and true interests. Self-interest, properly understood, is the good for human beings.

Thus, in effect, these traditions see two "selves" in every person. One is the self constituted by the conscious beliefs, wants, and intentions of the ego. The other self is the true nature that underlies this person's ego. "Know thyself" is the injunction to get beyond this surface self to figure out and realize our true underlying nature. Thus, traditions as diverse as Greek philosophy, Christianity, Buddhism, romanticism, and Marxism all see a process of self-realization as central to the good life.

Self-realization plays a similar role in Deep Ecology. But for the Deep Ecologists, the underlying self is the self that is one with the natural world. Self-realizing is a process of self-examination in which people come to understand themselves as part of a greater whole. It is a process through which a person comes to understand that "there is no firm ontological divide between humans and nonhumans," between self and other. It is the process through which we come to know ourselves not as individuals separate and distinct from nature but as a part of a greater "self." This self is the self described within metaphysical holism. If what we are as human beings, our nature, is constituted by our relations with other parts of the natural world, self-realization is a coming to understand and fully appreciate this oneness.

For many in the Western philosophical tradition, self-realization would be a means for developing a person's separate, individual, and personal nature. Deep Ecologists retain a commitment to self-realization, self-interest, and self-fulfillment, but they deny this individualistic understanding of the self. To distinguish their holistic and relational view of the self from the more individualistic model, Deep Ecologists typically use "Self" to refer to the holistic view and "self" for the individualistic view. Thus, "Self-realization" is a process through which "self comes to understand itself as Self" and "self-interest" comes to be seen as "Self-interest."

Devall and Sessions summarize these points.

In keeping with the spiritual traditions of many of the world's religions, the Deep Ecology norm of Self-Realization goes beyond the modern Western *self* which is defined as an isolated ego striving primarily for hedonistic gratification. . . . This socially programmed sense of the narrow self or social self dislocates us, and leaves us prey to whatever fad or fashion is prevalent in our society. . . . Spiritual growth, or unfolding, begins when we cease to understand or see ourselves as isolated and narrow competing egos and begin to identify with other humans from our family and friends to, eventually, our species. But the Deep Ecology sense of self requires a further maturity and growth, an identification which goes beyond humanity to include the nonhuman world.[19]

The second ultimate norm is that of biocentric equality. In Devall and Sessions's words, this intuition is that

all things in the biosphere have an equal right to live and blossom and to reach their own individual forms of unfolding and self-realization within the larger Self-realization. This basic intuition is that all organisms and entities in the ecos-phere, as parts of the interrelated whole, are equal in intrinsic worth.[20]

At one level, biocentric equality is the same insight described in Chapter 7 as biocentrism. Taylor's *Respect for Nature,* for example, also defends a biocentric ethics based on the notion of equal inherent worth. However, Taylor's bio-centrism is well rooted within traditional Western philosophy. It develops out of an individualism that views organisms as centers of individual lives. The biocentric equality of Deep Ecology grows out of metaphysical holism with equally old Western roots. Members of the biotic community possess equal moral worth, not because as individuals they have intrinsic worth, but simply because they are members of that community.

Is there a significant difference? If there is any, it seems that Deep Ecologists are less willing to make tradeoffs between human and nonhuman interests. When human interests conflict with nonhuman interests, Deep Ecologists are less inclined to favor the human interests. Taylor goes to some lengths to work out a means for rationally resolving conflicts. For Deep Ecologists, this is likely to result in hierarchies that inevitably will have human interests at the top.[21] Deep Ecology seeks a more democratic and less hierarchical equality.

We must recognize that the Deep Ecology platform allows humans to "reduce" biocentric richness and diversity in order to "satisfy vital needs." It is difficult to see how something like Taylor's distinction between basic and nonbasic needs would be hierarchical when this statement is not. Perhaps part of the answer lies in how "vital needs" are explained. For example, Naess suggests that unemployment in a country with a high standard of living would not violate a vital need. On the other hand, Devall and Sessions sug-gest that vital needs would include such things as "love, play, creative expres-sion, intimate relationships with a particular landscape (or Nature taken in its entirety) as well as intimate relationships with other humans, and the vital need for spiritual growth, for becoming a mature human being."[22] Thus, the ethical and practical implications of biocentric equality within a Deep Ecological perspective would differ from those generated by a more individ-ualistic philosophy.

What are these practical implications? Deep Ecologists are committed to promoting lifestyles that "tread lightly on the Earth." This means that humans ought to live in simple, relatively nontechnological, self-reliant, decentralized communities. Second, analogous to the concept of an ecosystem, communities ought to be organized regionally, existing as a "bioregion" rather than as more traditional political organizations. Our lifestyles ought to be simple in the sense that our consumer or material desires should be kept to a minimum. We need to recognize material wants as artificial products of human society. "We should live with minimum rather than maximum impact on the other species and on the Earth in general."[23] The ideal seems to be a situation in which local communities exist in a harmonious and self-regulating relationship with their surroundings. This ideal has been called an "ecotopia," a community that seeks harmony with rather than dominance over nature.

10.7 CRITICISMS

It sometimes seems that Deep Ecology acts as a lightning rod for environmental criticism and backlash. Because Deep Ecology does critique the dominant worldview, we should not be surprised to find significant critical reaction. Sometimes this criticism is fair, but other times it has not been.

As mentioned at the start of this chapter, Deep Ecology does not refer to one specific and systematic philosophy. It refers to an assortment of philosophical and activist approaches to ecological issues that share some fundamental ecocentric and nonanthropocentric assumptions. It is perhaps best thought of as a movement that encompasses both philosophical and activist sides.

Given this diversity, it is difficult to offer any precise criticisms of Deep Ecology. A critique of, for example, the tactics of Earth First! could be rebuffed by Deep Ecologists as beside the point because not all Deep Ecologists agree with these tactics. Likewise, a critique that accuses Deep Ecology of being too abstract and vague on issues like "Self-realization" might be rejected by Deep Ecologists who are more inclined toward political activism.

Of course, this ambiguity itself can be ground for criticism. In some ways, the claims of Deep Ecology are so sweeping and general as to become empty. A "movement" that can claim inspiration from such diverse sources as Taoism, Heraclitus, Spinoza, Whitehead, Gandhi, Buddhism, Native American cultures, Thomas Jefferson, Thoreau, and Woody Guthrie is certainly eclectic at best. At worst, it becomes unintelligible.

This ambiguity can be frustrating for critics as they try to focus on specific claims, only to find their target shifting. It can also lead to an end of dialogue because critics can be dismissed as missing the point, irrelevant, or misrepresenting Deep Ecology.[24]

Another criticism echoes the fascism charge raised against holistic and nonanthropocentric ethics in earlier chapters. Biocentric equality would seem to suggest treating human interests as equal to the interests of other living things as well as the more general biotic community. However, when this equality is combined with the metaphysical claim that individuals are not real and the charge that humans alone are responsible for significant environmental destruction, Deep Ecology can seem misanthropic (as hating humanity). Humans are no better than other living things and, in fact, are guilty of great environmental malevolence. Thus, human well-being is not a moral priority. Some of the more well-known examples of misanthropic remarks include Edward Abbey's claim in *Desert Solitaire* that he would rather shoot a human than a snake and Dave Foreman's suggestion that we should not aid starving Ethiopians and allow them to die.

Deep Ecologists disavow such claims. Fox, for example, points out that Deep Ecologists criticize "not humans per se (i.e., a general class of social actors) but rather human-centeredness (a legitimating ideology)."[25] This claim amounts to the view that Deep Ecologists do not deny intrinsic value to humans. They simply deny that only humans have intrinsic value.

But the same challenge can be issued here that was raised in Chapter 9. What is to be done when human interests conflict with the interests of elements of the nonhuman natural world, as so often is the case with environmental issues? In such cases, if we favor humans, we seem to abandon nonanthropocentric holism. If we favor the nonhuman world, we approach the misanthropic position that Deep Ecologists want to deny. Again, this requires Deep Ecologists to work out a clear hierarchy of vital needs.

Another challenge is raised in various forms by a diverse group of critics. The problem with Deep Ecology, in their view, is that it has overgeneralized in its critique of human-centeredness, anthropocentrism, and the dominant worldview. From this point of view, not all humans nor all human perspectives are equally at fault for environmental problems. When Deep Ecologists critique "the" dominant worldview, they fail to acknowledge that many humans are not part of that dominance. Thus, Deep Ecologists are too broad in their critique and, thus, overly broad in their positive program.

One version of this critique is raised by the Indian ecologist Ramachandra Guha.[26] Guha argues that despite its claims to universality, Deep Ecology is uniquely an American ideology, essentially a radical branch of the wilderness preservation movement. In Guha's view, if put into practice, Deep Ecology would have disastrous consequences, especially for the poor and agrarian populations in underdeveloped countries. Describing India as a "long settled and densely populated country in which agrarian populations have a finely balanced relationship with nature," Guha reasons that a policy of biocentric equality and wilderness preservation would effectively result in a direct transfer of wealth from poor to rich and a major displacement of poor people.

Applying the Deep Ecology platform to societies in underdeveloped countries smacks of Western imperialism. "We (environmentalists in the West) know what is best for you. Let us generalize from our experiences and our culture and tell you why you should live in ways that we suggest. Stop treating nature as resources, even if you are living at a mere subsistence level. Preserve and respect nature for its own sake."

Guha also faults Deep Ecology for its appropriation of Eastern philosophies and traditions. Citing Hinduism, Taoism, and Buddhism as if they are a single consistent Eastern worldview and one that is more in tune with environmentalism "does considerable violence to the historical record." Eastern cultures, as well as Western cultures, have manipulated nature and caused significant ecological destruction.

Accordingly, Deep Ecology is not very helpful to the environmental concerns of peoples of underdeveloped countries. At best, it is irrelevant. At worst, it can be harmful to the very people who already are victimized by social and political dominance.

Similar critiques of Deep Ecology have been offered by thinkers associated with two other movements within environmental philosophy, *social ecology* and *ecofeminism*. These perspectives agree that in the search for the "deep" underlying causes of the environmental crisis, Deep Ecologists have focused their attention at too abstract a level. The more significant causes can be located at a much more localized level: the social, economic, and patriarchal structures of contemporary societies. Each philosophy claims that, in faulting anthropocentrism, Deep Ecologists fail to recognize important distinctions between people. If there is "a" dominant worldview, Deep Ecology must recognize that many humans are also oppressed by it. Not all humans are equally at fault for environmental destruction, and not all humans were included in the "human-centered" dominant worldview. Instead of looking at some abstract dominant worldview, these critics seek to specify the particular practices and institutions that dominate both human and nonhuman alike. Guha calls our attention to the perspective of people, especially poor people, in underdeveloped countries. Social ecologists look to the dominance of social and economic elites and a materialistic consumerist culture as a primary cause of environmental destruction. Ecofeminists suggest that the causes of environmental domination and the oppression of women are connected.

Thus, these views all fault Deep Ecology for overgeneralizing in its critique of anthropocentrism. Holding all humans equally responsible for environmental problems, as the rejection of anthropocentric ethics suggests, does serious injustice to people in underdeveloped countries, the poor and oppressed, and women. Some of these critiques are developed in Chapter 11.

10.8 SUMMARY AND CONCLUSIONS

This chapter presented an overview of the most common philosophical themes and concepts involved in Deep Ecology. Deep Ecology represents the first explicit attempt to develop a systematic environmental philosophy that is both ecocentric and nonanthropocentric. Perhaps more than any other approach, it requires us to understand that environmental issues are not simply ethical issues. Environmental issues raise fundamental questions of philosophy, including questions of metaphysics, epistemology, ethics, and political philosophy.

Notes

1. Michael Martin, "Ecosabotage and Civil Disobedience," *Environmental Ethics* 12 (winter 1990): 291–310.

2. Bill Devall, *Simple in Means, Rich in Ends: Practicing Deep Ecology* (Layton, Utah: Gibbs Smith Publishing, 1988), p. 3.

3. See, for example, the distinction between "deep" and "shallow" offered by Donald VanDeVeer and Christine Pierce, *People, Penguins, and Plastic Trees* (Belmont, Calif.: Wadsworth, 1986), pp. 69–70. Here "shallow ecology" is taken as the view that "nature has no value apart from the needs, interests, and good of human beings," and "Deep Ecology holds that nature has value in its own right independent of the interests of humans."

4. See Arne Naess, *Ecology, Community, and Lifestyle*, trans. and rev. David Rothenberg (Cambridge, England: Cambridge University Press, 1989), and Bill Devall and George Sessions, *Deep Ecology: Living as If Nature Mattered* (Salt Lake City: Peregrine Smith Books, 1985).

5. Arne Naess, "The Shallow and the Deep, Long-Range Ecology Movement," *Inquiry* 16 (1973): 95–100.

6. Arne Naess, "A Defense of the Deep Ecology Movement," *Environmental Ethics* 6 (fall 1984): 264.

7. Devall and Sessions, *Deep Ecology: Living as If Nature Mattered*, p. ix.

8. For these citations and others, see *Deep Ecology for the Twenty-First Century*, ed. George Sessions (Boston: Shambala Publications, 1995), p. ix.

9. This description relies heavily on David Rothenberg's introduction to Naess's *Ecology, Community, and Lifestyle*.

10. This platform is presented in Devall and Sessions, *Deep Ecology: Living as If Nature Mattered*, ch. 5, as the "basic principles" of Deep Ecology. They are also presented as a "platform" in Naess, *Ecology, Community, and Lifestyle*, ch. 1.

11. Naess, *Ecology, Community, and Lifestyle*, pp. 26–27.

12. Ibid., 39–40.

13. Ibid., 130–33.

14. For one sustained account of the "dominant modern worldview," see Devall and Sessions, *Deep Ecology: Living as If Nature Mattered*, ch. 3.

15. Warwick Fox, "Deep Ecology: A New Philosophy for Our Time?," *Ecologist* 14 (November–December 1984): 194–200, as quoted in Devall and Sessions, *Deep Ecology: Living as If Nature Mattered*, p. 66.

16. Harold Morowitz, "Biology as a Cosmological Science," *Main Currents in Modern Thought* 28 (1972): 156. The material quoted here is quoted and discussed in J. Baird Callicott, "Metaphysical Implications of Ecology," *Environmental Ethics* 9 (winter 1986): 300–15. Callicott's essay suggests that a "consolidated metaphysical consensus" might be emerging from ecological science that would supplant the mechanical model that emerged from seventeenth century physics.

17. Naess, *Ecology, Community, and Lifestyle*, p. 66; the emphasis is in the original.

18. Ibid., 70–71.

19. Devall and Sessions, *Deep Ecology: Living as If Nature Mattered*, pp. 66–67.

20. Ibid., 67.

21. See the discussion of Devall and Sessions, *Deep Ecology: Living as If Nature Mattered*, p. 68.

22. See Naess, *Ecology, Community, and Lifestyle*, p. 30; the quote from Devall and Sessions can be found in *Deep Ecology: Living as If Nature Mattered*, p. 68.

23. Devall and Sessions can be found in *Deep Ecology: Living as If Nature Mattered*, p. 68. For another description of this lifestyle, see Naess, "Ecosophy, Technology, and Lifestyle," ch. 4 in *Ecology, Community, and Lifestyle*.

24. For example, George Sessions dismisses a range of critics in less than one page in his preface to *Deep Ecology for the Twenty-First Century*, pp. xii–xiii. Criticism of Deep Ecology is "based on misinterpretation and misunderstanding." It seems to me that this is a theme in many Deep Ecologists' responses to critics.

25. Warwick Fox, "The Deep Ecology-Ecofeminism Debate," in Sessions, ed., *Deep Ecology for the Twenty-First Century*, p. 279. This is a version of an essay of the same title previously published in *Environmental Ethics* 11 (spring 1989): 5–26.

26. Ramachandra Guha, "Radical American Environmentalism and Wilderness Preservation: A Third World Critique," *Environmental Ethics* 11 (spring 1989): 71–84.

Discussion Questions

1. Would civil disobedience in the defense of the environment ever be justified? If so, when and why? Is tree spiking a defensible means for preventing logging of old-growth forests?

2. What is an individual? What is an individual living thing? Does the meaning of this word change in different contexts? What implications for ethics follow from your answer?

3. Is the statement "This is a tall tree" any more objective than the statement "This is a majestic tree"? Explain how both might be defended as true.

4. Classical economists such as those discussed in Chapter 3 claim that humans are always motivated by self-interest. In light of the discussion of the "self" and "Self" in this chapter, do you agree with that view of human motivation? Would the Deep Ecology view of "Self-realization" require that human nature be rewired as Baden and Stroup claim in Chapter 3?

5. Is there enough uniformity and consistency in human cultures that talk of a "human-centered" worldview makes sense? Which specific beliefs and values are particularly anthropocentric?

Further Reading

John Davis, ed., *Earth First! Reader* (Salt Lake City, Utah: Peregrine Smith Books, 1991), collects a wide variety of essays on and by radical environmentalists. A helpful collection of essays on environmental activism from less radical sources is Don Marietta and Lester Embree, eds., *Environmental Philosophy and Environmental Activism* (Lanham, Md.: Rowman and Littlefield, 1995).

Dave Foreman, *Confessions of an Eco-Warrior* (New York: Harmony, 1991), by the best-known radical environmentalist.

George Sessions, ed., *Deep Ecology for the Twenty-First Century* (Boston: Shambala Publishing, 1995), a recent and comprehensive anthology of Deep Ecology sources.

CHAPTER

11

Social Ecology
and Ecofeminism

DISCUSSION

The World Bank Memo
and the Chipko Movement

The following memo was circulated at the World Bank in 1991. Lawrence
Summers, the chief economist of the World Bank at that time, went on to
become Secretary of the Treasury under President Clinton.

Date: December 12, 1991
To: Distribution
From: Lawrence H. Summers
Subject: GEP[1]
   'Dirty' Industries: Just between you and me, shouldn't the World Bank be
encouraging MORE migration of the dirty industries to the LDCs [Less Developed
Countries]? I can think of three reasons:

1. The measurements of the costs of health impairing pollution depend on the
foregone earnings from increased morbidity and mortality. From this point of
view a given amount of health impairing pollution should be done in the country
with the lowest cost, which will be the country with the lowest wages. I think the
economic logic behind dumping a load of toxic waste in the lowest wage country
is impeccable and we should face up to that.

2. The costs of pollution are likely to be nonlinear as the initial increments of pollution probably have very low cost. I've always thought that underpopulated
countries in Africa are vastly UNDERpolluted; their air quality is probably vastly
inefficiently low compared to Los Angeles or Mexico City. Only the lamentable

facts that so much pollution is generated by nontradable industries (transport, electrical generation) and that the unit transport costs of solid waste are so high prevent world welfare enhancing trade in air pollution and waste.

3. The demand for a clean environment for aesthetic and health reasons is likely to have very high income elasticity. The concern over an agent that causes a one in a million change in the odds of prostrate cancer is obviously going to be much higher in a country where people survive to get prostrate cancer than in a country where under 5 mortality is 200 per thousand. Also, much of the concern over industrial atmosphere discharge is about visibility impairing particulates. These discharges may have very little direct health impact. Clearly trade in goods that embody aesthetic pollution concerns could be welfare enhancing. While production is mobile the consumption of pretty air is a nontradable. The problem with the arguments against all of these proposals for more pollution in LDCs (intrinsic rights to certain goods, moral reasons, social concerns, lack of adequate markets, etc.) could be turned around and used more or less effectively against every Bank proposal for liberalization.[2]

Worldwide, the Chipko Movement has become one of the best-known examples for environmental and feminist activism. *Chipko* is taken from the Hindi word for "hugging," and it refers to the practice of villagers in northern India, many of whom were women, who literally hugged trees to prevent commercial logging. This movement calls attention to a complex interplay of economic, political, environmental, feminist, and ethical concerns.

The northern mountain region of India extends from the great central plains to the Himalayan peaks that stretch into Tibet and Nepal. Most people in these regions live in small villages and for generations have survived through a combination of subsistence farming, raising livestock, foraging in adjacent forests, and some trading of forest products.

Traditionally, the women of the villages did much of this work. In addition to the typical domestic chores of cooking, cleaning, and raising children, women are expected to cultivate crops, tend livestock, and gather firewood for cooking and heat. As has happened in so many societies, as the Indian economy has become more industrialized and agriculture on the central plains has expanded, the demand for labor has increased. Increasing numbers of village men are leaving the area to find employment on the plains and in the cities. Of course, this has left even greater local responsibility to the women.

Until the nineteenth century, local people enjoyed unrestricted access to the forests and existed in a stable economic and ecological relationship with them. Beginning in the nineteenth century but expanding rapidly in recent decades, the government (initially the British colonial government, but since independence, the Indian government) took control of the national forests. The government's primary aim was to manage these forests as a commercial resource, although in recent years the Indian government has begun to show some interest in protecting these areas as nature preserves.

In the early 1970s, two separate events set in motion what was to become known as the Chipko Movement. In 1970, the monsoons caused significant flooding and landslides throughout the region. Many people died, hundreds of homes were destroyed, and crops and livestock were lost. Some of the worst damage occurred in villages located below hillsides that had been logged intensively. (Devastating floods and landslides followed again in 1973, 1977, 1978, and 1979.) Because women were responsible for most of the household work, these events were especially hard on women and their children. Local people recognized that the widespread logging and deforestation occurring under government policy was intensifying the flooding, landslides, and erosion.

Some years earlier, workers in the region had formed a cooperative, the Dasholi Gram Swarajya Sangh (DGSS), to promote local industry and local employment. DGSS would bid at government auctions for the right to harvest local timber and other forest products and use these resources in its local industries. In 1973, the government denied a DGSS request to cut approximately one dozen ash trees for use in making farm tools. At the same time, the government granted a commercial firm permission to harvest many more trees for use in the manufacture of sporting goods. DGSS organized protests to resist this decision, with many protesters promising to hug the trees to prevent commercial logging. The threat of significant protests prevented any logging at that time.

The following year, the government again announced the auction of logging rights for major forests throughout the region, including the Reni forest. This announcement was again met with threats of major protests. Both the recent floods and the DGSS episode had combined to create a strong unified opposition to large-scale commercial logging. During the week leading up to the scheduled logging, the government arranged to have DGSS leaders attend a meeting in a different region and invited the men of Reni to travel to another city to discuss a long-standing financial dispute.

While most of the men were away, the loggers moved into the region to begin cutting. When word of what was happening spread, a local woman, Gaura Devi, organized the village women to go out into the forest to protest the logging. In what undoubtedly was the best-known incident involving the Chipko Movement, Devi and her followers faced down the loggers, forcing them to retreat without cutting down any trees. The women used the Chipko technique, patterned after the nonviolent civil disobedience championed a generation earlier by Mahatma Gandhi.

Reni forced the government to reexamine its logging policies. When a study concluded that the Reni forest was ecologically sensitive, the government imposed a ten-year moratorium on commercial logging. In subsequent years, the Chipko Movement spread to other regions and continued its success in preventing massive logging. Throughout these events, women continued to play a major role and partially as a result began to enjoy greater political participation as well.[3]

11.1 INTRODUCTION

This chapter examines one approach to ecological and environmental issues, called "social ecology," and a variety of approaches that together can be identified as "ecofeminism." Although social ecology and ecofeminism have many differences, these approaches share important similarities that make it appropriate to examine them in one chapter.

Social ecology is associated primarily with the work of one person, Murray Bookchin, and consists of a relatively unified theoretical perspective.[4] Ecofeminism, in contrast, reflects the diversity that exists among feminist thinkers and might better be thought of as a general perspective on ecological issues rather than as a unified "theory" of ecophilosophy. In general, ecofeminism involves the use of any of the diverse feminist philosophies in the analysis of ecological issues. Because feminist philosophy embraces many different perspectives, we can expect to find diverse ecofeminisms.[5] Nevertheless, ecofeminism and social ecology and the various perspectives within ecofeminism have important similarities.

To help understand these similarities, we can distinguish two facets of social ecology and ecofeminism. Each approach includes *analytical* aspects that offer analyses of the causes and issues underlying the contemporary ecological crisis. Each also has more *programmatic* aspects that offer alternative visions of an ecologically sound future. Social ecology and ecofeminism have much in common in their general analysis of ecological problems. Each sees ecological destruction as related to social problems of control and dominance. They differ in the specific explanations offered for these social problems and in their programs for social change.

Social ecology and ecofeminism look to society to find the underlying causes of the environmental crisis. They do not, like Deep Ecology, identify the roots of ecological destruction as a dominant philosophy or worldview. Each would hold that Deep Ecology is concerned with factors that are too abstract and too general, ignoring the specific human and social causes of environmental destruction. Each denies that *human* centeredness is the cause, arguing instead that specific human institutions and practices—*unjust* institutions and practices—are more critical. Each might also fault Deep Ecology for overemphasizing wilderness concerns while ignoring the human costs of environmental harms. They do not believe that the fundamental cause lies only in a failure of traditional ethics, either in the scope or application of those theories. Traditional theories of social justice can be adequate for analyzing environmental problems.

Social ecologists and ecofeminists argue that the root of our ecological crisis lies in certain social factors. Specifically, social ecologists and ecofeminists believe that the domination and degradation of nature arise from social patterns of domination and hierarchy, patterns of social life in which some humans exercise control or domination over others. Thus, both approaches shift philosophical attention away from questions traditionally associated with metaphysics and ethics and onto questions traditionally associated with social and political philosophy. Social justice becomes the primary focus of these philosophies.

A central insight of these views concerns the relations between individual humans and the patterns of social organization in which they live. Remember that societies are human creations, organized and structured by human beings in ways that serve human ends. Thus, when examining social problems such as environmental destruction, we should ask about the ends or purposes served by the particular institutions causing the problems. We also need to ask questions about what a particular arrangement is doing *to* those humans who are living within it. That is, we need to ask not only what does society do *for* people, but also what does a particular society do *to* people. Who is benefiting from and who is being harmed by our social practices? In the views of social ecologists and ecofeminists, many social structures serve to oppress some members of society for the benefit of others. This oppressive social structure in turn works to reinforce a way of thinking and living that encourages domination in all forms, including the domination of the natural world.

Bookchin summarizes this point as follows. "The very notion of the domination of nature by man [Bookchin is deliberately gender specific here] stems from the very real domination of human by human."[6] In a similar vein, Rosemary Radford Reuther, one of the first feminist thinkers to address ecological issues, has written,

> Women must see that there can be no liberation for them and no solution to the ecological crisis within a society whose fundamental model of relationships continues to be one of domination. They must unite the demands of the women's movement with those of the ecological movement to envision a radical reshaping of the basic socioeconomic relations and the underlying values of this society.[7]

In this view, environmental and ecological destruction is best understood as a form of human domination, in this case the human domination of nature. To understand this crisis more fully, both social ecologists and ecofeminists agree that we need to understand more general patterns of human domination of other humans. In this way, an adequate understanding of the ecological crisis must address fundamental questions of social and political philosophy. We must identify and analyze patterns of domination and oppression within societies and evaluate these patterns in terms of philosophical accounts of justice. An alternative ecological vision in turn should be based on a model of social justice in which all human beings are free from oppression and domination.

We can initially distinguish social ecology from ecofeminism by looking to their analyses of the various types of social domination and alternative conceptions of justice. Social ecologists liken environmental destruction to what they see as general and widespread forms of domination and hierarchy. These would include such social practices and structures as racism, sexism, and class structures as well as private ownership, capitalism, bureaucracies, and even the nation-state. These social practices and institutions establish social hierarchies in which some humans exercise power and domination over others. Social ecologists typically defend an anarchist conception of justice in which human freedom, understood as the absence of external control and psychological manipulation, is the essential element of justice.

Ecofeminists, on the other hand, identify the oppression of women as a principal form of social domination.[8] Ecofeminists identify many close connections between the oppression of women and the oppression of nature. As a result, they believe that the goals of the feminist movement closely parallel the goals of the ecological movement. However, ecofeminists offer various analyses of women's oppression and appeal to various accounts of social justice in critiquing this oppression and developing alternative nondominating models of society.[9]

In characterizing these parallel feminist and ecological concerns, philosopher Karen Warren emphasizes

> the concern about connections—historical, empirical, conceptual, theoretical, symbolic, and experiential—between the domination of women and the domination of nature. According to ecofeminists, a failure to see these connections will result in the continued exploitation of both women and non-human nature and in the development of policy, theory, and practices which is grossly inadequate from a feminist point of view.[10]

11.2 THEORIES OF SOCIAL JUSTICE

Earlier chapters described ethics as addressing this fundamental question: How should we live? But this question is ambiguous in that we can refer either to each of us individually or it can refer to all of us collectively. In the first case, ethics is sometimes referred to as *morality*. Whereas in the second case, ethics refers to social justice. Justice is concerned with how we all should live together. Justice can be understood as the first principle of social and political philosophy. "How should we live together?" and "What is justice?" are, in this approach, the same question.

In one sense, moral philosophy provides the background against which a theory of justice develops. Moral philosophy considers, among other things, the responsibilities that each of us has toward others and the rights that we possess against others. So a partial answer to the question of justice is that we ought to respect the rights and responsibilities that each of us individually possesses. But moral philosophy does not exhaust issues of justice. Living together in community creates benefits and burdens that exist only within community. Further, social institutions and practices influence individuals. Justice must address these further topics as well. How should the benefits and burdens of society be distributed? How should social institutions treat people? What do people deserve from society?

In general, we can say that justice is concerned with giving each person his or her due. Theories of justice differ in determining exactly what people deserve. In the Western philosophical tradition, most discussions of this question begin with Aristotle's claim that justice requires treating equals equally. What is often called the "formal principle of justice" requires that people be treated equally unless they have differences that would justify unequal treatment. This remains a formal principle. We can give alternative interpretations to what it means to treat people equally and the implications that follow from this principle.

For example, utilitarian justice argues that we should treat the interests of each person as of equal value (each is to count as one and only one) and then apply the impartial rule of maximizing the overall good to the question of distributing social benefits and burdens. As discussed in earlier chapters, the utilitarian might argue that environmental resources should be distributed in ways that maximize the overall satisfaction of individual interests, perhaps including the interests of future generations and animals. The memo from Lawrence Summers that opens this chapter provides an interesting example of the sort of policy that utilitarian justice might support. Overall world happiness could be increased if the wealthy countries that produce pollution were to export that pollution for a price to poorer less developed countries.

But many philosophers, especially those sympathetic to the Kantian approach to ethics, have offered serious challenges to utilitarian justice. They argue that the utilitarian principle of maximizing overall happiness fails to treat individuals with the respect due each person. Justice, in this view, requires that individuals not be treated as mere means to the end of producing beneficial social outcomes. The utilitarian goal of maximizing overall benefits is unjust if the price of those benefits involves a distribution of burdens that is unfair or unjust. Instead, justice demands that benefits and burdens be distributed fairly and impartially among all citizens. Requiring poor societies to carry the costs of pollution generated by wealthy countries, is in this view, unfair and unjust.

The American philosopher John Rawls has developed one of the most powerful and influential accounts of justice.[11] Rawls offers a contemporary development of the social contract theory of justice in the tradition of John Locke and Immanuel Kant.

Rawls's theory of justice consists of two major components: a method for deciding on the principles of justice and the specific principles derived from that method. The method itself is a version of the hypothetical social contract used earlier by Locke and Kant. Imagine rational and self-interested individuals having to choose and agree to the fundamental principles for their society. To ensure that the principles are fair and impartial, imagine further that these individuals do not know the specific details of their own lives. They do not know their abilities or disabilities and talents or weaknesses. They are, in Rawls's terms, behind a veil of ignorance and must choose principles that they will abide by when they come out from behind the veil. To ensure that each individual is treated as an end and not as a means, imagine finally that these individuals must unanimously agree on the principles. These initial conditions of impartiality, what Rawls calls the "original position," guarantees that the principles chosen are fair.

Rawls derives two fundamental principles of justice from this original position. The first principle states that each individual is to have equal rights to the most extensive system of liberties. Individuals would demand as much freedom as possible, but no rational and self-interested individuals would be willing to sacrifice their own equality simply to secure more liberty for others. The second principle holds that social and economic benefits and burdens should be distributed equally unless an unequal distribution would benefit the least advantaged members of society and only if those benefits are attached to positions for which each person has an equal opportunity. Rawls believes that people would accept these principles because rational people would follow a "maximin" strategy. That is, if you did not already know your position in society and you had to agree to a distribution of benefits and burdens, you would adopt the conservative strategy of trying to minimize your potential harms rather than trying to maximize your potential benefits. (Consider: Is it more rational to take a great risk for the possibility of a great benefit—using all your savings to buy lottery tickets—or a slight risk for a slight gain—keep your money in an insured savings account?)

Given this brief discussion of justice, return to the question that social ecologists and ecofeminists ask about society. How are the benefits and burdens of society distributed? Who gets the benefits? Who bears the burdens? Are the current distributions of benefits and burdens fair? Further, what kinds of people—what character traits, values, and attitudes—are being reinforced by society?

More specifically, what are the environmental benefits and burdens? Consider some of the topics mentioned in this book: air and water pollution, toxic waste dumps, pesticide poisoning, overpopulation, wilderness loss and development, and global warming. Who carries the burdens of environmental harms, and who benefits from the practices that cause them? Who would benefit from the policies promoted by environmentalists? Who would bear the burdens for these policies? Both social ecologists and ecofeminists criticize those who would answer these questions in terms of some general humanity, as in "humans suffer from environmental destruction" or "humans would benefit from wilderness preservation." Such general claims miss important distinctions between people. We need instead to examine more precisely who benefits from, who pays the price for, and who is at fault for environmental problems and environmentalist solutions.

11.3 ENVIRONMENTAL JUSTICE
AND ENVIRONMENTAL RACISM

Environmental justice investigates the social distribution of environmental benefits and burdens. A society that distributes these benefits and burdens unequally is prima facie unjust. According to many observers, the Summers memo reprinted at the beginning of this chapter was simply the most glaring example of an environmental policy that distributes benefits and burdens unjustly. More specifically, all too often society places the burdens on people in the least advantaged positions—the poor and people of color, for example. Thus, these policies are more accurately described as examples of environmental racism. Further, as the Chipko Movement suggests, there is some evidence that women often bear a greater environmental burden than men. Hence, we need also be concerned with environmental sexism.

Although a full review of environmental justice concerns is beyond the scope of this section, a brief survey to highlight the extent of such concerns is offered. This will provide a practical context for the more philosophical claims advanced by social ecologists and ecofeminists.

Consider the distribution of health and safety risks associated with pollution and toxic wastes. Since the mid-1970s, a number of researchers and activists have called attention to the disproportionate risks faced by communities of color. Sociologist Robert D. Bullard has been at the forefront of this research. Time and again, Bullard finds toxic waste dumps, landfills, incinerators, and polluting industries being located in communities and neighborhoods with a high density of poor and minorities. Bullard cites a 1992 study conducted by the *National Law Journal*, which concludes,

> There is a racial divide in the way that the U.S. government cleans up toxic waste sites and punishes polluters. White communities see faster action, better results and stiffer penalties than communities where blacks, Hispanics and other minorities live. This unequal protection often occurs whether the community is wealthy or poor.[12]

From prevention to clean up to punishment of offenders, this study found that enforcement of environmental laws is systematically lax when it concerns minority communities.

This research confirmed an earlier study conducted by the United Church of Christ Commission on Racial Justice. This 1982 study, *Toxic Wastes and Race in the United States,* concluded that race is the best predictor in identifying those communities and neighborhoods most likely to be the location of toxic waste sites. The evidence is strong. If you are a person of color, you are much more likely to live in an area where toxic dumps, landfills, incinerators, and polluting industries are or will be located. It is also less likely that the pollution will be cleaned up, and polluters probably will face lighter punishments than if they were located in white neighborhoods.[13]

Similar results are found at the international level. Poor countries are more likely to suffer environmental degradation—deforestation, desertification, and air and water pollution—than wealthy countries, and the poorest residents of those countries, the poorest of the poor, are likely to suffer most. Part of the explanation for this is the historical legacy of colonialism. During the past few centuries, many countries that today are underdeveloped were governed as colonies or near colonies, supplying the natural resources to fuel the industrial growth and living standards of Europe and the United States. The colonists exploited the resources of these countries with little or no regard for the environmental costs to the local community.

But the legacy of such injustices live on, often implicit within the economic thinking examined in Chapter 3. If we conduct a cost-benefit analysis, we find that distributing environmental risks to people and places with the least value is more efficient. It simply costs less. For example, if we are planning to build a trash incinerator, it makes economic sense to build it in an area with low property values. In this way, costs are minimized.

Philosopher Laura Westra finds a clear example of such reasoning in the World Bank memo. Westra quotes the World Bank's chief economist, Lawrence Summers, as arguing,

> The measurement of the costs of health-impairing pollution depends on the foregone earnings from increased morbidity and mortality. From this point of view a given amount of health-impairing pollution should be done in the country with the lowest cost, which will be the country with the lowest wages. I think the economic logic behind dumping a load of toxic waste in the lowest-wage country is impeccable and we should face up to that.[14]

When we understand that the World Bank effectively controls the administration of international debt and thus exercises tremendous control over the economies of most underdeveloped nations, we can see some real problems with this attitude. Except, perhaps, within the most crude form of utilitarianism, it would be difficult to find any theory of justice that would accept any of these examples as just or fair. Certainly, most would fail Rawls' restriction that inequalities can be justified only if they benefit the least advantaged members of society. Because the people burdened by these decisions seldom even have a voice in making them, these examples may well violate Rawls' first principle as well.

We do not need to look far to find other policies that would reinforce environmental injustice and environmental racism. Many prescriptions for controlling population growth strike many as disproportionately burdening the poor and minority communities. Those who target population growth as a major cause of environmental destruction often ignore cultural and economic factors that encourage the poor, especially poor women, to value more rather than fewer children. Given the history of oppressive population control policies targeted against minorities, a history that includes slavery, Nazism, and apartheid, minority people have reason to be skeptical of population policies advanced by wealthy white environmentalists.

In a classic article on world hunger and population growth, ecologist Garrett Hardin argues that overpopulation is a serious threat to the survival of all humans.[15] Using the metaphor of a lifeboat, Hardin claims that overpopulation is threatening to sink all of us as population surpasses the carrying capacity of the earth. Hardin recommends against food relief to victims of famine and other starving people. Such help would only lead to a greater population explosion among the poor and place a greater burden on the earth's productive capacity.

Critics point out that such policies harm the most disadvantaged human beings, the people least able to protect themselves. Such a policy would also protect the interests of the most advantaged peoples (those already aboard the lifeboat). A policy like Hardin's implies that people in developed countries, especially those in positions of power and privilege, can maintain their comfortable standard of living while the least advantaged human beings are allowed to starve. It is not just that we are in the lifeboat and they are not. There is less room in the lifeboat because we have brought with us all the creature comforts of our consumerist society. Again, it would be difficult to find a theory of justice willing to claim that such policies give people what they deserve.

Many preservationist policies also appear to benefit social elites while harming the most vulnerable. We have already seen a version of this in Guha's critique of Deep Ecology in Chapter 10. This issue was also a major theme at the 1992 Earth Summit in Rio de Janeiro. Many environmentalists from the industrialized countries of Europe and North America promoted policies at the summit that would limit development and population growth while preserving wilderness areas, rain forests, and biological diversity. Of course, these policies were most often aimed at less developed countries. To many people from countries in the less industrialized southern hemisphere, such policies serve the interests of the industrialized north at the expense of the less advantaged in the south. It sounded as if northern environmentalists were saying, "Our culture wreaked environmental havoc so that we might attain a comfortable and healthy lifestyle. Now that we have that, you should not seek a comparable standard of living because that would jeopardize the remaining wilderness areas, rain forests, and biological diversity. We did not value these things more than our own economic development, but you should."

Finally, some observers point out that in most of these examples of environmental injustice, women and children actually bear the brunt of the harms. The potential harms caused by exposure to pollutants, pesticides, and toxins fall disproportionately on women.[16]

Throughout much of the developing world, women have a threefold responsibility. They are primarily responsible for domestic chores such as cooking and maintaining the home, they have primary responsibility for the care of children, and they work outside the home, typically being responsible for tending domestic crops and livestock. Worldwide, women have less mobility than men to escape pollution and unsanitary conditions. Women have greater responsibility for the nonmechanized harvesting of crops and thus face risks associated with exposure to pesticides. Women have primary responsibility for gathering fuelwood and water. Thus, they suffer from loss of access to forestlands and water pollution. One estimate suggests that 34.6 percent of all childhood deaths in underdeveloped countries result from the lack of access to clean water.[17] As the Chipko Movement demonstrates, environmental destruction and development in many underdeveloped countries create particular burdens for women. Of course, population policies also typically burden women in ways not experienced by men. Women and children suffer more from the harms of overpopulation, whereas the responsibility for controlling population growth typically is thought to belong to women.[18]

11.4 MURRAY BOOKCHIN'S SOCIAL ECOLOGY

Murray Bookchin is a social theorist who has been writing about the connections between social domination and the domination of nature for more than four decades. His views have been characterized in a number of ways, including "libertarian social ecology," "eco-anarchism," and, most commonly, "social ecology." In what follows, we will limit the phrase "social ecology" to the social philosophy developed in Bookchin's writings.

Social ecology has its roots in a variety of philosophical traditions, including Marxian socialism, libertarian anarchism, and the "Western organismic tradition" associated with philosophers like Aristotle and Hegel. Although a full description of these diverse traditions is well beyond the scope of this textbook, we will need to consider them in order to understand social ecology.

First, we need to examine what Bookchin means by social domination and how this is connected to ecological problems. Specifically, Bookchin is concerned with *hierarchies,* which he explains as

> the cultural, traditional and psychological systems of obedience and command, not merely the economic and political systems to which the terms class and State most appropriately refer. Accordingly, hierarchy and domination could easily continue to exist in a "classless" or "Stateless" society. I refer to the domination of the young by the old, of women by men, of one ethnic group by another, of "masses" by bureaucrats who profess to speak of "higher social interests," of countryside by town, and in a more subtle psychological sense, of body by mind, of spirit by a shallow instrumental rationality.[19]

Thus, hierarchies imply the existence of at least two groups, one of which holds power over the other. This power enables the "superior" group to command obedience from the "inferior" group. Hierarchies promote social systems of domination in which the superior group is able to manipulate the inferior group to serve the purposes of the superiors while preventing the inferiors from pursuing their own true ends.

In this quotation, Bookchin distinguishes his views from those of traditional Marxists and traditional anarchists. Unlike the Marxists, Bookchin does not believe that the primary form of social hierarchy and domination rests with economic classes. Unlike the anarchists, Bookchin also does not believe that the modern nation-state is the primary agent of social domination. In his view, we are likely to find structures of domination within societies that lack economic classes and the bureaucratic nation-state.

This quotation also suggests that physical domination and power are not the only means of social control. Hierarchy "is also a state of consciousness" as well as a social condition. People can be oppressed by their consciousness, their understandings and beliefs, as much as by external forces. Thus, Bookchin speaks of people who "internalize" social structures of hierarchy and learn to accept a life of "toil, guilt, and sacrifice" while their "superiors" enjoy a life of pleasure and satisfaction.[20] As this quote from Bookchin suggests, human freedom involves more than just the absence of external controls. In his classic book, *The Ecology of Freedom,* Bookchin offers a history of the diverse forms of hierarchy and domination that have existed in societies from the Paleolithic era to the modern world.

But the most pertinent aspect of Bookchin's views concerns his assertion that the domination of nature "stems from" these patterns of social hierarchy and domination. How exactly should we understand this claim?

An initial point to note is that Bookchin essentially has reversed a standard Marxist interpretation. In the view of many Marxists, the human ability to dominate nature in the appropriation of private property allowed the creation of wealth and class structures that in turn led to class conflict and oppression. Bookchin suggests that social structures of domination preceded the domination of nature.

Bookchin also distinguishes his views from a Marxist view by denying any necessity or determinism to the connection between social domination and the domination of nature. He allows for the possibility that hierarchical societies might actually have rather benign relationships to nature and that non-hierarchical societies might abuse their natural environment.[21] Rather, he seeks to uncover how patterns of social domination can foster "a broad cultural mentality" or "ideology" that supports the domination of nature.

In summary, societies characterized by a high degree of hierarchy are also likely to abuse and damage their natural environment. Social hierarchies provide both the psychological and material conditions—the motivation and the means—for exploiting and dominating nature. In hierarchical societies, social institutions and practices (which would include, for example, forms of agriculture and technology) are designed in ways that facilitate control. You might think of the concept of economic efficiency as one such social ideal. In such a society, success is understood in terms of dominance and control. The more people who work for you, the more wealth, power, and status that you have, the more successful you are. Such a society also identifies human success with the domination and control of nonhuman nature. To understand the analysis further, it will help to discuss briefly another facet of social ecology, what Bookchin refers to as the "organismic tradition."

The organismic tradition in social philosophy focuses on the relations between individuals and their society. It seeks a middle ground between those who believe that individuals are simply the products of their society and those who believe that society is nothing more than a collection of individuals. An organic society or what is more often called a "community" exists in what philosophers call a "dialectical relationship" with individual human beings. That is, communities are created by human actions and human decisions, but humans are also created by their community. Social institutions, practices, values, and beliefs all influence the person I become. My identity is constituted to a large extent by my social roles, social history, and social circumstances. But the organic tradition does not reify the society, making it some "thing" out there that shapes and controls humans. Society is a product of human action and human decisions. Thus, the dialectical relationship sees humans as creating their society while being created by it.

Given this understanding of social history, we can now understand Bookchin's primary social and ethical value. Humans cannot help but be shaped and created by their social history. But this can occur in two ways. Humans can go through life being created by and in turn creating their social world without fully recognizing this reality, or they can be fully conscious of and responsible for this history. The preeminent human value is fully conscious "self-determining activity" because it is only through this type of action that humans most fully attain their natural potential as conscious thinking beings. This value is Bookchin's anarchist conception of freedom.

How is fully conscious self-determining activity possible? It is possible only when humans are free from all forms of external control and domination, which include not only physical but social, legal, psychological, intellectual, and emotional forms of coercion. Thus, the only truly just society is one in which humans are free from all forms of control or domination. This, then, is the goal of Bookchin's "libertarian anarchism." Philosophical anarchism holds that no coercive authority is ever justified. Put another way, philosophical anarchism maintains that all claims of authority are simply disguised forms of power or coercion.

In this model, the just community is one that is created to serve common needs and goals. It is a community that eschews domination in any form, whether domination of humans or nature. It would be a community in which democratic values such as full participation and freedom are the norms. Bookchin characterizes this just community as one that avoids institutions and customs that place one person or group of people in positions of authority over others. They would be communities in which decision-making authority is decentralized, where individuals complement and cooperate with each other but do not dominate each other. Indeed, the ideal "anarchistic community would approximate an ecosystem; it would be diversified, balanced, and harmonious."[22]

Given these philosophical goals, we can see how practices like sustainable agriculture would play a central role in Bookchin's ideal social and ecological community. He sees sustainable agriculture not as a collection of solutions to specific farming problems but as part of a lifestyle in which both humans and their natural surroundings can live free from dependence on dominating institutions and practices. Sustainable agriculture decentralizes and diversifies decision-making authority. In this sense, it is truly a democratic practice. Decisions are made directly by the people most affected by them. Sustainable agriculture reinforces a lifestyle in which local communities become sustainable and self-sufficient. In this type of world, humans experience true freedom, and only in this type of community are humans able to live in harmony with their natural environment. It is not coincidental, according to Bookchin, that nature's freedom from human domination can come about only in a world in which humans are also free from domination.

11.5 CRITICAL REFLECTIONS

Several challenges can be raised against Bookchin's social ecology. One concerns the alleged connection between social domination and the domination of nature.[23] A second focuses on the role that humans play in guiding the evolutionary development of nature.[24]

Bookchin explicitly denies that there is a necessary connection between social hierarchies and social domination on the one hand and attempts to dominate nature on the other. The former does not *cause* the latter. But what is the relationship? Bookchin's answer is not always clear. Yet, without a clear answer, social ecology loses much of its persuasive force, especially when considering its practical implications.

A strong causal connection between social domination and the domination of nature would suggest that we will be unable to meet environmental challenges unless we first abolish social hierarchies. In this interpretation, our policy demands are clear. We must address social questions before ecological ones. Yet, if the connection is less clear, then so, too, should be our policy priorities. If we can address ecological problems first and independently of addressing social hierarchies, the very relevance of social ecology is open to question.

In fairness to Bookchin, his view is more subtle than this challenge allows. As he sees it, the connection is less than a necessary causal connection but more than a mere accident. Bookchin speaks of the historical connection between real social hierarchies and the *idea* of dominating nature.[25] This suggests that, as a matter of historical fact, hierarchical societies encourage humans to identify social progress with control of and domination over nonhuman nature. Eventually, the connections can be thought of as mutually reinforcing. By implication, we need to address both, and to address one is also to address the other. Changing to a more benign relationship with the natural world will provoke changes in social arrangements (as the discussion of the political nature of sustainable agriculture might suggest). Changing our social relationships to less hierarchical, more decentralized associations will encourage a more felicitous relationship with nature (as the discussion of sustainable agriculture might suggest).

A second challenge to Bookchin focuses on the role that he allows humans in guiding natural evolution. Bookchin casts humans as "stewards" of evolution, capable of consciously serving and directing natural evolution. To some critics, this suggests a willingness to privilege human interests over nonhuman interests, to allow humans to "seize the helm of evolution" and direct nature to human ends.[26] Critics reject such anthropocentrism as being exactly the attitude that created much ecological destruction in the first place.

This criticism grows out of Bookchin's description of human rationality and human society as products of natural evolution, a "nature-rendered self-conscious." On this basis, Bookchin rejects any view that calls for humans to remove themselves from the natural world or that "denies or degrades the uniqueness of human beings." He lists both biocentric ethics and Deep Ecology among the philosophical views that degrade the rational abilities of human beings. He describes social ecology as "humanistic in the high Renaissance meaning of the term," which requires "a shift in vision from the skies to the earth, from superstition to reason, from deities to people—who are no less the products of natural evolution than grizzly bears and whales."[27]

Bookchin distinguishes "second nature," which includes such features of human evolution as rationality, communication, culture, and society, from "first nature," which refers to the nonhuman natural world. Although he emphasizes that this distinction is one of degree rather than kind, nevertheless it also suggests that humans are not simply the "equal biotic citizens" described in biocentric ethics, the land ethic, and Deep Ecology. The implications of this trouble critics, especially when Bookchin elaborates as follows.

> Natural evolution has not only provided humans with the *ability*, but also the *necessity* to be purposive interveners into "first nature," to consciously *change* "first nature" by means of a highly institutionalized form of community we call "society. . ." Taken together, all of these human traits—intellectual, communicative, and social—have not only emerged from natural evolution and are inherently human; they can also be placed at the *service* of natural evolution to consciously increase biotic diversity, diminish suffering, foster the evolution of new and ecologically valuable life-forms, reduce the impact of disastrous accidents or the harsh effects of mere change.[28]

Bookchin explicitly denies that he is suggesting that humans should take command of nature and control it for anthropocentric ends. As it exists today, second nature is thoroughly shaped by social hierarchies and ideas of domination. Hence, it would be a mistake simply to pass control of the natural world over to this type of thinking and reasoning. Further, in a spirit reminiscent of Leopold's, Bookchin emphasizes the complexity of first nature and strongly recommends a conservative and prudent approach to any activity that changes nature. Nonetheless, he does not shy away from the ramifications of his initial claim. Humanity as a part of natural evolution and the only part capable of sophisticated, rational thought has a responsibility to act as steward of the natural evolutionary process.

During the late 1980s, an acrimonious debate developed on this issue between Bookchin and several Deep Ecologists. Deep Ecologists accused Bookchin of anthropocentrism and attributed to him the view that "human beings are a *higher* form of life."[29] Bookchin, for his part, had accused Deep Ecology of advocating an oppressive and misanthropic philosophy.[30] A short review of this debate can provide a helpful summary of Bookchin.

Bookchin's critique of Deep Ecology can be generalized to apply to any biocentric or ecocentric ethics that attributes "equal moral worth" to human and nonhuman life-forms. During these debates, Bookchin highlighted the extreme views of members of Earth First! and several Deep Ecologists. These views suggested that famine and AIDS, for example, were "nature's revenge" for overpopulation and ecological destruction. The implication was that starving children in places like Ethiopia and Somalia should be allowed to die in the name of some natural ecological law concerning carrying capacity and population dynamics. Bookchin forcefully rejected these views as unjust, claiming that they followed straightforwardly from the philosophy of biocentrism.

> If the Deep Ecology principle of "biocentrism" teaches that human beings are no different from lemmings in terms of their "intrinsic worth" and the moral consideration we owe them, and if human beings are viewed as being subject to "natural laws" in just the same way as any other species, then these "extreme" statements are really the *logical* conclusion of Deep Ecology philosophy.[31]

One problem with the principle of biocentric equality is that it tends to treat all humans as equally responsible for ecological destruction. The cause of the ecological crisis is attributed to "anthropocentrism," a human-centered ethics. As an alternative, a biocentric or life-centered ethics is developed. But Bookchin rejects the view that "humanity" is at fault, that "we" are destroying the natural world.

> But, I have to ask, who is this "us" from which the living world has to be protected? . . . Is it "humanity"? Is it the human "species" per se? Is it people, as such? Or is it our particular society, our particular civilization, with its hierarchical social relations . . . ? One of the problems with this asocial, "species-centered" way of thinking, of course, is that it blames the victim. Let's face it, when you say that a black kid in Harlem is as much to blame for the ecological crisis as the president of Exxon, you are letting one off the hook and slandering the other.[32]

We can see the central insight of Bookchin's philosophy in these challenges to Deep Ecology and biocentrism. To understand the roots of our ecological crisis, we need to look to how societies are organized. Society is a human creation, and some forms of society can lead to an attitude that encourages humans to dominate and destroy the natural world. But because society is a human creation, human beings can also change it. Bookchin reminds us that although human decisions and human values have played a major role in ecological destruction, they can be a major part of ecological solutions as well.

11.6 ECOFEMINISM: MAKING CONNECTIONS

Ecofeminism identifies a variety of approaches that also see a connection between social domination and the domination of nature. Since the term was first used by Françoise d'Eaubonne in 1974, ecofeminism has generated a significant amount of interesting writing and research.[33] As described by Warren, ecofeminism or ecological feminism

> is the position that there are important connections—historical, experiential, symbolic, theoretical—between the domination of women and the domination of nature, an understanding of which is crucial to both feminism and environmental ethics.[34]

Ecofeminism is a recent development among environmental philosophers, and as this quote suggests, much of the work is still concerned with simply exploring the connections between the feminist and ecological movements. Nevertheless, this approach has already made significant philosophical contributions.

Because feminists offer a wide diversity of viewpoints concerning the nature and analysis of women's oppression, they also have diverse views concerning the connections between the domination of women and the domination of nature. What follows is a review of some of the connections that have been made between the domination of women and the domination of nature and an overview of their philosophical and environmental significance.

We begin with a discussion of the most general features of any system of domination or what Warren has called the "logic of domination."[35] This logic of domination is a pattern of thinking in which two groups (for example, men and women) are distinguished in terms of some characteristics (for example, men are rational and women are emotional), a value hierarchy is attributed to these characteristics (for example, reason is superior to emotion), and the subordination of one group is justified by its lack of this superior characteristic (for example, men ought to be in positions of authority because they are more rational and less emotional than women). This is the most general pattern of thinking that feminists reject. Different feminisms can be distinguished by their analyses of this logic of domination.

One framework for organizing feminist thinking that has influenced many ecofeminists was developed by philosopher Alison Jaggar.[36] Jaggar distinguishes liberal, Marxist, radical, and socialist forms of feminism. Each offers an account of the oppression of women and an alternative social philosophy.

Liberal feminists, for example, deny that any relevant difference between men and women exists. Liberals (like the utilitarians, Kant and Rawls) argue that all humans possess the same nature as free and rational beings and any unequal treatment of women would deny this moral equality and would, therefore, be unjust. As a result of this analysis, liberal feminists devote much of their energy to locating discrimination and fighting for equal rights and equal opportunity.

Marxist feminists argue that women are oppressed because they are relegated to domestic and, therefore, dependent forms of labor. These feminists argue, for example, that the Lockean theory of private property rights makes sense only within a context in which women's labor is ignored. A necessary precondition for a "man" to "mix his labor" with some unowned land is that there exist women who are performing full-time domestic labor, allowing the man the free time necessary to accumulate land. Domestic labor, of course, did not give women property rights of ownership over the home. Only by becoming full participants in independent and productive forms of labor do women become liberated from economic and political exploitation.

Socialist feminists reject the strict class analysis offered by Marxists and claim that a complex web of social relationships underlies the oppression of women. These relationships include both economic factors and the traditional patterns of gender roles and identities. Both Marxist and socialist feminists would likely describe the women of the Chipko Movement as becoming liberated from economic and social oppression to take a more autonomous and responsible role in their own lives.

Radical feminists believe that biological and sexual differences between men and women have been made the basis of women's oppression. This type of feminism is "radical" in the sense that it denies that women's oppression can be reduced to some other more basic form of oppression. Women have been culturally defined in terms of their biology. This biological difference has been used to justify a wide-ranging gender system that ensures that women remain dominated by men, primarily by being cast exclusively in roles of mother, wife, and sex object. Because of their roles in childbearing, child raising, and human sexuality, women have been characterized as more controlled by their bodies, more passive, and more emotional than men. Given the logic of domination, it is a short step from these gender distinctions to the conclusion that men, by being more reasonable and active than women, ought to be in positions of authority over women.

Recognizing this pattern of thinking, some radical feminists conclude that women can escape oppression only when traditional gender roles are abolished. Some early radical feminists argued that women should strive for a "unisex" or androgynous culture, whereas others advocated a separatism between women and men. Still other radical feminists turned this logic of domination on its head. Rather than denying biological, sexual, and gender differences between men and women, these feminists seek instead to encourage and celebrate the female. Accepting the view that women do experience, understand, and value differently than men, some radical feminists seek to develop an alternative feminist politics, culture, and ethics.

A significant amount of work on ecological issues has come from this branch of radical feminism. What has been called "cultural ecofeminism"[37] accepts the view that there do exist authentic and particular "women's ways" of experiencing, understanding, and valuing the world. Cultural ecofeminism holds that women's perspectives historically have been and remain closely identified with nature and that women, like nature, have been systematically oppressed in the process. But rather than denying the link between women and nature (as liberal ecofeminists, for example, might), cultural ecofeminists aim "to remedy ecological and other problems through the creation of an alternative "women's culture" . . . based on revaluing, celebrating and defending what patriarchy has devalued, including the feminine, non-human nature, the body and the emotions."[38]

The connections between alternative women's cultures and ecological concerns have been explored in a number of ways. We will briefly consider two: an ecological ethics based on care and relationships and a women's spirituality movement.

One contrast between masculine and feminine that has been a part of the oppression of women views men as rational and objective while viewing women as emotional and overly concerned with the personal. Consistent with this contrast, the dominant models in ethics construe the moral realm in terms of abstract, rational, and universal principles. The traditional theories of natural law, utilitarianism, and deontology are prime examples of ethics perceived in this way. The domestic roles of women as mothers and wives meant that those values important to women—caring, relationships, love, responsibility, and trust—remained outside of mainstream ethical theorizing.

In recent decades, some feminists have brought many of the values traditionally associated with women's roles, summarized as an "ethics of care," into the forefront of ethical theorizing. Drawing on the work of Carol Gilligan, Nel Noddings, Sara Ruddick, and others, these feminists seek to articulate and defend a perspective that de-emphasizes abstract rules and principles in favor of a contextualized ethics focusing on caring and relationships.[39] Traditional ethical concepts such as moral laws, rights, duties, obligations, and justice presuppose a world in which interests conflict, the demands of justice restrict and limit human freedom, and morality battles egoism. An ethics of care begins with a moral universe in which cooperation replaces conflict, relationships replace confrontation, and caring for the other replaces rights and duties. It is a moral universe in which mothering and friendship serve as moral ideals rather than abstract principles like individual autonomy and freedom from interference.

Feminists offer different explanations for why an ethics of care is particularly a women's perspective. In general, feminists such as Noddings and Ruddick understand an ethics of care as more compatible with the life experiences of women, specifically as those experiences follow from both reproductive biology and experiences in mothering. Abstract ethical principles and rules seem irrelevant in a life of childbearing and child rearing. The vocabulary of rights and duties, autonomy and justice, and rules and laws is highly artificial and inappropriate within the context of a mother-child relationship.

Some cultural ecofeminists build on these observations concerning an ethics of care. These thinkers acknowledge that women historically have been portrayed as closer to nature than men. But rather than criticizing this portrayal as the basis for much of the violence done to women, as feminist Susan Griffin has, some ecofeminists build on this identification as a basis for a benevolent relationship between humans and nature.[40] From this perspective, the ethics of care covers human-nature relationships as appropriately as it covers mother-child relationships. Women, as those who are taught to experience this caring more directly and more immediately than men, are the more appropriate voices for nature's interests.

To briefly develop this description of an ethics of care, reflect on some issues of virtue and character discussed earlier in this book. The care perspective moves beyond an ethics conceived of as abstract universal rules that we can apply to specific problems and from which we can deduce what decisions we should make. The moral person is not conceived as a free and independent individual who must answer "What should I do?" The care perspective focuses on specific relationships in all their detail, seeking to uncover the full nature of these relationships and affiliations. In such particularity, an ethics of character or an ethics of virtue appropriately replaces abstract and general principles. The good person, for example, the loving mother, is what an ethics of care seeks to describe. Moral actions would be those performed by the good person rather than those conforming to abstract general principles.

How might this be relevant to environmental issues? Again, reflect on some earlier issues. Many philosophers have raised challenges concerning our duties to future generations in large part because people of the future do not conform to certain abstract and general conditions for moral standing. An ethics of care can shift our focus away from such abstract questions and start from the reality that many people do in fact care about what happens to people of the future. So, too, an ethics of care does not get encumbered with abstract questions concerning the moral standing of animals that characterizes so much of the animal liberation discussion. Rather more central questions for ethics are do we care about animals? Do we have relationships to them? What is the basis for our attachments to animals?[41] The discussion of moral standing and moral considerability is similar. We can and do exist in relationships with our natural surroundings, and an abstract ethical theory that ignores that will be inadequate. A view consistent with an ethics of care is Leopold's injunction that we must first come to "love, respect, and admire the land" before applying the more abstract principles of the land ethic. Finally, the powerful image of the Chipko women literally embracing trees to protect them from violence testifies to the ethics of care as an experience of women.

The women's spirituality movement is a second area in which cultural ecofeminists have explored a bond between women and nature.[42] Within much mainstream Western religion, God is seen as outside of or transcending nature. Nature is mere matter: passive, inert, shapeless, and dead. God created, formed, and breathed life into the dust. In much of this tradition, women again are associated with nature because they are so dependent on their bodies and are so passive. Thus, organized religion often sees women as lacking the special spirituality that would qualify them as priests, rabbis, ministers, popes, and so forth. Thus, within much of this mainstream, we again can witness the dual denigration of women and nature.

Many cultural ecofeminists seek a spiritualism or theology that reverses these trends.[43] We should instead observe and honor the identification of women, nature, and the divine. Often looking to ancient religions in which God was identified both as the earth itself and as a woman, some cultural ecofeminists honor a spirituality that views the Goddess as immanent in nature and the natural world as revealing the divine. Thus, the earth itself is worshipped as divine, and caring for or loving the earth is a spiritual as well as an ecological responsibility. Celebrating Mother Nature or the Greek goddess Gaia, for example, becomes the way for women's spirituality to rejoice in the sacredness of women and nature.

11.7 ECOFEMINISM: RECENT DEVELOPMENTS

Despite these developments, many feminists are reluctant to accept the strategy of those who embrace the view that distinctive and separate "women's ways" of understanding, experiencing, and valuing the world do exist. They fear that by accepting the dualism implicit in viewing women as "closer to nature" than men that these feminists only reinforce the way of thinking that underlies hierarchies and the logic of domination. Philosopher Val Plumwood calls this "the feminism of uncritical reversal" and sees it as "perpetuating women's oppression in a new and subtle form."[44] Ynestra King suggests that an "unwitting complicity" in a patriarchal mind-set underlies the culture-nature split that this view assumes.[45]

In place of cultural ecofeminism, with its roots in radical feminism, Plumwood and Warren seek a "third wave" of feminism that "is an integrative and transformative feminism, or that moves us beyond the current debate over the four leading versions of feminism and makes a responsible ecological perspective central to feminist theory and practice."[46] Although this approach is still very much in the early stages of its development, the remainder of this section sketches some directions in which this "transformative feminism" might be developing.

The view that we are considering can be found in the writings of Warren and Plumwood.[47] To introduce this third wave of feminism, it will be helpful to follow Plumwood's review of the first two waves. Feminism's first wave, typified by liberal feminism, seeks to end discrimination and attain equality for women. The problem with this view is that in a culture in which masculine traits and characteristics dominate, equality for women amounts to little more than requiring women to adopt these dominant male traits. In effect, women can be equal to men only if they become masculine, and to the degree that strong cultural forces work against this, women always fall just a little short of full equality. (This point parallels the critical discussion in Chapter 6 concerning animal liberation. Only those animals fortunate enough to resemble humans are granted moral standing.) The ecological implications of this first wave can be devastating. Women can liberate themselves from an oppressive identification with nature only if they, like men, become oppressors of nature.

The second wave of feminism is represented by the "uncritical reversal" of some feminists. This perspective promotes and celebrates a distinctive female point of view. However, as suggested earlier, this perspective risks being co-opted by the dominant male culture by accepting the dualisms that male culture has used, via the logic of domination, to justify women's oppression.

The third wave seeks an alternative to both liberal and radical versions of feminism. This alternative sees the domination of nature and the domination of women as inextricably connected. They are connected in more ways than simply being two types of a more general pattern of domination. Women have been identified as closer to nature, and nature has been identified as feminine. These identifications have mutually reinforced the oppression of each. Thus, environmental philosophy and feminism need to develop in unison, each recognizing parallel interests.

Plumwood and Warren suggest that at a most general level, both feminism and the ecological movement need to address a cluster of dualisms and dualistic ways of thinking that underlie the logic of domination. This is not to suggest, of course, that distinctions are not to be made nor differences recognized. But we should challenge those distinctions that are designed to reinforce superior-inferior, oppressor-oppressed frameworks. This type of ecofeminism challenges both feminists and environmentalists alike to uncover the patterns of domination common to the oppression of women and nature and begin exploring alternative and nondualistic ways of thinking about both human and nonhuman nature. This type of ecofeminism is also quite similar to Bookchin's more general analysis of hierarchies and domination.

Some of these dualistic ways of thinking that are especially relevant to ecofeminism involve the split between masculine and feminine, human and nature, reason and emotion, mind and body, and objectivity and subjectivity. Each dualism typically gets used within our culture in contexts that support domination: masculine over feminine, human over nature, reason over emotion, mind over body, and objectivity over subjectivity. The goal, therefore, is to weed out dualisms and develop alternative patterns of thinking.

One of the most interesting directions in which this type of analysis has proceeded concerns science, technology, and a scientific understanding of nature. As pointed out, a number of feminist scholars have chronicled the many ways that culture has identified women with nature. But much interesting research has also been conducted on how that identification has influenced Western science.[48] Science has typically been identified with the dominant part of these dualisms: masculine, human, rational, mental, and objective. Feminist scientist Evelyn Fox Keller has detailed the ways in which a particular way of understanding nature, women, and even marriage has also helped shape the early development of Western science.[49]

Fox quotes the early scientist Francis Bacon to show how many of the models and metaphors of early science betrayed an aggressive attitude toward both women and nature. According to Bacon, science seeks to "establish a chaste and lawful marriage between Mind and Nature. . . . I am come in very truth leading to you Nature with all her children to bind her to your service and make her your slave." Science and technology do not "merely exert a gentle guidance over nature's course; they have the power to conquer and subdue her, to shake her to her foundations."[50] Bacon's images are clear. Nature is a woman, and she is to become married to man who will subdue her and turn her into a slave. Bacon associates nature not only with women and marriage but with a particularly dominating and abusive type of marriage.

Sensitivity to these kinds of images should alert us to similar attitudes within modern science. Typically, scientific theories are judged by their ability to explain and predict natural phenomena. But all too often the ability to predict natural phenomena is simply the first step in developing a technology to control natural phenomena, to "conquer and subdue her" and "make her your slave." This is a science and technology that sees value only in instrumental terms. How can we humans use nature for our own interests? Seldom does this science and technology consider noninstrumental values in nature, typically rejecting these values as a matter of "emotion" or "feelings" and, therefore, "subjective" and scientifically irrelevant.

Recent feminist scholarship alerts us to many of these subtle but oppressive patterns of thinking and patterns of acting. This scholarship also offers suggestions for alternatives. Keller has also written a biography of the geneticist Barbara McClintock, *A Feeling for the Organism: The Life and Work of Barbara McClintock.* In this work, Keller describes an approach to science that exhibits this "feeling for the organism," an approach that is often called and then dismissed as "a woman's way of thinking." Keller does not suggest that mainstream science be abandoned in favor of this more particularized approach to knowing but that science done only from the control-and-dominate perspective will likely miss much that is important. Review many of the discussions presented in this book to look for situations in which little feeling is exhibited toward nature by a science bent on domination and control. Look particularly at the science and technology involved in creating pesticides, harnessing nuclear energy, developing wilderness areas, experimenting on animals, conducting agribusiness, and eliminating varmints and predators. For alternatives, consider the science that would support sustainable agriculture.

A second direction for further environmental thinking encouraged by this type of ecofeminism develops from a much more modest conception of human action, ethics, and understanding. This third wave of ecofeminism encourages thinking that is *contextualist, pluralistic, inclusive, and holistic*.[51] It is contextualist in the sense that it seeks to avoid abstract and universal ethical pronouncements. This process of abstraction can prevent us from recognizing the rich diversity within both human and nonhuman nature. Too often, this process of abstracting to the universal has simply taken characteristics of the dominant group and turned them into ethical and philosophical ideals. We have already seen how this can reinforce oppression of women, animals, and the rest of the natural world.

This third wave of ecofeminism is pluralistic and inclusive in the sense that it respects diversity and difference. Perhaps the key aspect of a dominating ideology is the belief that there is only one right way of being, thinking, and acting. A philosophy that self-consciously avoids hierarchies and domination will celebrate diversity and resist attempts to establish one "correct" environmental theory.

Finally, this ecofeminism is holistic in the sense that it encourages us to understand human beings as essentially a part of their human and natural communities. (Note how this common way of speaking already assumes a dualism, as if human communities are not "natural.") This ecofeminism rejects the view that humans are abstract individuals, fully constituted by their private consciousness, thoughts, and choices. Humans are created by and are an inextricable part of their social and natural environments.

11.8 SUMMARY AND CONCLUSIONS

Like Deep Ecology and, to a lesser extent, Leopold's land ethic, both social ecology and ecofeminism advocate a radical shift in the ways in which the major and dominant sectors of the contemporary world think about and understand the relationships between humans and the rest of the natural world. But social ecology and ecofeminism are more specific about the roots of environmental and ecological devastation. The domination of the natural world is part of more general patterns of domination and control. Until all patterns of domination are eliminated, we can expect little real progress to be made on the environmental front.

Both social ecology and ecofeminism face serious philosophical challenges. How exactly are we to understand the connections between human domination of other humans and the human domination of nonhuman nature? Has one caused the other? Are they mutually reinforcing? Should one have ethical priority? Are they simply parallel developments with little direct connection? What are the ethically and philosophically preferable strategies for resisting these forms of domination? What are the connections between the domination of women and other forms of social domination? Is ecofeminism a branch of social ecology?

Ecofeminism especially resists attempts to construct a unified and over-arching environmental philosophy, and we need to be careful about this when raising challenges to these views. Many of these challenges seek the type of universal and abstract answers that ecofeminists (and social ecologists) iden-tify as part of the problem. Ecofeminism is also in the early stages of growth and development, and it would be unfair to expect too much in the way of answers at this point. But social ecology and ecofeminism have already made significant contributions to environmental ethics and environmental philoso-phy. No longer can these issues be discussed independently of discussions of social domination and control. Further, by calling attention to such issues, these approaches stimulate our understanding of the benefits of the type of alternative social arrangements typified by sustainable agriculture.

Notes

1. This memo exists in places in the public domain after being leaked to the press apparently from an internal World Bank source.

2. At the time of the memo reprinted here, Lawrence Summers was the chief economist of the World Bank. In 1999, Mr. Summers was appointed Secretary of the Treasury by President Clinton. After the memo was leaked to the public, Mr. Summers apologized and explained that it was intended as ironic. Later reports even suggested that Mr. Summers had not even written the memo, although it was circulated with his name attached.

3. For further information on the Chipko Movement, see Shobita Jain, "Standing Up for Trees: Women's Role in the Chipko Movement," in *Women and the Environment,* ed. Sally Sontheimer (New York: Monthly Review Press, 1991), and Ramachandra Guha, *The Unquiet Woods* (Berkeley: University of California Press, 1989). These two accounts are particularly interesting because Jain sees the Chipko Movement more as a women's movement and Guha interprets it more as a peasant uprising.

4. For Bookchin's ecological views, see especially *The Ecology of Freedom* (Palo Alto, Calif.: Chesire Books, 1982) and *The Philosophy of Social Ecology* (Montreal: Black Rose Books, 1990).

5. A helpful resource for recent work on philosophical aspects of ecofeminism is the *American Philosophical Association Newsletter on Feminism and Philosophy* 90 (fall 1991). This issue contains an overview of ecofeminist issues by Karen Warren and a solid philosophical bibliography compiled by Warren and Carol Adams.

6. Bookchin, *The Ecology of Freedom,* p. 1.

7. Rosemary Radford Reuther, *New Woman/New Earth* (New York: Seabury, 1975), p. 204.

8. This is a general characterization. Descriptions of ecofeminism offered by Reuther, Val Plumwood, and Karen Warren suggest an understanding that sees the oppression of women as a major, but perhaps not the major, form of oppression. Other feminists argue that women's oppression represents the principal form of social domination. Radical feminists, for example, explicitly deny that women's oppression can be reduced to any other more basic form of oppression.

9. See especially Alison Jaggar, *Feminist Politics and Human Nature* (Totowa, N.J.: Rowman and Littlefield, 1988), for the best discussion of various feminist understandings of social justice.

10. Karen Warren, introduction to *Hypatia* 6 (spring 1991): 1.

11. John Rawls, *A Theory of Justice* (Cambridge, Mass.: Harvard University Press, 1971).

12. Marianne Lavelle and Marcia Coyle, "Unequal Protection," *National Law Journal*, September 21, 1992, as quoted in *Unequal Protection*, ed. Robert Bullard (San Francisco: Sierra Club Books, 1994), p. 9.

13. Bullard's work is a solid resource for these claims. In addition to the anthology mentioned in note 12, see Robert D. Bullard, *Dumping in Dixie: Race, Class, and Environmental Quality* (Boulder, CO: Westview, 1990). Other sources include *Environmental Justice*, ed. Bunyan Bryant (Washington, D.C.: Island Press, 1995), and *Faces of Environmental Racism*, ed. Laura Westra and Peter Wenz (Lanham, Md.: Rowman and Littlefield, 1995). Bullard and Bryant emphasize policy and activist readings, and Westra and Wenz are philosophers. For a general introduction to a justice perspective on environmental issues see Peter Wenz, *Environmental Justice* (Albany: State University of New York Press, 1988). See also United Church of Christ Commission for Racial Justice, *Toxic Wastes and Race in the United States* (New York: United Church of Christ, 1987).

14. Laura Westra, "A Transgenic Dinner? Ethical and Social Issues in Biotechnology and Agriculture," *Journal of Social Philosophy* 24 (winter 1993): 215–32. Quoted in Westra and Wenz, eds., *Faces of Environmental Racism*, p. xvi.

15. Garrett Hardin, "Lifeboat Ethics: The Case Against Helping the Poor," *Psychology Today* 8 (September 1974): 38–126. Reprinted in *World Hunger and Morality*, 2d ed., ed. William Aiken and Hugh LaFollette (Upper Saddle River, N.J.: Prentice-Hall 1996), pp. 5–15.

16. Leonie Caldecott and Stephanie LeLan, eds., *Reclaim the Earth* (London: Women's Press, 1983); Vandana Shiva, *Staying Alive: Women, Ecology, and Development* (London: Zed Books, 1988).

17. This estimate is from UNICEF, *State of the World's Children* (1988) as quoted in Vandana Shiva, "The Impoverishment of the Environment," *Ecofeminism*, ed. Maria Mies and Vandana Shiva (London: Zed Books, 1993), p. 81.

18. See Annabel Rodda, *Women and the Environment* (London: Zed Books, 1991), pp. 68–80, for extended discussions of these claims.

19. Bookchin, *The Ecology of Freedom*, p. 4.

20. Ibid., 4–8.

21. Much of what follows is taken from Murray Bookchin, "Recovering Evolution: A Reply to Eckersley and Fox," *Environmental Ethics* 12 (fall 1990): 253–73.

22. Bookchin, "Ecology and Revolutionary Thought," in *Post-Scarcity Anarchism* (Berkeley, Calif.: Ramparts, 1971), p. 80. This essay originally was published in 1965.

23. See, for example, Robin Eckersley, *Environmentalism and Political Theory* (Albany: State University of New York Press, 1992), pp. 148–54.

24. Ibid., 154–60. See also Eckersley's "Divining Evolution: The Ecological Ethics of Murray Bookchin," *Environmental Ethics* 11 (summer 1989): 99–116.

25. See, for example, Bookchin, "Recovering Evolution: A Reply to Eckersley and Fox," pp. 262–66.

26. Eckersley, "Divining Evolution: The Ecological Ethics of Murry Bookchin," p. 99.

27. Murray Bookchin, "Social Ecology Versus Deep Ecology," *Socialist Review* 18, nos. 1–2 (1988): 27–28.

28. Ibid., 28; the emphasis is in the original.

29. Judi Bari, "Why I Am Not a Misanthrope," *Earth First!*, February 2, 1991, p. 25. For other Deep Ecology critiques of Bookchin, see Christopher Manes, *Green Rage: Radical Environmentalism and the Unmaking of Civilization* (Boston: Little, Brown, 1990), and Warwick Fox, *Toward a Transpersonal Ecology* (Boston: Shambhala, 1990). An excellent overview of these debates can be found in Steve Chase, ed., *Defending the Earth: A Dialogue between Murray Bookchin and Dave Foreman* (Boston: South End Press, 1991).

30. See Bookchin, *Social Ecology Versus Deep Ecology* (Burlington, Vt.: Green Program Project, 1988), reprinted in *Socialist Review* 18, nos. 1–2 (1988): 27–28.

31. Chase, ed., *Defending the Earth: A Dialogue between Murray Bookchin and Dave Foreman*, p. 125.

32. Ibid., 30–31.

33. Françoise d'Eaubonne, *Le feminisme ou la mort (Feminism or Death)* (Paris: Pierre Horay, 1974). Among the most recent philosophically helpful sources are *Hypatia* 6 (spring 1991), the special issue on ecological feminism, and the *American Philosophical Association Newsletter on Feminism and Philosophy* 90 (fall 1991) and 91 (spring 1992). In addition to articles and interviews, the APA's newsletters contain helpful course syllabi and bibliographies.

34. Karen J. Warren, "The Power and Promise of Ecological Feminism," *Environmental Ethics* 12 (summer 1990): 126.

35. See Karen J. Warren, "Feminism and Ecology: Making Connections," *Environmental Ethics* 9 (spring 1987): 3–20, and "The Power and Promise of Ecological Feminism," *Environmental Ethics* 12 (summer 1990): 125–46. In the earlier article, Warren takes the logic of domination as characteristic of patriarchal frameworks, whereas in the more recent paper, she has revised her views to include all "oppressive" frameworks. In this respect, the second article seems to parallel more closely Bookchin's general discussion of hierarchies.

36. This classic discussion of liberal, Marxist, radical, and socialist feminisms can be found in Jaggar, *Feminist Politics and Human Nature*. For a discussion of these models as they relate to ecological issues, see Warren, "Feminism and Ecology" and Carolyn Merchant, "Ecofeminism and Feminist Theory," in *Reweaving the World*, ed. Irene Diamond and Gloria Feman Orenstein (San Francisco: Sierra Club Books, 1990), pp. 100–105; and Val Plumwood, "Feminism and Ecofeminism," *Ecologist* 22 (January-February 1992): 8–13.

37. This follows the usage of Val Plumwood, "Current Trends in Ecofeminism," in *The Ecologist* 22, no. 1 (January–February 1992): 10.

38. Ibid.

39. Carol Gilligan, *In a Different Voice: Psychological Theory and Women's Development* (Cambridge, Mass.: Harvard University Press, 1982); Nel Noddings, *Caring: A Feminine Approach to Ethics and Moral Education* (Berkeley: University of California Press, 1984); Sara Ruddick, *Maternal Thinking* (New York: Ballantine, 1989).

40. Two of the earliest and best sources that explore the women and nature connections and the oppression and violence against women are Susan Griffin, *Women and Nature: The Roaring Inside Her* (New York: Harper and Row, 1978), and Carolyn Merchant, *The Death of Nature: Women, Ecology, and the Scientific Revolution* (New York: Harper and Row, 1980).

41. A helpful bibliography, "Women and Animals," is part of the thorough bibliography, "Feminism and the Environment," ed. Adams and Warren, that appears in the *American Philosophical Association Newsletter on Feminism and Philosophy.*

42. Diamond and Orenstein, eds., *Reweaving the World,* contains several articles on women's spirituality and includes another helpful bibliography. See also Carol Christ, *Laughter of Aphrodite: Reflections on a Journey to the Goddess* (San Francisco: Harper and Row, 1987); Reuther, *New Woman/New Earth;* and Starhawk, *The Spiral Dance: A Rebirth of the Ancient Religion of the Great Goddess* (San Francisco: Harper and Row, 1986).

43. Two classic sources for exploring the more general issue of women's spiritualism are Reuther, *New Woman/New Earth,* and Mary Daly, *GYN/Ecology: The Metaethics of Radical Feminism* (Boston: Beacon, 1978). Neither Reuther nor Daly subscribes to the particular overview of spiritualism described here, however.

44. Plumwood, "Feminism and Ecofeminism," p. 12.

45. Ynestra King, "Feminism and the Revolt against Nature," *Heresies* #13: *Feminism and Ecology* 4 (1981): 15.

46. Warren, "Feminism and Ecology: Making Connections," pp. 17–18. The phrase "third wave of feminism" is from Plumwood, "Feminism and Ecofeminism," pp. 12–13.

47. For Warren's views, see the citations in notes 5, 10, 34, and 35 as well as *Ecological Feminism* (New York: Routledge, 1994). Plumwood's more recent thinking appears in her *Feminism and the Mastery of Nature* (London: Routledge, 1993).

48. See especially Merchant, *The Death of Nature: Women, Ecology, and the Scientific Revolution,* and Evelyn Fox Keller, *Reflections on Gender and Science* (New Haven, Conn.: Yale University Press, 1985).

49. See especially Keller's "Spirit and Reason at the Birth of Modern Science," ch. 3 in *Reflections on Gender and Science.*

50. Ibid., 36.

51. Adopted from Warren, "The Power and Promise of Ecological Feminism," pp. 141–45.

Discussion Questions

1. Critics sometimes describe environmentalists as "tree huggers." Clearly, this is intended to ridicule environmentalists. What might the source of this ridicule be? How does this compare to the sense of tree hugging as it originated with the Chipko Movement?

2. Must a public policy intentionally discriminate before it can be described as racist or sexist? Is discrimination always a matter of intent? In your opinion, what is the intent behind decisions on where to locate waste dumps? Do you think that the Lawrence Summers memo was racist or classist?

3. Review the common dualisms (for example, mind-body, reason-emotion, and objectivity-subjectivity) mentioned in this chapter. Discuss and evaluate the value hierarchies that are implicit within them.

4. Bookchin claims that human beings cannot help but be, nor should they seek to avoid being "purposive interveners" in nature. That would seem to conflict with many preservationists and Deep Ecologists who believe that humans should let nature take its course. Discuss how these different views might evaluate policy on the Yellowstone fires, Olympic goats, Chipko Movement, and population control.

5. In his recent book *Earth in the Balance*, Vice President Al Gore described the infamous nineteenth century Irish potato famine as resulting from monoculture farming techniques. That is, the Irish overrelied on a single imported species of potato so that a single infestation destroyed their entire food supply. This brings to mind the claim of some Deep Ecologists that famines often are "nature's revenge" on humans for their abuse of nature. In his book, Gore also notes that other foodstuffs, including wheat and sheep, were being exported to England even as Irish people were starving. How might a social ecologist analyze the causes of the Great Hunger in Ireland?

6. In Chapter 1, we quoted scientist Amory Lovins as saying that the "answers you get depend upon the questions you ask." What different questions might be asked by someone taking a feminist approach to science and technology regarding such issues as nuclear energy, population policy, pesticide use, and animal agriculture?

Further Reading

The debate between social ecologists and Deep Ecology and Earth First! is reviewed by Murray Bookchin and Dave Foreman in Steve Chase, ed., *Defending the Earth* (Boston: South End Press, 1991).

Janet Biehl, *Rethinking Ecofeminist Politics* (Boston: South End Press, 1991), offers a critique of ecofeminism from the perspective of social ecology. Although helpful for understanding some differences between social ecology and some forms of feminism, this book is not always fair to the wide variety of ecofeminist positions.

Robert Bullard, ed., *Unequal Protection* (San Francisco: Sierra Club, 1994), provides an excellent starting point for investigating environmental racism and environmental injustice.

A substantial bibliography of ecofeminism was compiled by Carol Adams and Karen Warren for the *Newsletter on Feminism and Philosophy* 90 (fall 1991) published by the American Philosophical Association. A helpful and more recent selected bibliography can be found in Greta Gaard, ed., *Ecofeminism: Women, Animals, Nature* (Philadelphia: Temple University Press, 1993).

Pluralism and Pragmatism

AGREEMENT AND DISAGREEMENT IN ENVIRONMENTAL ETHICS

After this intellectual journey through a variety of environmental philosophies, an obvious question arises. Which if any is right? Describing theories like biocentrism, the land ethic, Deep Ecology, social ecology, and ecofeminism is only one-half of the philosophical task. Should we not now determine which is ethically and philosophically the most valid or true? If we do not, are we not left with disarray, disagreement, and contradiction? We return to the skeptical question raised in Chapter 2. Who is to say what is right or wrong?

At this point, the relativist's answer might seem attractive. We have looked at a variety of environmental philosophies and have seen much disagreement among them. Animal rights philosophers disagree with the land ethic, Deep Ecologists disagree with social ecologists, and social ecologists disagree with ecofeminists. Further, the field of environmental ethics seems to be entirely defined in terms of a variety of conflicting dualisms: anthropocentrism versus nonanthropocentrism, holism versus individualism, and intrinsic versus instrumental value. Environmental ethics seems to offer little more than disagreement and controversy. If we cannot determine a single right answer, then—as the relativists have claimed all along—ethics has no objectivity. Environmental ethics should then be relegated to the domain of mere opinion.

Before drawing such skeptical conclusions, we should recognize the agreement among these theories as well. It may be helpful to step back and review some areas in which a strong consensus does exist—the diagnosis of environmental problems and some guidelines that need to be followed when resolving these problems.

Environmental philosophers have reached a strong consensus that the narrow worldview of classical economics and the preference utilitarianism that underlies it must be rejected. We should not allow consumer demand alone to decide environmental policy and determine environmental value. Valuing the natural world as a mere resource to be manipulated and consumed for the short-term consumer preferences expressed in economic markets is at fault for much environmental destruction. We would find wide agreement on this among anthropocentric and nonanthropocentric approaches, biocentric and ecocentric theories, those concerned with future generations and those concerned with animal welfare, and those concerned with social justice for the poor and marginalized.

Different environmental philosophies would offer different explanations for why this approach is wrong. Some would point out that it misunderstands or ignores important human values. Some would argue that it distorts and ignores the interests of human beings in the near and distant future. Others argue that people at society's margins—the poor, oppressed, and minorities—are systematically excluded from markets. Still others point out that it is contemptuous of the respect due plants, animals, and other parts of the natural world. Of course, it might be that they are each right in their criticisms. Nevertheless, they would all agree that the assumptions and values of the economic worldview are philosophically and ethically unsound.

Further, although these various philosophies offer differing prescriptions for what needs to be done, a consensus is emerging around several ecological judgments. All recognize that the capacity of natural ecosystems to produce essentials such as clean air and water, food, and fertile topsoil has limits. All recognize that natural ecosystems have a limited capacity to assimilate wastes and pollutants and rebound from disruptions and destruction. The natural world and natural ecological processes, at least those necessary for human survival, are more fragile and more connected than we previously understood. Human activities need to proceed with less arrogance and more humility for our own sake if not for the sake of future generations and other living beings. Even those who endorse a narrow anthropocentrism with only instrumental value attributed to the natural world acknowledge this.

MORAL PLURALISM AND MORAL MONISM

Nevertheless, the lack of agreement among environmental philosophies is troubling. Certainly, there are good reasons to seek a unified ethical perspective. Chapter 1 introduced ethics with Socrates' observation that "we are dealing with no small thing but with how we ought to live." Irresolvable conflict about such important matters does seem to threaten the foundations of an ethical life. Without a determinate procedure for making decisions, we seem to lack any guide for making them. Further, to live without a unified and consistent ethics seems to be a life without integrity, principles, and commitments.

Within moral philosophy, these questions are part of a debate between moral monism and moral pluralism. Monists claim that there can be only one valid or correct moral theory. Pluralists accept the possibility that more than one basic approach can be legitimate. Because of the wide-ranging disagreements over environmental policy and the diversity of environmental perspectives, the debate concerning moral pluralism has intensified among environmental philosophers in recent years.[1] Pluralism is a useful theme for some final reflections for this textbook.

One strong motivation behind moral monism is the fear of the alternative. Without a single unified and coherent ethical theory, we seem relegated to ethical relativism. The alternatives seem to be either a single ethical theory or abandoning the quest for a rational ethics.

But this either-or dualism is what moral pluralists deny. Pluralism is an alternative to monism and relativism. Rejecting the monist view that there is only one correct answer in ethics, pluralists also reject the relativist claim that there can be no right answer. Instead, moral pluralists maintain that there is a plurality of moral truths that cannot (perhaps unfortunately) be reconciled into a single principle. According to monists, this is the same as relativism.

We have observed a plurality of environmental values at many points in this textbook. Indeed, the very structure of this textbook suggests a continuing expansion of ethical values. Some issues, such as water pollution and pesticide contamination, directly threaten human beings and thus raise familiar ethical concerns. Other issues, such as nuclear waste storage and global warming, extend these familiar concerns to future generations. Issues such as wilderness preservation increase our concern for aesthetic, spiritual, historic, and symbolic values. Other topics challenge us to consider the moral value of nonhuman natural objects such as animals, plants, and even ecosystems or the earth itself. The landscape of environmental ethics appears to be populated by a value diversity that rivals the biological diversity of natural landscapes.

We have also examined several strategies for maintaining a monistic approach in the face of diverse values. The distinction between basic and non-basic interests that characterizes the animal welfare debates is one attempt to bring unity to a diversity of values. Paul Taylor's set of procedural rules for resolving conflicts in the interests of living beings is a similar project. J. Baird Callicott's image of concentric circles of moral sentiment is yet another. Each project attempts to bring unity and consistency to a range of values that, at least at certain points, seem to conflict. These strategies share the assumption that an ethical theory is incomplete unless we can find a single way to reconcile conflict and prioritize competing values.

But perhaps a diversity of values is not as bad as it appears. Chapter 1 also warned not to be misled by scientific models when making ethical judgments. Science and mathematics may require certainty and unambiguous answers as their standard of rationality. But perhaps this is a case of the misapplication of scientific and mathematical standards to ethics. Perhaps we are asking too much when we seek clear, unambiguous, and certain decisions on ethical matters. Perhaps we can be rational about ethical matters without having unambiguous certain answers.

Christopher Stone uses such strict standards in his recent writings on moral pluralism and environmental ethics. Stone tells us that a monistic theory involves "a single coherent set of principles capable of governing all moral quandaries" and yielding "for each quandary one right answer." Because all traditional ethical theories seem incapable of doing this and because relativism is unacceptable, Stone concludes that pluralism is the answer.[2]

Why should we expect ethics to be so mechanical in generating answers? With the exception of mathematics, logic, and perhaps the mathematical sciences and engineering, few intellectual disciplines produce certain results. When we confront a problem in mathematics, we know that if we apply the relevant rules in the correct way, we will arrive at a single correct answer. (This is what computers are so good at doing.) But consider a science like medicine. Although medicine can sometimes provide a single right answer for diagnostic or prognostic questions, several alternative answers often are equally valid. Good doctors have many diverse tools in their bag: surgery, a wide variety of medications, exercise, rest, nutrition, and counseling. Medicine is not a mechanistic science of applying unambiguous rules to specific situations and seeking one right answer. Deciding when and where to apply which tool is the essence of being a good physician. On the other hand, it is also important to note that the alternative to determinate rules is not chaos. There is still a big difference between a good physician and a quack.

Suppose that we were to ask the doctor this question. Of all the diverse treatments in your repertoire, which is the best for protecting and preserving good health? The best answer surely is none and each. No one answer is the best in all situations, but each is, in particular situations, the best. Perhaps this is how we ought to think about the diverse environmental philosophies considered in this book. No one has all the right answers in every situation, but each has something important to bring to environmental ethics. Each provides a different perspective from which we can understand the values of and the place of humans within nature.

When we think about ethical issues in general and environmental controversies more specifically, we should consider whether ethics is more like mathematics or medicine. Perhaps it would be nice if we could get unambiguous answers in either medicine or ethics. But it would appear that neither health nor the good life is open to such determinations.

Here, again, we might learn something from the history of philosophy. At the beginning of his writing on ethics, Aristotle reminds his readers not to demand more precision and accuracy than a subject matter allows. It is one thing to demand rigorous proof from a mathematician and another to demand such proof of a rhetorician. "Virtue and justice—the subject matter of politics—admit of plenty of differences and uncertainty, so much so that some have thought them to be matters of convention rather than being natural and true."[3] Lacking rigorous scientific proof is not a sign that ethics is merely a matter of convention. It may reflect the fact that ethics involves complex and subtle matters. In this case, it may be irrational to insist on unequivocal answers.

Aristotle reminds us that ethics involves practical reason with which we judge not what is true but what we should do. Often, practical decision making is exclusive. If we do one thing, we are precluded from doing another. Thus, this is the real attraction of monism. Because I can do only one thing, ethics should give specific and unequivocal advice. But pluralism resists that attraction, holding that several different actions may be equally rational and equally justified.

Consider what is involved in being a good parent. Parents are constantly confronted with decisions, some easy and some difficult. It would be peculiar to insist that good parents must hold to "a single coherent set of principles" that would yield "for each quandary one right answer." Obviously, some acts are ruled out. A good parent is not abusive. But just as obviously, some quandaries have no single right answer. For example, good parents try to encourage self-confidence in their children, yet they also should provide comfort and a safe haven. Sometimes these principles may offer conflicting advice. Being a good parent sometimes requires backing away to allow a child to face difficulties alone. Sometimes it requires stepping in to provide comfort and support. There is no mechanical way to decide this (and it certainly is not the sort of thing a computer could do). Pluralism acknowledges this complexity and characterizes the ethical life as involving many situations in which diverse, equally important, values must be balanced.

According to Aristotle, such situations are best left to older, more mature people who have had greater and more diverse experiences. His theory relied on the judgments of the "good man." For ethical guidance in the face of uncertainty and complexity, we should rely on the judgment of the person with experience, wisdom, and moral character. This is not unlike how we might proceed when faced with complex medical or parental decisions. Perhaps the best we can hope for is to rely on the judgments of experienced, knowledgeable, and caring people.

In this way, we can think of the theories considered in this textbook as the various tools that we find in a doctor's repertoire. They are resources that we can use to diagnose and treat environmental illness. Although no single one provides all the right answers, we need them all. A responsible citizen should be familiar with the values that each articulates, as well as with the limitations of each. Especially in a democracy, we should be prepared to encounter a variety of perspectives and values. This perspective, along with important virtues such as courage, humility, and care, may be the best for which we can hope.

ENVIRONMENTAL PRAGMATISM

In recent years some environmental philosophers have turned their attention to a more pragmatic approach to environmental issues.[4] Environmental pragmatism takes moral pluralism seriously and articulates a middle ground between a single monistic theory and an anything goes relativism.

The words "pragmatic" and "pragmatism" have two related meanings in ordinary usage. On one hand, to be pragmatic is to be practical and aim for what can be achieved rather than for some unattainable ideal. A pragmatic person is realistic, sensible, down-to-earth, and willing to compromise. On the other hand, pragmatism refers to the particular philosophical tradition developed by American philosophers such as William James and John Dewey in the nineteenth and early twentieth centuries. Philosophical pragmatism is skeptical of monistic theories in both epistemology and ethics. Instead, pragmatism focuses on context-dependent practical accounts of both truth and value. Pragmatism is sometimes described as a radical empiricism. Empiricism holds that all knowledge is derived from experience. Pragmatism emphasizes the particularities of experience. If we take experience seriously, we must recognize that the world of experience is a world of diversity, change, and pluralism.

These two meanings of pragmatism can be found in recent discussions among environmental philosophers. Some believe that environmental philosophy is so focused on abstract conceptual issues that it has become irrelevant to the pressing concerns of environmental policy. On this view, it is time for philosophers to be more concerned with real-world practical issues such as pollution, environmental destruction, and environmental justice. Philosophers should come down out of the clouds (to use Aristophenes's image of Socrates) and become more pragmatic. Some of these observers also believe that the explicit philosophy of American pragmatists can be useful in contemporary environmental debates.

Pragmatism echoes some of the themes discussed previously. Like the physician, pragmatists recognize that determining the appropriate methods and tools will depend on the specifics of each situation. No single approach can be known to be correct independent of the particular context. Like Aristotle, pragmatists shift attention in ethics from what is *true* to what is *practical*, and they understand that practical reasoning may not always offer unambiguous advice. Pragmatism also supports democratic values such as tolerance and respect for diverse opinions and the commitment to free and open procedures for deciding rather than seeking the single true decision.

A recent personal experience may help in understanding environmental pragmatism. Over the last few years, I was a member of a local task force appointed by our mayor and charged with drafting an environmental ordinance to govern economic development and the preservation of environmentally sensitive natural areas. Our city had recently merged with a surrounding township. The land within the original city limits was mostly developed, and the land in the surrounding township was mostly agricultural and rural. The challenge to this task force was to decide how this rural land should be developed. As one might expect, members were appointed to represent the various constituencies: land owners, farmers, real estate developers, builders, representatives from the Sierra Club and the Audubon Society, and officials from local and state government agencies.

In some ways, this was not a diverse group at all. All of the members were white, European-Americans, most came from the middle and upper-middle economic class, most had college degrees, and slightly more than one-half were men. Yet in terms of their environmental philosophy, this was a very diverse group. Several members believed that developers already faced adequate environmental regulation and opposed any new regulation at all. Some members argued that 50 percent of any new development should be set aside as open space. Some thought that economic markets and the demand for new housing should determine what land gets developed and how. One person even argued that every available piece of land should be developed and brought onto the tax rolls to benefit the entire community. Of those who wished to preserve open spaces, some argued that wild animals and trees deserved protection, and others argued that wild spaces should be preserved as habitat for hunting and fishing. Some argued that ecologists should decide what areas remain protected, and others thought the City Council should decide.

For the first two years of its work, the task force resembled much of the field of environmental ethics. Most participants thought that their "theories" (seldom explicitly articulated) should determine the policy. Each brought their own theory and principles to the table, applied them to this specific case to determine what ought to be done, and then tried to convince others to accept their conclusions. For the first two years of its work, the task force got nowhere. Not only did people disagree (and they did, significantly), but some had a difficult time even understanding the opposing side. This time was chaotic, frustrating, and totally unproductive. In the meantime, of course, development continued under the old regulations, which meant that no land was being protected.

At a certain point several members sought to revitalize the group by listing the issues on which there was general agreement. Many were surprised by the result. There was widespread agreement that several natural areas within the city ought to be preserved, even if the city needed to purchase them to do it. Likewise, several areas were acknowledged to be prime sites for commercial development. There was also wide agreement that more housing developments, especially affordable housing, were needed within the city. There was also agreement that open spaces ought to remain in those areas being developed. People agreed that ecologically trained naturalists and scientists ought to be consulted in deciding boundaries for the protected areas. The task force then created development guidelines for achieving these goals and was able to complete its work within a few months. In effect, agreement on principles followed agreement on practice.

This experience captures many of the insights of environmental pragmatism. Disagreement reigned when people approached the challenge seeking to apply preconceived theories and principles. The diversity and abstractness of these starting points effectively prevented agreement and understanding. It also led to animosity and frustration among participants. Further, while we were debating the efficiency of markets or the moral status of a rare northern cactus, unregulated development continued. The alternative began with the practical matter of getting things done, and it did this by starting with specific issues on which people agreed. Ultimately, "theory" followed practice in the sense that the final governing principle was developed out of the agreed on starting points. In effect, the task force was monistic in terms of its practical conclusions, but remained very pluralistic in terms of its theories about why we ought to adopt these conclusions. Members agreed on what should be done, but disagreed on why it should be done. In this sense, pragmatism has elements of both monism and pluralism. Of course, a different community likely would have begun with different agreements and, therefore, likely would have ended with a different policy.

The solution was a practical compromise. The new ordinance creates a process that each planned development must go through. An initial survey identifies all the natural areas that are ecologically sensitive and historically significant. Native prairies, rare woodlands, riparian corridors, and habitat of rare species top the list. If a planned development impacts one of these areas, the developer and city planners enter negotiations aimed at preserving the natural area. As part of the bargaining, the city is legally empowered to offer compromises on other zoning regulations (for example, street width, housing density, and so forth) in order to minimize the financial impact of preserving the natural area. The procedure offers no guarantees to either side and relies a great deal on the good faith efforts of many people. So far, it seems to be working.

No one got all that they had originally desired and neither side "won." Yet as one member pointed out, the real winner was democratic citizenship. People came together, argued, debated, and eventually found common ground. The compromise "worked" in the sense that most everyone concluded that they could live with it. In a democracy—indeed, in any situation in which diverse perspectives conflict—it is unrealistic, unreasonable, and perhaps unfair to expect or desire one side completely to triumph over others. This is, in many ways, the "pragmatic" solution.

While environmental pragmatism has many articulate defenders, criticisms remain. The practical compromise that characterizes pragmatic solutions can be, in the opinion of critics, little more than a wishy-washy capitulation to the status quo. If we test environmental policy against what "works" and what is "practical" within a specific situation, we may be doing little more than conforming to the expectations and values of the status quo. Assuming that we do face real environmental challenges that have arisen in part from this very status quo, this pragmatic approach might prove counterproductive at best. A second criticism holds that the context-dependent nature of pragmatic solutions means that pragmatism never fully escapes ethical relativism.

In response to the first challenge, pragmatists would point out that a pragmatic solution does not privilege the status quo in the way suggested by this criticism. In the words of Anthony Weston, values and practices "co-evolve."[5]

Neither has an absolute priority over the other. As values are brought in line with practices, they evolve to guide future practices, which in turn shape future values. Our practices elevate some values and principles and discount others. In my community, for example, it would be very difficult to defend an "environment-be-damned" attitude after the compromises reached by the task force. The consensus has legitimized certain values that no doubt will shape future development. The criticism assumes that practices never change and never progress.

Pragmatists also have a response to the challenge of relativism. Pragmatic solutions are relativistic only if we assume that ethical evaluations must fit an either/or, true/false dichotomy. But pragmatism rejects this monistic view of value. We can return to Aristotle's reminder that ethics involves practical reason which judges not what is true but what we should do. The criterion in ethics is not truth as much as it is reasonableness. For the pragmatist, two incompatible ethical judgments might each be equally reasonable. Only for the monist must at least one be wrong. Since only one can be left standing, there is a tendency among ethical monists to seek confrontation, conflict, and triumph. If, as pragmatists hold, many competing views can be equally reasonable, the tendency will be toward tolerance, respect, compromise, and getting along. Pragmatists argue that there are standards for reasonableness—intellectual and moral openness, intellectual and moral care, and attention to detail—and that these standards prevent the collapse of pragmatism into relativism.

CONCLUSION

In light of this discussion of pluralism and pragmatism, we need exercise care in our final evaluation of the relevancy of philosophical ethics. Ethical theory and analysis have important roles to play in environmental issues, but perhaps not, as the pragmatists advise, as independent principles to be imposed from on high to resolve environmental controversies. But being applied in this way is not the only way for abstract theoretical thinking to guide our lives. Without careful analysis and care and attention being paid to the detailed and sophisticated theories of environmental ethics, we can hope for little more than an opinionated and biased environmental ethic. An environmentally sustainable future, as well as our own intellectual integrity, demands more.

Notes

1. Much of this recent debate was provoked by Christopher Stone's book, *Earth and Other Ethics: The Case for Moral Pluralism* (New York: Harper and Row, 1987), and a later essay, "Moral Pluralism and the Course of Environmental Ethics," *Environmental Ethics* 10 (summer 1988): 139–54. Stone's view was soon challenged by J. Baird Callicott, "The Case Against Moral Pluralism," *Environmental Ethics* 12 (summer 1990): 99–112. My own thinking on these issues owes much to Peter Wenz, "Minimal, Moderate, and Extreme Pluralism," *Environmental Ethics* 15

(spring 1993): 61–74, and Bryan Norton, *Toward Unity Among Environmentalists* (New York: Oxford, 1991).

2. Christopher Stone, *Earth and Other Ethics: The Case for Moral Pluralism* (New York: Harper and Row, 1987), p. 116.

3. Aristotle, *Nicomachean Ethics*, in *Basic Works of Aristotle*, ed. Richard McKeon (New York: Random House, 1941), book 1, ch. 3, 15–17.

4. The single best resource for environmental pragmatism is *Environmental Pragmatism*, edited by Andrew Light and Eric Katz (New York: Routledge, 1996). Several of the essays reprinted there were originally published in the journal *Environmental Ethics*.

5. Anthony Weston, "Before Environmental Ethics," *Environmental Ethics* Vol. 14, No. 4 (winter 1992), reprinted in Light and Katz, eds. *Environmental Pragmatism*, pp. 139–160.